MEASURING THE INTENTIONAL WORLD

MEASURING THE INTENTIONAL WORLD

Realism,
Naturalism, and
Quantitative Methods
in the Behavioral Sciences

J.D. TROUT

New York   Oxford • Oxford University Press   1998

Oxford University Press

Oxford   New York
Athens   Auckland   Bangkok   Bogota   Bombay   Buenos Aires
Calcutta   Cape Town   Dar es Salaam   Delhi   Florence   Hong Kong
Istanbul   Karachi   Kuala Lumpur   Madras   Madrid   Melbourne
Mexico City   Nairobi   Paris   Singapore   Taipei   Tokyo   Toronto   Warsaw

and associated companies in
Berlin   Ibadan

Copyright © 1998 by J.D. Trout

Published by Oxford University Press, Inc.
198 Madison Avenue, New York, New York 10016

Oxford is a registered trademark of Oxford University Press

Library of Congress Cataloging-in-Publication Data

Trout, J.D.
Measuring the intentional world : realism, naturalism,
and quantitative methods in the
behavioral sciences / J.D. Trout.
p.   cm.
Includes bibliographical references and index.
ISBN 0-19-510766-7
1. Psychology—Statistical methods.
2. Social sciences—Statistical methods.
3. Realism.   I. Title.
BF39.T76   1998
300'.1—dc21   96-40149

1 2 3 4 5 6 7 8 9
Printed in the United States of America
on acid-free paper

In memory of my mother,
Marie Regina Marciante
1927–1971

Preface

In the last 100 years or so, the psychological and social sciences have enjoyed brisk progress. This progress coincided with the development of sophisticated quantitative methods and, where possible, lab studies. This book argues that a measured realism about the social and psychological sciences is warranted in light of the reliable role of quantitative methods in those domains. I propose a theory of measurement—Population-Guided Estimation—that connects natural, psychological, and social scientific inquiry. In doing so, I advance a version of epistemological naturalism that allows us to assimilate the essentially scientific notion of measurement into familiar epistemic categories.

Realist interpretations of the entities, laws, and theories of the natural sciences have become familiar fare for contemporary philosophers of science. Along with their empiricist and various antirealist opponents, realists typically draw their evidence exclusively from the mature sciences of physics, chemistry, and biology. This focus is understandable. In doing so, scientific realists attempt to select the clearest evidence of referential success for central theoretical terms and approximate truth of laws and background theories. Antirealists propose philosophical arguments against realist construals of the most mature sciences, reasoning that the undermining of the strongest cases for realism is also the most damaging to the realist. The cumulative effect, however, has been the nearly universal neglect of the social sciences and psychology in this dispute.

There is a history explaining philosophical neglect of the social sciences and psychology, along with the neglect of their emerging quantitative approaches. For the better part of this century, scientists and philosophers of science were weaned on a logical empiricist model of scientific theories. During that period, philosophers of science held up physics as the measure of respectability for all sciences, in part due to its obvious successes and in part because, given reigning empiricist standards, philosophers regarded syntactic reducibility to physics as a measure of the success and maturity of other working theories such as biology and psychology. At the same time, humanistic responses to the scientism of the logical positivists, embodied in narrative and affiliated hermeneutic traditions, provided an understanding of psychology and the social sciences that was little better than empiricism at accommodating the insights of naturalism. This book offers an alternative to these extremes.

With the introduction of quantitative, particularly statistical, methods, reliable and truly cumulative research could be undertaken, overcoming the impressionistic presentations and unprincipled theoretical shifts of narrative approaches. It is the chief aim of this book to explain those intellectual methods and to articulate some of the semantic, epistemological, and metaphysical lessons of this sophisticated quantitative research. The position I advance, Measured Realism, does not require that the instrumental reliability of quantitative methods in the social and behavioral sciences be explained in terms of the approximate truth of theories, as more robust versions of realism do. At the same time, Measured Realism is stronger than mere realism about some theoretical entities of the social and behavioral sciences—so-called entity realism—because its focus on theoretical improvements in measurement procedures depends not just on the existence of some entities but also on the approximate truth of some theoretical laws. Accordingly, Measured Realism provides a model of significant theoretical advances that are not yet definitive, thus yielding a sense of progress that places quantitative psychological and social sciences among the domains whose secrets nature is rapidly surrendering to us.

It would be peculiar, if not pointless, for a naturalistic philosopher to write a book defending scientific realism about the behavioral and social sciences that scientists or philosophers couldn't read. The first step toward measured realism about the social and psychological sciences begins with careful attention to particular representative lines of research on vision, audition, language, concept acquisition and structure, memory, party affiliation, and market segmentation, with the resulting admiration and respect that palpable progress always inspires. Books with a unifying, naturalistic perspective often contain more descriptive material than any particular specialist reader would like, and I'm afraid this book is no exception. To provide the necessary philosophical background for behavioral scientists, I have supplied introductory discussions of realism, empiricism, naturalism, and confirmation that are already familiar to philosophers of science. Philosophers with expertise in this field may wish to skim chapters 1 and 4. For philosophers to appreciate the progress in the psychological and social sciences, I have included lengthy sections describing noteworthy methodological, substantial, and integrative advances in those fields. Readers with the relevant scientific background may wish to skim those sections.

I BEGAN THINKING about the issues of this book while a Mellon Postdoctoral Fellow at Bryn Mawr College. Special thanks to Michael Krausz for his help and encouragement. I then took my first full-time position in philosophy and had the good fortune to work with the historian of science, Jim McClellan. His scholarship is a model of care and elegance I can only hope my own work in philosophy approximates, but his kindness I know I can never match. During a visiting position at Virginia Tech, I spent hours enjoying the company of John Christman and Mary Beth Oliver. I then participated in an NEH Summer Seminar at Johns Hopkins University on methodological issues in nineteenth-century physics. Many thanks to the director, Peter Achinstein, for his patient and incisive comments, and to the other talented members of that group. Shortly after my arrival in Chicago, Arthur Fine allowed me to sit in on a realism seminar he was teaching at Northwestern University. I hope the humor he finds in my realist attachments is adequate compensation for that generosity.

Much of this book draws on research in psychology. I began doing speech perception research in graduate school, and I am indebted to a number of distinguished psychologists and linguists with whom I did graduate coursework or research, among them Frank Keil, Roger Shepard, Bill Poser, and Michael Kelly. I have since been fortunate to land at a university that houses the Parmly Hearing Institute, a distinguished center for comparative sensory research. The Parmly Hearing Institute has supported my speech perception research, including regular travel to Acoustical Society meetings, which I appreciate. Thanks especially to Bill Yost, the director of Parmly. Parmly's research meetings, friendly atmosphere, and demand for excellent science provide a model of what science at its best can be like.

I had the pleasure of presenting earlier versions of parts of this book at various conferences and colloquia. I presented part of chapter 3 at a 1994 meeting of the Philosophy of Science Association. I presented versions of chapter 5 at the University of Chicago's Colloquium Series for the Committee on the Conceptual Foundations of Science (in conjunction with the Fishbein Center for the History of Science and Medicine), at Virginia Tech, the University of Illinois at Chicago, and the Tenth International Congress of Logic, Methodology, and Philosophy of Science in Florence, Italy, in 1995. At the Florence conference, Robyn Dawes made useful suggestions, several of which took root. I presented a version of chapter 6 at a 1992 American Philosophical Association Pacific Division meeting and at a 1991 Society for the History and Philosophy of Science meeting of the Canadian Philosophical Association. I am grateful to these audiences for their friendly and helpful comments.

My debts to Paul Moser are too numerous to list. He has read and commented on drafts of every chapter and, along with Richard Boyd, has been a helpful participant in discussions about the topic of this book. My graduate seminars at Loyola University of Chicago have also provided a valuable source of feedback and enthusiasm. More generally, Loyola has provided a supportive and stimulating research environment. I received support in the form of a summer stipend in 1994, and I am grateful.

For help, conversation, and encouragement, thanks go to Irene Appelbaum, Jason Beyer, Mike Bishop, David Buller, Aaron Bunch, Richard Burian, Sue Cunningham, Walter Edelberg, Richard Farr, Arthur Fine, Phil Gasper, Stuart Glennan, David Malament, Vandana Mathur, Erik Midelfort, Dwayne Mulder, Peter Pruim, David Reichling, Norma Reichling, Marya Schechtman, Alan Sidelle, Scott Tindale, Jonathan Vogel, Rob Wilson, Bill Wimsatt, and David Yandell. Among these, Rob Wilson, Richard Farr, Phil Gasper, and David Yandell deserve special mention. Rob read a very rough draft of the entire book and made incisive and detailed criticisms (and I'm grateful for the Goldilocks allusion). Richard, Phil, and David read individual chapters and provided valuable philosophical and editorial comment. More recently, I have benefited from correspondence with Paul Meehl, whose influential work on statistics and design informed and enlivened the topics of this book. Thanks also to Scott Tindale, who checked the statistics, and to Professor Erik Midelfort of the University of Virginia, who kindly supplied references for some of the material on Martin Luther. An anonymous reviewer for Oxford University Press supplied specific suggestions for improvement, and persuaded me that the penultimate could be made leaner. Cynthia Read, Gene Romanosky, and MaryBeth Branigan of Oxford University Press handled the manuscript with care and grace. I am grateful to all of these people, and the errors that remain are, of course, my own.

Parts of this book draw on my recent publications. Part of chapter 3 draws on "Austere Realism and the Worldly Assumptions of Inferential Statistics," *PSA 1994*, volume 1 (1994). Part of chapter 4 draws on "Theory-Conjunction and Mercenary Reliance," *Philosophy of Science* 59 (1992). Part of chapter 6 draws on "Robustness and Integrative Survival in Significance Testing: The World's Contribution to Rationality," *British Journal for the Philosophy of Science* 44 (1993). Part of chapter 7 draws on "Diverse Tests on an Independent World," *Studies in History and Philosophy of Science* 26 (1995). I would like to thank these publishers for allowing me to reprint this material, most of it substantially revised.

Finally, I want to thank my wife, Janice Nadler. My life with her continues to be immeasurable fun.

Chicago, Illinois   J. D. T.
Spring 1997

Contents

MEASURING THE INTENTIONAL WORLD

Introduction

Realism and Naturalism in the Philosophy of Science

This introduction has three purposes: (1) to present just enough conceptual and historical background to contemporary philosophy of science and enough material describing progress in the psychological and social sciences so that nonspecialist philosophers and other readers can see the promise that their own methodological concerns will be addressed in the chapters that follow, (2) to elucidate the role of various philosophical theses, such as holism, in the demise of the foundationalist epistemology and radically normative conception of confirmation held by logical empiricism, and (3) to explore the way in which the nonindependence characteristic of confirmation relations determines the naturalistic, abductive form of argument favoring the measured scientific realism advanced in this book.

The Background

Early logical empiricism—in many ways still the dominant outlook among methodologically reflective psychologists and social scientists (but not philosophers) in this century—states that scientific knowledge is restricted to observable phenomena and that theories are mere instruments for generating hypotheses to be tested by observation.[1] Scientific realism is the alternative view that our best scientific

---

1. Later variants of logical empiricism abandoned instrumentalism. See Hempel (1966). It is not clear whether these later variants of logical empiricism have managed to abandon instrumentalism in a way that is either faithful to a core empiricist outlook, or consistent with their own proposed empiricist strictures.

theories should be understood as approximately accurate descriptions of a mind-independent reality, in both its observable (empirical) and unobservable (theoretical) aspects. Both of these views attempt to account for the special epistemic status of our best sciences. Naturalism is the doctrine that philosophy is methodologically continuous with the natural sciences.

This is a book about a special form of scientific realism and philosophical naturalism, formulated to characterize a kind of theoretical success in the behavioral sciences that is as uneven as it is indisputable. The contemporary emergence of a thoroughgoing philosophical naturalism has forced our attention to the methodological and substantial details of science. Consequently, the philosophy of science has become richer and more interesting, particularly in the philosophy of the physical and biological sciences. In this connection, the methods of measurement have provided a secure basis from which to extract metaphysical lessons about the natural kinds of those domains and epistemological lessons concerning the rationality of certain methods of inquiry. But when philosophers and others consider the morals that might be drawn from the social and behavioral sciences, there is an apparent crisis of philosophical imagination. Rather than marveling at the advances in the social and behavioral sciences made in a comparatively shorter time than those in the natural sciences, and rather than searching for a common basis of scientific estimation, many thinkers evidence a spectacular resignation, or a desperation that approaches the theatrical, about the prospects for a properly scientific analysis of intelligent behavior and of social structures. These gloomy reflections are familiar from the literature in social theory and elsewhere. The following passage is representative:

> Now the time seems ripe, even overdue, to announce that there is not going to be an age of paradigm in social science. We contend that the failure to achieve paradigm takeoff is not merely the result of methodological immaturity, but reflects something fundamental about the social world. If we are correct, the crisis of social science concerns the nature of social investigation itself. (Rabinow and Sullivan 1979, p. 4)

Some intellectuals have devoted much of their scholarly effort to showing why there cannot be a science of human behavior or of human institutions. As a matter of fact, it is an interesting research question why they are so broadly pessimistic, often in the absence of information about ongoing research in the social and behavioral sciences or in light of only a domain or two. One sometimes hears similar pronouncements made by practicing experimental psychologists and social scientists, though typically after 10 P.M. or after a week of abortive experimental work.

Although I take these worries seriously, I believe that the popular, wholesale rejection of the social and behavioral sciences—which are recognizably methodologically continuous with the natural sciences—has at its source either intellectual impatience or a mistaken conception of what science requires. The methods of science have a quantitative function. Statistical designs in the social and behavioral sciences serve this function and are not for this reason any less able to deliver understanding or insight than the nonstatistical methods of interpretive social science. (In fact, one might argue that when the latter succeed, it is because they are accurate estimators of the magnitudes of psychological and social factors.) It is measurement (or, if one prefers, estimation) of the properties of a *physical arrangement* that sustains the connection between the sciences of physics and biology on the one hand and psychology, sociology, and economics on the other.

The philosophical naturalism to which measurement is central holds that humans are part of the natural order. The measured realism defended in this book connects scientific realism and philosophical naturalism. Measurement relations are natural relations; they depict physical dependencies between specific instruments (or particular applications of methods) and physical quantities, whether or not the latter are described in a physical vocabulary.

Modern philosophers of science have become, as their ancestors were even a century ago, natural philosophers—although now without commitment to a first philosophy (for a nice, tightly argued review, see Kitcher 1992). Typically, contemporary philosophers of science have one hand in philosophy and the other in science. This naturalistic tendency, vibrant at the moment, has awakened from several philosophical generations of dormancy. During the first half of the twentieth century, it was difficult to find in philosophical training the view that philosophy was continuous with the natural sciences, even among those with sound training in science, from Russell, Carnap, and Reichenbach to Whitehead, Braithwaite, and Ramsey. At that time, if a person with a science degree turned to philosophy, it was probably the result of a wrenching epiphany or the leisurely desire to satisfy long-standing interests. And if a credentialed philosopher had turned an eye toward scientific training, it was usually to satisfy an independent interest or to ensure financial stability; it was not because empirical science was thought to be relevant to the formulation of epistemic principles. For reasons I will survey in this introduction, the distinction between science and philosophy of science is now much more difficult to sustain. The philosophical movements leading to this renewed naturalism are traced below.

Although the abandonment of logical positivism left us without either a model or a systematic philosophical conception of science, it had an uneven influence on our philosophical assessments of the various special sciences. The crisis thereby produced in the philosophy of physics was perhaps tempered by the sheer instrumental success of physics. Nice as it would be to have a model, no one worried that our inability to articulate the reasons for its success provided ground for doubting that physics was successful or could enjoy progress. The social and behavioral sciences, however, did not survive the fall of logical positivism in such presumptive favor, partly because psychology, sociology, history, economics, and political science have not achieved the level of (at least) predictive success of physics. More important, the peripheral treatment of psychology and the social sciences at the hands of philosophers of science is an artifact of philosophical training.

Traditional philosophical training has been distinctly humanistic, a feature associated with the legacy of the Enlightenment. The Enlightenment tradition harbors the persistent intellectual assumption—call it the narrative view—that social and behavioral inquiry involves a special, narrative art, essentially different from natural scientific inquiry. This perspective is found in the Verstehen tradition and in a host of other approaches such as participant observation (see Collingwood 1959; Riley 1974; Truzzi 1971, 1974; White 1973, 1987). Narrative authorship may demand special storytelling skills, a flare for anecdote, or an eye for cultural and personal detail. But reading and understanding these narratives certainly should require no special training, just a liberal education and an openness to the understanding of persons and cultures. The narrative view is most resilient and influential in philosophical discussions of social, historical, and psychological phenomena. One might class among these narratives nearly everything written on human behavior prior to the late 1800s, and the narrative tradition has persisted to the present. Exemplars are Tocqueville's *Democracy in America*, Freud's *Civilization and Its Discontents*, and Malinowski's *Argonauts of the Western Pacific*. Each of these works is typical of a body of literature we now associate with history, sociology, anthropology, political science, and psychology.[2]

Take, for example, a regrettable but representative work in narrative history. Whether a Hegelian legacy or not, a number of the great historical works of the first half of the twentieth century were prone to sweeping generalization, speculation about recurring and cyclical patterns in history, and abstract forecasts compatible with evidence of virtually any kind. In Arnold Toynbee's classic work, *A Study of History*, we find a straightforward and representative case of a base-rate fallacy, a failure to appreciate the relative frequency with which relevant events occur in a population. Like many narrative historians, Toynbee was disposed to advance claims of historical recurrence, often without specifying the dimensions of historical events along which repeating sequences could be clearly identified. Toynbee assigned these claims of recurrence a weighty evidential role in his account of the origin of the universal state:

> 'Every schoolboy knows'—Macaulay's optimistic estimate—that on four occasions, separated from one another by just over one hundred years, the English (or British) people, taking advantage of the comparative immunity afforded by their island fast-

---

2. In case there is any question that the humanistic, narrative tradition has a powerful hold on philosophical training in the social and behavioral sciences, one need only survey texts in the philosophy of social science. With a few notable exceptions—Papineau (1978), Little (1990), Kincaid (1996), (the much more demanding) Glymour et al. (1987), and especially recent work in the philosophy of economics—there are no philosophy of social science books that describe what the majority of social scientists actually do. Instead, they address certain topics that can interest, or be discussed by, a philosophical audience without any training in science. (I would place in this group such books as Thomas 1979, Trigg 1985, Macdonald and Pettit 1981, and Rudner 1966, to name just a few. This impression can be confirmed by a simple library search of philosophy of social science titles, selected arbitrarily.) The result is often a very good book on Davidsonian philosophy of language applied to the challenge of understanding and interpreting alien cultures, or on the relation between rock-bottom individuals and social wholes, or on rational decision theory applied to social choice, or on the value-ladenness of social science. But often the topic of quantitative methods—statistical analyses, experimentation, or measurement—does not even arise, even though most social and behavioral scientists spend their days immersed in these activities. One could not hope to understand what resources are available to handle the understanding of alien cultures, group phenomena, and the value-ladenness of inquiry without having some familiarity with quantitative methods.

ness, first repelled and then helped to destroy a continental Power which was offering, or threatening, to supply Western Christendom with a universal state, or at any rate was, in traditional language, 'upsetting the balance of power'. On the first occasion the offender was Spain—Spanish Armada, 1588; on the second occasion, the France of Louis XIV—Blenheim, 1704; on the third occasion, the France of the Revolution and Napoleon—Waterloo, 1815; on the fourth occasion, the Germany of Wilhelm II—Armistice Day, 1918—subsequently recrudescent under Hitler—Normandy, 1944. Here is an unmistakably cyclical pattern, viewed from an insular angle, a set of four 'great wars', spaced out with curious regularity, each one larger than its predecessor, both in the intensity of its warfare and in what we will call the area of belligerency.

Each of these four wars for the prevention of the establishment of a Modern Western universal state had been separated from its successor and from its predecessor by a time-span of about a century. (1957, p. 270)

This postulated cyclical feature is no idle or peripheral interest of Toynbee's; it is a centerpiece of an account of history that is both comprehensive and substantial. About its comprehensiveness, he claims that "an examination of the war-and-peace cycles in post-Alexandrine Hellenic history and in post-Confucian Sinic history yielded historical 'patterns' curiously similar in their structure and in their time-spans to those here described in the course of Modern Western history" (p. 271). In substance, the cyclical theory "is not simply a case of a wheel revolving four times *in vacuo* and coming round each time to the position in which it has started. It is also a case of a wheel moving forward along a road in a particularly ominous direction" (p. 271). About its significance, he states that four times Britain rebuffed efforts to create a larger cultural community by conquest or that the nation in question was attempting to "upset the balance of power." Moreover, Toynbee seems to associate some measure of Britain's success with its insular island status. He further argues that there are similar cycles throughout history, proof for which "can be set out in tabular form" (p. 271). He then provides just such a table supposed to supply the evidence for an account of history that is both progressive and endowed with a putatively cyclical character that for Toynbee seems to take on mystical proportions.

Toynbee would have us infer from the "curious" cyclical character that it is theoretically interesting as well, a "pattern" worth explaining. But how curious is it? More specifically, how frequently would one expect a pattern of interest to arise? An answer to this question depends on how one defines a pattern that appears curious or surprising against a background of other events. If the historian first *predicts*, on the basis of his or her theory, that a 100-year cycle of particular sorts of wars will emerge from the archival data, then we might begin to assign provisional significance to the cycle. Only a pretty good theory of history, one would have thought, could specify the mechanisms of historical procession finely and accurately enough that one could predict precisely which patterns an archival search would pick up. But this is patently *not* what Toynbee does. Instead, he first muses indistinctly about the significance of patterns and then, having satisfied himself that an apparent pattern has postcedently emerged from the data, claims its significance. There is no prediction, prior to the search, that a 100-year cycle would be found, let alone any indication where. Given the sheer number of possible patterns, the burden of identifying correlations is light.

But neither is there any 100-year cycle. If we take a closer look at the relevant 300 or so years spanning 1588 A.D. to 1918 A.D., this "unmistakably cyclical pattern" of war every 100 years or so is hardly clear or periodic. In fact, it is difficult to distinguish this sequence from the relative frequency with which such 100-year sequences can be found both throughout history and during the same 300-year period using arbitrarily selected 100-year intervals. As we shall see, the assignment of some special status to Toynbee's *particular* intervals requires that we identify far fewer intervals satisfying Toynbee's loose and hedged descriptions than could have been found. For example, although Toynbee begins the first 100-year interval at 1588, in 1602 the Spanish Army surrendered to English troops in Ireland. War began again with Spain in 1624, just thirty-six years after the English victory over the Armada, and, together with Portugal, England defeated Spain again in 1665, this time seventy-seven years after the Armada and a full thirty-nine years before the end of Toynbee's first interval. Perhaps some of these exchanges do not meet the criteria that Toynbee expounds, but the criteria are so vague it is unclear exactly how the warring exchanges I have mentioned fail to meet his standards for significant or relevant war. The 300-year period defined by Toynbee was rife with warring between Britain and the other states, and without an independent reason for selecting the particular wars he does, his selection is ad hoc. The point here is not to charge that Toynbee was a terrible historian but rather to identify a very general defect in a historiography that Toynbee shared with others, such as Spengler, and handed down to many popular, contemporary historians. I will return to this example in chapter 8, when I argue that measured realism and population-guided estimation can diagnose, and often correct, many such ills in narrative texts.

This book contends that people can be the objects of scientific study, and the requisite science is not of a special sort. In particular, the methods of the natural sciences can be extended to the "human," psychological, and social sciences. In the last 100 years, we have learned far more about psychological and social life than in the previous 2,000 years, by any measure. But when we consider the most definitive achievements of the psychological and social sciences in recent history, the methods used were not narrative but quantitative, more closely associated with the methods in the natural sciences than those in the hermeneutic or interpretive tradition of the human sciences. It is my contention that this fast progress began with the introduction of quantitative, largely statistical and experimental, methods.[3] Experimental design and statistical measurement are concerned with

3. In a criticism of traditional behavioral and social texts, it would be unfair to attack practitioners for failing to make use of mathematical and theoretical insights that their history and culture had not made available to them. Just as it would be foolish to criticize Zeno for not having made use of the calculus to solve the paradoxes, it would be silly to derogate Weber for not using the techniques of causal modeling, or Wundt for failing to use repeated measures ANOVAs. When illustrating a frailty of a traditional narrative, my intent is not to claim that the frailty could have been avoided given

the estimation of magnitudes, of causal factors central to prediction and explanation of social and psychological phenomena. Research on visual perception—on the rotation of mental images, visual search and attention, and visual psychophysics—makes essential use of experimental design and statistical analysis of reaction times, classification schemes, and scaled responses. Other examples of progress can be cited in contemporary research on frequency selectivity in audition, on word recognition in speech perception and psycholinguistics, on problem solving and the relation between memory and processing load in cognition, on party affiliation in political science, on self-esteem effects in social psychology, and on the history of witchcraft. I discuss examples of this research in "A Survey of Sciences Worthy of the Name" in this chapter.

If quantitative methods have been so successful, what makes the narrative view so resilient, particularly in our philosophical understanding of social and behavioral research? A single idea, with many modifications, underlies the durable narrative view and has shaped modern philosophical treatments of the social and behavioral sciences: the idea that humans are, in some important and relevant respect, special objects in the natural order, unfit for study using the methods of the natural sciences. To use the apt phrase of Charles Taylor, we are "self-interpreting animals."[4] On one side of the great phylogenetic divide, there is the world of physics, a world of objects without passion, hope, fear, or meaning. On the other side, there we stand, objects full of intention and significance. It is one thing to understand how our bodies navigate through the world, another to understand how we understand our movement through the world, how we interpret ourselves. The idea that self-interpretation is a defining feature of human psychological and social life gives systematic voice, not to mention solace, to those who diagnose in humans characteristics unsuitable for proper scientific study.[5] Such intentional characteristics require investigation in terms of sympathetic understanding or homey anecdotal explanation, methods too orthogonal to

---

resources available at that time. Rather, I will use such cases simply to demonstrate how unreliable exclusive dependence on narrative methods can be, compared to the methods we now have available. This is not to say that traditional narrative works are worthless or irresponsible; it is to say that, in general, their methods should not be emulated.

4. See Charles Taylor (1985b), and for his version of naturalism, see his introduction in Taylor (1985a).

5. Another basis for the irremediable difference between the human and natural sciences, a difference that invites some to make special pleas on behalf of narrative methods, is driven by a metaphysical view that distinguishes two putatively irreducible types of causes: mechanical and teleological. The concept of mechanical causation is appropriately applied to the deterministic interaction of organizationally simple, macroscopic objects (like billiard balls), while the concept of teleological causation is applied to organizationally complex systems (like biological systems or societies), with properties of redundancy. But the distinction looks irreducible only if you attend to the difference between archetypal cases of mechanical causation and archetypal cases of teleological causation. Whether or not this distinction is irreducible is an a posteriori question. And the distinction is certainly more complicated than the one between nonintentional and intentional systems, for some teleological systems are nonintentional (like a cell or clusters of them). There may be no clear line, and it may be a crude understanding of causation that would endorse such a distinction.

those of the natural sciences to be easily assimilable to a naturalistic conception of social and behavioral phenomena, according to which objects with intentionality are part of the natural order.[6] The humanistic biases of philosophical training systematically distort philosophers' understanding of what social and behavioral scientists do and make them unprepared for what they see when they look.

Defenses of scientific realism have been proposed on the basis of evidence from the natural, but never from the social and behavioral, sciences. When one turns, however, to extant versions of scientific realism for an analysis of the psychological and social sciences, those versions are either too strong to find support in an immature subject matter or too weak to capture even the modest achievements of the social and psychological sciences. One especially robust and aggressive version of scientific realism (Boyd [1983] 1991a) states that the instrumental reliability of scientific methodology in the mature sciences can adequately be explained only if we suppose that theories in the mature sciences are at least approximately true. Other more timid versions of scientific realism (Hacking 1983; Humphreys 1989) argue that the instrumental use of postulated items as tools in the production of further effects gives us legitimate grounds for ontological commitment to theoretical entities but no more. Both robust and modest versions of realism are abductive, arguing that either the approximate truth of background theories, or the existence of theoretical entities, provides the best explanation for some fact about the scientific theory or practice.

The first purpose of this book is to defend an interpretation called Measured Realism. This account is measured in two distinct senses: it focuses on the epistemic category of measurement in the case for scientific realism, and it charts a middle course between the robust realism (sometimes dubbed "theory realism") developed by Richard Boyd and the more modest "austere realism" proposed by Paul Humphreys and "entity realism" advanced by Ian Hacking. At the same time, the account is realist because the reliability of quantitative methods in the social and behavioral sciences is explained in the standard abductive realist way, in terms of theoretical knowledge, claiming that our knowledge concerning some central processes and laws in the psychological and social sciences provides the best available explanation for the modest but undeniable successes in those fields. Our background social and psychological theories need not be approximately true but only good enough to support weak cases of abduction. The best available explanation of the kind in question need not be approximately true. According to Measured Realism, no claim of approximate truth is warranted for theories in the social and behavioral sciences, but more is required than theoretical commitment to the existence of some selected posits. If we are to explain the reliability

---

6. After all, even if the capacity of self-interpretation is *a* difference between humans and an atom in the void, it is not immediately clear why this one—among the many differences—should be a difference that prohibits the scientific study of people. Some have suggested that our special cognitive capacities have made us unpredictable. But certain quantum mechanical and chaotic systems are at least as unpredictable as people, and the former physical systems have been the proper objects of scientific study for some time now. So perhaps the foiling feature lies elsewhere.

of quantitative methods in the social and behavioral sciences, we must suppose that we have theoretical knowledge of some laws and warrant for some of the central posits of those theories. Although I will set out the central features of Measured Realism in chapter 4, I want to portray this version of scientific realism as more than just a philosophical doctrine. In the hands of the naturalistic philosopher, Measured Realism is a description of a scientific research program.

The second purpose of this book is to advance a novel version of naturalism about the psychological sciences, according to which the normative judgments about the epistemic status of behavioral generalizations are given not by any favored philosophical principles but by the standards of sound estimation in the particular field. Although modern philosophy at least until Kant was stimulated by a concern with science, this concern prompted no widespread, thoroughgoing naturalism. The conception of scientific epistemology proposed here may not favor philosophy with the sort of intellectual priority that some philosophers desire, but it is the only conception that can yield the appropriate kind of justification. The nature of this justification is closely associated with the doctrine of realism itself, and so a good part of the naturalism depicted in this book derives from its development of a realist conception of measurement—here designated Population-Guided Estimation—that assimilates statistical measurement in the behavioral sciences to measurement generally, including physical measurement. Standards of independence are important here, for it is the independence of measurement outcomes from particular theories that establishes Measured Realism as an appropriate analysis of the epistemic status of behavioral generalizations. Of course, the continuity of physical, psychological, and social measurement is precisely what a naturalistic conception of scientific methodology would lead us to expect. But it is important that realists present a unified model of measurement that is firm and illustrative so that they can respond decisively to initial charges that a naturalistic account of social and behavioral measurement is inconceivable or hopelessly implausible.

Empiricist Analysis of the Social and Behavioral Sciences

The story I tell in this introduction offers a general overview of the two systematic positions in contemporary philosophy of science—logical empiricism and scientific realism—that prima facie take seriously the use of quantitative methods in the social and behavioral sciences. I give special attention to the relation of those positions to current philosophical conceptions of psychology, sociology, political science, and history and to the form that philosophical naturalism about the social and behavioral sciences should take. Like all overviews, the present one paints in broad strokes and yet is selective in the topics it discusses. This feature will make it accessible to practicing scientists, as well as to interested philosophers, with little or no background in the philosophy of science.[7]

---

7. Several very nice and quite different introductions to the philosophy of science have appeared. Klee (1997) offers a thorough discussion of contemporary issues, clear and accurate descriptions of

The story begins with the largely admirable motivations of logical empiricism.[8] The history of twentieth-century philosophy of science, until about the mid-1960s, just is the history of logical empiricism. The development of logical positivism, and the logical empiricism into which it evolved, can be traced at least as far back as the early years of the twentieth century, when Bertrand Russell and others reacted against the British idealism of Bradley and McTaggart. Science had an increasingly high profile on the intellectual scene in the late 1800s and early 1900s, and, given the instrumental knowledge it yielded, philosophers attempted to extract general epistemological lessons from the best examples of empirical knowledge available—those provided by science.

Throughout history, philosophical pedagogy was driven by narrative methods; it required instruction in several languages and classic philosophical, historical, and literary texts and often theological training or at least an earnest familiarity with the dominant religious tradition. This philosophical tradition was comfortable with metaphysical vocabulary that allowed protracted and solemn discussion of claims about values, gods, souls, angels, and essences, all hidden from casual inspection. But there were broader cultural, social, and political forces that led philosophers to nod in ceremonious approval to the weighty (if obscure) pronouncements of such figures as Hegel, Fichte, and Schelling. After all, such tolerance for mystery reflects a perhaps appropriate, conversational imagination, when

---

scientific practice, and candid judgments on historical figures and positions in the philosophy of science, all in a lively style. Fetzer (1993) does an especially good job simplifying the often quite technical treatments of confirmation and explanation. Kosso (1992) is a somewhat less systematic treatment of issues in recent philosophy of science, but the discussions are unusually novel for an introduction, made accessible by the author's elegant style. Laudan (1990) offers a useful discussion of contemporary issues in a dialogue format. At the more advanced level, Salmon et al. (1992) presents wonderful overview essays central to current disputes, and Boyd, Gasper, and Trout (1991) provides important articles that define contemporary philosophy of science, as well as substantial introductory material.

8. The presentation of the empiricist program that follows is not advanced as exegesis but as an accurate description of its actual impact. Recently, realist presentations of logical empiricism have been criticized for misrepresenting logical empiricism as both philosophically monolithic and naive. This literature rationally reconstructs logical empiricism, drawing a narrative line through the Kantian tradition in which logical empiricist themes can be seen as having been distilled and amplified by such figures as Wolff and Heidegger. One central suggestion in this literature is not just that there is an unclaimed philosophical legacy leading from Kant to Carnap but that it was in some way irresponsible to have missed it.

The treatment of logical empiricism as defined by the principle of verifiability and the observation/theory distinction is not an invention of realists but of honest empiricists, such as Hempel (1965a) and later van Fraassen (1980), who carried out an internal critique of these tenets of traditional logical empiricism. Of course, there may be some level of abstraction at which, say, the Carnap who wrote "Testability and Meaning" could be seen as involved in an oblique philosophical exchange with traditional metaphysicians, but this in no way undermines the claim that the chief philosophical impact remains as we have always supposed. Whatever the history of intellectual debt or the motivation of the program, the canons of logical empiricism were used routinely by figures such as Carnap and Neurath as blunt instruments against philosophical programs of metaphysical presumption. There is no reason to doubt that logical empiricism was a complex and philosophically interesting movement, in much the same way that the lesser saints could be seen as building in an intellectually intricate way upon an Aristotelian legacy.

all that is at stake is faithfulness to the heroes of one's philosophical tradition. (For a more sympathetic vision of Hegel, see the introduction to Beiser 1993.) But philosophers and the social thinkers they inspired often had grander aims, with the result of grounding social policy in philosophical declarations so obscure they could be recruited in support of the most intolerant measures, from virulent nationalism to open racism. In the early twentieth century, the largely German and Austrian logical positivists contested vague but common declarations of "the greatness of the state" and "the inferiority of the Semitic people." A leisurely, polite tolerance for vagueness seemed inappropriate given the offensive content (either political or personal) of the declarations. When combined with the broader recognition that the development of the philosophical tradition had not achieved the kind of consensus and epistemic success—a body of accumulated wisdom—enjoyed by the emerging scientific tradition, some philosophers who were open to the morals of scientific methodology urged clarity in the explication of statements claimed to have empirical support.

In light of this history, the demanding epistemological standards ultimately advanced by the logical positivists were neither cavalier nor unmotivated. Moreover, to the extent that the science of the time reflected general intellectual standards valued in philosophical and other disciplines, the scientism of logical positivism was understandable. The logical positivists, following their interpretation of the Humean dictum that all nontautological knowledge arises from experience, attempted to formulate a way of distinguishing claims that have empirical content—and thus could be adjudicated objectively and neutrally by appeal to observable evidence—from those that do not have empirical content. In doing so, they hoped to secure a way of catching and identifying those claims that are metaphysical and thus on their view empirically meaningless. The resulting *principle of verifiability* was formulated in a variety of ways (for an early version, see Ayer 1946; for the rationale that was in the air at the time, see Schlick [1932/33] 1991). The principle asserted that the meaning of a statement is determined by the set of observation statements that nonvacuously entail it. Though a semantic principle, it was most often used in a way that was aggressively normative; it was used in an attempt to endorse certain types of statements and theories as properly empirical and subject to scientific investigation and to reject those that appeared by empiricist standards to be nonscientific, pseudoscientific, or otherwise "metaphysical" or meaningless. In its normative function, it provided the following test for meaningfulness: The (empirical) meaning of a statement or theory is given by the set of procedures used to test and thus confirm or disconfirm the statement or theory. An epistemic correlate, also wielded normatively by its proponents, claimed that knowing the meaning of a statement or a theory consists in understanding the circumstances under which one would be empirically justified believing it or its negation.

The difficulties facing applications of the principle of verifiability were both internal and external, involving both logical peculiarities resulting from its syntactic formulation and philosophical questions concerning the metaphysical status of the principle itself. For our purposes, the gravest criticism of the principle of verifiability is one it shares with an associated doctrine of the time, that of operationalism. In short, the principle of verifiability, no matter how well motivated, could not accommodate the actual, epistemically reliable practices of scientists; indeed, it contradicted those practices. It is now an adage that, when reliable scientific practice meets exacting philosophical principle, philosophical principle always yields or faces embarrassment.

Recognizing the patently metaphysical character of theoretical discourse in science, operationalists attempted to provide definitions of theoretical terms entirely by appeal to observable circumstances (Bridgman 1927). Operational definitions are identity statements that link each observable measurement procedure with a single type of unobservable quantity. To their credit, empiricists eventually rejected this account of theoretical measurement as incoherent (see Hempel 1965a). The primary problem arises as follows. According to unreconstructed scientific practice, a single theoretical quantity can be measured in a variety of ways. But according to operationalism, the particular procedure is definitive of the theoretical quantity, and thus one would have to postulate a different quantity for each different observable procedure that was (perhaps even could be) used. Should the normative feature of this rational reconstruction be taken seriously, it would recommend an improper methodology. It was precisely because empiricists recognized and respected that the same theoretical quantity persisted under diverse measurement procedures that they rejected early operationalist accounts of theoretical definition.

In this sense, operationalism can be seen as a foundationalist precursor to the verifiability principle.[9] Orthodox histories of this period often diagnose the allure of the verifiability principle in terms of the common attraction to foundationalist epistemology.[10] It is important to notice, however, that it was a special kind of

9. Foundationalism is often presented as a doctrine that makes nothing more than a modest claim concerning the structure of justification. Although this is a possible understanding of the term "foundationalism," it is important to recognize that foundationalist epistemologies, as actually proposed and defended in the history of philosophy, have made substantial claims about the content of the justificatory material. Phenomenalists claimed that the content was sensory and should be describable in a vocabulary of sensations, for example. Operationalists claimed that the meaning of theoretical terms was defined by, or identified with, observed measurement procedures. Phenomenalism ran afoul of privacy problems, operationalism of improvement apparently based on theoretical considerations.

10. By itself, foundationalism is the doctrine that all knowledge depends for its justification on certain "basic beliefs." However, positivist formulations normally cast the required source of justification as some sort of sensory content or sense data, sometimes referred to as "the given." One such basic belief might be "this liquid appears red" or "this metal rod is hot." The requirement that there be such basic beliefs gets its primary force from what is widely believed to be one of two disastrous alternatives, either infinite regress or circularity. Among logical empiricists, it was common to understand justification in terms of the relation between the premises and conclusion of a deductive argument, in which the premises provide the justification for the conclusion. If justification does not terminate in doxastic states that are in this sense basic or foundational, then either the justification of some premises depends on other premises and those on still others, producing an infinite regress, or some premises must be self-justifying, thereby yielding claims to justification that are circular. So foundationalists take solace in the apparent inevitability of one of these consequences and conclude that, if beliefs are ever to be justified, some beliefs must be basic and not depend on any other beliefs

foundationalism that motivated the principle of verifiability, a kind of foundation-alism that assigned observation the definitive epistemic function in theory choice and confirmation and that found its chief expression in the choice between em-pirically equivalent theories.

Early logical empiricists attempted to analyze the centrality of observation (and the extraneous character of metaphysics) to scientific objectivity by formulating an illustrative thought-experiment envisioning empirically equivalent theories. Imagine that we have a theory, T_1, designed to explain some specified class of natural phenomena such as chemical bonding. It does so in terms of the theoreti-cal notion of valence. By appeal to this unobservable property, and in conjunction with certain auxiliary hypotheses, we are able to generate observational predic-tions concerning the behavior of particular solutions. However, it is possible to formulate a different theory of the same observable phenomena, T_2, that specifies different unobservable causal mechanisms but has all the same deductive observa-tional consequences. Suppose, for example, that T_2 postulates certain conscious features of personal attraction and repulsion between elemental phenomena but is rigged to yield all the same predicted outcomes as T_1.[11]

Although the consideration of empirically equivalent theories had an innocent philosophical origin, it fed the philosophical appetite for generality and abstrac-tion. As a way of indicating how observation can play an important role in set-tling theoretical disputes in experimental settings already highly constrained by received collateral information, the empirically equivalent theories account per-forms well. But as an account of relevant reasons to doubt the particular conclu-sion drawn from a particular experimental test, the idea that a test must survive the strain of empirical equivalence applies standards too abstract either to guide experimental design or to endorse methods that are epistemically reliable.

With similar concerns about identifying and diagnosing intellectually disrepu-table practices, Karl Popper proposed the principle of falsifiability—that the hall-mark of a scientific theory is that it is falsifiable under empirical testing. Put more formally, a theory is potentially a scientific theory if and only if there are possible observations that would falsify or refute it. The principle of falsifiability differs from the principle of verifiability in two important ways. First, the principle of falsifiability is not a semantic tenet. Rather, it is a standard of demarcation that proposes to distinguish science from nonscience, not statements with meaning from those without. The fact that a statement fails the test of falsifiability does not show that the statement is meaningless. What it does show is that the state-

---

for their justification even if other beliefs may depend on basic beliefs. I will address this concern in the discussion of naturalism below. For a sophisticated coherentist alternative, see Bon Jour (1985).

11. Glymour (1980, chapter 9) usefully considers just such a concocted theory, in the case of "the gorce-morce theory of force." Glymour proposes that the evidence is stronger for our familiar, single-factor theory of force because it is better tested than its two-factor alternative. This type of reaction to austere empiricist accounts of evidence derives from confirmation theory, in which strength of evidence is normally analyzed not in terms of metaphysical notions like correspondence truth or our causal relations to underlying factors but in terms of methodological features such as severity of testing.

ment is not properly scientific. Second, the principle of falsifiability is profoundly anti-inductivist. Although defenders of the principle of verifiability would take an instance of a metal rod that expands when heated as (some) confirmation of the universal generalization that all metal rods expand when heated, it is not so according to Popper. For Popper, a theoretical hypothesis is not confirmed by experimental test; instead, it is said to be "corroborated"—in short, it fails to be refuted. It is not clear how many times a hypothesis needs to survive attempts at refutation before theoretical commitment is warranted. Indeed, it would seem that our most secure theoretical posits in physics deserve greater epistemic esteem than Popper's corroboration allows. It is too weak an expression of the success of these posits to say that the "postulated" existence of, for example, molecules and their bonding properties has till now merely survived efforts at refutation. Despite this defect, the principle of falsifiability, for a time, embodied the desired standard of severity to separate genuine science from pseudo-science.

The approaches of falsifiability and verifiability are alike in four important ways. First, both assign a less central epistemic role than they should to the auxiliary hypotheses or background theories required to test the target statement or theory (see Putnam 1974). Second, both are deductivist about theory testing; theories isolate hypotheses to test by deducing observational predictions. Third, with its Humean roots, the doctrine of falsifiability, like the doctrine of verifiability to which it was widely regarded as the only alternative, assigned a fundamentally empiricist and foundationalist significance to observation. So we find Popper analyzing the concept of falsifiability by claiming that "statements or systems of statements, in order to be ranked as scientific, must be capable of conflicting with possible, or conceivable observations" (1963, p.39). Finally, they are both aggressively normative. We have already seen this feature of the verifiability program. To see it in Popper's falsifiability method of demarcation, one need only look at the opening pages of his *Conjectures and Refutations*, in which it is announced that Marx's theory of history is empirical but has been refuted, Adler's individual psychology is irrefutable by crucial experiment and thus pseudo-scientific, and Einstein's theory of general relativity is a paradigm of a genuine scientific theory.

Fortunately, scientists weren't much bothered by the fact that successful sciences failed to meet one or all of the standards set out by the verificationist and the falsificationist. In this, an irony was missed by logical empiricists. Philosophers in the middle of the twentieth century were still telling scientists their business—this time in the form of a rational reconstruction—despite the facts that the history of epistemology over the last 2,000 years illustrates little consensus concerning the conditions of epistemic justification and that science was, perhaps uniquely, distinctive for the security and the scrupulousness with which it tested its own knowledge claims.

Logical empiricists proposed to resolve the tension between their austerely antimetaphysical constraint on cognitive exchange and the metaphysically potent vocabulary of science by subjecting scientific practice and discourse to philosophical scrutiny and explaining the apparent centrality of theoretical commitment in other terms—to reconstruct the practice and discourse of the sciences so that it could be viewed as rational. This rational reconstruction was carried out in a number of ways. One approach, fostered by Rudolf Carnap and others, sharply distinguished observation and theory. This approach collapsed under the strain of a series of difficulties. Another, more contemporary version introduced by Bas van Fraassen (1980), reformulates this distinction as one about the attitudes of the scientist, who can accept a theory as empirically adequate rather than believing a theory as approximately true. We will consider selected aspects of this view in greater detail in chapters 3, 4, and 5.

The accurate description of scientific practice, of course, occurs prior to rational reconstruction. So it is not surprising that the empiricist use of it should do a miserable job at depicting actual science. However, under the banner of ontological purity and philosophical clarity, rational reconstruction came to play a powerful normative role in determining the acceptability of a systematic, philosophical conception of science. Although the positive aim of rational reconstruction concerns the improvement and clarification of what is best about scientific methodology, philosophers in the twentieth century have made ambitious negative use of it. Rational reconstruction is often used to reject epistemological views that do not have prima facie antimetaphysical consequences or that endorse explanations for the success of scientific methodology in terms of the (approximate) truth of appropriate background theories.

The Move toward Holism and Naturalism

Owing to internal pressures within the movement, logical empiricism's central epistemic tenets were losing their grip on the philosophical audience of the time. In this process, Quine's attack on foundationalism marked a decisive turn in attitudes toward rational reconstruction. Cast first as an attack on the testing of hypotheses by the "tribunal of experience alone" (1963), it was transformed by Quine, in *Word and Object* (and later in his 1969 piece "Epistemology Naturalized"), into a positive version of naturalism, according to which there is no first philosophy and thus no privileged position that philosophers can arrogate to themselves.

In fact, Quine's holism, informed as it was by the work of Pierre Duhem, reminded philosophers of science of the theory dependence of scientific method and what might be called confirmation holism in the testing of hypotheses. If we observe scientific practice, we will notice that hypotheses (or statements) are never tested in isolation; they are tested in groups. If one wants to test a hypothesis concerning the location of light-sensitive cells in the visual cortex and does so by recording their impulses with an electrode, one depends not just on the best physiological theory of the time but also on the best physical theory that provided the basis for the design and use of the oscilloscope and electrode. If the prediction is supported by the experiment, then the collateral or background theories receive mild support as well. If the prediction is not supported by the experiment, it could be due either to the falsity of the hypothesis or to local errors in the mature collateral theories used in testing the hypothesis. In light of the deeply theory-dependent nature of scientific methods and the holism of confirmation, it is very difficult to locate credit for the routine success of a scientific theory anywhere but in the postulated entities, laws, and theories tested.

The theory dependence of scientific method evident in the testing of hypotheses was made even more salient by Thomas Kuhn's *The Structure of Scientific Revolutions* in 1962. According to Kuhn, perceptions and judgments of scientists are so dependent on the theories in which scientists were trained that the philosopher and the historian of science are driven to a dramatic conclusion about the relation between the scientist and the world: Theory articulation is best understood as a process of the construction of a (mind-dependent) world rather than the discovery of a mind-independent reality. Many philosophers of science have contested whether the ontological conclusion that Kuhn draws is warranted on the basis of the methodological evidence he recruits, but this controversy does not threaten the doctrine of theory dependence; the theory dependence of scientific method remains one of the most influential and durable themes in the philosophy of science. The aftermath of Kuhn's *Structures* gave rise to a variety of strategies to marry the normative aims characteristically pressed by the philosopher of science and the descriptive aims of the historian of science (see Lakatos 1970; Lakatos and Musgrave 1970).

The naturalism of this book is a variant of Quine's. Because there is no first philosophy, no special (typically a priori) philosophical principle is required to justify claims regarding the reliability of scientific methodology. However, this feature is sometimes claimed to produce a crisis of justification for the naturalistic epistemologist.[12] As Quine himself points out (1969, pp. 75–76), early logical empiricists treated as circular the appeal to psychology for justification of epistemic principles. If one conceives of epistemology as a separate foundation of empirical science, then empirical psychology would indeed be the wrong place to look for justification of epistemological claims. This charge of circularity requires closer examination.

The philosophical community was prepared for the rise of naturalistic treatment of knowledge by the emergence of naturalism in other areas such as the philosophy of mind. In action theory, Davidson's (1963, 1980a) and Goldman's (1970) explanations of the rationalizing power of reasons in terms of their causal efficacy paved the way for the routine adoption of causal explanation as a model for psychological explanation generally. The same powerful impetus to naturalism was provided by the appearance and articulation of functionalism in the philosophy of mind (Putnam 1960, 1973), according to which mental states are identified by their causal relations to input, output, and other mental states. Since mental states are here both deemed unobservable and accorded causal powers, the flourishing of functionalism is regarded by some as a crowning achievement of realism.

---

12. Like Quine, I hold that to do epistemology is to do psychology. Unlike Quine's naturalized epistemology, however, the version of naturalism I defend insists that the psychology that supplants traditional epistemology should be the best psychology of the time, judged by the best scientific standards (some of which are psychological) of the time. By these standards, models of internal processing are favored over behaviorism.

A survey of the way in which scientific theories classify their objects reveals a simple but important principle: Scientific taxonomy, at least characteristically, is causal taxonomy. Species are classified in part by their powers to interbreed, chemical elements are classified by their abilities to combine with certain other elements, subatomic particles are classified by their dispositional, interactive forces, and the list continues. Even domains thought to be "merely taxonomic," such as geology and paleontology, classify objects with respect to causally important features of objects in the domain. (There are, of course, other taxonomies that are not causal, such as mathematical ones, but these will not concern us.)

The articulation of a causal taxonomy, in whatever domain, is the result of actual empirical investigation; in the case of science, it is the result of experimental and theoretical work. In the area of the philosophy of language, appreciation of this fact led to causal theories of reference for names and for natural-kind terms. According to Putnam (1970) and Kripke (1971), the definitions of such terms are given by a posteriori investigation of their actual historical origin and the causal regulation of their use by social conventions and by interaction with their actual extensions. In the case of "gold," the term refers to the item that plays a systematic role in the causal taxonomy of chemistry. Only the actual investigations of chemistry, by which the extension is determined, can fully articulate its definition. In fact, in light of the refinement of a natural definition by the causal interaction of term and world, the causal theory of reference provides a model of epistemic refinement that explains the failure of other such relations of epistemic significance, such as operationalist accounts of measurement.[13] The routine correction and improvement—in short, the refinement—of measurement procedures can be plausibly explained only in terms of a reliable causal relation between an instrument and a quantity.

When this instrument is a knower, we have an illustration of the sort of relation that has motivated causal theories of perception and knowledge (Goldman 1967, 1976; Armstrong 1973). On a generic description of this view, an instance of knowledge consists in a causal relation between a reliably produced (approximately) true belief and some specific aspect of the world. Reliability in this context is taken to indicate a relation of causal dependence. This kind of naturalistic epistemology has seemed troubling to some, precisely because it leaves to the field of psychology the description of the mechanisms of justification. Two reasons for worry are often given. In the first place, it is thought to leave unaddressed the justification of psychology itself. Many have considered Quine's answer—"In induction nothing succeeds like success" (1969, p. 165)—to be unable to capture the normative distinction between good and bad methodology, to be a conception that would not necessarily count as poor a method that was predictively successful by sheer accident. Second, and more to the point, some foundationalist epistemologists worry that, if scientific testing and practice provide the final word on the

---

13. I am assuming here that the theory of reference—perhaps semantics generally—will find its final resting place in a suitably complete epistemology.

assessment of epistemological principles, we will have no basis for the independent appraisal of those scientific methods vindicating the proposed epistemological principles.

This requirement that epistemology be normative is most commonly claimed to break the back of a naturalized epistemology (see Moser 1993, pp. 147–151, and Moser 1991). I will argue that a naturalistic epistemology is normative, but not in the way that a foundationalist typically requires. The foundationalist worry can be framed as follows. If actual scientific practices and perspectives are the fundamental basis for the evaluation of epistemological principles, as the naturalistic epistemologist holds, then it is not clear what principles constitute the epistemological basis for the critical appraisal of scientific principles and practices. Suppose, for example, that some principle P is advanced as conducing to reliable judgment in a particular domain. Traditional epistemological standards would require that, if we are to explain why this application of principle P is worthy of trust, we must either advert to some other principle O in which the reliability of P is grounded (in which case justification hasn't yet terminated) or appeal to the general reliability of P itself (in which case the proposed justification is circular).

In a clear taxonomy of this naturalistic project, Philip Kitcher (1992, 1993) sets out naturalism according to the following four theses:

1. The central problem of epistemology is to understand the epistemic quality of human cognitive performance, and to specify strategies through whose use human beings can improve their cognitive states. . . .
2. The epistemic status of a state is dependent on the processes that generate and sustain it.
3. The central epistemological project is to be carried out by describing processes that are reliable, in the sense that they would have a high frequency of generating epistemically virtuous states in human beings in our world.
4. Virtually nothing is knowable a priori, and, in particular, no epistemological principle is knowable a priori. (1992, pp. 74–76)

Denuded of its familiar normative garb, traditional naturalism, as Philip Kitcher calls it, is criticized for its inability to offer a satisfactory answer to the skeptic. The most common charge is that such naturalism has no normative force, and giving it normative force makes it circular. Call this the grounding problem. The most common form of this problem arises when the naturalist conceives of epistemic principles as the province of psychology; on this view, the reliable processing of information is the subject matter of psychology. According to the grounding problem, if we appeal to the results of psychological research for justification of a belief, it is not clear what provides justification for our belief that psychology supplies results reliable enough to vindicate appeal to psychology. In this case, an irreducible appeal to psychology is circular, and a reducible one leaves our belief ungrounded. Unprincipled appeal to the challenge of skepticism is the primary cause of premature rejection of naturalism.

No epistemology, naturalistic or not, has yet accommodated the diverse styles of inquiry in science that Kuhn and others have identified. If a response to the skeptic is deemed unsatisfying apart from terminating justification in a priori principles, then the consistent naturalist should not comply; skeptics have yet to state the a priori principles that, if not honored, make naturalism untenable. If the antinaturalist proposal is that there are general (nonscientific) intellectual standards that scientific inquiry must display if it is to be properly scientific, then these standards have yet to be plausibly delivered. This radically normative program of intellectual hygiene has advanced such standards—in the form of the verifiability principle, the falsifiability principle, and a host of others—but to a principle these standards have failed on both normative and descriptive grounds.

I believe Kitcher's diagnosis of the current situation in epistemology is correct. A fully naturalistic epistemology must honor the social and the historical character of scientific judgment; it is not just the reliability of individuals on which we depend but the reliability of scientific communities and institutions as well. Traditional forms of epistemology lack the resources to handle such facts. In addition, the relevant notion of justification in any fully naturalistic epistemology must treat justification as an achievement that can only be properly characterized diachronically rather than synchronically, as the skeptic often demands. On this latter point, Richard Boyd (1981) has articulated the rationale for just such a diachronic condition, of reliable belief regulation rather than simply reliable belief production.

This is not a book about scientific epistemology, except to the extent that the historically contingent and subject-matter-specific features of measurement yield a model for the direction of epistemology. But several points are worth noting. The principles most central to theory testing, experimental design, and theory choice are all theory dependent; they are not home truths, conceptual truths, or otherwise associated with a priori status. The primary principles guiding theoretical judgment are a posteriori. If the foundationalist raises the familiar concern regarding the source of justification for *these* principles, this would amount to a simple demand, in advance, that justification be a priori, a demand that the principles of justification not be radically contingent. It is not a desire for presumptuous commitments or a flare for drama that drives the realist to the claim that the justificatory principles of epistemic naturalism are historically contingent; it is rather the need to explain a striking feature of scientific practice that cannot be rationalized in accordance with the sort of a priori principles characteristic of foundationalist projects. Those principles are normally presented as home truths or pieces of common wisdom, open to casual assessment. However, should the critic remain unconvinced that justification must be of a nonfoundationalist sort, consider the fact that the principles are not just theory dependent but arcane as well.[14] The principles guiding the assimilation of old evidence to contemporary taxonomic categories (Trout 1994), the determinations of appropriate experts on whom other scientists can depend (Hardwig 1985, 1991; Thagard 1993; Trout 1992), and judgments of simplicity, sampling, and representativeness (Boyd [1985] 1991b), turn on extremely detailed and technical considerations known only to a

---

14. This feature seems to be behind Richard Miller's (1987) emphasis on the "discipline-specific" character of methodological principles.

(typically) small and highly trained community; these principles are therefore based on information that is sufficiently arcane that their reliability cannot be accounted for by appeal to scientists' appreciation of a body of common lore, of a priori methods open to all.[15]

Failure to appreciate the arcane, contingent, and a posteriori character of justificatory principles in science is one source of the nearly universal assumption of this literature on naturalism that naturalistic epistemology must be purely descriptive—that there is no room in such an epistemology for normative requirements. (I except from this regrettable trend the work of such figures as Giere, Goldman, Kitcher, and Kornblith.) If this were required by naturalistic epistemology, philosophical naturalism would appear to be peculiarly inadequate for its original purpose, for it would fail to capture the very critical, normative component in scientific practice itself, apparently essential to its instrumental reliability. And it was the distinctive success of scientific methodology that motivated philosophical naturalism in the first place. Developed sciences are sufficiently successful that we should regard theoretical standards in science as the normative basis for scientific knowledge.

The upshot is that there can be a naturalistic epistemology that is normative, where the prescriptions come from the methodologies of science itself. This may not be the sense of normativity desired by a Humean foundationalist, but it is the only plausible one that doesn't make the demand a priori that providing explicit justification is constitutive of the role of justification in science; that one cannot *be* justified without *providing* justification. In addition, chapters 6 and 7 of this book sketch what a realist, naturalized epistemology would look like when it is normative. In particular, chapter 7 critically addresses, from a naturalistic perspective, a prominent style of skeptical argumentation to which philosophers and scientists are prone when criticizing unfamiliar research.

The charge that naturalistic epistemology is question-begging arises in part because an adequate understanding of the normative aspect of epistemology is thought to require a certain type of intellectual practice, namely *giving* justification. In this respect, the charge of question-beggingness fails to acknowledge perhaps the most compelling moral of the causal theory of knowledge: It is possible for us to be causally related to objects, and regulated by their properties, without necessarily knowing that we are so related.[16] Few who take scientific knowledge seriously doubt that such knowledge is justified in virtue of *some* facts; but this can be so without justification being characterized in the way envisioned by tradi-

---

15. Other themes in naturalistic epistemology will find support in the following pages. For example, the contents of many of the cognitive and perceptual states implicated in epistemic appraisal are not consciously accessible. But we should distinguish between the radical contingency of a methodological principle (in which the principle is esoteric) and its inaccessibility to consciousness in our application of it.

16. Population-guided estimation rejects internalism about the properties that confer knowledge. I don't intend to enter the fray here. For sympathetic versions of reliabilism, see Goldman (1992, chapter 9) and Sosa (1991, chapter 8). For a useful taxonomic discussion of internalism and externalism, see Alston (1989, chapters 8 and 9).

tional foundationalists. In particular, one might have justification for a certain belief, or be justified in holding the belief, but be unable to provide or articulate its conditions of justification. One might contend, for example, that the success of modern physics and chemistry was initially made possible by a series of developments that might be described as broadly historically contingent—namely, the adoption and articulation of the atomistic hunch at the time of Boyle and Newton. Once scientists appreciated the power of the hypothesis that at one organizationally important level the world in small is like the observable world in consisting of discrete concreta, the discoveries of modern physics and chemistry could commence (as long as other necessary factors were also in place, such as sufficient capital and labor to work out the project; see Kitcher 1993).

To the critic of naturalistic epistemology, this appeal to the radical contingency of the history of science may appear a desperate, ad hoc attempt to rescue the naturalistic program from a decisive objection. But actually this move is motivated by simple descriptive facts concerning the history of science. In the first place, we have been unable to find a priori principles by which to assess knowledge claims, and it hasn't been for want of trying. Consider, for example, the claims made on behalf of the adjudicating power of Bayes's theorem. The principles that seem to lead to the most impressive bodies of empirical information are themselves a posteriori; the history of science has shown us this if it has shown us anything. Put negatively, the central methodological principles, described at a level of specificity that renders them useful, are not a priori. This might explain why methodology interacts so richly with background theory. In fact, the sort of scientific methodology with which we are familiar might not achieve reliability without a sufficiently accurate background theory concerning the causal structure of unobservables. Now, it might be that in the social and behavioral sciences— and for similarly contingent reasons—we haven't arrived at such a Newtonian hunch, or we have but we lack the conceptual resources to exploit this hunch. Perhaps this could explain the slow progress of the social and behavioral sciences.

A problem of scale lurks here, which occurs whenever we don't spell out the standards of accuracy being employed. After all, in a sense the social and behavioral sciences did not start out as badly as physics, for four reasons. First, unlike the phenomena of primary interest in physics, many of the phenomena in the social sciences—perhaps most of the phenomena of interest—are observable. Many of the events and objects of interest, then, are open to casual inspection. Second, we may well be adapted to have the competencies to do at least the basic tasks in the behavioral sciences, in the form of various sorts of communication. So we have a pretty good background of tacit theory to constrain hypotheses and on which methodology can operate. Third, even if all of the phenomena we are studying and about which we are generalizing are observable, the methods themselves are hardly a priori. Economics is largely about observable phenomena, and yet the principles that determine financial exchanges depend upon contingent facts concerning specific features of the economy. Finally, no one doubts that psychology and social science have a subject matter—the existence of other minds was seldom disputed, though the existence of photons often was—and so it is puzzling that the critic should miss the fact that in the social and behavioral sciences we begin with theoretical posits that are more secure than those begun within physics. Given the routine success we enjoy in explaining each other's behavior in mundane contexts (Fodor 1986; Trout 1991), it is easy to feel betrayed by stumbling research programs in the social and behavioral sciences, since they begin with such cognitive advantages.

But there is an alternative explanation, one tied to the version of epistemological naturalism defended in this book. I will argue in the next chapter that some hypotheses can be tested by several different theories and are thus dependent on no single theory. This feature of a hypothesis I call being epistemically bite sized, and it underlies one plausible explanation for the slow and piecemeal progress in the behavioral sciences. It is possible that the units of progress are epistemically bite sized precisely because, given our routine familiarity with the objects of the behavioral sciences (in dramatic contrast to the routine hiddenness of the objects of physics), the history of the behavioral sciences is not as radically epistemically contingent as the history of the physical sciences. In other words, progress in the behavioral sciences does not depend on any Jamesian, Freudian, or other hunch about the theoretical structure of behavior in the way that physics depended upon the reception of the Newtonian hunch.

Other conceptions of naturalism exist, of course, and there remains considerable disagreement about what naturalism entails.[17] Some commentators suppose that naturalism about the social and behavioral sciences requires social and psychological events to be implicated in generalizations subsumable under natural laws (see, for example, Papineau 1978, 1993; Braybrooke 1987). This view and variants of it presuppose a reductionist account of the social and behavioral sciences that is certain to drive many of those doubtful of the prospects of reductionism into the warm sanctuary of narrative, Verstehen-type approaches. Therefore, criticisms of this version of the naturalistic approach are criticisms that one would have made of positivism and are hence correspondingly less illuminating. The naturalism I defend need not be reductive. Indeed, the naturalistic philosopher concerned to recruit trends in the history of science as support for naturalism must formulate a version at least compatible with the striking proliferation of scientific disciplines, a trend not predicted by the strong "unity of science" view of the positivists. So long as it is possible to specify the causal mechanisms responsible for reliable belief formation and transmission (etc.) in a satisfactory, nonmysterious way, nonreductive accounts are available to naturalists.

Because naturalism proposes to take the products and methods of science at face value, the resurgence of naturalism licenses the unreconstructed, metaphysical discourse in science, at least to the extent that science is metaphysical. Even in mundane, nonscientific contexts, we have always adverted to unobserved men-

---

17. For a suggestion to this effect, Philip Kitcher draws a useful distinction between the claim that psychology is relevant to the analysis of epistemic concepts and the claim that psychological results are relevant to the development of epistemic doctrines (1992, p. 62, n. 27).

tal dispositions in the explanation of behavior. One powerful form of argument for realism sprang from critiques of positivism.[18] If, contrary to positivist strictures, the distinction between observational and theoretical statements is not clear or is otherwise not epistemically significant, then one is inclined to realism if one is to avoid skepticism even about observables. If this background argument is sound, then one reason realism about the natural sciences has been treated as at least initially plausible (as an epistemological position, no matter what one's stance about realist modal claims concerning laws and necessity) is that the instrumental and theoretical success of the physical sciences has been pretty uncontroversial— that's part of the rationale for calling physics and chemistry mature. The realist infers the doctrine of realism not from instrumental success alone but from the epistemological parity of observational and theoretical claims as well. With some of the philosophical concepts now in hand, we can turn to a survey of scientific results meriting realistic interpretation. The appropriate version of realism is developed in chapter 4.

A Survey of Sciences Worthy of the Name

The survey offered in the present chapter does not purport to represent the subtlety and sophistication of theory construction and testing in these disciplines; no brief survey could. Indeed, a clear and detailed appreciation of the achievements of the social and behavioral sciences would be impossible without an elaborate study. Instead, I hope to convey the instrumental reliability of many areas of psychological and social research, their integration or tendency toward unification across disciplines, and their ability to generate their own research questions. So this brief survey of substantial experimental and theoretical accomplishments of selected social and behavioral sciences should stimulate the interest of philosophers who otherwise reserve their intellectual respect for physics and biology.

Psychology

VISION.   Many anecdotal musings on the faculty of vision, by philosophers and others, have noted that we are not aware of the complexity of visual processes. Phenomenologists sometimes note that we take in the scene all at once. Unfortunately, observations advanced in support of this sort of generalization are too coarse to isolate specific causal factors responsible for this ability. Do we have any reason to suppose, as Descartes and Berkeley apparently did, that lack of awareness of the operation of separate mechanisms is an indication that there are not separate temporal stages or distinguishable mechanisms operating? Not especially.

18. In her careful survey of arguments for and against scientific realism, Alison Wylie (1986, p. 287) has dubbed these "default arguments for realism."

In the words of contemporary researchers, "the immediacy and directness of an impression are no guarantee that it reflects an early stage of information processing in the nervous system. It is logically possible that we become aware only of the final outcome of a complicated sequence of prior operations" (Treisman and Gelade 1980, p. 98). The discrimination of separate stages or mechanisms in the visual process is made possible by a theory and method that partition the population of mechanisms under study into causally independent groups. Narrative focus on the phenomenology of vision is as questionable as impressionistic approaches elsewhere; narrative phenomenology delivers judgments about the fine-grained stages and mechanisms that are unlikely to have been guided by features of the population. Some of the evidence for distinguishable mechanisms comes from quantitative research in the physiology of vision.

RECEPTIVE FIELDS AND FEATURE DETECTORS.   Prior to the 1940s, early-stage accounts of vision proceeded on the assumption that a single neuron yielded very simple responses to very simple dimensions of sensory stimulation (e.g., light frequency, hue, etc.). Single neurons in the visual system were therefore thought to effect an elementary mapping from, for example, values of energy at some specific point of the sensory surface to response values transmitted to later stages of visual processing, where information could be integrated and structural information could yield a percept of the stimulus source. However, from the 1940s and into the 1960s, a series of studies on individual neurons showed that single neurons were selectively responsive to very specific, structurally complex patterns of sensory stimulation. Rather than responding to a single dimension of a light array, one sort of ganglion cell of the frog (Barlow 1953), for example, responds to a dark disk moving quickly back and forth through the receptive field, a notion introduced to describe this complex sensitivity. The motion of this dark target engages the frog's characteristic response to the detection of a bug—jumping and snapping its tongue. Similarly, feature-specific detection capacities were characterized by Hubel and Wiesel (1962) in neurons of the cat's visual cortex (also Kuffler 1953; Lettvin et al. 1959).

FEATURE DETECTORS AND ATTENTION.   At some point in the process of perception, information about the shape and color of an object must feed into the mechanisms supporting attention. We have the ability to acquire information about a single feature of an object by selecting and attending to that singular property. So at least some feature information is accessible to attention. Objects combine more than one feature, of course—for example, being vertical and green—and typically we must be able to distinguish between different types of objects that share at least one feature. This fact presents the visual system with the challenge of integrating separately processed features into the same object. In light of the earlier research on receptive fields in vision, then, an interesting question arises: Given the automatic responses of single neurons and the largely "executive," voluntary character of important aspects of attention, is attention deployed to combine features that have separate receptive origin?

According to the feature-integration account of attention, we must attend to each separable feature, such as shape or color, when distinguishing objects in a display that conjoins features—as, for example, a display of red and green circles (same shape, different color) or a display of green circles and squares (same color, different shape). Following a classic series of experiments (Treisman and Gelade 1980), a wealth of studies has characterized the role of attention in the perception of objects. For instance, if people are given a cognitively demanding task and at the same time are asked to view an array containing a red square and a green circle, they are vulnerable to what are called "illusory conjunctions"; that is, they regularly report seeing a red circle and a green square and do so more frequently than when there are no other demands on their attention (Treisman and Schmidt 1982).

No matter what the perceptual modality, the primary challenge in perception concerns the generation of a coherent percept from some sensory array. In the case of vision, when we first view a scene, feature information such as shape and color must be held somewhere while it is being integrated. It is held in a visual buffer, a type of visual memory that affords attentional mechanisms access to elemental visual processes. To account for feature integration and a host of other phenomena, psychologists and neuroscientists have appealed to patterns of activation and attention windows. The attention window selects a specific region of the visual buffer for close analysis. That region includes a pattern that has been activated by the stimulus (see Kosslyn and Koenig 1992, p. 55).

How do we test the hypothesis that some features of objects are processed separately and, in particular, processed before other features? Presumably in the same way we would identify separate observable objects. One way is to formulate experiments designed to detect separate causal contributions—marks of its degree of causal independence—if there are any signs of separation.

Early research on receptive fields provides the basis for theoretical integration between psychology and neuroscience, but the evidence of integration is now too diverse and plentiful to document fairly in a casual review. Any recent survey of the literature, even on as narrow a topic as visual attention, includes discussion of physiological features of neural activation, the anatomy of the visual cortex, the pathologies associated with visual breakdown, short-term visual memory, perceptual mechanisms in vision, and so forth. This type of integration is to be expected on the account of measurement described in chapter 2. But according to that account of measurement as population-guided estimation, agreement in the results of diverse procedures or programs is most plausibly explained by the existence of common causal factors with which we make epistemic contact. In such cases, we infer that the theory is guided by features of a common population.

COGNITION.   One of the most vigorous domains of cognitive research is in the area of memory. Its importance derives not just from its familiarity in everyday life—forgetting a date or a grocery list or misremembering the time of an appointment—but also from its role in nearly every perceptual and cognitive process.

Problem solving, visual-feature integration, and other cognitive tasks all include a role for various stages of the memory process.[19]

Contemporary descriptions of memory processes are imbued with a vocabulary of computation and representation. For example, rehearsal strategies are the most widely used techniques for memorization. (Rehearsal is actually a kind of mnemonic device.) Rehearsal is depicted as the process by which we maintain awareness of an item by continually reactivating the perceptual representation of spoken names of an item. That is why repeating a name or a number is thought to contribute to its memorization. As long as the rehearsed item is in awareness, or the representation is activated, the person has access to a representation—a model of sorts—that he or she can reproduce. There is a natural limit, amounting to roughly seven items, that can be recalled from a serially presented and rehearsed list. This limit is what George Miller (1956) was alluding to in his acclaimed title "The Magical Number Seven, Plus or Minus Two." When the list extends beyond seven items, it appears that people adopt quite a different method for remembering the sequence. Rather than waiting for the entire string to be completed before repeating the string (in serial fashion) from first item to the last, as they do with seven or fewer items, now subjects repeat each new item a few times in an effort to heighten its activation. In consequence, this task requires the perception of new words and the rehearsal of old ones, both of which compete for processing capacity and between which the subject must divide attention.

Perhaps the most well-established finding concerns the result of attempting to recall a list of more than ten words. This effort yields what might be called a "serial-position curve." The highest recall rates occur at the beginning and the end of the list, with performance falling off systematically as a function of the words' closeness to the medially presented item. This pattern of performance therefore produces a distinctive, bow-shaped curve. The primacy effect (high recall at the beginning of the list) and the recency effect (high recall at the end of the list) are explained in terms of the same mechanisms invoked in rehearsal. Roughly put, the earlier items are more accurately recalled because they receive more rehearsal, and the final items are more accurately recalled because their representations are still activated when the subject reports the list.

Our dependence on memory and our claims to its reliability are of practical as well as theoretical significance. On the basis of eyewitness testimony, itself merely a report of information recalled, men and women are judged, vilified or vindicated, sometimes even placed in jail. As can be seen, appeal to representational states and their activation is a crucial part of contemporary cognitive research. The description of transducer mechanisms alone will not bear the necessary explanatory weight in accounts of late-stage perception and higher cognitive functions. Representations are essential postulated mechanisms in memory research,

---

19. Early research made at least one feature of memory clear: memory is a complex faculty, subject to separable competencies. This moral can be extracted from a peculiar and interesting book by de Groot (1965): If chess masters are better at recalling possible board positions, it is not because they simply have better memories than the novices, for their memories were no better for the impossible-positions condition.

and attention research is no different in this respect. There are also memory and attentional subsystems that control and store features unique to a given modality. Visual phenomena of a conjunctive search engage a subsystem of visual attention, and so does visual memory. Representational states are at play in process descriptions of all of the sensory modalities. Like the representational states of memory described above, attentional states too can be primed or otherwise activated.

Input can activate multiple representations. Consider, for example, the important occurrence of priming. The speed with which we match a memory representation to some stimulus item—yielding a judgment, say, that a word on a screen and a semantic representation are the same—is in part determined by the representation's level of activation. The level of activation is raised by priming that representation. In a standard priming task, the subject is asked whether two stimuli presented in sequence are the same or different. The first stimulus is called the standard, and the second is called the probe. Subjects are able to identify two letters presented in sequence (such as A–A) as the same more quickly than they are able to respond to A–B as different. That is because the first occurrence of A primes all the stored features of the representation of A, raising its level of activation and making it more accessible than representations sharing fewer features with the standard (Proctor 1981). If fallacies of availability are abetted by accessibility effects of recency and priming, then the same reasons for concern over the availability bias should be thought to apply as well to processes whose contents are made available by priming and similar effects. Once a schema has been accessed, a connection is easily insinuated between a historical event and an explanation of that event that was preceded by similarities with the event recorded.

These mechanisms are unobservable, and the knowledge of them surveyed above has been acquired by theory-driven experimentation. As Measured Realism will suggest, their discovery and initial characterization depends not on possessing an approximately true theory of memory—let alone a complete one—but rather on an accurate description of their local causal powers and a general explanation of their apparent function. Of course, models of memory are now detailed and sophisticated, a consequence of the scientific tendency toward increasing accuracy and comprehensiveness. But failure to fit one specific model is rarely reason to reject the existence of mechanisms so characterized.

LANGUAGE.   Research on language has been similarly robust. Language, though not a separate sensory modality like vision or audition, appears to be a highly specialized subsystem having some of the same characteristics as the traditional modalities (Fodor 1983). Whatever its peculiarities, language, both spoken and written, is one of the most successfully mined fields of psychological research. Language studies fall into three broad areas: syntax (the study of grammatical form), semantics (the study of meaning in language), and pragmatics (the study of the contribution of context to linguistic meaning). Each of these categories has further subdivisions: phonetics, phonology, morphology, prosody, phrase, context, and others. The first two broad areas have been the most widely studied experimentally.

Let's begin with categorical perception in speech using the speech sounds

/ba/, /da/, and /ga/, heavily worked in phonetics research. These speech sounds vary along a physical continuum. But we perceive them as distinctive sounds. Our perceptual system must take the continuous signal and carve it into perceptually discriminable units. Suppose you take digitized speech and systematically change the frequency of the dominant component. We will come upon a point on the physical continuum that acts as a perceptual boundary: on one side we hear a /ba/ sound, and on the other we hear a /da/ sound. We do not, at that point, hear a sound that is described as "sort of" /ba/ and "sort of" /da/. This is an idealization, but what can be safely said is that various tokens of /da/ are more difficult to discriminate from one another than they are to discriminate from /ba/ or /ga/. (For more on this categorical feature of speech perception, see Repp and Liberman 1987; Rosen and Howell 1987; J. L. Miller 1990.) The engineering implementation of signal-processing theory is used in the digitization of speech; this intellectual cooperation reflects the kind of unifying power evident at the borders of psychology and "harder" disciplines.

Not only does the accumulation of this research constitute scientific progress, but the pace of this progress approaches that in more mature disciplines such as physics and biology. As late as 1920, there were still no experimental studies of phonetic categorization and language learning, and only anecdotal speculation about language pathology. (For the pioneering work on language pathology, see Head 1926.) There were, of course, many more descriptive works from previous centuries that transcribed and symbolized the sound patterns in particular natural languages, dictionaries that reported usage, and unregulated speculations about the origin and nature of language. But nothing was known about the mechanisms of activation, the pace and sequence of the child's syntactic development, or the processing capacities of a speech system so subtle that it can discriminate between two speech sounds differing in only (in the ideal case) one prominent spectral component.

PERSONALITY AND SOCIAL PSYCHOLOGY.   No matter how powerful and resilient the countervailing evidence may be, people manage to persist in the belief that they are above average in intelligence, looks, competence, and a legion of other properties. This tendency is part of a complex program, part affective and part cognitive, of self-esteem maintenance. A survey of 1 million high school seniors revealed that 70 percent believed they were above average in leadership ability. In the category of ability to get along with others, 25 percent believed that they were in the top 1 percent (College Board 1976–1977). As one might expect, people are also prone to attribute their failures to situational or external factors rather than dispositional or internal ones. This penchant for self-flattering interpretation is not a simple tendency but a cluster of dispositions, each of which may serve the same function of self-esteem maintenance in a different way. Just as we may enhance our self-esteem by overestimating the presence of selected positive properties, we deflect and manage negative ones. People control negative attributions made to them by "self-handicapping"—that is, by mentioning to the potential attributor in advance specific factors that might interfere with successful performance (in sports settings, "My shoulder is stiff"; "I borrowed this mitt"; etc.). These phenomena are thought to contribute to positive self-assessment and to the maintenance of self-esteem.[20] In serving these functions, they are integrated with well-understood cognitive effects.

These self-esteem effects in personality and social psychology emerge under standard experimental arrangements and statistical analyses of the data. Evidence of the existence of such self-esteem–maintaining mechanisms derives in part from their persistence under diverse experimental tests. Moreover, because these mechanisms are clusters of unobservable dispositions, our knowledge of them must reflect our ability to measure these theoretical quantities. Indeed, the reality of these mechanisms will supply the best available explanation of the improvement of the statistical designs in the field.

History

In historical research, we cannot construct a true experiment, so hypotheses must be tested by other means, explanations compared by other devices. One such example can be found in historical scholarship on European witchcraft. Early writings on European witchcraft did not collect sampling data of the sort described above. Instead, they offered close textual analyses of standard writs such as the *Canon Episcopi*, the *Malleus Maleficarum*, and the spate of other theoretical treatises on witches. From these works we might venture a composite profile, perhaps representative of those targeted for accusation. What emerged, not surprisingly, was the anecdotal stereotype of the aged sorceress. But the dangers of this style of historical inquiry should be just as clear as the advantages of the quantitative approach; among other facts leading to distortions, each of the primary sources was crafted by the hand of a medieval man. More specifically, one might want to determine how many of those prosecuted actually fit this dominant description or what the backgrounds, fortunes, and occupations were of those identified and ultimately prosecuted.

When quantitative care is taken, an interesting picture emerges from the historical data, even when aided only by percentages and a simple coding scheme. For example, Monter (1976) uses trial records of witchcraft prosecutions drawn from the Jura region during the sixteenth and seventeenth centuries to explore the profile of persons most likely to be accused. Legal records typically included the name and age of the accused, along with their occupation, marital status, and date of arrest or execution. In contrast to common lore, according to which accusations of witchcraft are independent events, Jura legal records indicate that clus-

---

20. See in particular Arkin and Maruyama (1979); Arkin, Cooper, and Kolditz (1980); Davis and Stephan (1980); Gilmour and Reid (1979); Lau and Russell (1980); Miller and Ross (1975); Tetlock (1980); Tetlock and Levi (1982); Weinstein and Lachendro (1982); Wiley, Crittenden, and Birg (1979). Much of this research is summarized and elegantly discussed in chapter 5 of Gilovich (1991). Further references can be found there. Also see Myers (1996).

ters of accusations punctuated long periods during which there were relatively few prosecutions. Those clusters, it turns out, represent particular witchcraft "panics" that would quickly spread through a region and just as quickly dissipate.

During the entire period, the disproportionate numbers of persons prosecuted were women, were older, and lived alone, either spinsters or widows (Monter 1976, pp. 115–126). Is there an explanation for this distribution of prosecutions? Here, we test explanatory hypotheses by determining whether implications of proposed hypotheses, in conjunction with our best social and psychological theories, are to be found elsewhere in the data. For example, Monter concludes that witchcraft accusations "can best be understood as projections of patriarchal social fears onto atypical women, those who lived apart from the direct male control of husbands or fathers. These defenseless and very isolated women became the group most often exposed to charges of witchcraft" (p. 124).

Moreover, by coding and recording the data we can examine possible causal influences—influences that are secondary to gender—and do so in a way that is systematic. It appears, for example, that while the majority of accused witches were poor, wealthy people were prosecuted with greater frequency during panic intervals than during other intervals, leading Monter to advance the hypothesis that an element of class resentment was exercised when terror suspended rules of social propriety, a hypothesis that can be assessed archivally. Indeed, without a partitioning of the population by gender, age, and social background, it is unlikely that any resilient trend would have emerged.

Of course, none of this is to say that Monter's patriarchal-projection interpretation of witch classification is unassailable. It is always possible that records that would have washed out this gender/age/marital status trend are missing, that the records were (unbeknownst to the historian) fraudulent, and so on. What it says is that the focus on quantitative parameters makes the historical analysis most subject to the influence of the historical evidence rather than to bias and unregulated speculation, a central theme of Measured Realism. (For further examples of the way in which raw percentages can be illuminating when theoretical dimensions are carefully selected, see Nauert 1977 and Braudel 1985.)

Sociology

I have cited quantitative research in sociology in a way that assigns intellectual dignity to the field, and more than one philosopher has dismissed the promise of scientific sociology with a territorial adage like "almost everyone makes fun of philosophers, and philosophers make fun of sociologists." When I have asked what was meant by "sociology," the picture that emerged was one of narrative social science, and a degenerate form at that. This attitude is not especially surprising, in light of the standard philosophical training described earlier. But a responsible philosophical assessment of progress in specific social sciences requires some exposition of the methods and content of those sciences, as we have supplied in the preceding sketches. Sociology and political science are also disciplines worthy of protracted philosophical analysis. Although the themes most important to the doctrine of Measured Realism are emphasized here, the primary function of these

research sketches is to initiate philosophical readers to particular brands of quantitative research in the social and behavioral sciences so that those disposed to
utter a similarly disparaging adage may at least present a realistic target.

Advances in sociology have illuminated nearly every area of collective human
and institutional action. The most notable developments have occurred in the
areas of administrative and organizational behavior, along with that of the interaction of labor markets with social and economic structures. In some of these
cases, improvements occurred because there are now methods that render theories
testable where there had been none before. In other cases, current theories have
replaced older, less powerful theories. Perhaps the most important development is
the introduction of causal modeling. Among other improvements occasioned by
this approach, causal models assign specific estimated values to unmeasured independent variables in a design. Because advance explicitness about causal variables
is part of the program, causal modeling allows us to trace the possible source of
interference, influence, confounding, and so forth without need for post hoc and
idle speculation about what might have gone wrong (or right) in a particular
design.

Researchers designed just such a causal model for the evaluation of the social
program of Headstart (Magidson and Sorbom 1982). According to this model,
variables such as parental educational level, occupation and socioeconomic status
and the child's cognitive ability are theoretically relevant and, in light of the best
affiliated research or (where there is no research) modest assumptions, assigned
specific values. Sometimes value and relevance assumptions are defended, and in
such cases it is by appeal to independently established evidence. Explicit causal
assumptions then determine the direction of causal dependence among these variables in the model. Because there is a record of these commitments, it is possible
to raise systematic and evaluable doubts about the theoretical commitments of
the model. For example, the Magidson-Sorbom model assumes that family socioeconomic status is a cause of parental education and family income. Glymour et
al. (1987, p. 201) raise questions about the plausibility of this assumption and
indeed whether the causal direction is not in fact reversed. Because the assumptions are explicit, estimable, and directional in the propagation of effects, these
claims can be evaluated, the recurring virtue of quantitative methods.

Suffice it to say that it is very difficult to practice experimental and quasi-
experimental sociology without methods of causal modeling. Focus on method as
a means of improvement here indicates the "data-driven" character of current
sociological theories, but substantial theoretical assumptions that prove successful
in one model get exported to others, a hallmark of realist interpretation. Therefore, one should not infer that contemporary sociology is bereft of theory or theoretical commitment. (For more on substantial social theory and design, see Blalock 1985a,b.)

Political Science

One of the most striking features of electoral systems such as those in the United
States is their stability; elected officials come and go, but the main political struc-

tures remain.[21] One explanation for this fact concerns the existence of political parties. Parties play a stabilizing role in the electoral process, helping to anchor the process against the vagaries of the individual styles of candidates and elected officials, as well as the temporary fancies of the electorate. Contemporary political research examines the relation between party affiliation and feelings of political efficacy, along dimensions such as race and class. The dominant approach to the study of the relation between politics and race focuses on racial differences in voting behavior. I will set out some representative studies of political attitudes and race.[22] But it is important to bear in mind that voting behavior is a very narrow and controversial method of measuring important political dispositions, and this fact will emerge in the discussion of these studies.

Party identification, feelings of political efficacy, and levels of political trust are just three dimensions along which relations between politics and race have been examined. In a comprehensive discussion of field studies, Abramson (1982) claims that two Michigan SRC panel surveys of party affiliation showed that, between 1956 and 1960, and between 1972 and 1976, "the white electorate has highly stable partisan attachments and that there is less partisan stability among blacks" (p. 99). However, these surveys used a three-party format (Republican, Democrat, and Independent). Often, there is either no Independent candidate or strong social pressure not to vote Independent ("You'll be throwing your vote away"). If we identify those Independents either as Democrat or Republican according to their partisan tendencies, and thus more closely approximate actual voting conditions, we find that "blacks, too, have a fairly high over-time consistency" in party affiliation (p. 102). It's not clear that the remaining African American versus white difference in partisan stability is statistically significant, and in any case no general explanation is offered here for this difference despite the fact that many possible causes suggest themselves (i.e., social, economic, educational, etc.).

One of the main panel studies of the American electorate compared African Americans and whites on the issue of the stability of feelings of political efficacy between 1956 and 1960. Negative answers to the following types of statements marked participants as "feeling politically efficacious": (1) "Politics and government seem so complicated"; (2) "Voting is the only way people can have a say";

---

21. This stability of political structures is, of course, a historically specific phenomenon. In Italy and Japan, parties that dominated the political landscape for decades have collapsed. It is important, then, for the relevant theoretical assumptions in political science to specify the period over which the generalizations range. One might treat parties as theoretically superficial, pointing out that the collapse of a party can be followed by the co-opting by other parties of its more durable political tendencies. This would explain shorter temporal fluctuations in the dominance of parties, as when the federal Conservative Party in Canada, which had been in office for almost a decade, won only two seats across the country. Notice, however, that none of this undermines interest in the phenomenon of political stability—even when (often-fleeting) parties figure centrally in the research—so long as the deeper question of political representation sustains the focus on parties.

22. Race is treated as a categorical variable in this literature, even though matters aren't that simple.

(3) "Public officials don't care what people think"; and (4) "People like me don't have any say." Other studies trace the over-time correlation (as a measure of stability) from 1952 to 1980, and for all but one of these four-year periods African Americans had a lower estimation of their own political efficacy than whites (Abramson 1982, p. 166).

Panel studies on stability (or over-time comparison) of political trust are available only for the intervals 1972–1974 and 1974–1976. Political trust was estimated by answers to questions on a "five-item political-trust index" (Abramson 1982, p. 227)—questions such as, "Do you think the government in Washington can be trusted?" and, "Do you think the government wastes tax money?" According to this survey, during this period whites have a higher level of stability of political trust than African Americans.

When sense of political efficacy is studied in the context of narrowly electoral settings, my argument for the power of quantitative methods finds strong support. In the first place, it can be argued that sense of political efficacy is a theoretical construct of little more than biographical interest. Methods relying on self-appraisals of potency are poor measures of real political impact, subject as those self-assessments are to obvious threats of deception from within and without. In addition to this criticism of invalidity, there is also a criticism of theoretical pertinence: It is a sterile conception of political power that treats it as the ability to influence an electoral system. The scope of political power extends far beyond electoral participation, to the education and organization of community and national groups, influence through boycotting, cartel formation and other forms of economic consolidation, and threats and acts of organized violence.

But notice how a critic might elaborate these attacks. What has been argued by social critics of bourgeois social science is not that feelings of political efficacy (or other such individualist values) measure nothing, or that it measures nothing unobservable, but rather that what it measures is not explanatorily important or of theoretical interest. This type of fact about theoretical criticism is central to the version of realism I defend, for it marks an important distinction between the two jointly exhaustive positions concerning the possibility of measuring psychological and social phenomena. Once it is conceded that something is being measured, the standard considerations apply to show that the objects are theoretical rather than merely observable. And notice that the quantitative approach allows us to attend to and formulate these concerns, a point about measurement that will be developed in chapter 2. So if one wants to dispute the progress of the behavioral and social sciences, one has a lot of explaining away to do. For those who nevertheless remain convinced that the research programs described above do not identify sciences worthy of the name, chapter 8 will show why narrative methods don't constitute a serious alternative to quantitative methods.

Abduction and Naturalistic Scientific Realism

How might one argue for a realist interpretation of these psychological and social accounts? In defending an interpretation of scientific theories, it will not do to model actual procedures of scientific justification on the structure of deductive argumentation, as we find in the verificationist and falsificationist traditions. Even doing so heuristically will be badly misleading, for justification in science is typically inductive (see Hempel 1965b; Boyd 1985a). The charge of circularity, then, cannot be cast in the standard form—in terms of the dependence of one premise on another—unless one is happy for it to be a mere lament that induction is not deduction. Good inductive arguments characteristically have nonindependent premises. That is, if one conceives of epistemic justification as inductive, then nonindependent premises may be integrated to yield reliable patterns of ampliative inference.

In fact, the most common form of inductive argument in science follows a striking pattern (sometimes called 'abductive'):

1. There is some class of observed phenomena O that have an effect E.
2. There is an unobserved factor (entity, process, state, event, property) U that (in light of our best theories), if present, would provide the best explanation of E.
3. Therefore, probably U.

When the observed phenomenon O in question is the instrumental reliability of some theory, then the abductive argument yields the sort of argument for scientific realism about theories that Fine ([1986] 1991a), Laudan ([1981] 1991), and van Fraassen (1980, 1985, 1989) have attacked. But the same form of argument is recruited in less ambitious purposes, in modest realist arguments for certain unobservable entities and states. Indeed, the best illustration of this pattern of argument concerns Perrin's establishment of the existence of atoms, where the class of observed phenomena consisted of the effects of alpha decay and electrolysis. There, Perrin argues that the existence of atoms provides the best explanation for the "remarkable agreement" between otherwise apparently disparate phenomena (1923, p. 215).

In chapters 3 and 4, I suggest that philosophical applications of abduction are vindicated by the success of abduction in science and address objections to the parity of methods implied by the comparison. On the contemporary philosophical scene, we find various abductive defenses of scientific realism. With due credit to nineteenth-century anticipations by William Whewell and Charles Peirce, the first published argument that gives explicit expression to the primary realist form of argument can be found in J. J. C. Smart's claim that the rejection of realism about the posits of modern science requires a belief in cosmic coincidences or "innumerable lucky accidents" (1968, p. 150). The most famous positive argument for realism, one that Hilary Putnam attributes to Richard Boyd and that, once properly formulated, Boyd develops in detail, is that realism is the only philosophy that doesn't make the success of science a miracle. Boyd's argument states that scientific realism provides the best explanation for the instrumental reliability of scientific methodology. This form of argument has been given many names and is claimed to be grounded in a variety of argumentative principles: abductive, explanationist, inference to the best explanation, and others. For the moment, let us call the strategy abductive.

As suggested earlier, abductive defenses of realism have been proposed on the basis of evidence from the natural, but never from the social and behavioral, sciences. I believe this fact is contingent; it has given many philosophers the impression that plausible realist arguments can't be formulated on the basis of carefully analyzed evidence in psychology, history, political science and sociology. This impression has been abetted by forces associated with, but inessential to, disputes surrounding the doctrine of scientific realism. Many of these arguments against scientific realism derive from constructivist historians of science concerned to do good, non-Whiggish history of science. Other strains of antirealist argument, also social constructivist, are particularly prominent in the sociology of science. Some of these antirealist arguments arise from concerns of social criticism; their proponents are vigilant of the applications of science and are worried that confidence in the truth of knowledge claims in science must amount to a giddy enthusiasm for its products. These arguments are challenging, but I will say little about them in this book. The antirealist arguments with which I will be primarily concerned have more direct, and less recognizably political, motivations. Some derive, though, from professed desires for intellectual tolerance.

Whatever positive argument for realism is given, it must be comprehensive, combining appropriate notions of explanation, reference, causation, measurement, knowledge, accurate descriptions of scientific practice, history of science, and other matters. There is a general expectation that (as a test of the adequacy of the account), if realism (or any theory of science) is true, then it should be robust—so it should be exemplified in a variety of ways. This view is part and parcel of an account of science that is unified, and unification is itself a value in science.

On the view that I will defend, specific scientific claims can be epistemically appraised on the basis of other scientific claims, and they can be so appraised in a non-question-begging way, but only if the claims are relatively independent of one another, and only if the question is not an idle skeptical one. Scientific claims in one domain, say historical geology, are largely independent of claims in, for example, the theory of magnetism. Thus, appeal to one in partial justification of another (as happens in evolutionary generalizations based on paleomagnetic dating) need not be question-begging. The only principles presupposed by both theories are relatively general, shared by a large number of areas of inquiry.

The epistemic value of theory-based independent testing is an important component of a scientific epistemology. But the naturalism I will call for is thoroughgoing, treating the study of science as itself subject to epistemic evaluation; this naturalism is subject to naturalistic assessment. Therefore, we can do better and worse jobs of studying science. After all, scientific theorizing is itself a natural process about which we can theorize. Scientists have a psychology, and the scientific community has a sociology. Indeed, naturalistic epistemology is often treated as a major component of a comprehensive theory of science that incorporates scientific theorizing as part of the natural world, enjoying its endowments and limited by its constraints. It casts the general reliability of our belief-producing mechanisms as the results of a complex evolutionary interaction between our perceptual and cognitive capacities and features of our environment.[23]

It may not be too peculiar to view contemporary philosophy of science as attempting to articulate a systematic and descriptively adequate picture of the practices and goals of scientists, whether cast in evolutionary terms or not. This picture must have a certain form, however. Scientific practices must be portrayed as rational, or at least as not systematically defective, since these practices are routinely sound. Modern science deserves this flattery because, whatever concerns one might have about its products and applications, science embodies the most impressive set of epistemic practices thus far known. At the same time, the general requirement that routine practices be rationalized adds a normative ingredient to this naturalistic account.

On the account I will defend, naturalism about the social and behavioral sciences is the doctrine that the methods of those sciences are continuous with those of the natural sciences. Whenever claims of continuity are involved, we must identify the relevant dimensions of similarity. In this case, for example, it is not that physics and sociology use the same types of instruments, or the same sorts of experimental designs, but that they are continuous in the sense that measurement is a central feature of both and that, at a level of generality that can be clearly elaborated, the methods of both estimate quantitative properties of a population.

I will contend that the most plausible version of naturalism finds the best fit with realism rather than with empiricism. The most thoroughgoing versions of naturalism appear to share two essential tenets:

1. The initial analysis of methodologically and epistemically important aspects of scientific practice must be descriptively accurate and (against logical empiricist rational reconstructions) must portray science as rational or as not systematically defective.
2. Scientific justification and knowledge are most faithfully explicated in a nonfoundationalist/causal manner. Such unobservable causal relations are most characteristic of instances of measurement.

Whether the version of naturalism most faithful to scientific practices presupposes realism or empiricism is, of course, a matter of evidence. One might note, however, that these two tenets incline us to take the routine practices and discourse of scientists at face value; and at face value, unreconstructed scientific practice and discourse are patently metaphysical.

Let us take each tenet in turn. Concerning tenet (1), the demand for a descriptively accurate account of science over its rational reconstruction now guides most recent analyses of developed sciences, and experimentation has been the centerpiece of these emerging philosophical accounts (Galison 1987; Giere 1988; Hacking 1983). What has developed is a broadly realist conception of scientific

---

23. For more on evolutionary epistemology, see Radnitzky and Bartley (1987) and the overview in Bradie (1986).

theories and of knowledge, based on arguments of vindication by experimental success. First, theoretical commitments guide decisions about appropriate experimental design. When instrumental success repays discriminating judgments of design, we are free to conclude that experimental knowledge reflects theoretical knowledge. Second, postulated theoretical entities are sometimes recruited as tools in the study of other theoretical effects. When such efforts are successful in uncovering a predicted effect, it is in virtue of our theoretical knowledge concerning the tool. To advert to the now infamous phrase about electrons that Hacking borrowed from an experimental physicist, "If you can spray them, they're real" (1983, p. 23). Evidence of manipulability is sufficient for ontological commitment.

Concerning tenet (2), much experimental knowledge is embodied in textbooks and computer programs, and no experimental scientist has the sort of observational knowledge required by the Humean foundationalist to provide a basis for experimental reasoning. In particular, scientists haven't observed the experimental results of studies reported in the journals, and often they don't gather the data themselves. Instead, they rely on technicians, graduate students, or other colleagues. These practices of reliance represent the very kind of reference and competence-borrowing procedures that defy the internalist, typically foundationalist understanding associated with logical empiricism (Hardwig 1985, 1991; Kitcher 1990, 1992, 1993; Trout 1992).

This fact places the foundationalist in the uncomfortable position of either carrying out a strained "rational reconstruction" of these practices (and thus adopting a peculiarly nonnaturalistic stance toward scientific theorizing) or arguing that these practices are simply irrational. In either case, the question arises for the foundationalist of how the behavioral and social sciences have achieved the level of success that they have—in the areas of vision, audition, cognitive dissonance, and attitude research, to name just a few—if the practices are so systematically irrational or if Humean foundationalist strictures are inviolable.

Although naturalistic epistemology typically describes the primary psychological processes and states in terms of belief, desire, and other folk notions, the question of the survival of these folk notions should be separated from the plausibility of naturalistic epistemology. After all, naturalistic epistemology treats its posits as subject to evidential appraisal, and it could turn out that we must revise central folk concepts. However, I believe that the core practices and concepts of an appropriately articulated folk psychology are scientifically respectable, and the prospects for the future look fine.

The most powerful considerations favoring folk psychology are best described in light of recent attacks predicting the elimination of folk psychology. Some philosophers are so critical of folk psychology that they have predicted that a developed neuroscience will eradicate the principles and theoretical kinds (belief, desire, etc.) implicit in our ordinary practices of mental state attribution. By examining several actual exchanges in mature neuroscience, I have shown (in Trout 1991) that neuroscientists routinely rely on folk psychological procedures of intentional state attribution in applying epistemically reliable standards of scientific evaluation. For example, when relying on another scientist's results, one scientist attributes to the other (all other things being equal) the belief that, if there were artifacts that a remote scientist believed to be problematic, the remote expert would have controlled for them. Such attributions are subtle and complex. Occasionally, the joint influence of belief and desire determines attributions of poor judgment to scientists whose judgments are otherwise reliable but for specific conditions of, say, personal pressure. If the effort is to demonstrate the epistemic reliability of folk procedures of intentional state attribution, then scientific contexts are preferable to ordinary ones; scientific contexts place folk procedures of attribution under *theoretical stress*, producing evidence of folk psychological success that is less equivocal than the evidence in mundane settings.

In the final chapter, I am deeply critical of narrative styles of social and behavioral inquiry, but that does not imply that I am correspondingly critical of folk psychology. Epistemic frailties are evident whenever we (unreasonably) expect more from a theory or method than it can deliver. Any theory, no matter how resourceful and well formed, applies to a naturally circumscribed domain. Newtonian mechanics fails if we apply it to phenomena at high enough velocities. Special relativity hardly constrains theories of embryonic development. In the social and behavioral sciences, these limitations emerge when narrative styles of inquiry, often implicating folk notions, are used to isolate and detect subtle theoretical factors in social settings or to estimate the degree of contribution one intentional factor makes in a context swamped by exogenous economic, political, and social causes. Folk psychology too has its proprietary domain, that of normal, instrumentally intelligent behavior. It is not a theory of society, of social development, of democratic participation, or of perception. It would not be a serious objection to folk psychology, then, that its notions were used by alchemists, any more than the core notions of contemporary physics are in doubt because they are used by some astrologers to give spurious intellectual respectability to their endeavors.

The argument of this book is set out in two parts. Part I sets out a realist theory of measurement (chapter 2) and its epistemic centrality and then explores arguments for three forms of scientific realism—minimal, robust, and measured. Chapter 3 argues that a very bare version of realism is warranted by a similarly modest version of abduction: we are entitled to infer a stable unobserved structure in explanations for observed outcomes or distributions. While a move in the right direction, austere realism does not go far enough as an interpretation of the social and psychological sciences, where rather specific theoretical models and generalizations are tested. Robust realism, on the other hand, is too strong, for many social and psychological theories are not even approximately true and yet merit some significant degree of epistemic approval. Accordingly, in chapter 4 I propose a measured realism about the psychological and social sciences, one that commits us to theoretical knowledge of some true lawlike generalizations and central theoretical entities. The evidence for Measured Realism is found in methodological and ontological independence, the relative autonomy of experiment from theory, the local character of confirmation, the special methodological role of diverse testing, the dependence of observed values on ontologically separate, unobserved ones, and the often mercenary recruitment of evidence from archaic and remote theories. Measured Realism is required to explain the current level of (modest) theoretical success in the social and psychological sciences. I conclude that those sciences reach levels of systematic and cumulative success great enough to merit equally systematic explanation.

Part II focuses on the quantitative concepts involved in social and behavioral measurement and on the program of epistemological naturalism required to account for the reliability and validity of such measurement. The scientific strategies deployed to secure this measurement success are all abductive, in keeping with the philosophical account of Measured Realism set out earlier, and many of the relations responsible for sound measurement are recognizably similar to traditional epistemological notions, particularly those in reliabilist epistemology. The narrative model of social and behavioral research generally flouts these standards of epistemic responsibility, and chapter 8 examines these frailties in widely respected work of the tradition. We will find there, as we did in the history of physics, that the call for intelligent inquiry in these fields is a call for measurement, in this case, the measurement of the intentional world.

PART I

SCIENTIFIC REALISM
Minimal, Robust, and Measured

Measurement as Population-Guided Estimation

> Do I then measure, O my God, and know not what I
> measure?
>
> Augustine, *Confessions*

> Many psychologists adopt the dictum of Thorndike
> that "Whatever exists at all exists in some amount"
> and they also adopt the corollary that whatever exists
> in some amount can be measured: the quality of hand-
> writing, the appreciation of a sunset, the attitude of an
> individual toward Communism, or the strength of de-
> sire in a hungry rat.
>
> J. Guilford, *Psychometric Methods*

This chapter (1) introduces the principles of Population-Guided Estimation and charts the manifest progress in behavioral measurement during the twentieth century, (2) presents the fundamental principles of the theory of measurement, relating them to traditional epistemological categories, (3) surveys contemporary methods of social and psychological measurement, (4) introduces the notions of adipose theory and epistemically local or bite-sized confirmation relations to explain the autonomous character of the products of measurement, and (5) explains theoretical progress in psychological measurement in terms of Population-Guided Estimation. This distinctly realist model characterizes measurement in the behavioral sciences at once as piecemeal and theoretically cumulative.

Introducing Population-Guided Estimation

Estimation is the commonest of human activities. How much time do we have to do the shopping? How much food can we afford to buy? How far can we comfortably walk with the groceries? Measurement is nothing more or less than controlled or regulated estimation. Guided by substantial background knowledge and principles of reasoning, we select a value from a population of possibilities: Will the groceries that we need to purchase be $85, $95, or over $120? Will the shopping take twenty, forty, or fifty minutes? We even estimate the strength of our own beliefs and desires in deciding what to do.

In this chapter, I sketch a general, realist account of measurement that characterizes measurement as Population-Guided Estimation (PGE), a relation between an estimation procedure and the true value of a population parameter of theoretical interest. PGE covers all domains of actual measurement; it is formulated to apply as much to the world of physics and biology as it is to the world of sociology and psychology. Our best theories identify the relevant populations—populations of theoretical interest—such as oak trees, endogenous pain control systems in humans, electrons, comets, capitalist democracies, and activation processes in semantic memory. The population parameters of the quantity or magnitude are definitive of the kind. The goal is to provide a naturalistic account of social and behavioral measurement, one that renders unmysterious the relation between the experimental or quasi-experimental conditions and the real value of a theoretically appropriate population parameter.

According to the traditional prejudice, now a piece of common lore, the difference between measurement in physics and measurement in psychology marks an epistemically significant distinction. This distinction has been drawn with more or less severity, between hard and soft measurement, scientific and unscientific measurement; these designations have the effect of minimizing the respectability of measurement in the social and behavioral sciences. Of course, if we consider the objects of measurement, there is a distinction between the respective relata of physical and behavioral measurement. But that is only a description of the difference in subject matter, not the distinction in methodological sophistication implied by critics of behavioral measurement. On any reasonably general description of measurement, this dichotomous view cannot be sustained. What allows us to measure a domain concerns relations equally available to the physical and behavioral sciences.

Population-Guided Estimation embodies at least four central claims typical of good cases of measurement:

1. The parameter values of natural populations are real, mind independent features of the world; they are not mere artifacts of our methods of measurement.
2. Parameter values of a natural population are stable relative to the method used to measure them, sufficiently so that measuring them does not routinely make the difference between significant and nonsignificant effects; quantities are not nominal essences that are defined conventionally.
3. The conditional dependence evident between the value of population parameters and the reports of reliable instruments or procedures represents a relation of causal dependence, to be analyzed dispositionally.
4. Measurement relations—which determine the estimate of the level of a magnitude—are typically inexact.

Each claim deserves some clarification. In (1), "natural population" is not to be contrasted with a population of artifacts. In the behavioral and social sciences, human artifacts and conventions are often the subject matter: rituals, automobiles, and so forth. Rather, "natural population" indicates that the set of objects under study are theoretically appropriate units of study. The populations are not theoretically phony or otherwise "hoked up"; complex objects such as my-dog-and-a-telephone or a book-and-elm tree are examples of phony population constituents (not to mention disjunctive phony kinds). By "real value," I mean only that the population has an unmeasured value, a value that is most naturally explained in terms of the stable properties of the constituents and the relations among them. Nor should (1) and (2) imply any sort of traditional essentialism, according to which objects of theoretical interest—natural kinds—have clear and timeless identity conditions. The idea of population-guided estimation is an instance of being guided by the world, particularly when one conceives of population parameters as identifying stable kinds, items of theoretical interest.

In virtue of what facts might the central property of (3)—conditional dependence between population values and measurement reports—be thought to hold? Like the production of ripples in water, the intervention of measuring techniques into a physical configuration takes place against a background of a stable unmanipulated configuration. Because the unmeasured population has a value, we are able to talk about what would have happened if some event would not have occurred. This is the relevant conditional dependence. Finally, (4) follows from general constraints on measuring instruments: that is, from the fact that some degree of error—whether systematic or random—is associated with any particular application of a measurement procedure.

Sound measurement is guided by theory, but certain canons of good testing can be set out abstractly. Diverse testing by many different methods guards against systematic error or bias. Random sampling attempts to ensure that errors in the observations are spread out fairly evenly. The use of experimental design, and in particular blocking, endeavors to balance error. All of these methods are designed to secure representative estimation; they attempt to ensure that peculiar or atypical objects in the population of interest are not overrepresented and that typical or representative objects are not hiding or otherwise obscured. Given the successful performance of these principles on observed samples, their reliability may not be revealed after one pass, but after many it will.

Although PGE is a relatively modest view that counsels us to attend to the most important statistical features of a sample and population, it has substantial consequences. This is a thin account of objectivity, which is all that is needed at the moment in the social and behavioral sciences. Robustly progressive claims made on behalf of the natural sciences require a thick account of objectivity, one committed to the radical contingency of the history of science. The identification of the relevant population is the province of our theory, but by following the tenets of PGE we can raise the probability that our theoretical commitments will represent features of the target population rather than incidental characteristics or artifacts of our own theoretical designs.

If the population satisfies (1) and (2), then the familiar estimators of population parameters should provide estimates of population parameter values. The value of some selected property of a sample from that population should converge on the true value of the parameter as the number of observations increases. As we will see, in a reliable measurement system population parameters form equivalence classes of quantities that are unobservable. PGE holds that some of our measurement procedures consist in relations to unobservable phenomena. An instrument validly measures a quantity, then, if the values yielded by the instrument are conditionally dependent on the values of the population parameters. The most natural way to understand these dependencies is causal. I will argue that the causal theory of measurement is the most appropriate analysis of PGE. And because some of these quantities are unobservable, PGE, little more than a codification of pervasive principles of good measurement, entails that at least some of the knowledge yielded by measurement is theoretical knowledge. Thus the claim that PGE supports a realist conception of measurement and knowledge. Privileging observable over unobservable phenomena in advance of settling epistemological questions is scientifically unnatural, since taxonomically interesting population parameters are of both sorts.

The epistemic features of the PGE account of measurement stand in stark contrast to those of the empiricist account of measurement that dominated for much of this century. According to the empiricist account, the epistemic power of measurement to test predictions and resolve disputes derived from the fact that measuring apparatus outputs are observable. Antioperationalist arguments ultimately raised difficulties for empiricist accounts of measurement by showing that the empiricist could not explain the improvement of measurement and detection procedures without recourse to theoretical notions that were unacceptable to the empiricist. While many of these antiempiricist arguments appealed in an impressionistic way to the regulating role of unobserved causal influences, there was no realist account of measurement to replace the empiricist one under scrutiny. As presented here, PGE is a sketch of that replacement, incorporating the realist insights of antiempiricist attacks, as well as the primary morals of causal modeling in the psychological and social sciences. It provides a rationale for, among other things, the indifference that scientists show about whether the postulated causal factor is an unobservable or just an unobserved observable. As mentioned earlier, population parameters are of both sorts.

Independence is one of the most basic requirements of explanation statements—as it is of measurement statements—that such statements not be ad hoc and thus that they figure in the explanation of phenomena other than those of interest at the moment. Statements of causal dependence, such as those in the causal account of PGE developed here, express the ontological separability of objects, properties, and states. These items, therefore, are available for the explanation of other states. But before we can assess the independence of measurement claims—the independence of which forms the basis of *Measured Realism*—we shall turn to a discussion of the nature of measurement.

What Is Measurement?

As with most common terms, there is no single definition of "measurement" agreeable to all practitioners. In the most general terms, measurement—a central epistemic activity in science—relates a number and a quantity in an effort to estimate the magnitude of that quantity. A quantity is typically a property of a physical configuration, such as length or weight, and determines a function that applies to a domain or class of objects. At this high level of abstraction, the description of the purpose and relation of measurement is metaphysically neutral, leaving open the question of whether the domain is observable (empirical) or unobservable (nonempirical).

We can determine and express the value of a quantity as long as we can describe the quantitative relationships that obtain between two or more objects. The familiar mathematical relationships of "greater than," "less than," and "equal to" are the most commonly used to express quantitative relations; these relations provide a basis for the articulation of other quantitative relationships such as "farther than," "shorter than," or "same heaviness as." Instruments most commonly allow us to discover and formulate the relationships expressed.

Measurement practice has a long history, is primarily occupied with astronomical inquiry and engineering concerns of volume, density, and speed, and is associated with the most notable figures in the history of science. Measurements were made with laboratory, telescopic, and navigational instruments until the nineteenth century, when probabilistic methods soon found their way into the estimation of population characteristics in the areas of demography, mortality rates, annuities, and epidemiology. In the middle of the nineteenth century, Quetelet applied the theory of errors to an array of social and biological statistics, attempting to construct a kind of "social physics," as it was sometimes called. Shortly thereafter, Fechner and others pioneered a psychophysical theory designed to measure sensory magnitudes. Later, Spearman introduced factor analysis, and other psychologists such as Stevens (1951) developed additional techniques for the systematic estimation of the magnitude of psychological properties. The twentieth century witnessed vigorous advances in the area of physical measurement, owing to sophisticated laboratory instrumentation. The development of a statistical theory of experimental design, proposed by R. A. Fisher, allowed statistical and laboratory instruments to be used with greater power.

Contemporary interest in measurement has generated two bodies of research. The first is primarily mathematical, concerned with the formal representation of empirical (that is, observable) structures and the deductive consequences thereof. The second is primarily philosophical, being concerned with the epistemological and metaphysical assumptions and lessons of the practice of measurement. The former we might call "measurement theory," and the latter, "philosophical theories of measurement." This chapter covers both.

Measurement Theory

The mathematical theory of measurement, though in principle a metaphysically neutral description of the measurement process, has been developed in a way that displays the distinct and deep influence of empiricism. Although measurement theory is compatible with the realist view that some of the objects of measurement are unobservable, contemporary treatments of measurement theory typically import the additional stricture that the domain be observational or empirical. The following discussion will reflect that empiricist orientation.

Representation of the Domain

To estimate the magnitude of a quantity—mass, charge, cell firing-rate, cognitive dissonance, and so on—we must have some systematic way of representing the relations among that quantity and others in a domain. (For a clear and thorough introduction to the technical apparatus used in measurement theory, see Wartofsky 1968, chap. 6.) Often, the objects, events, processes, properties, and states (hereafter, simply "objects") that we want to measure are unobservable or at least unobserved. If we are to draw out the order among objects in a class, we first must represent them in some way. (The most common and convenient way of representing qualitative order in the objects of a class is numerical. This by itself does not render the data themselves quantitative, even if numbers are used in their analysis.) When the objects in question are observable, their representation serves the purpose of keeping track of often complex and dynamic systems.

The process of measurement demands that we set up certain correspondences between a representational (typically numerical) system and an empirical, observational domain. These correspondences are fixed by relations of specific sorts, and, depending upon the nature of the measurement relation in question, we want to arrive at a mapping that preserves that relation. A mapping from one relational system to another that preserves all the relations and operations of the system is called a homomorphism. If there is a one-to-one homomorphism between the representational system and the domain, the relation is an isomorphism.

According to standard measurement theory (Krantz et al. 1971), we begin with a system U of observed, or empirical, relations and try to arrive at a mapping to a numerical relational system B that preserves all of the relevant empirical relations and structures of U. In the case of the measurement of temperature, for example, we attempt to find an assignment of numbers that allows us to preserve the relation "warmer than" so that the numbers assigned increase as the temperature increases.

If measurement is the representation of quantitative relations by numerical relations, what conditions must be satisfied if there are to be scales of various types? The most common sort of feature in terms of which objects are represented is a relation. Relations can be binary, triadic, quadratic, to n-adic. Binary relations are determined by ordered couples $<x,y>$, triadic relations by ordered triples $<x,y,z>$, and so on.

The first condition on the measurement of a quantity is that the objects in the domain can be ordered according to the relation chosen. Domains are often depicted as classes, or sets. The relation "same length as," for example, can be determined by ordered pairs of material objects. But, to compare the lengths of two objects in a class—that is, to depict the relative presence of some property or magnitude (in this case, length)—we must first define an equivalence class of that property or magnitude, such as all those objects with length. We then estimate the relative presence of that magnitude or property in two objects by defining equivalence classes of a unit. A unit of measurement defines an equivalence class of that magnitude. Objects in the equivalence class may be compared by an equivalence relation. Two classes of objects, a and b, can bear the equivalence relation to each other with respect to a specific property. The unit of one gram defines the class of all those things that are one gram, one meter the class of all those things that are one meter.

Measurement theorists differ in the notation they use, but the expressions below illustrate common uses. With respect to some class, a binary relation R is an equivalence relation if and only if it is transitive, symmetric, and reflexive. More formally, two objects, x and y, bear the relation R of "same length as" if and only if: (1) for every x, y, and z in the class, if $R(x,y)$ and $R(y,z)$, then $R(x,z)$ [transitivity], (2) for every x and y in the class, if $R(x,y)$ then $R(y,x)$ [symmetry], and (3) for every x in the class, $R(x,x)$ [reflexivity]. Any two objects compared for length that bear these three relations to one another will be of equal length.

Other orders can be determined by further sets of ordered pairs. With respect to some class, a binary relation R is

intransitive on a class if and only if, for every x, y, and z in the class, if $R(x,y)$ and $R(y,z)$, then not $R(x,z)$—being the mother of

asymmetric on a class if and only if, for every x and y in the class, if $R(x,y)$, then not $R(y,x)$—being the father of

antisymmetric on a class if and only if, for every x and y in the class, if $R(x,y)$ and $R(y,x)$, then x = y (that is, x is identical to y)—being at least as great as on the real numbers

irreflexive on a class if and only if, for every x in the class, not $R(x,x)$—being the brother of

strongly connected on a class if and only if, for every x and y in the class, either $R(x,y)$ or $R(y,x)$—being at least as great as on the natural numbers

connected on a class if and only if, for every x and y in the class such that x ≠ y, either $R(x,y)$ or $R(y,x)$—being less than upon the natural numbers

In the hands of many modern measurement theorists, the further empiricist demand is introduced that the homomorphism satisfies a function between a number and a formal representation of a domain that is empirical or observable. No additional epistemological argument has been offered that the domain in question must be observable, and therefore it is at this stage quite incorrect to understand the relevant formalism as an antimetaphysical feature of the theory of measurement.

It might be thought that this empiricist assumption of the representationalist-formalist approach is not just inadequately defended but false. The attempt to treat formalism as an antimetaphysical feature of a theory has failed for related projects. The representationalist-formalist approach is often criticized on the grounds that, despite its formal appearance, it does not divest itself of assumptions concerning the specific nature of the domain being measured. Measurement employs scales, and the grounds for use of those scales include substantial assumptions about the objects, observable and unobservable. According to standard criticisms of projects that attempt to eliminate appeal to unobserved causes, the antirealist goal is not achieved until the causal direction represented in the models of the empirical substructures (as well as other features of the model) can be determined without theoretical commitment. A similar difficulty arises on the syntactic conception of theories. There, the effort to eliminate theoretical terms was itself parasitic upon the complete articulation of that theoretical system. According to the representationalist-formalist view, the goal of the theory of measurement is the construction of an observable representation of the consequences of measurement axioms (a Ramsey sentence if you will). It is this feature that ties the formalist-representationalist approach to the empiricist tradition. For philosophers more aggressively empiricist, the function of measurement theory is eliminative; by providing an observable representation of the objects and relations in the domain, the model-theoretic, semantic approach allows one to appeal to embedded substructures as rendering superfluous the commitment to nonempirical components of the theory. Craig's theorem attempted to execute a similarly eliminative project for the syntactic approach to scientific theories. In such a case, this eliminativist project loses its original rationale. The initial motivation concerned the possibility of exclusive reliance on the observation statements of the theory. However, if the theoretical terms can be eliminated from the system only after the system has been developed, then theoretical terms appear to isolate an essential portion of a theory's content. It has been argued that, as a result, the eliminativist goals of Craig's theorem and Ramsey sentences foundered on this general difficulty.

The second conception of measurement might be called the causal (or sometimes, interactionist) approach. I shall have more to say about this approach in the discussion of philosophical theories of measurement.

Representation of Order and Scale

To achieve a representation of relations that is systematic, we can use scales. There are four basic scales, corresponding to four levels of measurement: nominal, ordinal, interval, and ratio. As we ascend from nominal to ratio scales, the scales increase in their power to represent characteristics of the data while preserving the ability to represent the data in accordance with the preceding level. The process of measurement attempts to estimate magnitudes, the amounts of the attributes or properties under investigation.

Not all scales represent magnitude or even order; some merely classify data. Nominal scales, for example, sort observations into different categories or classes. The classification of people into gender groups of male and female is an instance of nominal measurement, as is the categorization of subject responses into yes and no. Nominal scales cannot represent many important properties of objects in the class, but the importance of the nominal classification of objects into stable categories should not be ignored. Ordinal scales, by contrast, order objects along a dimension—or "rank order"—but do not indicate how great the difference is (along that dimension) between any of the objects. Such scales are common in surveys where choices range from strongly disagree to strongly agree. Although this scale depicts order, it does not capture information about magnitude; we don't know by how much "strongly disagree" differs from "disagree." Such scales do not have the power to honor the principle of equal intervals, a feature of interval scales. Interval scales allow us to infer specific differences among objects from differences in scale points. The most common example here is that of temperature; any ten-point difference on the scale has the same meaning. Ratio scales allow us to infer from numerical proportions among the representations of objects that one magnitude is twice or three times another. Ratio scales have a true zero point, unlike the other scales we have thus far seen. The musical scale, based on frequencies, is a ratio scale. The zero point in this case occurs when there are no cycles per second. One can say that middle C is half the frequency of the C an octave above.

There are two kinds of theorems in measurement theory: representation theorems and uniqueness theorems. Representation theorems state the conditions under which a numerical representation can be found for empirical structures; they thus state the existence of certain types of scales given that the nonnumerical relational structure of a domain satisfies certain conditions. Uniqueness theorems tell us whether the resulting scale is unique or whether there are permissible transformations from one scale to another. (What we are trying to establish is not uniqueness proper but uniqueness in some relevant sense.) The characterization of these transformations is important because they specify invariances among scales, and these invariances are thought to reflect important features of a property in the domain.

Providing an interpretation of the scale is a necessary condition for measuring the domain. Aiding in this interpretation was the theory of error, one of the most important contributions to the theory and practice of measurement. In light of certain fundamental statistical assumptions or axioms—most often the Kolmogorov axioms—the effects of measurement error could be estimated. These axioms can be used to calculate the probability that a certain distribution of measurement values could be expected by chance. In order to do so, we need some method for estimating variation. Therefore, we can estimate this probability by calculating the variance and the standard deviation. We begin with the sum of the differences between measurements and the mean value. The variance is the sum of the squares of these differences, and the standard deviation is the square root of the variance. Once supplemented with the theory of error, measurement theory might be understood as the effort to explore the deductive consequences of the Kolmogorov axioms of probability.

The estimation of the magnitude and direction of error is an important condition of valid and reliable measurement and makes explicit the routine inexactness of measurement. A measuring instrument estimates the value of a quantity, yielding a number, but does so only subject to a certain range of error. Therefore, the accuracy of the measuring instrument, be it a pH meter or a statistical design, can be assessed only in light of a theory of error.

Philosophical Theories of Measurement

There have been three main philosophical approaches to measurement: operationalism, conventionalism, and realism. Directly or indirectly, these approaches attempt to address the apparently realist character of measurement; measurement procedures are formulated in light of, and to operate on, quantities that are theoretical or unobservable. The thesis that measurement or its outcome is typically theoretical—in short, the theory dependence of measurement—did not set well with the empiricist epistemology that motivated the operationalist account with which this history begins. In light of their diverse epistemological, metaphysical, and semantic commitments, these three approaches attempt either to explain away this apparent theory dependence of measurement, to concede it but limit its significance, or defend its literal interpretation and its consequences.

Operationalism

Operationalism was an early logical empiricist approach to measurement that attempted to cleanse unreconstructed appeal to theoretical quantities and to define theoretical magnitudes exclusively in terms of observables. The resulting "correspondence rules" or "operational definitions" formed identity statements linking each observable measurement and detection procedure with a single term for a type of unobservable quantity. Empiricists eventually rejected this account of theoretical measurement as incoherent. The problem arises as follows. According to unreconstructed scientific practice, a single theoretical quantity can be measured in a variety of ways. But according to operationalism, the particular procedure is definitive of the theoretical quantity, and thus one would have to postulate a different type of quantity for each different procedure that was (perhaps even could be) used.

Consider improvements in the measurement of pH. Because these revisions constitute changes in operations, according to the operationalist empiricist they must reflect a change in what "pH" refers to; for each new type of procedure, a different type of quantity. But scientists clearly take themselves to be measuring the same quantity, no matter how many different types of procedures they use; and, the substantial continuity of their measuring procedures appears to vindicate this supposition. So, when applied to an instrument as familiar and well understood as a pH meter, the operationalist account of measurement, squarely within the logical empiricist tradition, supplied a disappointingly misleading account of scientific practice. Nevertheless, it was precisely because empiricists recognized and respected that the same theoretical quantity persisted under diverse measurement procedures that they rejected early operationalist accounts of theoretical definition.

In this description of an objection to the operationalist conception of measurement, another important feature of operationalism emerges. Because the operationalist holds that the particular procedure is definitive of the theoretical term, in this respect operationalism is an early conventionalist doctrine. Because the meaning of "pH" is associated with a certain convention—that we take the specific measurement procedure as definitive of the term—the term "pH" couldn't fail to refer.

Moreover, it became clear that any single measurement procedure tacitly depended upon a variety of auxiliary hypotheses in the design of the instrument. The pH meter employs a collateral theory of electricity, for example. The accuracy of the pH meter was therefore partly dependent upon the accuracy of the auxiliary electrical theory. The recognition of this fact about routine measurement led to the two most influential features of the critique of operationalism, features that set the terms of the dispute after the demise of operationalism. The first is the holistic character of measurement: Revisions and improvements to measurement procedures are made in light of background or auxiliary theories. The second is the realistic assumptions underlying those revisions and improvements. Increasingly successful measurement could be accounted for only in terms of the accuracy of our theoretical knowledge.

Many empiricists acknowledged the holistic aspect of measurement but were not prepared to accept the metaphysical consequences that define the realist program. For such empiricists, measurement is guided, if not dominated, by convention.

Conventionalism

Conventionalism about measurement states that the interpretation of measurement procedures reflects our conventions. Alternatively, measurement procedures do not provide evidence of quantities that exist independently of our efforts to measure. The conventional aspect of measurement is most forcefully illustrated in cases where two or more scales equally well represent the empirical order. In such cases, only pragmatic factors can determine our choice of a scale, factors such as the simplicity of the numerical laws. Indeed, on this view, the simplicity of our laws would be inexplicable unless we suppose it to result from our selection of a theoretical framework. Unless we take this stance, the conventionalist argues, we must suppose that the laws of nature, with all the complex details of their observational consequences, could be revealed to us through diverse experimental strategies and sundry instrumentation. The conventionalist argues that increasing success in measurement is not a reason for thinking that the measurement reflects accurate causal (typically theoretical) information; it is only a reason for thinking that the measurement procedure or instrument exhibits the empirical order in a way we find simple or otherwise aesthetically pleasing.

Conventions are employed in the introduction of a unit, as in the choice to use the familiar meter bar located near Paris as the standard meter. Conventions operate at a later stage as well in the application of those units and scales (see Ellis 1966). According to conventionalists such as Reichenbach, we must adopt certain conventions if we are to maintain simple laws. One such convention is that a measuring rod remains rigid when transported through space (to measure distances or objects at remote locations). In light of the underdetermination of theory by (observable) evidence, one might suppose that there are forces that operate in such a way that the rod changes length when transported. But such suppositions would generate less simple laws. A specific convention is therefore adopted—that forces operate uniformly on the measuring rod—to rule out such complicating possibilities.

At the same time, critics of conventionalism interpreted these conventions as reflecting not harmless stipulations but rather substantial theoretical assumptions. After all, judgments of simplicity, elegance, parsimony, or convenience, it has been charged, are themselves theory-dependent judgments, unable to be made on the basis of empirical or observational considerations alone. According to this criticism, a numerical law counts as simple only in light of certain theoretical considerations, and so the conventionalist, like the operationalist, cannot avoid the epistemic (as opposed to merely pragmatic) function of theoretical commitment in the selection of a scale or measurement procedure. For the realist, this theory describes causally important dimensions of the world.

Realism and Causal Analysis

A realist account of measurement treats the act of measurement as a product of a causal relation between an instrument (broadly interpreted) and a magnitude. The relation is one of estimation. These magnitudes or quantities (properties, processes, states, events, etc.) exist independently of attempts to measure them and are sometimes too small to detect with the unaided senses. Mean kinetic energy is one such theoretical magnitude.

From the realist perspective of unreconstructed scientific practice, a pH meter is thought to measure an unobservable property: the concentration of hydrogen ion in a solution. The term "pH" is then thought to refer to this unobservable quantity. This ungarnished account is openly metaphysical. The realist account that replaced operationalism treated the introduction of new procedures in exactly the way that scientists seemed to—as new ways of measuring the same quantities identified by earlier procedures, now improved in response to the instrument's increasing sensitivity to unobservable features of magnitudes (Byerly and Lazara 1973). The impressive pace and character of the developments in the natural sciences, particularly the fashioning of sophisticated instruments, seemed to warrant the realist claim of theoretical improvement in measurement procedures. This argument for a realist interpretation of successful measurement is based upon an inference to the best explanation: The accuracy of our theoretical knowledge provides the best explanation for the improvement of our measurement procedures.

According to realists, there is a core set of reasons, common to lab and life, that provide powerful general grounds for a realist rather than empiricist conception of measurement. The first reason we have already seen. Early empiricist accounts, most notably operationalism, cannot explain the routine use of diverse procedures for the measurement of (what we regard as) the same quantity.

Second, the interpretation of measurement error, compulsorily reported in nearly all behavioral and social science journals, is rendered obscure on an empiricist account of measurement. It is misleading to describe a measurement as inaccurate, or as in error, if there is no difference between measured and real (or unmeasured) value. It would seem that the only natural way of expressing the incorrectness of a measurement is in terms of its difference from a correct measurement. There are other, less natural ways that the empiricist might reconstruct the initial concept of a "correct" measurement—perhaps in terms of ideal measurements, infinite samplings, or the measured value at the limit of inquiry—but none of these alternatives has the kind of grounding in experience required by the empiricist. And were these notions invoked to explain any practice less central to science than measurement, they still would be anathema to the empiricist. By contrast, the realist holds that the typical quantities have a real value, independent of attempted measurements; error is the distance between the real and measured value, distance produced by limitations of knowledge, instrument design, and noise. So the realist can provide a consistent rationale for the estimation of measurement error. (The realist does not presume to know the objective value but merely states that there is one. The most familiar estimators of the true value of a quantity are biased estimators, such as the sample mean.)

Finally, early techniques for the measurement of certain kinds of magnitudes, such as pH, have been corrected and improved upon by later ones. For example, early methods of pH measurement did not correct for the fact that the same solution would yield different pH readings owing to differences in temperatures of the solution. More recent methods make more accurate estimates by accounting and correcting for the contribution of temperature in the measurement of pH. This fact of increasing accuracy is difficult to explain without supposing first that both the early and more recent measurements are of the same quantity and, second, that it is at least plausible to talk about the measured item as having an objective value toward which successive measurement procedures are converging.

Now that we have in hand general measurement concepts such as ordering relations and scaling, we can now replace rarefied, domain-neutral, quantitative directives with a brief survey of the particular methods in the behavioral and social sciences used in contemporary social and behavioral measurement.

Task and Quantitative Method in the Behavioral and Social Sciences

Tasks in psychology typically involve the presentation of stimulus items and the person's performance. The psychological magnitude of interest is measured by first associating a number with each subject response and then placing those responses on a scale. The methods and tasks I will discuss are psychophysics, reaction time, ratings and rankings, attitude surveys, and nonreactive techniques. These methods may overlap. While not theory neutral in application, these methods are sufficiently independent of any particular psychological theory that the use of these methods, together with various theories, does not guarantee the computation of a certain set of values. That is the test for the independence of a method or hypothesis.

Psychophysical Measures

In the last quarter of the nineteenth century, Wilhelm Wundt developed a sophisticated method, known as psychophysics, for abstractly relating stimuli and behavior. Since then, psychophysical techniques have been refined, and, despite the fact
that psychophysics was originally developed for sensory scaling, psychophysical
paradigms have been used in nearly every area of psychology.

In a traditional psychophysical design, subjects are presented with, say, a certain interval of time during which a tone, at random, may or may not be presented. Subjects are instructed to answer "yes" if they hear a tone during that
interval, "no" if they do not. Given two possible responses (yes and no) and two
possible stimulus conditions (tone present and tone not present), there are four
possible response conditions: yes/present (called a hit), no/present (called a miss),
yes/not present (called a false alarm), and no/not present (called a correct rejection). Psychophysics offers two measures of performance broadly corresponding to
two possible sources of a response. Sensory variables reflect one's sensitivity to the
presence of the signal (in this case, a tone) and is given by the psychophysical
measure d'. Bias variables reflect all other influences that might incline the subject to respond in a particular direction and is given by the psychophysical measure ß. (The formulae for the calculation of d' and ß, based upon relations of hits,
misses, false alarms, and correct rejections, are provided in many sensory psychology texts. For more on the interpretation of these measures, see the widely used
psychophysics text by Green and Swets 1988.)

There are two kinds of psychophysical procedures: objective and subjective.
One objective method, the method of discrimination, was developed to determine
(in this case) the smallest difference between two sounds that can be reliably
distinguished. This smallest detectable difference in known as the JND—just noticeable difference, or difference threshold. Objective procedures are able to determine when the subject is correct, because the experimenter has a way of knowing
when the signal is actually present and when it is not and about specific features
of its character. The threshold for judgements of loudness could be arrived at by
presentation of two tones at two different decibel levels. We can establish the
threshold from the functional relationship between some measure of the subject's
performance (such as the percentage of correct discriminations of high and low
decibel trial) and an objective, physical feature of the sound (such as the sound's
amplitude). The conditions can be manipulated to reduce the influence of bias
variables on subject performance. Subjective techniques, on the other hand, are
typically used to arrive at perceptual scales. These scales may reflect the influence
of both sensory and bias variables. The subject might, for example, be presented
running speech with noise mixed in and asked to report the speech quality—from
very poor to very good—of selected sequences.

Reaction Time

One way to estimate the characteristics underlying performance is to measure the
amount of time that elapses between the presentation of stimuli and the execu-

tion of the task. Reaction time is most commonly measured by a timing device designed to start at the presentation of a stimulus and to stop when an appropriate button or key is pressed. This method has been used in nearly every corner of psychological research, from work on motor skills to memory and psycholinguistics. Significant differences in reaction times for different types of stimulus items indicate the deployment of different processing mechanisms or differences in item accessibility. These differences are then explained in terms of the storage of that item in some position within our cognitive or perceptual organization. One need not assume a simple relation between reaction time and accessibility: A number of experimental designs can be used to separate considerations of speed from those of accessibility. One might try to measure the same ability by different tasks— such as lexical access by a classification task or a recognition task—and in doing so attempt to determine whether performance interacts with task. If significant differences emerge between tasks, then, given the accuracy of some further theoretical assumptions, it may be reasonable to infer that different levels of processing reflected in that performance or inhibitory mechanisms are at play.

Ratings and Rankings

Here, subjects are asked to rate, rank, or estimate the level of some property. For example, a subject might be asked to rate synthetic "computerized" speech on a scale from "unintelligible" to "easy to understand." These methods place demands on memory and attention and so are appropriate only when the experimenter can estimate the influence of these cognitive factors and the influence of exogenous ones.

Attitude Reports

In the designs of many disciplines, subjects are asked to report their attitudes, typically in terms of positive or negative reaction, and the strength of that reaction. If we assume that, other things being equal, people are capable of accurately reporting the strength and character of their attitudes, then the values associated with the scaled attitude reports can be used to measure (the strength of) the unobserved dispositions that determine the subject's report.

Nonreactive Methods for Attitude Measurement

The measurement of attitudes based on subject responses is especially tricky when subjects are likely to modify their responses in light of their beliefs about how an interviewer (or other observers) might react. Often, people are too ashamed or otherwise reluctant to publicly and honestly report their real attitudes, particularly attitudes concerning very emotional or controversial issues such as political and religious affiliation and feelings about race, gender, or various sexual activities. Imagine an interviewer asking someone, face to face, "Do you subscribe to any tenets of Nazism?" or, "Are you sexually aroused by scenes of violence?" Responses that subjects give to these questions in face-to-face settings are different from those in situations designed to insulate the honest subject from the disapproving reaction they fear they will receive from an interviewer (see Hatchett and Schuman 1975–1976).

The threat of embarrassment can perhaps be reduced by presenting subjects with questionnaires, to be completed alone and returned anonymously (with a subject code for scoring the responses). But here too there is a concern that subjects would still dissemble, knowing that their results will be evaluated. So the measurement of attitudes concerning highly emotional or controversial topics is difficult to bring off. If one insisted on using an interview or questionnaire format, perhaps the questions could be formulated in a way to minimize distortion due to evaluation apprehension. More speculatively, one might persist in using reactive measures but assume as a constant some average quantity of distortion due to evaluation apprehension and subtract or add that quantity to the responses. The first remedy merely attempts to avoid reactive responses as much as possible, but it is often difficult to estimate with what success. The second technique would be extremely difficult to motivate, for the magnitude of the distortion is unknown, and it must be estimated if it is to provide the basis for the correction.

The optimal arrangement would be for the subjects to engage in some behavior centered on the attitudes of interest but not let them know that they are being evaluated for that behavior. It is this demand for valid measurement of reactive attitudes that prompted the introduction of the "lost letter technique." Introduced in Milgram, Mann, and Harter (1965) and widely used since, the lost letter technique is used to infer attitudes about a variety of (typically emotional or controversial) issues. According to this technique, addressed, sealed, and stamped envelopes are placed in various public places. Envelopes are addressed in such a way that, if mailed, they will go to the experimenter. When someone happens upon an envelope, he or she can decide whether to mail the letter, ignore it, or throw it away. The most striking finding of Milgram et al. is that the return rates varied greatly according to the nature of the address (in this case, the type of organization) listed on the envelope. The experimenters inferred that the finder made some type of judgment concerning the importance or purpose of the letter on the basis of this address and would then decide whether to mail the letter, ignore it, or destroy it. The technique therefore yields a unique return rate for each address used.

Because the mailing behavior is anonymous (the person who finds the letter has no suspicion that anything they are doing regarding the letter is being monitored in any way), it is probably safe to suppose that any principled judgment they make, whether conscious or not, reflects an attitude they have concerning the addressed organization. In fact, sometimes a cohort (a person recruited by the experimenter) is watching, so the experimenter can gather information about more specific units than just address; they can manipulate factors of the finders, such as whether they are white or African American.

Clinical Caveats

With all the literature on psychological testing, why not appeal directly to the evidence embodied in such classics as Anastasi (1988) or in the encyclopedic Minnesota Multiphasic Personality Inventory? Doesn't this research represent progress and form the basis of an argument for realism? I would contend that the relative success of testing methodology is tentative support for realism about the behavioral sciences but not for any particular behavioral theory used in those fields.

There are at least two ways in which to relate the vast literature on psychological testing to realism about the behavioral sciences. First, one might examine the particular applications of psychological tests. There are, for example, IQ tests, neuropsychological tests, occupational tests, and tests of clinical disfunction. In any particular test, there is a question of whether there is a particular property, such as intelligence, creativity, Broca's aphasia, or paranoia, whose presence is being detected. Some complex capacities or traits no doubt represent a variety of separable but jointly stable features. A pertinent example may be IQ. The controversy surrounding IQ tests arises not from the contention that IQ tests don't detect anything but rather from the claim that there is no single feature, no monolithic property of intelligence, that test values represent. Instead, the claim proceeds, the results of familiar IQ tests represent a number of causal sources such as economic status, social background, attention, and motivation. With so many sources, the variables must be confounded. This worry, however, is best understood as a lament that we do not have a good enough theory of cognitive function to isolate the factors contributing to problem-solving (and other cognitive) virtue. But we should distinguish between a bad test and a bad theory. If we cannot establish test validity, it is because our theory is either too inaccurate or too undeveloped to determine when the measured value approximates the real value of a faculty. The criticism is not necessarily that the test is unreliable; for most such tests the distribution of scores is reasonably repeatable.

When assessing the evidence for realism here, we must separate the above evidence—yielded by particular applications of particular tests—from the general question of whether the canons of test structure allow behavioral tests to respond systematically to psychological variables, confounded or not. The ordinary standards of convergent and discriminant validity, to be discussed more thoroughly in chapters 6 and 7, can isolate causal factors, even though we may not possess a theory that cites specific mechanisms demonstrably responsible for test results. Rather, such standards are able to answer abstract questions about general perceptual, cognitive, and social factors. Intelligence quotient tests designed to measure a monolithic property in fact afford repeatable prediction of a variety of factors such as social class. This may not have been the original intention, but the discovery of a confound is a step in the right direction. Similarly, we can suppose that clinical diagnostic tests are capable of isolating behavioral patterns, even if we do not embrace the specific theory held by those implementing the test.

HISTORY. Unlike many of the disciplines we have thus far discussed, history does not allow true experimental design. What has already transpired cannot be manipulated. But as we shall see in chapter 5, the manipulation of an independent variable is just one among many ways of estimating the relevance and strength of causal influences. Simple sampling information may be useful, even for causal inference, if formulated carefully. In some disciplines, explanatory practices are so impressionistic, unchecked, and otherwise degenerate that any quantitative concepts would show the way to less dependence on idiosyncrasies of the recorder.

Because randomization and treatment are not available to historians, their most potent corrective of narrative biases is simple critical attention to the quantitative parameters and techniques. Although the use of quantitative information is never theoretically neutral, the methodological directive that we attend to quantitative parameters is not especially controversial. The most devoted narrative theorist would concede that the discovery that their central examples were unrepresentative of the population would, all else being equal, render problematic their interpretation of events. When generalizing about a population, the researcher must critically evaluate the basis for such generalizations. Is the sample size large enough? Is the scheme for coding data sufficiently representative of the theoretically interesting categories?

When data is uncategorized and unscaled, as is so frequently the case with historical data, it often does take much to get the smoke to clear. In a morass of demographic information about the migration of immigrants, for example, a pattern can quickly emerge if we partition the population into ethnic categories or into class categories. In doing so, we might find that what initially looked like an undifferentiated group of people coming into the United States has settled into different geographic regions according to ethnic background. If we then take a specific ethnic background as the relevant population, we may find a further relation between specific religion and class affiliation that can be expressed in the structure of an ethnically specific neighborhood. Therefore, even rudimentary partitioning and scaling can yield improvements in the understanding of causal factors that account for the distribution of observed properties.

However, history is not limited to the use of crude percentages. Perhaps the most sophisticated quantitative methods used in history can be found in economic history and other areas in which cliometric approaches have dominated. There, the values of theoretically interesting variables are determined by data, along with certain causal assumptions about how those variables are related. The quantitative imperative in history is the same as that in other disciplines that are traditionally resistant to quantitative approaches: Our computational limitations, along with the complexity of the information, make it impossible to formulate reliable estimates of the impact of relevant causal factors without the aid of equations and computational aids. For example, as an alternative to speculation that U.S. slavery was undermined because it became increasingly unprofitable, historians attempted to identity the expense and income sources associated with the slave economy. One component of the cost is the purchase price of the slave. The prices slaves brought depended in part on gender, and so as part of this quantitative effort, the following sort of relationship was proposed by Fogel and Engerman (1974, p. 33) to express the factors determining the price of a male slave of a given age:

$$P_{sx} = (R_f) \sum_{t=1}^{n} \frac{\psi_t \, \lambda_t}{(1 + i)^t}$$

The assignment of an equation to the purchase of a person no doubt stimulates unseemly associations. But the fact that slavery is morally deplorable makes the equation no less a depiction of the factors guiding the sale of slaves and the ultimate profitability of slavery.[1]

POLITICAL SCIENCE.   Much of the research in contemporary political science concerns the structure of, and participation in, political systems. When those systems are electoral, designs are used to examine phenomena such as voting patterns and class affiliation or, as we have seen above, to investigate feelings of political efficacy. Electoral research, for example, groups individuals by political party. Party affiliation is then tracked over time, to estimate the influence of various factors such as change in economic status or age on party affiliation and stability of partisanship. However one esteems research on the electoral participation in the U.S. political system, the quantitative methods are stunningly sophisticated, concerned as they are with the dicta of population-guided estimation. In the United States, some race- and class-based differences in social roles (e.g., such as country club membership, private school enrollment, etc.) are so robust they are open to casual observation. But more subtle causal relations, as well as changes over time, are less detectable by casual inspection. To explore the possible existence of such effects, sociologists, political scientists, and economists use experimental and quasi-experimental designs.

In a classic design (Schuman, Steeh, and Bobo 1988), national opinion survey data are used from the forty or so years preceeding the study, along with carefully gathered survey data of the authors' own, to chart trends in racial attitudes among blacks and whites. Most of the survey questions require "yes-no" or "same-different" answers and concern topics such as the subjects' attitudes toward school busing, separate accommodations, laws against intermarriage, segregated transportation, residential choice, and many others.[2] Much of the data had been collected in surveys from years before, when researchers were not quite so concerned about the obtrusive nature of the survey questions or about the evaluation apprehension

---

1. Although slavery is no longer practiced in the United States, it is still a major component of the economies of many trading partners of the United States. For a useful discussion of the various kinds of slavery practiced on the contemporary international scene, see Sawyer (1986).

2. One brief discussion of the tasks can be found in Schuman, Steeh, and Bobo (1988, pp. 57–61).

that normally attends such interview settings. Indeed, one of the major concerns about the validity of social research is whether someone's knowing they are being observed causes them to act differently. For instance, if asked in a personal interview whether they disapprove of interracial marriage, white people might give what they regard as the "socially correct" response rather than the response that reflects their true attitude; they react to a perceived expectation of propriety. Researchers try to avoid this "reactivity" by a variety of techniques. Or they at least try to estimate the value of its impact (by comparing the behavior during personal interviews with that during videotaped sessions, for example).

Because we are not in the position to manipulate the independent variable in such archival cases, we must use one of a variety of quasi-experimental strategies to identify causes in the correlational structure of the data. Model fitting has been used in such post hoc cases. Briefly, Schuman, Steeh, and Bobo formulated three models of racial attitude change over time—no change, linear change, and curvilinear change—each model projecting different values (or frequencies) for responses on the survey questions. When there is no statistically significant difference between actual responses and those predicted by the model, then that model is said to "fit" the data. I refer the reader to this research. As always, in a critical evaluation of this research the pertinent question is not whether an intelligent initiate to the literature can dream up possible confounds or other imagined difficulties in the design. Rather, if choosing between quantitative and traditional narrative, anecdotal approaches, the question is whether the latter could justify its conclusions better than the former. Can the narrative theorist demonstrate that an innovative approach is an improvement in accuracy of generalization? Standards of reliability, validity, and other design considerations offer just such a demonstration in the case of quantitative approaches.

SOCIOLOGY.   The same sort of constraints on field study research obtain in sociology as well. In fact, aspects of social research are indistinguishable from those of political science, as we would expect when two disciplines have overlapping subject matter. Among the chief topics in sociology are social stratification, social mobility, the causes of deviance, the influence of religion and education on social variables, as well as that of science and technology, social change, and urbanization. Since these influences often must be studied in the field, and the cacophony of causal influences in natural social settings do not afford control, we rely on our best social theory to estimate the magnitude of the most plausible interfering influences. This theory may consist of little more than the commitments of social common sense, commitments we acquire during childhood and reliably deploy in adulthood. Attitude surveys are grounded in just such folksy competencies. These competencies may be remarkably subtle, and so to call them folksy is not to degrade them. Moreover, even if they aren't especially sensitive, this may pose no difficulty for the method in question as long as the phenomenon under study is robust enough. Many quantitative approaches begin with ungarnished, common-sense assumptions, but they do not end with them. We are often surprised by what such inquiries reveal, even if it is an unsurprising, familiar account that guided the selection of controls. Nevertheless, on this modest basis the most sophisticated quantitative techniques have been developed.

In the next chapter, I will argue that statistical methods support at least modest assumptions about the existence of unobserved structure. These reliable methods are used to analyze outcomes on tasks like reaction time, survey response, psychophysical judgment, and the rest. Let us now examine a realist theory of measurement that accommodates the reliable and accurate estimation of social and behavioral magnitudes.

Sketching the Realist Theory of Measurement

That terms of conditional dependence provide the most natural expression of the relation of measurement can be seen in routine definitions of measurement concepts, such as an instrument's sensitivity:

> sensitivity = scale deflection/value of measured quantity causing deflection (Morris 1991, p. 53)

The fraction on the right side of " = " represents a quantitative relation between deflection and value, where the degree of scale deflection depends asymmetrically on the measured quantity. So one can see counterfactual dependence at work. If the measured quantity hadn't been of value X, the scale would not have been deflected Y. This is precisely the relation between the statistical distribution and the disposition that produces it, as we shall see in property (C) of chapter 3. In fact, this expression of instrument sensitivity is just a special case of the dependence of observed on real value in the case of any reliable methodology. In chapter 6, I will argue that statistical designs are instruments of a sort, so the above sensitivity ratio applies more literally to the statistical case than one might have at first imagined.

The dependence relation becomes more apparent as the account of measurement becomes more satisfactory. Something like the following account captures part of our unreconstructed conception of measurement:

> X has some property P of magnitude M, and instrument i measures P if and only if it reports the actual value of M.

As stated, however, this simple account of measurement would be inadequate. In the first place, it would count coincidentally correct reports by defective instruments as instances of measurement, allowing that a stopped clock measured the time simply because the hands indicate the correct time twice a day, or a thermometer stuck at 100.4 degrees will report a person's temperature correctly whenever that person has a fever of 100.4, and so on. So we need to add a further condition in order to rule out coincidentally correct reports by defective instruments:

> X has some property P of magnitude M, and instrument i measures P if and only if it reports the actual value of M and i would not have reported that value unless M had that value.

But now it would seem that the account of measurement is too strong, ruling out as measurement cases in which the reported value is incorrect but within an acceptable margin of error. So we need to add a clause that tolerates some amount of systematic and random error:

> X has some property P of magnitude M, and instrument i measures P if and only if it reports the actual value of M and i would not have reported that value unless M, within certain well-understood parameters of error, had that value.

Spelling this distinction out, however, will yield an analysis that treats measurement as a relation of causal dependence. This relation can be expressed by following the form of the counterfactual analysis of causation:

> the counterfactual analysis of causation: P causes Q if and only if (1) P obtains, (2) Q obtains, and (3) Q would not be the case if P were not the case.

> the counterfactual analysis of measurement: Instrument i measures P if and only if i reports the approximate value of M and i would not have reported that value unless M, within certain well understood parameters of error, had that value.

The above analysis of measurement does not require that the real value of M be known in order for the parameters to be well-understood.[3] For example, calibration occurs against a standard, and that standard is devised in light of our best theory (like a standard used to calibrate a pH meter).[4] A regress is avoided because we have diverse and increasingly better ways of measuring pH, time, and other objects.

Difficulties remain for the realist account of measurement. In the first place, it is not clear that a counterfactual analysis of causation requires realism even if other dependence relations do, as we shall see. Second, although the above analyses of causation and measurement treat counterfactual support as transitive, it has been claimed that counterfactual analyses of causation founder; causation may be transitive, the charge proceeds, but counterfactual dependence is not (see Lewis 1973, pp. 31–36). More ambitious critics charge that causation itself is not transitive. It may be, however, that both causation and counterfactual dependence are transitive; that is, apparent failures of transitivity occur due to pragmatic features of the sentences expressing those relations. Consider the following example of Robert Stalnaker's, discussed by Lewis:

(1) If J. Edgar Hoover had been born a Russian, he would have been a Communist.

(2) If he had been a Communist, he would have been a traitor.

---

3. The qualification concerning well-understood parameters of error is what distinguishes reports that are true by accident or by dumb persistence from those by sound design and application. In fact, the properties of validity and reliability help us to distinguish the latter from the former.

4. The instrument may be appropriately calibrated even if the total background theory is not approximately true, as long as that part of the theory used in calibration is sufficiently accurate. So this analysis of measurement does not imply a version of realism I might find too strong.

(3)   If he had been born a Russian, he would have been a traitor. (Lewis 1973, p. 33)

Such sentences rarely occur together, even though it is true that one can cleverly contrive counterfactual conditionals that fail transitivity. Nothing follows about the nature of causation from this fact alone. As in the causal case, the apparent failure of transitivity in the counterfactual case may result from a pragmatic feature of implication; in the "J. Edgar Hoover" case, there may be a fallacy of four terms, equivocating either on 'he,' in which the third-person pronoun could be interpreted as referring to two different individuals or on 'traitor,' whose satisfaction is relative to citizenship. I do not propose here a definitive answer to the charge of failed transitivity; instead, I simply suggest the pragmatic tangle between causation and its analysis as a possible source of weakness in the charge. For our more general purposes, however, the important point is that there is a dependnece relation in causal cases that must be respected, no matter what specific analysis of this dependence is advanced.

Fortunately, counterfactuals have other functions besides depicting relations of causal dependence. Consider the following two analyses:

P = placing the lid on the container
Q = the container exploding
R = my injury

the causal analysis: Placing the stop in the flask caused the container to explode. The container exploding caused me to be injured. Therefore, placing the stop in the flask caused me to be injured.

the counterfactual analysis: If I had placed the stop in the flask, it would have exploded. If the flask had exploded, I would have been injured. Therefore, if I had placed the stop in the flask I would have been injured.

No matter what specific analysis of dependence is advanced, our concerns are more general: There is a dependence relation in causal cases that must be honored. As we will see, in the case of measurement this dependence relation is best accounted for by a realist understanding of the objects related.

If the above account of measurement includes a condition of asymmetric dependence, it also offers a compensating parity in the treatment of the instruments to which it applies. The above, realist, account of measurement applies equally to proper lab instruments and statistical instruments.

In the latter case, there is a causal relation, typically elaborate, between the instance of statistical design and the population parameters that the sample statistics estimate. According to this view, the statistical instrument measures the relevant parameter if and only if the instrument reports the approximate value of the magnitude and the instrument would not have reported that value unless the magnitude, within certain well-understood limits of error provided by statistical theory and experimental design, had that value. The continuity between statistical and proper lab instruments asserted by PGE depends only on the observation that there is a relation of causal dependence of the procedure's or design's measurement report for the sample on the real value of a population parameter. All the rest is taken up by whatever ingenuity is required for the reliable and valid estimation, the illuminating "tweaking," of that part of our world.

Measurement relations are theoretically local. For this reason, the causal theory of measurement developed here can support Measured Realism, thereby endorsing a carefully circumscribed theory-realism. In chapters 3 and 4, we will consider the notions of causal independence and causal isolation as they occur in confirmation. At the moment, however, we should notice that measurement statements depict two circumstances: the conditions obtaining and the values those conditions produce. On the inoffensive assumption that x cannot be identical to y if x causes y, then x and y are sufficiently causally isolated from one another that x can exist without y. It is this feature that makes the objects and effects of measurement theoretically local and can render some aspects of theory adipose.

Adipose Theory and Epistemically Bite-Sized Commitment

So far, little has been said about the size of the units of theory to which measurement procedures are applied. Indeed, the notion (and act) of measurement is itself neutral on this issue. There is a little-told side of the measurement story, whose omission has allowed realists too blithely to move from the theory dependence of measurement to the approximate truth of those theories from which the measurement hypotheses are drawn. On this story, the remarkable improvements of measurement are so deeply dependent on the specific theory in the field that measurement successes confirm the entire theory, not just those parts involved in the computation of the expected measurement value. But there is nothing about theory testing or confirmation proper that requires that every part of a theory from which a measurement hypothesis is drawn is confirmed. In fact, if evidential relations are essentially causal, as many realists hold, then the evidence we can have for a theory or any part of it will only be as local (or piecemeal, at any rate) as the theory's dimensions of causal relevance will allow.

The successful role of diverse testing provides converging evidence in favor of the existence of theoretical quantities. Two or more different methods or instruments can isolate the same causal pattern, a common occurrence in the history of science (see, for example, the various tests of Avogadro's hypothesis or of August Weismann's "germ plasm" vs. William Bateson's "genetics"). This actuality indicates that we do not need to hold the same theory in order to isolate the same phenomenon. Accordingly, not every part of a theory is equally implicated in such measurement. And certainly those parts of the two theories that are inconsistent with the other are not essential to the measurement. We can call that part of the theory that is disengaged from the confirmation "adipose theory."

Here we have a fact of scientific practice that conflicts with more dramatic portrayals of measurement as so theory dependent that measurement outcomes confirm only that theory in whose terms the measurement hypothesis was explicitly formulated. If we are correct in supposing that diverse testing is epistemically valuable, then we must accept the following consequence: Many of the theoretical claims tested by measurement procedures are epistemically bite-sized. But if this is true for diverse testing, then it is also true for other epistemically central scientific practices that expose adipose theory. These include archaic confirmation, mercenary reliance, and the autonomy of experiment.

Although it is not initially apparent, then, the success of diverse testing is a testament to the autonomy that measurement has from particular theories. But that autonomy can be demonstrated only if we can isolate and characterize an object by different methods of measurement. To explain most naturally how this is possible, we must suppose that some kind of contact, characterized de re, is made between the object and our recognitional capacities. It is possible to detect an object dimly, in the same way that causal accounts of perception elucidate some justification relations in terms of a person's appropriate, unreduced causal relations to an object. Some forms of scientific realism, recently termed "theory centrist" (see Burian and Trout 1995), are committed to the specific details of particular scientific theories. Such accounts typically assume that confirmation for particular hypotheses reaches to detailed corners of the particular theory that prompted the test. This tendency toward theory centrism leads to extreme confirmational holism as well. How does the preceding realist sketch of measurement, once freed from extreme holism of confirmation, apply to the social and behavioral sciences? Let us begin by tracing its evolution, because PGE arises as a specific alternative to epistemologically troubled empiricist accounts of estimation.

Old Empiricist Accounts of Behavioral Measurement

Now that we have set out a general theory of measurement, we must determine how such an account would look when applied to the social and behavioral sciences. Although we have seen a number of difficulties associated with empiricist accounts of measurement generally, if the realist theory of measurement is to be preferable as an account of behavioral and social measurement specifically, we must show that it has the resources to handle these complications. In light of PGE, we can readily diagnose the problems with old empiricist accounts of behavioral measurement, and this constitutes the first step in presenting the realist alternative.

In response to the failings of operationalism and to the experimental demands of the special sciences, specific and more sophisticated empiricist accounts of measurement emerged. The psychological literature on construct validity displays all of the tensions one would now expect from methodologically competent efforts to balance empiricist strictures and the realist act of measurement. The notions are introduced as though designed to satisfy empiricist ends: A construct is an abstract variable that is normally taken as a measure of an unobservable psychological object intervening between stimulus and behavior. Constructs, it was said, are postulated to explain the distribution of (observable performance) scores on an experimental task. The construct is valid just to the degree that it measures what it purports to measure. Construct validation is achieved when diverse methods yield the same values for the measured trait—when independent methods converge on the same result.

The introduction of "construct" as a general experimental term reflects the lingering influence of empiricism. This legacy is first evident in its treatment of an unobservable process (object, etc.) as postulated solely on the basis of what is observed: "A construct is some postulated attribute of people assumed to be reflected in test performance" (Cronbach and Meehl 1955, p. 283). The empiricist twist is even more pronounced in the official treatments of recent texts. Construct validity is used as

> a measure of a psychological property of individuals for which, in fact, there is no existing, real-world measure (criterion). Mental abilities such as general intelligence, mechanical aptitude, and spatial relations; and personality characteristics such as sociability, dominance, the need for achievement, and introversion fall in this category. Since such things are hypothesized to exist, but have no direct real-world counterpart (That's why they are hypothesized to exist!), the variables in question are called constructs, and hence the term construct validity. (Ghiselli, Campbell, and Zedeck 1981, pp. 280–281)

This distinction belies the doubtful epistemic status that the empiricist tradition has always conferred on unobservable phenomena. Selective and tentative treatment of knowledge claims concerning unobservables is then parleyed into a case for the diminished ontological status of unobservables. The following sort of qualification is common in psychology and social science texts: "Although the terms used by social scientists do not have ultimately 'true' meanings . . ." (Babbie 1992, p.135) or "Tests of construct validity, then, can offer a weight of evidence that your measure either does or doesn't tap the quality you want it to measure, without providing definitive proof" (p. 133). The process of physical measurement does not imply that definitive proof is a reasonable standard in other disciplines.

Appealing to this evidential incompleteness, empiricists have been enormously resourceful at reconstructing the scientist's theoretical discourse until it is apparently purged of ontological commitment.[5] And once again, psychology and philosophy developed parallel solutions to the problem of theoretical definition, a common form of semantic holism. The particular anti-metaphysical strategy employed by psychologists casts construct validity not as a causal relation between an explanatory concept and the world to which it corresponds but as a concept defined solely by other concepts in the theory; no reference is made to a mind-independent world. Since there is no truly independent or unmediated way of establishing the validity of a measure, agreement with other test measures provides the only evidence that a construct reflects a real, causal influence. Coherence with other test outcomes seemed the best measure that experimentalists could hope for, leaving them with Thurstone's conviction that "validity studies in the cognitive functions now depend on criteria of internal consistency" (1952, p. 3).

---

5. Ramsification is another sort of empiricist attempt to evade the ontological commitment ordinarily attendant upon the use of theoretical concepts. It eschews the relation between concept and world, in favor of definitions that terminate in relations to other concepts of the theory.

In philosophical reconstructions, the metaphysically deflationary implication of holism is expressed in the logical empiricist treatment of scientific theories as formal languages. Of course, on this received view, constructs such as "introversion" appear as theoretical postulates in that formal system. The definition of this construct term, and the interpretation of theoretical terms generally, was to be given by a list of observation statements. As Hempel (1965a) showed, a complete interpretation for such terms cannot be given in a first-order language; among other problems, familiar disposition terms cannot be fully defined in terms of observables. But rather than abandon the logical empiricist account of theoretical definition, Hempel revised its aim: The nonobservational terms of a cognitively significant theoretical system need only be partially interpreted by observational claims. The balance of the definition can be completed by theoretical statements. But once we abandon the effort to define isolated theoretical terms entirely by observation statements—and in so doing abandon an important part of the traditional empiricist program—the psychologist's talk of "internal consistency" or "coherence" of measures finds its philosophical analog in high empiricist accounts that treat cognitive significance as a property of an entire interpreted system (Carnap 1956; Hempel 1965a), and in the later "law-cluster" theory of meaning. This excessive holism, too, is designed to evade metaphysical presumptions and is criticized in chapter 4 in light of the Minimal Connection and Minimal Detachment principles; the metaphysically simple among us might understand construct validity as an indication that a test measures a real, unobservable feature of the subject matter.

If we understand the validity of a theoretical construct as one product of successful diverse testing, then the epistemic and ontological restraint displayed in the empiricist literature appears to be methodologically unnatural. The reasons are by now familiar. All agree that the methods of diverse testing—"triangulation," as it is sometimes called—operate reliably on observable phenomena, providing reason for thinking that causal generalizations based on those methods are approximately true. We could, for example, estimate the length of an observable object in a variety of ways, and though the additional procedures over and above, say, the use of a ruler, may be redundant they need not be. The empiricist would have us doubt the reliability of those methods as soon as they applied to items too small to see, too quiet to hear, and so forth, even though scientists don't modify their conception of diverse testing when applying it at the unobservable level or think the causal properties of objects change in a relevant way at the unobservable level.

Construct validity is a distinct and substantial conception of theoretical definition. It must therefore compete with others. One might, for example, conceive of definition as a natural, causal relation one bears to both observable and unobservable aspects of the world.

One purpose of this chapter is to show that the application and improvement of tests reflect our approximate knowledge of unobservable causal factors and that this process is the only one that adequately explains what we do when we measure. Indeed, it may be due to the methods' demonstrated sensitivity to unobservables that empiricists fell silent when asked why we are able to increase (or improve upon) construct validity. Improvement in construct validity is just as troubling for the empiricist as the increasing precision of operational definitions. Approximate knowledge of unobservables is embodied in two forms in the practice of experimental design, one positive and one negative. On the negative side, our current theories identify a class of methods to avoid, particularly when the underlying causal factors are well understood. For example: Don't use a repeated measures design without also controlling for order effects (to block artifacts of learning). On the positive side, scientists assume that statistical tests can be sensitive to unobservable dispositions of members of the population, as well as to dispositions of the population itself.[6]

To reject these considerations favoring PGE is, in the end, to reject the idea that there is a mind-independent reality. After all, there are unsampled, perhaps undiscovered, members of a population, and their influence provides a perfectly sound example of the population guiding our judgment.

Components of a (Naturalistic) Epistemology of Measurement

If measurement or reliable estimation provides the basis of knowledge in science, then traditional epistemology could have much to learn by taking measurement relations as a model of justification relations. This is, I believe, the analogy toward which naturalistic epistemologists have been dimly gesturing since the late 1960s. Any plausible naturalistic epistemology of measurement will include a subsidiary model of concepts such as measurement de re, inexact measurement of natural quantities, population discrimination, confounding, and epistemic refinement. Below I make more explicit the components of this picture and show how they can be assimilated to traditional epistemological notions.

Evidence and Measurement De Re

If measurement has any purpose at all, it is to provide knowledge about a quantity. That is the kernel of truth in Lord Kelvin's otherwise unduly stern declaration that "when you can measure what you are speaking about and express it in numbers you know something about it; but when you cannot measure it, when you cannot express it in numbers, your knowledge of it is of a meagre and unsatisfactory kind; it may be the beginning of knowledge, but you have scarcely, in your thoughts advanced to the stage of science, whatever the matter may be" (quoted in Thomson, 1891, pp. 80–81). It is not surprising, then, that knowledge relations

---

6. One caveat: Some measurement descriptions, like Reichenbach's abstracta, really don't have corresponding quantities. Consider centers of gravity. The process of "measuring the center of gravity" of some object is not one in which we isolate an instance of a kind by applying principles of PGE. Because a center of gravity is an idealized location used merely for calculation, there needn't be an "object" to which the term corresponds. In such cases, by integrating over values at various locations in the object, we arrive at a mathematical construct. The calculated value of the "center of gravity" represents a relational property that is the result of measuring other magnitudes at other locations in the object.

can be plausibly treated as a species of measurement relations. In fact, the diagnostic features of causal dependence in measurement relations can be assimilated to those in reliabilist theories of knowledge, so that we view relations of causal dependence as those of reliability. On such a view, the relation between evidence and its conditions is said to be causal, and the fundamental notion of justification is one of reliable regulation; epistemic mechanisms can malfunction, but justification requires only that the relevant cognitive state be the product of a reliable mechanism or process (see Boyd 1981). Therefore, on the reliabilist account, justification need not be internalist; we need not have conscious access to the principles in virtue of which a belief is held in order for the belief to be justified. Nor is this account prone to the empiricist's selective skepticism; the object of reliable regulation can be either observable or unobservable.

There is nothing especially suspicious about the notion of justification without conscious access to the operation of the mechanisms involved in the epistemic relation of observation. As a matter of course we are causally related to things we can't see, hear, or sense in other ways, an insight of the causal theory of perception and an uncontroversial result of much experimental work in perception and cognition. Therefore, a causal theory of measurement is a simple illustration, elaboration, and extension of this view. For example, my ordinary visual beliefs are justified because my eyes are reliable visual mechanisms, and this can be so even though I have no articulated understanding of visual transduction, a process necessary for our visual perception. This process is described by our best biology and psychology, on which our best evidence for a causal theory of knowledge depends. This is not an especially novel view; many reliabilist and otherwise naturalistic accounts of knowledge attempt to describe the causal conditions thought to supply the required justification.

The previous section on empiricist accounts of measurement represents a putative consensus concerning issues about which there is in fact no agreement, for example, that a foundationalist epistemology is correct in light of its decisive role for observation. Here is an alternative story about how confirmation might work, one that takes a page from the book of the causal theory of perception. According to this account, justification consists of a causal relation between a belief and some set of conditions. Now, suppose I have a belief, on the ordinary sort of evidence, that there is a table in the room and I am challenged to defend this belief. I appeal to the fact that there is a table in the room as part of my explanation for why I believe there is a table in the room. I further appeal to the reliability of my eyes and of my other organs of transduction.

One way of putting this point is that I stand in an appropriate causal relation to the table (see Goldman 1967, 1976). Now, is there any reason to restrict the permissible justification conditions of events, processes, objects, properties, and states to those that are observable? In virtue of what more specific facts do I stand in the appropriate or reliable causal relation to the table? In virtue of the fact that the process of visual transduction, among others, is representation preserving. But it is also an unobservable process. So some of the causal relations that regulate (and thus justify) my belief that there is a table in front of me are unobservable.

At the same time, some of the features of the table that regulate my belief are at best unobserved, if not unobservable. In the human visual system, like other perceptual systems, the subject's discriminative capacities are sensitive to changes in theoretical states, even when those changes are not themselves introspectible and do not themselves reach threshold. Some perceptual studies are in the business of showing how performance can be made worse by degrading stimuli in ways that subjects are not consciously aware of (Fodor 1983).

Our theoretical beliefs, then, are justified to the extent that we bear an appropriate causal relation to the evidence. On this view, discovery is much more like confirmation than ever imagined. The entrenchment of our beliefs by routine testing is, like the inception of a new idea, a process initiated and regulated by our causal ties to the world. Those causal ties may be conceptualized or not, our beliefs about them de dicto or de re. Discoveries may produce ripples or waves; but scientific changes are not revolutionary or discontinous simply because communication becomes difficult across theories; progress and theoretical continuity can survive ruptures so long as our relevant cognitive and perceptual practices are regulated by the domain de re.

Inexact Measurement of Natural Quantities

Successful and precise measurement does not happen all at once. A familiar pattern of measurement occurs in unreconstructed scientific practice. An instrument that crudely measures a quantity is developed, and the instrument gets refined in such a way that, over time, it becomes a better and better detector of that quantity. This is the story of the pH meter, the magnetometer, and other instruments. The domains that these disciplines study and whose objects these instruments measure—chemistry and physics—are by now theoretically articulated and instrumentally successful. But they weren't always. This is an important observation because, in past disputes concerning ontological commitments in science, realists and antirealists alike have assumed that only a mature discipline is even prima facie deserving of a realist interpretation. But this needn't be so. It is implausible to suppose that there was some point in the history of chemistry at which ontological commitment was unwarranted and then, moments afterward, warranted. It is no less implausible to suppose that, at one point in the history of chemistry, chemists' judgments were unreliable and, at the next, reliable. The relation is incremental because the epistemic reliability of a method of measurement and ontological commitment to the quantities measured must be one of joint and increasing precision. At the start, measurement is inexact, and realists have not had an account of inexact (theoretical) measurement to help them articulate such early stages of empirical inquiry. We have always designed and offered arguments for unobserved (theoretical) structure, and these descriptions have always been couched in a theoretical vocabulary. Determinations of degrees of inexactness will be theory dependent, and we will have a univocal manner of comparison only when the standard and measurement are compared along the same theory-dependent dimensions. But this does not imply that all evidence of approximation relations is utterly theory bound. After all, the process of denotational and episte-mic refinement under confounding conditions sometimes occurs across theories. The behavioral and social sciences are (with the appropriate caveats about the unevenness within disciplines) now at the stage of early modern physics and chemistry.

If there is one theme in realist arguments that does the realist case a disservice, it is the exclusive focus on detailed theoretical understanding or the ability to use certain causal factors as tools. On this basis, one might be led to believe that, to defend realism about theoretical entities, our knowledge of them must be nearly complete—our measurement achievements must be secure. But surely we can have a realist argument based on inexact measurement. For although chemistry was incomplete in the 1930s, as indeed it is now, we had some imprecise knowl-edge of compounds and ions. We measured pH—perhaps not as accurately as we do now—but our old measurement procedures reflect some sort of theoretical knowledge of those chemical unobservables.

Although there is a common lore that the difference between the physical and the social sciences is that the former have laws that are exact and the latter inexact (as Hempel 1988 argues), the role of ceteris paribus clauses and provisos render inexact the laws of both domains. It is not, then, the inexactness of nomic generalization that is at the bottom of the critic's concern but the nonindepen-dence of the notions employed in their idealization approach. However, if there are good and routine inductive inferences based upon nonindependent premises, as the late nineteenth-century electrodynamics case seems to show, then noninde-pendence by itself cannot be the sole source of concern.

There is a thread sewn through developments in the last 100 years of electro-dynamics, taking us from fairly gross errors about basic components (such as the electron's charge) to our current level of sophistication. At the same time, those old accounts had approximately accurate calculations for some of the associated magnitudes (such as mass). So surely it must be acceptable to idealize in some way before our science has reached maturity. It is important to recognize that good science, such as classical mechanics, has often done just that, idealizing before all of the relevant sources of perturbation (such as magnetic influences on the pendulum) were known. What, then, should we say about the pendulum-magnetism case or the electron-gravity case? In the latter example, in 1874 Stoney identified discrete charges and in 1891 he correctly determined their mass but erred in assigning their charge. Six years later J. J. Thomson calculated that, after exiting the cathode, electrons travel at roughly one-fifth of the velocity of light. Thomson's calculation depended on the voltage applied and the degree to which the tube had been evacuated. If it were impossible (or at any rate, extraor-dinary) for an immature science to use idealization reliably, then the successes during Thomson's time, not to mention their contribution to our current state, would appear serendipitous or without rationale. But they clearly do have an explanation, in terms of scientific methodology's power to provide increasingly accurate accounts of the causal structure of the world.

Population Discrimination, Confounding, and Epistemic Refinement

The most distinctive feature of measurement is its apparent tendency to produce and accumulate scientific knowledge, and scientific realists have a guiding interest in explaining this fact. For sufficiently sophisticated theories, accumulation occurs, according to the realist, in spite of changes in theory; threats of incommensurability have been exaggerated. Realists have described in some detail the causal mechanisms that would serve to establish ontological continuity between different theories. Partial denotation occurs when the reference of a term is divided between two or more entities (Field 1973; Devitt 1981). According to a view of similar motivation, heterogenous reference potential exists when the conceptual resources of the scientist, along with prevailing theoretical demands (culminating in "initiating events"), "relate the term to different entities" (Kitcher 1978, p. 544). These proposals have the common goal of characterizing the apparently cumulative and continuous change in our ability to detect and refer to theoretical kinds. On a naturalistic account of language, the act of reference defines a practice that ultimately finds its place in an epistemological theory.

I am no less able to provide a realist account of the mechanisms of epistemic refinement in the case of statistical designs. Of course, the reliable operation of these mechanisms often requires that collateral claims (though perhaps not entire theories) be at least approximately true; but this is so for the mature sciences as well. My claim is that the character of statistical designs is no *special* impediment. If proper lab instruments secure increasingly accurate detection, then so can statistical instruments. Consider first the normal direction of confounding, which has a linguistic analog in partial denotation. Consider next the increasing discriminative capacity of designs, an epistemic relation akin to the semantic relation of denotational refinement. There can be no better evidence of theoretical progress than the discovery and correction of such epistemic conflation.

This epistemic refinement reflects theoretical knowledge, not just observational knowledge, as the empiricist would have it. If my analogy is correct, one could not accept the realist account of instrument calibration and consistently deny the implied theoretical knowledge. The changes occur in the direction of producing better and better techniques for detecting real causal factors in the world. This fact suggests the following picture. Statistical designs constitute a set of mechanisms that we have reason to think will, over time, converge on the causal factor of interest if there is one. We can think of the measurement practices as (imperfectly) indicating the presence of the studied causal factor, akin to the idea of partial denotation or reference potential. Statistical methods allow our cognitive practices to converge on significant causal factors. Typically, these methods don't secure reference all at once; instead, they identify complex and robust but confounded causal factors. In time, continued applications of variants of a design then separate contributing causal factors, not unlike the process of denotational refinement central to realist accounts. This process of epistemic refinement begins with an explanatory concept that is too general but that at least succeeds in locating some class of properties that covary with the property under study. Ordinary standards of discriminant and convergent validity, relying as they do on causal dependence, ensure that statistically significant results don't hide separate but uncontrolled causal factors that operate in the same direction as the studied factor.[7]

Such confounding effects occurred in attitude surveys concerning the feelings of political (narrowly electoral) efficacy of various ethnic minorities when researchers failed to control for the effects of class background on attitude. Feelings of political inefficacy among certain ethnic minorities were thought to derive entirely from their treatment as an outgroup. But these groups often occupied the same disadvantaged economic class as well, and part of the measure of political inefficacy could be attributable to low economic power (see Abramson 1982).

Now notice that, although these early studies failed to separate causal factors, the conflation occurs in the correct direction; outgroup treatment and low income appear to be causally related. Here is an instance of a familiar pattern of concept formation in the identification of a theoretical kind. Of course, only the benefit of hindsight allows us to dub an influence "confounding," a term of methodological derogation. In the early stages of research, a single variable may reflect the impact of several factors, but as long as these factors are causally related, a method that identifies such undifferentiated impacts is better than one that detects none at all. Thus we have a nonlinguistic correlate to the relation of partial denotation.[8]

What is interesting here, among other facts, is that scientists may see themselves not as producing better causal factor detectors but rather as merely improving controls, for instance. The process by which measurement procedures are improved is largely inexplicit; in fact, the improvements often get embodied in subsequent instrumentation.

Now, there is no question that we believe that our improved designs reflect theoretical knowledge; indeed, our best current theories tell us so. But how do we know that we have really secured improvement? Couldn't future scientists (or, more likely, future philosophers) add our current "accomplishments" to the litany of failed epistemic commitment in the history of science, akin to the many instances of failed reference?

This eventuality is certainly possible, but this concession doesn't show much, except that any level of ignorance, no matter how small, brings with it some epistemic risk. In the first place, measurement procedures often survive changes in theory; the instruments continue to detect real causal factors and do so with greater accuracy. Second, instruments do not detect nonexistent (but theoretically postulated) causes. As I pointed out earlier, it is a testament to this fact that instruments used in the practice of alchemy did not become alchemical detectors.

Our reasons for thinking that there is epistemic refinement are general, and so

---

7. Epistemic refinement is best illustrated when aging instruments are superseded by ones more sensitive and accurate. Compared to the new instrument, the outdated one confounds separate variables. The improvement in the instrument depends upon improved theoretical understanding.

8. For a representative example, see the conflation charge that Glymour et al. (1987, p. 201) levels against Head Start research for having only one variable ("socioeconomic status") for at least two likely factors ("occupation" and "income").

claims of progress do not depend on having a satisfactory, let alone complete, theory of reference. We now have in hand a family of austere arguments of extremely modest presumption that indicate our epistemic grasp of unobserved causal structures.

Causal Direction in Measurement

Unreduced appeal to causal notions figures in the components of a naturalistic theory of measurement. We shall consider one final way in which causal dependence is represented in analyses of measurement. Eschewing dependence as an unreduced causal relation, the model-theoretic approach analyzes the relation of measurement as a formal structure:

> [W]e call system Y a measurement apparatus for quantity A exactly if Y has a certain possible state (the ground-state) such that if Y is in that state and coupled with another system X in *any* of its possible states, the evolution of the continued system (X *plus* Y) is subject to a law of interaction which has the effect of correlating the values of A in X with distinct values of a certain quantity B (often called the "pointer reading observable") in system Y. (van Fraassen 1980, pp. 58–59)

According to an empiricist account of theory construction, how do the results of measurement affect theory? Particularly relevant for our purposes is the mediating role that van Fraassen assigns to models on his semantic conception:

> To present a theory is to specify a family of substructures, its models; and secondly, to specify certain parts of those models (the empirical substructures) as candidates for the direct representation of observable phenomena. The structures which can be described in experimental and measurement reports we can call appearances: The theory is empirically adequate if it has some model such that all appearances are isomorphic to empirical substructures of that model. (p. 64)

Drawing upon Suppes's collaborative experimental test of a linear-learning model, van Fraassen states that, when the theory in question is statistical, the semantic conception employs a standard "goodness-of-fit" test for empirical adequacy: "A statistical theory is empirically adequate if it has at least one model such that the difference between predicted and actual frequencies in the observable phenomena is not a statistically significant one" (pp. 195–196). The theory (for our purposes, of a given measuring instrument) is confirmed, disconfirmed, and modified in light of the outcome of this test, in virtue of the fit between the model and the actual (observed) frequencies (or values).

So while realists have been quick to claim that theoretical considerations guide the revision of models, the empiricist has an alternative: Improvements are made possible by refinements and subsequent testing of the empirical substructures of models of the domain, and those are observable. The apparent theoretical knowledge expressed in successful instrument design could then be understood as parasitic on the engineer's acquaintance with at least something observable—empirical substructures of the model.

I now want to make several sketchy suggestions about the difficulties with the empiricist theory of an instrument, or, in van Fraassen's terms, a "measurement apparatus." When constructing a model of a theoretical domain, the scientist indicates not just the empirical substructures subject to influence but also the direction of the influence. But notice that nothing is stated above concerning the direction of causal influence among parts of the model. Curious, then, that when the difference between predicted and observed frequencies reveals a distinct pattern, we can surmise the direction that modifications should take. Specifying the direction of causal dependence among, say, two parts of the model depends on prior theoretical/causal assumptions that often are not made explicit elsewhere in the model (Hausman 1983). Restricting itself to observed regularities in the outcome, the model may employ empirical substructures that may visually represent some events as preceding others, some as following others, and some as co-occurring. As the Humean moral counsels, such information is insufficient to specify the direction of causal dependence. Theoretical assumptions about the world, in both its observable and unobservable aspects, order the model, and to suppose otherwise is to have the model wagging the world. But for the empiricist, it is precisely this reliance, tacit or not, on theoretical information, that is illicit.

Another possible line of empiricist defense would be to suggest that improved controls result from past failures in design, and such failures are doubtless observable. But this approach fails to account for the reliability of projectibility judgments. Experiments fail for myriad reasons. Without already having access to accurate theoretical information, scientists could not adequately constrain the possible causes of a failed design so that they could arrive, as they often do, at a specific improvement. On the basis of observation, all we would know is that this particular design failed, not how we might improve it.

At any rate, the foregoing account of measurement as Population-Guided Estimation should put to rest a prominent view that the social and behavioral disciplines are not properly scientific because unable to provide a mathematical model of their subject matter. This is an overly restrictive standard, for it would rule out much in science (such as early qualitative chemistry), but psychology and the social sciences are capable of such models; indeed, in psychology, psychometrics does just that.

Conclusion: Theory, Law, and Measurement

Any account of measurement improvement would be incomplete if it didn't give its due to the role of theory in guiding measurement. In assessing the validity and reliability of an instrument or procedure, our best theory tells us which errors are theoretically relevant. Error assessment takes place against a background of theory. Our theory may tell us that a certain causal influence might be ignored, for it may conflict with another one of roughly equal magnitude. Or, if such conflict yields insensitivity of a sort that we would like to avoid, our theory may tell us how to eliminate those causal influences, already judged by the theory as irrelevant to the quantity measured.

The realist account of measurement as PGE states that quantitative procedures, routinely applied in light of our best theories, exploit the relation between (1) theoretically important dimensions of the population and (2) the products of measurement procedures and instrumentation, according to which the former reg-ulate the latter. First, when a procedure or instrument accurately measures a quan-tity, the values yielded by that procedure or instrument are conditionally depen-dent on the real values of the population dimensions. Therefore, it might be thought that the most natural way in which to understand these dependencies is causal. Second, some of the theoretically important population dimensions form equivalence classes of quantities that are unobservable, and measurement proce-dures are refined with respect to these unobservable phenomena. The causal as-pect of measurement not only explains the standard asymmetry of explanation but also accounts for (1) the apparent dependence of the measured value on the real value in valid measurement systems, (2) the counterfactual dependence evi-dent in the statement of measurement relations, and (when interpreted realisti-cally) (3) the indifference that scientists show about whether the postulated causal factor is an unobservable or just an unobserved observable.

Realists regard the typical quantities measured in science as natural kinds. For this reason, measurement outcomes are thought to represent real, enduring, or stable features of the population. We can measure objects that are perhaps not eternal but stable enough to support generalizations; such objects include quanti-ties in psychology and social science. Even so, philosophical analyses of measure-ment have always been devoted to special features of physical measurement.[9] These early analyses, however, were profoundly influenced by empiricist attempts to syntactically reduce higher- to lower-level theories and to produce reductive definitions in terms of observation. Freed from these special philosophical con-cerns, a generic realist account of measurement covers the social and psychologi-cal as well as physical sciences.

The pressure for realism moves by abduction from the success of measure-ment—which depends at least upon local laws and theoretical structure—to the approximate truth of laws and from the embedding of laws to the approximate truth of theories. This abductive move has been widely criticized by antirealists, and its most ambitious application can be found in scientific realist interpretations of the mature sciences. We can now assess the separate cases for varieties of realism and in particular examine their suitability as systematic analyses of the fledgling behavioral sciences.

9. All measurement depends on standards of one sort or another, from the standard meter to the rate of radioactive decay. One distinction that has gained some prominence in the literature is between fundamental and derived measurement. Fundamental measurement, as the name suggests, depends on no further standard. There, the measurement depends on a direct comparison of the object to the standard. If a measurement is not fundamental or direct in this sense, the measurement is derived. Density is the most familiar derived measurement, for density is the product of volume and mass, the two more basic measures.

THREE

Realism
Minimal and Robust

This chapter sets out two opposing versions of realism—minimal and robust. Both have appropriate domains of application. Minimal realism provides an adequate explanation for the reliability of inferences from statistical features of populations to the existence of general dispositional features of those populations, and robust realism supplies an adequate explanation for the instrumental reliability of mature scientific theories such as physics. But as an analysis of modestly successful, though relatively undeveloped, psychological sciences, minimal realism is too weak and robust realism is too strong.

PGE and Statistical Measurement

Population-Guided Estimation makes clear why we must separate questions of truth from questions of evidence: Configurations have an unmeasured (true) and a measured value. As we saw, empiricist accounts of measurement could not sustain this distinction. The same moral applies to theories of science. Lest we fall prey to verificationism, we must separate the issue of the truth of scientific realism from the issue of the evidence we have for it. Once we acknowledge this divide, it is possible for a particular version of realism to be more or less supported by the evidence. If realism is formulated too strongly, requiring for example the truth of all of the claims in the target domain, then that version of realism will have no evidence in its favor, for we have no such flawless theories. So it is unwise to cast an exacting version of realism when the evidence is so uneven, just as it is inadvisable to formulate a hypothesis more specifically than the sensitivity of our measuring apparatus will allow. At the same time, it is possible to formulate a version of realism so weak that it cannot recruit all of the pertinent evidence and resources available to address the most challenging empiricist criticisms. I will argue that there is just such an austere version of scientific realism, committed to little more that the existence of an unobserved structure whose properties we can barely characterize.

Austere realism is supported by the persistence of experimental correlations produced by careful manipulation. The inference to unobserved structure is abductive but well supported, for no working philosophy of science holds that there is *no* unobserved structure or even that nothing need be known about the unobserved structure to explain the persistence of the observed correlations. Typically, we select the theory that postulates an unobserved disposition as the cause of the observed performance or correlation. This comports with scientific practice generally, and the appropriateness of the inference to bare unobserved structure is minimally required to provide a rationale for scientific practice and an explanation for the reliability of certain quantitative principles, even as they operate on observables. However, austere realism is too weak to do justice to the theoretical knowledge reflected in substantial portions of the social and behavioral sciences. There, ontological commitments—to prototypes, nodes, lexical encodings, and schemas—are well articulated, extending beyond modest claims that some unobserved structure or other is responsible for an observed distribution. For these more ambitious claims about specific theoretical structure, we need Measured Realism, set out in chapter 4.

Inferential statistical tests—such as analysis of variance, t-tests, chi-square, and Wilcoxin signed ranks—now constitute a principal class of methods for the testing of scientific hypotheses. In particular, inferential statistics (when properly applied) are normally understood, for better or worse, as warranting a theoretical (typically causal) inference from an observed sample to an unobserved part of the population. These methods have been applied with great effect in domains such as population genetics, mechanics, cognitive, perceptual, and social psychology, economics, and sociology, and it is not often that scientists in these fields eschew causal explanation in favor of the statement of brute correlations among properties. However, the appropriateness of a particular statistical test and the reliability of the inference from sample to population are subject to the application of certain statistical principles and concepts.

In this chapter, I will consider the roles of one statistical concept (statistical power) and of two statistical principles or assumptions (homogeneity of variance and the independence of random error) in the reliable application of selected statistical methods. It is a truism repeatedly found and often demonstrated in statistics texts that the results of particular tests are reliable only if they satisfy certain assumptions. So, for example, the distributions to which a parametric test such as the Analysis of Variance (ANOVA) is applied must have equal variance if we are to legitimately infer from sample characteristics to the population characteristics.[1] But the conformity of statistical tests to these concepts and assumptions entails at least the following modest or austere realist commitment:

> (C) The populations under study have a stable theoretical or unobserved structure (call this property T, a propensity or disposition) that metaphysically grounds the observed values and permits replication and supports lawlike generalization; this structure therefore has a fixed value independent of our efforts to measure it.

(C) provides the best explanation for the correlation between the joint use of statistical assumptions and statistical tests, on the one hand, and methodological success on the other. The claim that (C) provides the best explanation, however, depends on the following naturalistic constraint on explanation:

> (E) Philosophers should not treat as inexplicable or basic those correlational facts that scientists themselves do not treat as irreducible.

Without (C), the methodological value of such assumptions as homogeneity of variance and concepts as statistical power would be an inexplicable or brute fact of scientific methodology. Without (E), the philosopher of science is able to design fanciful rational reconstructions of scientific practice; such reconstructions were popular in the logical empiricist tradition, guided by a priori principles of rationality that often designated as irrational typical and successful scientific practices. Along the way, I will consider possible empiricist interpretations of the reliability of these principles and assumptions. I will deploy the notion of a dispositional arrangement mentioned in (C). This dispositional arrangement is ontologically autonomous and independent of particular theories. But let us first turn to the considerations that weigh in favor of (E).

Austere Realism: Dispositional Structures in Statistical Practice

A handful of statistical practices, entrenched in the physical, behavioral, and social sciences alike, depend on assumptions about the nature of the unobserved world. Without these assumptions, familiar statistical practices would be without a rationale. In what follows, I will describe several such assumptions embedded in good methodological practice. By "good methodological practice," I mean practice that displays vigilance concerning the standard virtues of experimental design, virtues such as sensitivity and power. If we acknowledge that these principles and concepts are central to good methodological practice, then traditional empiricists cannot both deny that the appropriate domains have property T and still hold that we are sometimes justified in making inductions from samples to populations, even when those inductions concern (unobserved) observables.

The naturalistic constraint on explanation (E) mentioned above in part expresses a desire for deeper explanations. This plea for explanatory depth, however,

---

1. I believe my argument works for many other statistical methods—for example, regression. For a nice philosophical introduction to regression, see Woodward (1988).

is not new. Leibniz appealed to it when voicing his criticisms of Newton's purely mathematical description of the relation between Earth and the Sun. Newton's equations, Leibniz said, do not explain how the Sun and Earth attract one another through space. Instead, they describe an observed relationship that, if left without explanation, must be deemed a "perpetual miracle." In a more contemporary context, Jonathan Vogel notes that, "[w]here explanation is concerned, more is better, if you get something for it" (1990, p. 659). This should not be taken to imply that an explanation is inadequate until all of the facts on which the explanation depends are themselves explained. It is the governing theory that tells us when the explanation has gone far enough. Also, reigning theory tells us when any further detail would be extraneous or would yield a misleading picture of the sensitivity of the system. A naturalistic philosophy of science avoids rational reconstruction. Accordingly, the explanatory standards of our best (relevant) sciences settle the question of the depth at which an explanation should terminate.

Some pleas for deeper explanation range over ordinary and scientific contexts. The sparest arguments for realism have always begun with modest explanatory presuppositions seemingly shared by all. In its austerity, the present contention resembles the conclusion of a clever argument for the existence of unobserved structure, proposed by Paul Humphreys. I quote him at length:

> Consider an experimental situation S in which regularity R has been isolated, one in which a single observed factor A is uniformly associated with a second observed factor E; i.e., E regularly appears whenever A is present. Then introduce a third factor B which, in S, in the absence of A, is uniformly associated with a factor F. Now suppose that we claimed that a straightforward Humean regularity was sufficient, in the simple situation we have described (together with certain additional features such as temporal succession—what these are does not matter here), to identify A as a cause of E and B as a cause of F. Suppose further that neither E nor F is observed when both A and B are present and that the situation is completely deterministic. Now ask what happened to E. Why is it not present when B appears together with A? Now, as I mentioned earlier, it is possible for someone to deny that an explanation of this fact is called for. In such a view, there are three brute facts: situations with only A also have E present; situations with only B have F present; and situations with A and B have neither E nor F. I assume, in contrast, that the burden of proof is always on those who deny that an explanation exists for a given fact. And the case we have in mind should be taken to be the most routine, everyday kind of situation, with no exotic quantum effects. (1989, pp. 58–59)

Humphreys's argument shows that there is an austere, minimal realist position one might adopt and that the explanatory considerations in its favor are quite modest.[2] The natural explanation for the absence of E when A and B are present is that B prevents A from causing E, where event B is itself unobservable. This

---

2. The position I initially defend has affinities to that found in Humphreys (1989), as well as to Devitt's (1991) "weak realism" and Almeder's (1991) "blind realism," though my evidence derives from the successful use of statistical concepts and principles. Other realist arguments for modest knowledge of unobserved structure can be seen in Hausman (1983, 1986). On the basis of other, perhaps more specific and detailed evidence, a stronger version of realism may be warranted.

minimal realism justifies its ontological commitment by appeal to relatively enduring, unobserved structures[3] but does so without advancing ambitious claims concerning the approximate truth of theories or providing detailed descriptions of specific theoretical properties. As the above example indicates, austere realism is achieved rather by appeal to ordinary, explanatory demands. Recall that the principal question raised by experimental situation S is why E is not present when B appears together with A. If one rejects appeals to unobserved causal factors preventing E as epistemically illicit, then the observable correlations stated above must be regarded as explanatorily basic or irreducible; they just occur, presumably in virtue of nothing knowable.

Similarly, evidence for (C) can be found not just in the experimental settings of the sort described above but also in the success of those statistical concepts and principles that depend for their justification on the population's possession of property T. We thus find intimations of the Measured Realism to be advanced in chapter 4. And like austere realism, the more ambitious Measured Realism avoids dependence on any particular theory. Several theories of the same phenomena may isolate similar unobserved structures and arrive at similar generalizations about them. Below, the relevant principles and concepts are the independence of random error, statistical power, and homogeneity of variance, but others could serve to exemplify property T just as nicely, such as the unbiasedness and efficiency of an estimator.

The Independence of Random Error

Random fluctuations in the behavior of objects in study populations are thought to be tractable to statistical methods. A process is random if each of the possible outcomes (or values) has an equal probability of occurring. Random error is not a threat to design validity precisely because random error is unsystematic; that is, it is not the result of bias. It is in this sense that random errors are independent. Two events (or processes, properties, states, etc.) are statistically independent if a change in the probability of the one event has no effect (either positive or negative) on the probability of the other event.

Typical statistics texts mention that no two events are perfectly independent; appearances to the contrary derive from the idealization most closely realized in games of chance in which outcomes are equipossible (Humphreys 1985). The

3. The values of some sample statistics, such as the sample mean, often aren't found among any of the scores in the sample. So we have no reason to suppose that population parameters are any different, particularly in light of the fact that some populations are finite and so reflect some of the central properties of samples. They are not natural kinds, for the members of the population are too heterogenous for the mean, or any other measure of location, to represent a central tendency; therefore, just because you can count all the members and determine the value of each does not mean that the resulting value is "real." Here "real" is being used in the sense of "taxonomic in science" or "natural kind" or "an isolable object that can act as a cause" (supposing otherwise is an instance of the "average man" fallacy)—but this is an indictment of the specific measure chosen rather than a rejection of the concept of a real value.

correlation between two variables never completely reaches zero or, in null hypothesis testing, the null hypothesis is always, strictly speaking, false. This fact depends on a conception of causal relations according to which they are promiscuous and far reaching. Causal relations breed statistical nonindependence.

The principle of the independence of random error concerns, among other issues, the bias-diluting or bias-reducing effects of random error. On the one hand, the choice of research problems, samples, controls, and so forth is guided by our best theories. On the other hand, the independence of each random effect on each subject in a sample (or on each measurement of an instrument) reduces the likelihood of patterned results; that is what makes certain patterns in the data, when they do recur under diverse tests, particularly striking and theoretically interesting. This latter principle depends on the assumption of the canceling effects of error, an assumption stated (and sometimes even justified) in any standard statistics text. For sheer clarity and simplicity, it is hard to improve upon Guy's statement of the assumption, fashioned over 150 years ago: "[T]he errors necessarily existing in our observations and experiments (the consequence of the imperfection of our senses, or of our instruments) neutralize each other, and leave the actual value of the object or objects observed" (1839, p. 32).[4]

What must the population be like if reliable theoretical judgments can be made based upon the principle of the independence of random error? The assumption is that random errors (observed and unobserved) have opposing values and equal magnitudes, and so they are assumed to have values independent of measurement. Moreover, the independence of random error concerns the inference from a sample to a population because the assumption is that the error structure is the same in both the observed and unobserved parts of the population. The population's possession of property T therefore offers the most plausible explanation for the holding of the principle of the independence of random error.

Power and Sensitivity

After all the time and effort expended to design and run an experiment, the researcher wants to be confident (at least about factors in the design over which the experimenter has control) that the experiment is in fact sensitive to the dependent variable so that an effect will reach significance if the latter is present. The power of a test, then, is the probability of correctly rejecting a false null. (So, power = $1-\beta$.) Power is affected by a number of factors: (1) the probability of a type I error, in which we reject the null hypothesis when it is true, (2) the true alternative hypothesis, (3) sample size, and (4) the specific test to be used.

---

4. For another clear statement of this assumption, see Humphreys (1989, p. 48). Not all error need be observed; to suppose so is to conflate, in verificationist fashion, the concept of error with the experiential grounds for identifying error. One qualification: When the "errors necessarily existing in our observations" (as Guy says in the passage quoted above) are large, they may conflict and thus cancel out, leaving us with a statistical test that is less powerful and consequently less sensitive to the variable under investigation.

There are a number of ways in which the concept of statistical power can be loosely illustrated. Using a test with low power (say, due to small sample size) is like trying to catch fish of various sizes with a large-mesh net: You won't catch many, but the ones you do catch will be large. On the other hand, you will miss many smaller fish (commit many misses, or accept the null hypothesis when it is false). It is indeed due to the strict nonindependence of events (along with considerations of power) that we can construct "overly" sensitive tests. By increasing the sample size, we increase the probability that the postulated effect will be detected if it is there. And where the sample size is extremely large, it is highly probable that arbitrarily selected pairs of variables will yield correlations that reach significance (for more on what has been called the "crud factor," see Meehl 1990b).

What must the populations be like if we are to suppose that selected factors such as sample size and size of uncontrolled error affect sensitivity and power? If we are to honor (E) rather than simply insist that an equation holds or an observed correlation obtains, we must suppose that there is some discriminable, stable property of each object such that, by introducing it into the sample, the test increases in statistical power.

Homogeneity of Variance

When comparing two populations, we are attempting to estimate the value of the same quantity in both populations; otherwise, it would make no sense to infer that a change in the value of the quantity on the treated sample is due to the introduction or manipulation of the independent variable. In tests that depend on variance, we estimate the magnitude of that influence by a ratio that conforms to the appropriate distribution (t, chi-square, etc.). Where σ^2 is variance, homogeneity of variance is indicated by the relation

$$\sigma_1^2 = \sigma_2^2 = \sigma^2$$

in which the subscripts signify the particular population.

There are parametric tests (such as the t test and ANOVA) and nonparametric ones (such as the Wilcoxin). Parametric tests make three demands on the data they apply to: (1) the data must be drawn from a normal population, (2) the populations (when it appears that there are more than one) must have equal variances, and (3) the variable of interest must be measured on an interval scale described in chapter 2.

To see how the concept of homogeneity of variance plays a crucial methodological role in deciding what test to run, we must first explain the notion of variance. We determine the variance of a population by first calculating the deviation score $(X - \bar{X})$ (the difference between each score and the sample mean). After summing the squared deviation scores, we divide the sum by the number of scores. The result is the variance of the population. Now, if tests of dispersion (such as ANOVA) are to show that, with respect to a certain variable, some set of scores was drawn from a different population—and thus there is a significant difference between them—the two populations must have roughly equal variances. Otherwise, the appearance that the two sets of scores belong to different populations could be an artifact of the inequality of variance rather than of performance differences with respect to the test variable despite the populations' being otherwise the same.

In order to determine homogeneity, an F-ratio test is run. The F ratio represents the relation between the two estimates of variance: the variance between the means of the groups studied to the variance within the groups studied. This relation is expressed as follows (S^2 is the symbol for variance):

$$F = \frac{S_b^2}{S_w^2}$$

For a t test, we calculate the F ratio as a preliminary to a test that compares the means of two groups. The t test makes an assumption of equal variance—that is, that the two groups are drawn from populations with equal variances. There is a rationale for the prior F test, for we want to make sure that any substantial difference in the means is a consequence not of initial differences in population variance but of mean performance upon the introduction of the treatment.

Now, what properties must such populations possess if it is permissible to infer the suitability of a parametric test from the outcome of the F-ratio test? Minimally, it must be the case that the populations have enduring properties in virtue of which they can be systematically distinguished. And because the distribution is replicable—that is, the distribution is the result of a process that would produce a relevantly similar distribution under repetitions—the unobserved properties must be stable enough to permit such replication. By (C), this feature is best explained in terms of the population's possession of property T.

Explanation and Irreducible Facts

There is a remarkably durable, empiricist conception of theory testing according to which the epistemic interpretation of these statistical notions is exhausted by their observational content; their meaning can be defined, and their use given a rationale, solely in terms of their observational content. Indeed, population parameters are often treated by statisticians as certain sorts of mathematical fictions, as the result of indefinite or (near) infinite samplings (for a brief review, see Suppes 1984, pp. 82–83; for a discussion from the perspective of statistical inference, see Barnett 1982).

After all, the values that provide an apparent basis for knowledge possess features that violate traditional empiricist conceptions of knowledge; traditional empiricists have been loathe to rely on idealizations. In the case of knowledge borne from statistical inference, the standard empiricist understanding of statistical assumptions takes a form of the frequency interpretation: The "real" values are simply idealizations concerning the observed values yielded under an indefinite (or infinite) number of samplings or potentially infinite sequence of trials (for the standard view, see Mises 1957). The difficulties with a frequency interpretation of probabilistic claims are well known (see, for example, Hacking 1965). Consider the .5 probability a fair coin has to come up heads. Because the frequency interpretation defines "probability" in terms of observed frequency, no probability (of coming up heads or of coming up tails) can be assigned to an unflipped coin. The most natural explanation for the .5 distribution is that the coin has a propensity or tendency to produce a distribution of .5 heads. Let us concede that explanatory appeal to such a propensity may be vacuous when it is invoked to account for only a single (type of) observed effect, because the propensity gets framed in terms of the observed effect: The coin yields a .5 heads distribution because it has the propensity to yield a .5 heads distribution. Such explanations, however, are not vacuous as long as the propensities are manifested in diverse ways and thus can be independently characterized.[5] So the propensity said to explain a fair coin's .5 heads distribution may explain other observed effects as well—for example, other effects concerning its center of gravity. On the frequency interpretation, by contrast, the fact (and the correctness of our expectation) that a fair coin will yield a .5 heads distribution is not explained in terms of an unobserved, independently specifiable disposition or propensity. Rather, that fact is basic or irreducible, not explicable in terms of any deeper causal fact. The approximation of sample values to population values in the estimation of parameters such as variance appears to be a similarly irreducible fact for the empiricist, while it is explicable to the realist in terms of a propensity or tendency of the objects to produce certain observed values. Notice, a robust realism about theories is not required here, just a minimal realism about the existence of a property.

Explanations cite particular factors manifested in a variety of ways in observation. Without an explanation in terms of theoretical entities or laws, these various observable manifestations appear to be unconnected, and so one class of observational data does not provide inductive support for claims about the relations to other classes of observational data that represent other manifestations of putatively theoretical objects. For example, in cognitive psychology, prototype studies in the 1970s revealed just such a robust phenomenon. When asked to rate how representative an object is (e.g., robin, chicken, etc.) of a certain class (e.g., bird), subjects' performance was the same on both ranking and reaction time tasks (Rosch and Mervis 1975; Mervis and Rosch 1981). The convergent results of these two different test methods are taken by psychologists to indicate that the prototype effect represents a real (nonartifactual) feature of mental organization. Statistical methods were used in both sets of studies representing both measures.

There are a number of empiricist reinterpretations of the argument for C (the claim that some populations have property T). One might claim that I have not distinguished between objects that fall outside of the range of our sensory and perceptual powers and those that we could observe with the unaided senses were we properly situated at the time. The empiricist might claim that the argument

---

5. I hold that such propensity explanations are not vacuous even if no such independent specification can be found. Minimally, citing a propensity as a cause informs us that the effect is, in general, nonaccidental.

for C has no force, since one ought not treat with epistemic parity claims about unobserved and unobservable phenomena. However, the argument I have presented trades on the success with which these statistical concepts and assumptions have been implemented. This empiricist response, I believe, cannot bear the weight it places on this distinction. If the empiricist is to preserve the claim that induction is ever successful, the claim must range at least over unobserved observables. Meager as this power might be, without T this reliability of induction over unobserved observables is mysterious. The empiricist might contend that such instrumental reliability needs no explanation, but such a rejoinder runs afoul of (E).

On the other hand, one might deny that the sciences that employ statistical methods are successful, but that view has never been defended, and for good reason: These principles have been used to draw conclusions concerning observables, proving reliable in circumstances in which population values are already known. This is a common point among realists. Clark Glymour states that bootstrap principles "are principles we use in our science to draw conclusions about the observable as well as about the unobservable. If such principles are abandoned *tout court*, the result will not be a simple scientific antirealism about the unobservable; it will be an unsimple skepticism" (1985, p. 116). Michael Devitt states that the fundamental issue separating the realist and empiricist "is selective scepticism; epistemic discrimination against unobservables; unobservables' rights" (1991, p. 147). The sweeping consequences of selective skepticism have been noted elsewhere. Richard Boyd replies to attacks on realist applications of abduction by pointing out that "the empiricist who rejects abductive inferences is probably unable to avoid—in any philosophically plausible way—the conclusion that the inductive inferences which scientists make about observables are unjustified" ([1983] 1991a, p. 217). If we want an explanation for the reliability of these statistical principles and concepts at all, we must suppose that we have at least modest theoretical knowledge.

The argument I advance for an austere realist interpretation of statistical practice depends on similar explanatory considerations and makes a specific suggestion concerning the explanatory item: a propensity or a dispositional property invoked to account for the (observed) results of statistical applications. But for the modern philosophical vocabulary and specific measures of empiricism, there is nothing new in this general picture, and in holding it I am in sound statistical company. Lagrange, Laplace, and Gauss all had confidence that the populations worth studying had parameters with real values,[6] and inaccuracy or error arose not from

---

6. The sense in which a population has a "real value" is, as presented in this chapter, far weaker than one might have thought some scientific realists are committed to. The above methodological concepts and principles do not presuppose that these values always license causal inference, that they are permanent (rather than just stable), or that they are exact. The fact that these assumptions play a central role in making discriminating judgments about appropriate design is insufficient to support all of the epistemological claims of scientific realism—in particular, the claim that we can have detailed knowledge of the specific nature of those unobservables.

the absence of a true value but from both the nature of the true causes—which could be stochastic—and from our ignorance. Given this confidence in the stability of an unobserved world, it was also quite common for these eighteenth- and nineteenth-century figures to believe that under repeated samplings statistical methodology will bring our beliefs into conformity with the world.

The virtue of the present argument—in addition to its illustration of the austere realism represented in the reliability of statistical principles and concepts—is its demonstration that the empiricist's selective skepticism is abetted by (indeed, may depend upon) the empiricist's tolerance for brute facts or irreducible correlations. This tolerance is unnatural once philosophical standards of explanation are assessed by those of science—that is, by (E). Likewise, we should not blithely regard as inexplicable, or in need of no explanation, the correlation of the use of statistical methods and the improvements in diverse fields incident upon the introduction of these methods. To be more specific, we should not take as irreducible the coincident use of statistical principles and the reliability of inferences from samples to population characteristics. In light of the general epistemic reliability of these statistical, quantitative methods—in the social and behavioral sciences, as well as biology, chemistry, and physics (for the latter, see Eadie et al. 1971)—we should want to understand why they work when they do. Once achieved, this understanding leads to realism. Therefore, to the extent that one adopts the naturalistic conception of explanation, one will reject as unduly mysterious the empiricist account of the reliability of selected applications of statistical methodology, treating as a brute fact a correlation that the realist and scientist alike would explain.

Manipulability and Entity Realism

As satisfying as it might be to have articulated a generic realist view, a view presupposed by any design, this austere realism hardly seems strong enough to accommodate the detailed and sometimes daring descriptions of theoretical phenomena we commonly find in professional journals. Rather than identifying the reliability of selected statistical methods as a source of warrant for ontological commitment to some unobserved structure or other, another tradition of economical or modest realism focuses instead on the manipulability of theoretical causes. A selective realism, based on the manipulability of entities, shuns commitment to knowledge of theoretical laws and approximate truth of theories and does so on grounds different from those of the generic, austere realist. The centrality of manipulability was first explicitly presented by Douglas Gasking:

> [M]en found out how to produce certain effects by manipulating things in certain ways: how to make an egg break, how to make a stone hot, how to make dry grass catch fire, etc. . . . When we have a general manipulative technique which results in a certain sort of event A, we speak of producing A by this technique. . . . Thus a statement about the cause of something is very closely connected with a recipe for producing it or for preventing it. (1955, pp. 482–483)

Gasking is obviously concerned with the semantic analysis of statements of the form "A causes B," and says little about the epistemic status of those claims. This is not especially surprising, given the tendency during this period to assimilate all epistemological and ontological claims to semantic ones, but the core causal insight is still easy enough to extract: Manipulability provides a special kind of evidence of reality. As subtle as theoretical arguments about unobservables can be, manipulative interactions are decisive; one can offer reasons for postulating the existence of black holes, but electrons and ions we can manipulate.

Physicists do not explain the effects of electrolysis in terms of the operation of some stable, unobserved structure or other but rather in terms of specific features of electrons. Continuing this tradition of "manipulability" realism,[7] Ian Hacking elaborates the manipulability condition, a sufficient condition for legitimate ontological commitment. Hacking is surely correct in claiming that manipulability is diagnostic of reality. As he puts the point with respect to the electrons emitted by the polarizing gun: "So far as I'm concerned, if you can spray them then they are real" (1983, p. 23; emphasis deleted). Hacking does not rest content with the consequences of antioperationalist accounts of measurement; the successful introduction of controls does not represent clear evidence of theoretical knowledge. After all, it is theory that guides calibration: speculative and historically revisable theory. Hacking demands further evidence for realist conclusions—not just measurement proper, but manipulability:

> Determining the charge of something makes one believe in it far more than postulating it to explain something else. Millikan gets the charge on the electron: better still, Uhlenbeck and Goudsmit in 1925 assign angular momentum to electrons, brilliantly solving a lot of problems. Electrons have spin, ever after. The clincher is when we can put a spin on the electrons, polarize them and get them thereby to scatter in slightly different proportions. . . .
>
> Hence, engineering, not theorizing, is the best proof of scientific realism about entities. (p. 274)

Hacking's "manipulability condition" is advanced as a sufficient condition for theoretical commitment: If we can manipulate X, then X exists. By itself, the manipulability condition of entity realism is compatible with a more aggressive version of realism, according to which the instrumental reliability of methods responsible for such achievements as manipulation require for their adequate explanation *the approximate truth of the laws and theories* on which they are putatively based. So why not just embrace this more robust realism, if it appears to be required anyway?

Hacking would insist that his entity realism is not restrictive, claiming that manipulability is a sufficient but not necessary condition for realist commitment.

---

7. On this view, we are ontologically committed to anything held as a cause, and we acquire knowledge of causal factors by our efforts to manipulate them: "What makes p a cause-factor relative to the effect factor q is, I shall maintain, the fact that by *manipulating* p, i.e. by producing changes in it 'at will' as we say, we could bring about changes in q." (von Wright 1975, p. 107).

It is worth noting, however, that Hacking offers a number of reasons for rejecting more ambitious versions of realism, among them metainductive considerations familiar from Putnam's work (1978). In particular, Hacking claims that nonexperimental settings provide evidence that is insufficient for ontological commitment, implying that the "overall drift" of his book *Representing and Intervening* is "away from realism about theories and towards realism about those entities we can use in experimental work" (1983, p. 29).

What sorts of considerations, then, should incline us to accept realism about theoretical entities? Hacking traces his conviction as follows:

> Long-lived fractional charges are a matter of controversy. It is not quarks that convince me of realism. Nor, perhaps, would I have been convinced about electrons in 1908. There were ever so many more things for the sceptic to find out: there was that nagging worry about inter-molecular forces acting on the oil drops. Could that be what Millikan was actually measuring? If so, Millikan goes no way towards showing the reality of electrons. Might there be minimum electric charges, but no electrons? In our quark example we have the same sorts of worry. Marinelli and Morpurgo, in a recent preprint, suggest that Fairbank's people are measuring a new electromagnetic force, not quarks. What convinced me of realism has nothing to do with quarks. It was the fact that by now there are standard emitters with which we can spray positrons and electrons—and that is precisely what we do with them. We understand the effects, we understand the causes, and we use these to find out something else. The same of course goes for all sorts of other tools of the trade, the devices for getting the circuit on the supercooled niobium ball and other almost endless manipulation of the "theoretical." (1983, pp. 23–24)

Therefore, to the extent that Hacking's entity realism is more than just the manipulability criterion, it rules out robust realism, restricting us to an ontologically selective version of scientific realism.

There are a number of initial difficulties with this view, and they vary in degree of seriousness. First, all of the reasons we have for thinking that the entities we are manipulating are the ones we *think* we are manipulating depend upon experimentally prior laws and theories. After all, the devices used to spray positrons are designed in light of a theory of what positrons are like. We can toss theory away when we are through with it, but we shouldn't ignore our indebtedness to it. Put psychologically, it may be the flashy achievements of technical manipulation that convince us of entity realism, but this may be so only because our cognitive resources prevent us from appreciating the rich involvement of theory and experiment all at once. Second, it is not clear why such manipulability should mark a principled distinction between worthiness of ontological commitment and unworthiness. Indeed, the notions of manipulability and tool are themselves graded notions, and there would seem to be no magical point at which the apparent manipulation of a postulated entity becomes so effective that the postulate deserves ontological commitment.

Third, in light of Hacking's own epistemic standards reflected in his concern over metainduction, it should be a worrisome possibility that some mediating mechanism that researchers attempt to use as a tool should turn out to have properties very different from what researchers had supposed. In such a case, *something* is being used to systematically explore something else, but we may not know what. It does not appear that this modest "entity" realism has the resources to address such a metainductive challenge. The resources required to block the meta-induction can only derive from a naturalistic epistemology, one worked out more explicitly than here. And the epistemological naturalism required for a satisfactory rejoinder to the metainduction is most defensible on a more robust version of realism, a sweeping realism that entity realism was originally designed to avoid.

More important, separating warrant for entities from warrant for the approximate truth of laws and theories threatens a trusted thesis in contemporary philosophy of science: the theory dependence of design, measurement, and other activities of ontological consequence. How do we explain the reliable manipulation of particular theoretical entities if not by the guidance of theory? In short, entity realism underestimates the role of theory in guiding manipulation.

According to the measured realism I will defend, belief in some entities is independent of any particular theory, but not because the relation of manipulability is somehow irreducibly warranting in the way that Hacking suggests. Rather, warranted belief in some entities can be independent of any particular theory because warrant for such belief typically depends on more than one theory, and so not on any particular one.

Perhaps the most puzzling feature of the restrictive character of entity realism concerns the role of abduction. Whether or not Hacking has articulated the premises in the argument for realism about entities, the structure of the argument is clearly abductive: The existence of positrons provides the best explanation for our apparent ability to manipulate them. But why is this abduction permitted while abductions to the approximate truth of laws and theories are shunned? If my claims about the theory dependence of manipulative technology are correct, then Hacking cannot consistently defend this selective skepticism. Indeed, if our understanding of the effects and causes of a particular theoretical entity indicates knowledge, warranted ontological commitment to a particular theoretical entity consists at least in knowledge of true generalizations about those phenomena and thus to knowledge of at least some laws. Hacking must approve at least some applications of the no-miracles argument, since he appears to hold that our manipulative successes involving the positron gun would be miraculous were there no positrons. Yet, the ability to design positron-spraying instruments without the benefit of very accurate laws and theories about the relevant causal features of positrons would be, if not miraculous, surprising indeed. And so, because Hacking avoids appeal to laws or theories in the defense of entity realism, our manipulative success appears irreducible and mysterious, as did the reliability of our use of statistical notions such as homogeneity, power, and the independence of random error.

One might plump for a more aggressive law or theory realism to account for the more impressive successes in science. For example, the success of theory conjunction, a phenomenon to be discussed in chapter 4, depends not just on the existence of postulated entities but also on something like the deductive closure of laws and theories under the union operation. After all, theories, and not entities, are being conjoined.[8] The fact that the approximate truth of theories is preserved under the taking of unions is therefore still inexplicable on a version of realism—such as entity realism—that eschews the approximate truth of laws and theories. Only a stronger version of realism can vindicate the success of theory conjunction, and the adoption of this stronger version of realism will have dramatic philosophical consequences.

So far in this chapter, we have recorded a series of realist assumptions of statistical technique. We have seen in detail why the empiricist treatment of the observed value/expected value distinction is untenable. In short, the empiricist analysis of these assumptions is fragmented, providing different explanations for each phenomenon of scientific practice. By contrast, the realist can offer a unifying account of these assumptions in terms of the causal, unobserved disposition underlying sample performance. It is this feature that at once explains the canceling effects of random error, the homogeneity of variance, and the increase in power by increase in sample size.

Much of this chapter has been devoted to a defense of an austere realist explanation for the reliability of statistical methods. Measurement statements typically express the presence and magnitude of a disposition, estimated on the basis of an instrument's response to exposure to the relevant object. At a minimum, then, measurement statements reflect the property (C); the distribution of observed values is explained by the presence of an unobserved distribution. The relative independence from theory of austere measurement claims results from the ontological distinctness of dispositional arrangements.

We have determined that a minimal, austere realism is required to account for the reliability of statistical principles and that this assumption is deeply embedded in social and psychological theory testing. At the same time, the manipulability condition leads to a realist claim of similar modesty: The apparent manipulation of unobserved structures implies the reality of structures under the tested theoretical description or of ones causally similar to them. But we may ask whether the evidence sustains a far stronger version of realism: robust realism. After all, our ability to manipulate unobservable structure appears to depend on the accuracy of specific theoretical information—for example, in designing instruments to manipulate theoretical entities. Although I will argue that robust realism is not adequately supported by evidence of modest theoretical success in the social and behavioral sciences, much of what I shall say about abduction will be salvageable in my defense of Measured Realism—a realism about laws—a version of realism better suited as an interpretation of the social and psychological sciences.

---

8. It is true that descriptive adequacy demands an account of theory conjunction that permits something like approximate deductive closure, but of course this isn't a special problem for the realist; the empiricist, who agrees that theories are routinely and reliably conjoined, must at least produce an account of the approximate closure of the theories' joint observational consequences.

Premature Reports of Realism's Death

In contrast to austere and entity realism, robust realism makes the ambitious claim that the approximate truth of our background theories and the (at least partial) reference of relevant theoretical terms best explain the tendency of scientific methodology to identify predictively reliable theories. If the recent press is to be believed, robust realism—advanced in various forms by Richard Boyd, the early Hilary Putnam, and William Newton-Smith—has fallen on hard times. To its critics, the bold abductive expression of scientific realism vacillates between awesome implausibility and outright incoherence. Arthur Fine announces that "[r]ealism is dead" (1986a, p. 261). Larry Laudan apparently believes that, when death is inevitable, mercy requires a swift dismissal, calling the abductive argument for realism "just so much mumbo-jumbo" ([1981] 1991, p. 232). Van Fraassen holds that realism is a cowardly proposal; inasmuch as it goes beyond commitment to observable phenomena, realism is "empty strutting and posturing," a "display of courage not under fire" (1985, p. 255), purchasing nothing additional for its bravado. At the same time, defenders of realism are cast as witless participants in a comic philosophical tragedy, stamping their feet in childish insistence that the claims of science are really true (Fine 1986a, p. 271). The comfort lent by belief in an external world appears to be of almost clinical interest (pp. 274–275), perhaps the result of latent mechanism. As curious as it is that an arcane philosophical dispute should generate such affect, the emoting is misplaced.[9]

What prompts so strong a reaction? Surprisingly enough, it is a pattern of argument common in science and philosophy: abduction, or inference to the best explanation. According to this form of argument, we infer the existence of an entity, or the approximate truth of a law or theory, on the grounds that it provides the best explanation or descriptive account of some class of phenomena. Darwin argues abductively for the theory of natural selection: "It can hardly be supposed that a false theory would explain, in so satisfactory a manner as does the theory of natural selection, the several large classes of facts above specified" (Darwin 1859, p. 476). As we will see, Avogadro draws an inference to the best explanation for the existence of molecules. Pasteur infers the existence of anaerobic microbes as the most plausible explanation for fermentation, as many of his time appealed to the approximate truth of a germ theory of disease to best account for the spread of cholera and other epidemics.[10] In the history of philosophy, we often find a philosopher defending a comprehensive position on the grounds that

---

9. For a deft survey of the contours of this dispute, see Wylie (1986). The overall argument of this book is one of thoroughgoing scientific naturalism. While this version of naturalism is normative, the normative standards are not to be found in traditional philosophy. Therefore, I will not be especially concerned with the subtle metaphilosophical maneuvers that participants make in distinctly philosophical attempts to justify abduction.

10. For more historical examples and philosophical analysis of inference to the best explanation, see Thagard (1978).

it provides the best or most unified account of a diversity of evidence. Widespread as abduction is, its plausibility is questioned when it is applied to arguments for scientific realism.

Our discussion of robust realism has two purposes, one negative and one positive. On the negative side, I shall contend that the objections to abductive defenses of realism—objections offered by Arthur Fine, Larry Laudan, and Bas van Fraassen—are at best inconclusive and typically depend upon dubious assumptions about what is required to satisfactorily establish the conclusions of inductive arguments. On the positive side, I will argue that philosophers are entitled to the same explanatory strategies as those employed in science, and abduction is applied with routine effectiveness in science. Therefore, realists are entitled to the use of abduction in their defense of realism. The standard philosophical criticisms of abduction typically contend that it fails to meet certain rational principles of argumentation. I will contend that, in light of the fact that these critics hold abduction to be infirm, they have too little to say about the pervasive and successful role of abduction in scientific theorizing.

Debates about the status of inference to the best explanation inevitably engage disputes about the nature of explanation and its centrality in scientific theorizing. Empiricist explanations are weaker, more modest than realist explanations. Realist explanations implicate unobservables that ground observed correlations; empiricists rest content with observed correlations or with theoretical stories said to play a merely pragmatic role. I will call this empiricist tendency to withdraw from (theoretical) commitment at the crucial moment "explanatory timidity." Abductive arguments for scientific realism make a distinctive plea for (what I will call) confirmational independence. At present, let's briefly consider them in turn. The independence requirement is a consequence of the routine methodological injunction against ad hoc explanation, that it figure in the explanation of other phenomena. We saw a modest application of abduction earlier in this chapter, where property T was advanced as the best explanation for an observed distribution of performance.

Abduction, Realism, and General Form

The most robust abductive argument for scientific realism states that (given the theory dependence of scientific method) a realist interpretation of our most mature scientific theories provides the best explanation for the success of science. But before we describe the type of abductive argument pertinent to defenses of scientific realism and deployed in scientific practice, it is important to recognize that appeal to unobservables is not an essential feature of abduction. In fact, no matter what one's level of confidence in the theoretical inferences of mature sciences, some widely respected inferences to the best explanation represent reasoning from observables to observables. One such argument is familiar from our philosophical tradition: We infer that middle-sized objects exist, because their existence provides the best explanation for the patterns in our sense experience. The objects are observable, the patterns of sense experience are observable (in the sense that they are introspectible), and so inference to the best explanation (hereafter, IBE) is neither necessarily the arcane province of scientists nor necessarily a special philosophical pattern of reasoning uniquely adapted for the establishment of theoretical entities.

This fact about abduction is no insignificant detail. If there are reliable abductive patterns that move from observables to (sometimes unobserved) observables, then it is not the form of abduction that is suspect. Put in other words, if IBE performs well for observed populations and there is no objection heard in those cases, then the injunction against it reflects, as realists have always suspected, skepticism about the possibility of knowledge concerning unobservables. A second feature of IBE's instrumental reliability concerning observables indicates that, contrary to critical commentary, IBE is not especially speculative or problematic. It is perhaps this latter property of IBE to which realists are adverting when they have replied to critics that IBE is not prima facie suspect in the way that astrology is. For, the unreliability of astrological projection is demonstrable on observed populations. As we will see, this reply is neither question-begging nor an admission of religious devotion to realism. The justification for this realist reply, like all other conclusions of inductive arguments, depends on the independent establishment of each of the premises recruited in a full expression of the realist argument. Of course, an argument of the following form is at best question begging: The abductive argument for realism is reliable because abduction is reliable (or at least not prima facie unreliable). But this is not the realist response; the realist would treat the above argument as extremely enthymematic. Once the argument is properly spelled out, the realist then makes use of a variety of resources, each of which has in its favor an independent argument.

In barest outline, the form of abductive argument in dispute is:

1. There is some class of observed phenomena O, that have an effect E.

2. There is an unobserved factor (either unobservable or unobserved observable) U that, if present, would provide the best explanation of E.

3. Therefore, probably U.

Two importantly related points must be made about IBE. First, even in this schematic form, it is clear that the above argument form is inductive, and that should give pause to those critics locating the fatal flaw of abduction as a formal deductive defect, such as circularity or question-beggingness. Second, some instances of this argument form are demonstrably bad. These two points are related because it is the theory-dependent and inductive, ampliative character of abduction that makes poor instances possible. If our background theories are poor enough, for example, it is possible that the best explanation will be pretty bad. We find this out only after the fact, but such is the nature of empirical inquiry.

As the above remarks suggest, much depends on what is meant by "the best" in premise 2. Should it mean (1) the best explanation theoretically available at the time or (2) the best possible explanation that would be provided by the relevant completed science? The second option clearly won't do, since theory choice does not await the completion of science and confirmation does not have access to such a theory. The plausible option seems to be the first. However, we have not considered anything but a schematic version of IBE, so it remains to examine what version of IBE one should defend. Peter Lipton presents one straightforward description of IBE: "According to Inference to the Best Explanation, our inferential practices are governed by explanatory considerations. Given our data and our background beliefs, we infer what would, if true, provide the best of the competing explanations we can generate of those data (so long as the best is good enough for us to make any inference at all)" (1991, p. 58). One might suppose, as Peter Achinstein does, that the closing parenthetical phrase is designed to indicate that "a bad hypothesis, even if it is the only one available, or the best of the lot, is not inferable" (1992, p. 356). This restatement is not equivalent to Lipton's original, however. It is not a consequence of Lipton's remark that a bad hypothesis (presumably by some specific measure or set of measures) is not inferable but rather that, if we are to make any inference at all, the hypothesis must be good enough. There is no reason to suppose that a bad hypothesis couldn't be good enough to make some inference or other, no matter how qualified and modest. Conceptions of IBE such as Lipton's can permit that a bad hypothesis is inferable, so long as the bad hypothesis that is nevertheless the best of the lot is good enough to make any inference at all.

This issue is not just a textual quibble, for any plausible account of IBE must permit that a hypothesis that is poor by measures such as precision can yet be good enough to warrant an inference of some generality. We may now find our theories acceptable, but we would not accept archaic theories as adequate. Nevertheless, we got here from there, and this fact is difficult to account for if a bad but serviceable hypothesis is not inferable. In the early history of science, bad is all we had.

Second, the strategy of IBE has narrower and broader interpretations. Achinstein understands the best explanation as establishing high probability for a hypothesis (1991, chaps. 4, 9). But it is not clear what sort of epistemology would license such a requirement. In addition, this strong demand on IBE departs from the historical applications of IBE. Departure from the historical record may not trouble some philosophers, but it should at least concern those attempting to use the history of science as a source of evidence for philosophical positions. At any rate, in the history of science, some bad hypotheses still warranted inference. In such a case, the best explanation would not require establishing high probability but would require higher probability than its plausible rivals.

Achinstein's "high-probability" interpretation appears to be domain sensitive; it will permit abduction in some fields, presumably well-developed ones, and not in those that are primitive and unreliable. However, the other objections surveyed concern the very form of abduction. Laudan ([1981] 1991) and Fine (1986a) charge question-beggingness, while van Fraassen (1989) offers an intricate argument that abduction fails to meet certain ideal standards descending from his epistemology. At the moment, van Fraassen's conception of IBE is most pertinent.

Recognizing that IBE is inductive, van Fraassen subsumes it under an aggressively normative conception of inductive inference that, he claims, pretends to satisfy certain conditions of the "ideal of induction":

(a) that it is a *rule*,
(b) that it is *rationally compelling*,
(c) that it is *objective* in the sense of being independent of the historical and psychological context in which the data appear, and finally,
(d) that it is *ampliative*. (1989, p. 132)

Van Fraassen claims that "Inference to the Best Explanation is not what it pretends to be, if it pretends to fulfill the ideal of induction" (p. 142). But since IBE strikes no such pose in the literature, van Fraassen is criticizing a straw target. In addition, van Fraassen's analysis of IBE turns heavily on his (controversial) distinction between acceptance of a theory as empirically adequate and belief in its truth. According to van Fraassen, IBE entails belief in the best explanation, not just acceptance of it. And since for van Fraassen no theory or theoretical statement merits a doxastic attitude any stronger than acceptance, IBE is an unjustifiable pattern of reasoning. Although I will reserve discussion of most of the more general features of van Fraassen's constructive empiricism until later in this chapter, at the moment we should note that, even if we can distinguish between acceptance and belief—in the way that we can distinguish between night and day—actual doxastic attitude comes in degrees. When deciding which hypothesis to infer, or which theoretical horse to back, scientists make subtle, discriminating judgments based upon considerations ranging from availability of resources to the trustworthiness of an auxiliary expert or theory. Frequently the evidence is ambiguous. Those inferring target hypotheses are therefore often less than fully confident. It is not clear that in such cases the scientists hold that the (inferred) hypothesis providing the best explanation is true, approximately true, more likely than not, or unlikely but the best of a bad lot.

Despite the fact that we do not know precisely the considerations that are supposed to support (a)–(d), we can agree with van Fraassen that "Inference to the Best Explanation is not what it pretends to be, if it pretends to fulfill the ideal of induction." But if that is a telling point, it is a point conceded at little cost to the realist. From our own analysis of IBE, and the applications to follow, it is clear that actual applications of IBE bear no resemblance to the ideal van Fraassen devises, and there is no defense of IBE that I am aware of that even purports to satisfy all conditions (a)–(d). This fact might be disturbing to one bent on satisfying certain pretheoretic philosophical goals concerning reasoning, but no one serious about either the actual judgments of scientists, or about the success of IBE at the observable level, would be bothered by IBE's failure to meet such (inappropriately) high standards.

In van Fraassen's hands, what began as a question about whether there are reliable applications of IBE has been recast as one about whether it meets certain formalized, ideal epistemological standards. But these two issues are separable and should be separated. In the first place, even if we grant that it would be ideal to be in an epistemic situation satisfying van Fraassen's ideal of induction, actual conditions falling far short of those van Fraassen describes nevertheless support induction. In the second place, one need not agree that van Fraassen's four desiderata offer an appropriate analysis of an ideal epistemic situation. In particular, one needs a special defense of (c), a conception of objectivity in terms of independence of the historical and psychological context in which the data appear. Van Fraassen includes (c), I presume, out of respect for the traditional idea that the warrant for a belief should not depend on its genesis; how a belief was produced does not affect its probability. However, if what we mean by a belief's genesis is how that belief was produced, then van Fraassen's conditions at the very least rule out, a priori, extant versions of reliabilism. According to reliabilism, the justification for a belief just is given by the mechanism or method that produced it. The history of science is notoriously uneven. In scientific applications of IBE in the history of science, it is not clear why such rules must always be rationally compelling and independent of the historical and psychological context.

The argument against abductive versions of realism cannot be made by raising inappropriately abstract worries that applications of IBE deviate from a formal ideal. Why should we suppose that scientists themselves deploy IBE? At the risk of annoying an opponent, one might claim that attributing this pattern of argument to scientists proves so successful in providing a rationale for their behavior that such attributions must be approximately accurate. I will argue that the only way an inductive inference can be truly enumerative is to depend on no further background principles. And since every inductive inference fails this condition—surely all instances of scientific inductive inference do—then all relevant scientific inductive inferences are abductive. But there is an important qualification that signifies an obvious fact about inductive inferences, and this qualification has received little attention in disputes about abduction: Although abductive arguments have a common form, they depend in very different degrees upon more or less controversial background principles. It may be that all of the hypotheses in the field of testing are all unlikely to be true, as must have been the case with alchemical theories of the 1400s in Europe. And so, not all "best explanations" are very good. Against this weak, "availability" interpretation of IBE, van Fraassen claims that "[w]e can watch no contest of the theories we have so painfully struggled to formulate, with those no one has proposed. So our selection may well be the best of a bad lot" (1989, p. 143).

Here is the problem, according to van Fraassen: If a hypothesis is the best available of those historically given, then in light of underdetermination, it cannot provide a sufficient basis for belief. And if a hypothesis must be truly best in order to merit belief, then in light of the epistemic contingency of induction, no hypothesis in the history of science has merited belief, in which case the friend of IBE can have no evidence. But again, what should one require of belief rather than acceptance? Perhaps van Fraassen supposes that the answer to this question requires no systematic empirical investigation; it can be adjudicated by anecdote or conceptual analysis. In any case, the grounds for this distinction between belief and acceptance is not clear. Is van Fraassen's connection between belief and the judgment of being more likely true than not an empirical claim? Or does it follow from the very concept of belief?[11] Put another way, what is this psychological property that relates cognizer and evidence in such a way that we can distinguish between the psychological state of belief and the psychological state of acceptance? However unclear its basis, van Fraassen answers this question with ease: "To believe is at least to consider more likely to be true than not. So to believe the best explanation requires more than an evaluation of a given hypothesis. It requires a step beyond the comparative judgment that this hypothesis is better than its actual rivals" (1989, p. 143).

In the end, van Fraassen's stated aim is surprisingly modest: "My diagnosis is part and parcel of an approach to epistemology . . . in which rules like IBE have no status (*qua* rules) at all" (1989, p. 147). The realist's use of IBE does not depend on its being a rule in van Fraassen's sense. Rather, IBE is an informal pattern of reasoning, and its success depends at least as much on the reliability of the background theories with which it is conjoined as it does on this pattern's approximation to a formal ideal. In fact, I propose to understand IBE or abduction as one of the standard inductive canons of scientific methodology. In what follows, I will illustrate the inductive character of IBE. But to the extent that a naturalistic philosophy of science must (at least initially) take seriously any method that is pervasive and effective in science, the question of whether IBE satisfies certain philosophical prescriptions is beside the point. In fact, if failure to meet these standards entails that the method is suspect, that is reason to suppose that either the method is not being properly understood or the analysis is insufficiently naturalistic. Let us be clear. Naturalistic philosophy of science can be normative, and the regulative principles are themselves empirical.

Once IBE is seen to be scientifically routine and legitimate, then it is reasonable to ask when an inductive argument of this form is strong. This is a more discriminating and interesting question, and it can be answered in terms of the independent establishment of hypotheses used in the premises of the abductive argument. Of course, not just specific events in science need explanation; certain features of scientific theories themselves need explanation as well. One such feature is the instrumental success of our best scientific theories, or the instrumental reliability of scientific methodology.[12] The instrumental success of science is itself observable, and one would have thought that it is impressive enough that it mer-

---

11. The weight that van Fraassen's constructive empiricism places on undefended and controversial claims about the psychological states of belief and acceptance has been freshly criticized in Devitt (1991, chap. 8).

12. Another, according to Newton-Smith, is "smoothness":

The smoother the theory the more its failures can be covered by a single auxiliary hypothesis. If a theory is smooth in this sense it means that there is something that is systematic about its failures. There is hope of discovering what it is that is wrong about the theory with a view to correcting it. In this case it looks as though the theory, while having some erroneous aspect, is in fact onto something. If it is not smooth and requires a diverse range of unrelated auxiliary hypotheses to explain the failures, this suggests that the theory is not headed in the right direction. (1981, p. 228)

its attempts at explanation if any phenomenon does. Therefore, when the observed phenomenon O in question is the instrumental reliability of some methodology, then the abductive argument yields the sort of argument for scientific realism about theories that Fine, Laudan, and van Fraassen have attacked.

There is a package of relatively independent epistemological and semantic commitments associated with scientific realism; critics of scientific realism have tended to underestimate the resources of this package. As a way of breaking out of this circle, scientific realists have recommended that the merits of each competing view be assessed in terms of its adequacy as an overall package.[13] By employing relatively modest standards of instrumental success and comprehensiveness, philosophers of science can compare the relative epistemic merits of their respective accounts of the evidence. The evidence would devolve not just from the fit that realism or instrumentalism finds with an epistemology and semantics—whose (relatively) independent plausibility would themselves be assessed—but also from facts of scientific practice and the course of the history of science. It is for this reason that the attack has so often been mounted only against slogans. Putnam's version was an early target:

> The positive argument for realism is that it is the only philosophy that doesn't make the success of science a miracle. That terms in mature scientific theories typically refer (this formulation is due to Richard Boyd), that the theories accepted in a mature science are typically approximately true, that the same term can refer to the same thing even when it occurs in different theories—these statements are viewed by the scientific realist not as necessary truths but as part of the only scientific explanation of the success of science, and hence as part of any adequate scientific description of science and its relations to its objects. (Putnam 1975, p. 73)

Smart's "cosmic coincidence" argument also received much attention:

> One would have to suppose that there were innumerable lucky accidents about the behavior mentioned in the observational vocabulary, so that they behaved miraculously *as if* they were brought about by the non-existent things ostensibly talked about in the theoretical vocabulary. (Smart 1968, p. 150)

Without an explicit defense of abduction and an explication of the epistemic principles required for its defense, these arguments convey little more than the flavor of the abductive argument for scientific realism and the desire for a theoretical explanation of science's instrumental success. But the implication of these passages is clear.

Of all the versions of scientific realism targeted by critics, the most comprehensive, carefully articulated, and often-cited account can be found in a series of articles by Richard Boyd (for the most thorough overviews, see his [1983] 1991a

---

13. Horwich (1991) does not address this defense of realism and cites approvingly Fine's argument (1986a) that the abductive argument for realism is question begging.

and 1990). In Boyd ([1983]1991a), we are invited to consider the doctrine of scientific realism "as embodying four central theses":

(i) 'Theoretical terms' in scientific theories (i.e., nonobservational terms) should be thought of as putatively referring expressions; scientific theories should be interpreted "realistically."

(ii) Scientific theories, interpreted realistically, are confirmable and in fact often confirmed as approximately true by ordinary evidence interpreted in accordance with ordinary methodological standards.

(iii) The historical progress of mature sciences is largely a matter of successively more accurate approximations to the truth about both observable and unobservable phenomena. Later theories typically build upon the (observational and theoretical) knowledge embodied in previous theories.

(iv) The reality which scientific theories describe is largely independent of our thoughts or theoretical commitments. (p. 195)

Each thesis has a role to play in what is thought to be the best explanation for the instrumental reliability of scientific methodology. Of course, a view can be described without offering reasons in its defense. What reason have we to believe that theses (i)–(iv) are true? Boyd offers an elaborate defense of each thesis, defenses too detailed to reconstruct here. But taken together, the truths of these theses constitute the best explanation of the reliability of scientific methodology.

This robust version of scientific realism is understood to apply specifically to the mature sciences, certainly physics and chemistry, and to selected areas of biology. The successes here have been pretty uncontroversial—the theory of magnetism, the theory of gases, genetics, and so forth—and is conceded even among those who doubt that realism is required to explain this success. Of course, there have been failures, but most are the result, at least in part, of the admirable penchant for epistemic risk. In the next chapter, I will defend a relatively modest version of scientific realism—Measured Realism—designed to apply to the relatively immature social and behavioral sciences. The argument for measured realism is abductive, and so I will first argue that we needn't be gravely concerned over the arguments by Laudan, Fine, and van Fraassen that oppose the abductive defense of realism and resist the methodological principle of IBE. Abduction operates not just in philosophy of science but in science itself. So accusing abduction of a formal defect of philosophical argumentation such as circularity or question-beggingness implies that abduction violates an otherwise reliable scientific practice. By raising considerations of independence, philosophers are able to appraise the entire packages of empiricist views and realist views in the same way that scientists are able to assess a complex position.

Few philosophers of science—whether empiricist, constructivist, or realist—hold that such facts of predictive success require literally no explanation. Background theory, controlled experiments, and engineering applications produce nuclear reactors, magnetic resonance imaging, and intracellular recording devices, but the reliability of these impressive testaments to modern science, and of the methods that yielded them, requires no explanation. If this were so, then their predictive reliability would be an irreducible fact.

At the same time, if we bow to the demand for an explanation of the reliability of methodology, what kind of explanation would do, short of one that involves theoretical commitment? One might, for example, claim that the reliability of scientific methodology has an instrumental explanation, an explanation citing only observable causes. But such explanations are themselves unduly mysterious, even if they constitute an improvement over stubborn insistence that there is nothing about the apparent reliability of scientific methodology that merits explaining. We may now examine the way in which timid empiricist stances toward explanation are recruited to block realist applications of IBE.

No-Miracles Arguments for Scientific Realism

Philosophy need do no special pleading for abduction, for it is firmly grounded in the methods of science. In Perrin's work on Avogadro's number, we find an abductive argument for realism about molecules, an argument based upon the widely acknowledged principle of diverse testing:

> Our wonder is aroused at the very remarkable agreement found between the values derived from the consideration of such widely different phenomena. Seeing not only that the same magnitude is obtained by each method when the conditions under which it is applied are varied as much as possible, but that the numbers thus established also agree among themselves, without discrepancy, for all the methods employed, the real existence of the molecule is given a probability bordering on certainty. (Perrin 1923, pp. 215–216)

If one has objections to abductive arguments for realism, then it must not be due to grave doubts concerning the use of abduction in science.

In the philosophy of science, we find an unabashedly abductive argument for the existence of the relevant theoretical entities postulated by physicists. Giere's expression of this view is quite representative: "The only remotely plausible scientific account of what these physicists are doing requires us, as students of the scientific enterprise, to invoke entities with roughly the properties physicists themselves ascribe to protons and neutrons" (1988, p. 112). This account could even be understood as required by a scientific psychological or sociological explanation of scientists' behavior, a strikingly naturalistic consequence. Salmon extracts the following moral:

> It seems clear that Perrin would not have been satisfied with the determination of Avogadro's number by any single method, no matter how carefully applied and no matter how precise the results. It is the "remarkable agreement" among the results of many diverse methods that supports his conclusion about the reality of molecules.
>
> If there were no such micro-entities as atoms, molecules and ions, then these different experiments designed to ascertain Avogadro's number would be genuinely independent experiments, and the striking numerical agreement in their results would constitute an utterly astonishing coincidence. To those who were in doubt about the existence of such micro-entities, the "remarkable agreement" argument constitutes strong *evidence* that these experiments are not fully independent—that

they reveal the existence of such entities. To those of us who believe in the existence of these sorts of micro-entities, their very existence and characteristics—as
specified by various theories—*explain* this "remarkable agreement." (W. Salmon
1984, pp. 219–220)

Commenting approvingly on an earlier version of Wesley Salmon's argument,
McMullin says of Avogadro's number that

> One can by means of the same postulate account for a multitude of other phenom-
> ena of quite disparate sorts, such as electrolysis and alpha decay. The postulated
> microentities come out in each case to exactly the same number per mole. The
> number is so large and so precisely known that it seems altogether unlikely that
> different sorts of entities could be involved; a single kind of entity, the molecule,
> exerting several different kinds of causal agency, seems to be the only reasonable
> explanation. The instrumentalist ploy fails here because it can assign no plausible
> reason why the theoretical construct invoked to explain Brownian motion should
> turn out to be conceptually identical with the entity that explains electrolysis.
> (McMullin 1984, p. 213)

My point is not, of course, that this abductive strategy must be defensible on the
mere grounds that lots of philosophers use it. This abductive argument for scientific realism is persistent and durable, and it is grounded in a variety of scientific
practices and philosophical standards.[14] It might be this stable grounding in diverse applications that explains its persistence and durability, and chapter 7 will

---

14. J. J. C. Smart is primarily responsible for the early popularity of the "no-miracles" version of
realism. Here he restates the initial formulation:

> The realist's most general argument against instrumentalism is that he can explain the success
> of microphysics in predicting facts on the macro-level. The instrumentalist just has to accept
> this success as brute fact. Why should things happen on the macro-level just *as if* there were
> electrons, neutrinos, and so on, if there really is no micro-level and if discourse that appears
> to be about unobservable micro-entities is not to be taken at face value? The scientific realist
> holds that his opponent is left with something like a cosmic miracle. That theories work, or
> that certain generalizations on the observational level hold true, is something for which his
> instrumentalist opponent can give no explanation. (1982, p. 364)

A somewhat more obscure version of an abductive argument for scientific realism, giving special focus
to experimentation, can be found in the work of Roy Bhaskar (1975, 1982):

> A *real* distinction between the objects of experimental investigation, such as causal laws, and
> patterns of events is thus a condition of the intelligibility of experimental activity. Now as
> constant conjunctions must in general be artificially produced, if we identify causal laws with
> them, we are logically committed to the absurdities that scientists, in their experimental activ-
> ity, cause and even change the laws of nature! Thus the objects of scientific inquiry in an
> experiment cannot be events and their conjunctions, but are (I suggest) structures, generative
> mechanisms and the like (forming the real basis of causal laws), which are normally out of
> phase with them. And it can now be seen that the Humean account depends upon a misidenti-
> fication of causal laws with their empirical grounds. (1982, p. 343)

The weak, austere version of realism discussed earlier in this chapter shares a similar motivation and
conclusion, arguing for the existence of unobserved structures without much specification of their
nature.

show how this persistence and durability is unlikely to be a mere artifact of the sociology of science. The more important point, for my purposes, is that this abductive strategy is even more indispensable to scientific arguments to the (approximate) truth of theoretical hypotheses than it is to philosophical arguments concerning empiricism and realism.

The sorts of inferences to unobservables licensed by abduction are central to scientific methods. It is therefore important to clarify the dialectical status of the no-miracles argument, for in doing so we also trace the burden of proof. If someone objects to a no-miracles argument that purports to establish the existence of some theoretical entity, process, or state, it will no longer be an adequate rejoinder to simply point to some theory in the history of science that was false but instrumentally reliable. For now there is a requirement that the empiricist must satisfy as well: The empiricist must either account for a host of successful scientific activities regarding the target phenomenon, such as its predictive reliability and unifying power, its role in measurement and the calibration and improvement of instrumentation, and its ability to be used as a tool in the study of other phenomena, or else treat the phenomenon in question (or its occurrence) as an irreducible or unexplained fact about the world.

Abduction has been used at least as often by empiricists and other antirealists or irrealists—not, of course, for conclusions appealing to unobservable entities but in endorsing certain methodological conditions on theory testing. In realist hands, however, the no-miracles argument is used to license a further inference, an inference to the best explanation.

Confirmation Theory and Intolerance of Miracles

As we have seen, the standardly criticized version of the abductive "miracle" argument for realism states that, given the theory dependence of scientific methodology, realism must be at least approximately true because realism's approximate truth provides the best explanation for the predictive reliability of scientific methodology. Confirmation theory is an area of orthodox philosophy of science that is perhaps distinctive for its trenchant neutrality on metaphysical issues. But even here, many of the qualitative and quantitative accounts of confirmation depend on abductive, no-miracle argument forms.

The most important concept in confirmation theory in determining goodness of test concerns the independence of hypotheses. However, considerations of independence are typically buried beneath the details of miracle arguments, for independence is so common a methodological demand of theory testing that it is often a forgotten feature. In his discussion of Perrin's experimental derivation of Avogadro's number, Peter Kosso says:

Perrin measured the same physical quantity in a variety of different ways, thereby invoking a variety of different auxiliary theories. And the reason that Perrin's results are so believable, and that they provide good reason to believe in the actual existence of molecules, is that he used a variety of independent theories and techniques and got them to agree on the answer. The chances of these independent theories all

independently manufacturing the same fictitious result is small enough to be rationally discounted. (1989, p. 247)

The idea is that the fictitious confluence of results under apparently independent
tests is rationally negligible, leading to the belief that surprising results confer
special confirmation on a theory so long as those results can be explained on the
theory in an intellectually satisfying way.[15]
    Does the kind of nonindependence expressed in abductive arguments make it
impossible to rationally justify scientific realist conclusions? Substantial principles
in modern atomic physics have allowed us to construct clocks of increasing accuracy (when compared to an old standard), and the new atomic clocks are then
used to measure the duration of physical reactions. Is there a vicious circularity
lurking here, using physics to test physics? It wouldn't seem so, as long as the
reliability of the hypotheses used in the construction of the atomic clock can be
tested and established independently of the specific hypotheses employed regarding the temporal measurement of physical reactions. To suppose that the auxiliary
and target hypotheses are insidiously nonindependent because they fall under the
rubric "physics" is to draw a deep philosophical conclusion from a superficial or-
thographic similarity. After all, disciplines are often historically individuated, and
the phenomena covered by the term "physics" certainly differ in enough respects
that diverse names are warranted, and indeed we find them: plasma physics, quantum electrodynamics, solid state physics, and so on. These areas are distinguished
by the nature of the specific subject matter but, more important, by causal taxonomy.

Conclusion: The Role of Independence in No-Miracles Arguments

All induction that is of any use to science is abductive; one must hold this view
or else have no way of accounting for the constraints on inductive inferences.[16]
Where an inductive argument is not simply enumerative (on the assumption that
it ever is), it begs some question or other, for it invokes premises that are nonindependent. But such arguments are not, therefore, viciously circular. Because the
probability of one premise affects the probability of another, they are nonindepen-

---

15. This is a general problem with any position that treats observationally accessible patterns as
epistemically fundamental. We find this very difficulty in Fine (1991b). Though critical of abduction,
Fine evidently suspends this concern long enough to offer a reasonable treatment of dispositions,
arguing that the instrumental reliability of scientific theories should be interpreted dispositionally and
that dispositions ground the empirical correlations between applications of scientific methodology and
successes. But it is difficult to defend the move from empirical correlation to unobserved disposition
without recourse to abduction. Perhaps Fine's intention is to merely restrict the range of legitimate
applications of abduction, but Fine's criticisms of realist applications of abduction appear less qualified
than this.
16. There is nothing new in this basic idea, no matter how infrequently it is openly defended.
This is the core view in Harman (1965).

dent, but they can be as independently testable as hypotheses ever are in science. So it is not clear why the realist philosopher of science isn't permitted the same argument form as the scientist is.

Richard Boyd responds to the circularity objection by appealing to the powerful considerations of independent evidence: "I suggest that our assessment of the import of the circularity in question should focus not on the legitimacy of the realist's abductive inference in isolation, but rather on the relative merits of the overall accounts of scientific knowledge which the empiricist and realist defend" ([1983] 1991a, p. 217). In science as in philosophy, independence is best represented in cases where two disciplines make contact via methods unique to each discipline. We can find just such points of contact between biochemistry and membrane biology, electrodynamics and neuroscience, motivational psychology and attitude research in social psychology, voting studies in political science and ideology-shaping institutional forces in sociology. Who would have thought that two disciplines, with different histories and with scientists of disparate training, would have merged in ways that agree on the existence of certain theoretical entities or on the approximate truth of particular laws? In fact, the evidence for independence is most dramatic in cases where the disciplines are too remote from one another to be regarded as neighboring sciences at all—and so even less likely to suffer argumentative reliance on the commitments of that remote discipline. But if one is attempting to establish not just that scientific judgments are objective because suitably independent but also that there has been cumulative and sustained theoretical progress, then cases of remote reliance can be less persuasive illustrations of the accumulation of knowledge (this time, by unification); for, the success of their joint application is so striking it may appear somewhat serendipitous. And although the realist may hold that major advances in the history of science are radically contingent, few realists would sustain an account of theoretical success that made progress in general any less than the result of scrupulous and earnest application of routine methods. The usual contact made between neighboring theories leaves less mystery surrounding the possible mechanisms of intertheoretic contact, more details about causal interaction that convey the appropriate sense of the accumulation of theoretical knowledge.

With attacks on abduction now stayed, we can examine the reliability of abduction on a case-by-case basis. But it remains to explain why independent tests are valuable. Because confirmation theory dominated the philosophy of science and purported to be unconcerned with metaphysical issues, the concept of independence as a requirement on testing has been assimilated to a largely epistemic and semantic role. This is not especially surprising, given that logical empiricism disallowed metaphysical considerations in theory choice. But there is a causal notion of independence, and it is this feature of the world that explains the peculiar epistemic features of the conditions of good tests proposed in confirmation theory. In particular, it explains the good effects of enforcing this requirement. In the two chapters that follow, I will discuss independence as a metaphysical notion, and it is this feature that is distinctive about arguments for realism. As an epistemological property of test settings, the requisite independence is an expression of metaphysical independence, in particular of causal independence.

Because robust realism presupposes the approximate truth of background theories, its units of evaluation are not epistemically bite-sized. We have seen how the concept of relative independence ratifies a particular application of abduction as good, and this ratification shows how a global argument for scientific realism can have nonindependent premises and still be epistemically reliable. A metaphysical account of independence is required to ground the epistemic/methodological independence we find in good science, the ability to test a hypothesis by diverse means. Without such a notion, the why-question concerning both the fact and the success of diverse testing goes unanswered. Without a suitable notion of metaphysical independence, these epistemological/methodological features of scientific practice appear as irreducible properties of the world: Diverse testing, for example, just is reliable. But the focus on metaphysical independence has a more important consequence for the range of realisms one can plausibly argue for. The fact of metaphysical independence makes possible a defense of a more modest, measured version of realism. According to this view, a hypothesis can be determined to be well supported even if the background theory is not approximately true. A taxonomic generalization or law can be confirmed as approximately true even if the theory in question leaves much to be desired. Laws, as well as the objects they mention, are metaphysically independent and so (epistemically) independently accessible and testable—in short, epistemically bite-sized. This version of realism will provide a partial explanation for the plausibility of the robust realist interpretation of the mature sciences whenever it is plausible but, more important for the theme of this book, this measured brand of realism will explain the modest success and theoretical progress of the immature social and behavioral sciences. We will now turn to this measured realism.

Measured Realism

Then she tried Baby Bear's porridge. It was just right.
Goldilocks and The Three Bears

This chapter introduces Measured Realism, a doctrine designed to navigate between minimal and robust realism. Measured Realism embraces theoretical structure and our knowledge of it, but avoids the sweeping demand that theoretical knowledge rests upon the approximate truth of current psychological and social theories, or full reference of central theoretical terms. In the second section, I set out the doctrine of measured realism. The next two sections identify and characterize the independence of laws and set straight the misleading and highly idealized talk about confirmation. The balance of the chapter advances an illustration of the sort of independence made available by testing epistemically bite-sized hypotheses. I focus on the cooperative efforts between paleontologists and physicists and on those between psycholinguists and signal-processing engineers. The epistemic relation of mercenary reliance provides a clear and novel illustration of adipose theory and bite-sized theoretical commitments, two features characteristic of cases that merit a measured realist analysis.

Finding the "Right" Test of Measured Realism

It is quite easy to formulate a hypothesis in such a way that it will be unsupported by the evidence: Simply make the hypothesis so strong, so specific that, given the (in)sensitivity of the current instruments and methods, it is unlikely that the result will fall within the predicted, narrow interval. By the same token, one way to guarantee that a philosophical position such as realism will turn out to be unsupported by the historical and methodological evidence is by formulating it in such strong terms that it is true on no body of evidence.

We must arrive at a formulation of scientific realism that is appropriate to the subject matter and relevant to the evidence. This is not a plea for a cheap maneuver, crafting realism so that it is confirmed. Rather, it is a simple matter of properly formulating a hypothesis. Here, it is instructive to notice what scientists do when, in retrospect, a hypothesis is judged to be unduly specific or otherwise inappropriately stringent. Scientists do not conclude that the guiding conception of causal factors is entirely mistaken. Instead, they reformulate the hypothesis in such a way that the specificity of the hypothesis matches the sensitivity of the test.

This issue of appropriate formulation is especially important to a defense of scientific realism about the social and behavioral sciences, because the version of robust scientific realism discussed in the preceding chapter is sure to yield an unsatisfactory interpretation of the social and behavioral sciences. We cannot simply substitute "social and behavioral sciences" for "mature sciences" as it occurs in Boyd's expression of scientific realism. It is not the case that our current social and psychological theories are at least approximately true, nor is it unguardedly the case that the central theoretical terms of social and psychological theories typically (fully) refer.

As disheartening as this may be, the realist has no reason to despair, at least the realist who is a naturalist. A naturalistic approach predicts that the appropriate formulation of scientific realism will be different for different domains. After all, disciplines differ in the level of organization of their appropriate objects, and the contingencies of culture and history mete out the resources and motivations for the execution of research differently.

In the section that follows, I will present a version of scientific realism most appropriate to the evidence in the social and behavioral sciences and naturalized in the way that the methodologies there dictate. The next section proposes that what makes progress both possible and demonstrable in the social and behavioral sciences is the relative independence of the various methodologies from any particular theory. The notion of adipose theory permits us to see how methods are applied in ways that are theory dependent and yet not so fully dependent upon the detailed reaches of a specific theory that a hypothesis can only be confirmed through the use of that particular theory; some aspects of the theory are confirmationally superfluous or adipose, indicating that the proprietary properties of objects picked out by one theory are relatively causally isolated from other properties of objects in the domain. Because these properties and relations are theoretically local, they are also epistemically accessible by those holding different theories; they are epistemically bite-sized. That is why commitments to them are best expressed not as commitment to entities, or to the approximate truth of theories, but to the existence of laws that are at least mildly counterfactual supporting. The epistemically bite-sized character of confirmation relations allows us to show how objections to realism often turn on interpretations of confirmation that are, from the perspective of scientific practice, unnatural and so, not surprisingly, not in evidence; instead, they are most common in idealized philosophical talk about theories. The roles of adipose theory and epistemically bite-sized features—prime warrant for Measured Realism—are expressed variously in any serious review of scientific research, though not under those descriptions. Below, we will find them in the autonomy of experiment, confirmation of current theory by archaic evidence, and mercenary reliance on one scientist's expertise by another in a remote domain. All of these are, in effect, kinds of diverse testing, and the virtues of diverse testing are essential ingredients in the realist theory of measurement presented in chapter 2.

The Shape of Measured Realism

The contingencies of the history and subject matter of social and behavioral theories have made them too weak and undeveloped to aid reliably in the improvement of affiliated theories; progress has indeed been uneven. Imagine someone—following the realist argument about core areas in physics—trying to defend the claim that only the approximate truth of some sociological account could explain reliable applications of some particular quantitative method. Rather, many other plausible explanations exist for this apparent reliability. Maybe the point-interval prediction is too weak. Maybe the hypothesis is too vague. Maybe the standard of significance is too lax. Therefore, although there is adequate evidence for a realist interpretation of the social and behavioral sciences, it is a more modest, measured realism than that warranted by the natural and physical sciences. The Measured Realism I defend includes four theses:

1. At least some of the quantitative methods and practices of science reliably detect and identify some of the central posited entities, processes, states, properties, and events in the social and behavioral sciences.
2. Sometimes behavioral and social scientific theories, more often the generalizations that constitute them, are confirmed by the application of accepted methodological standards in the field. This process of confirmation is most evident in such activities as the refinement of measurement procedures and in the successful introduction of controls.
3. In our best psychological and social theories, confirmation relations important to theoretical progress in those sciences are epistemically bite-sized, and, accordingly, some parts of the tested theory are typically confirmationally adipose or extraneous. The methodological independence (or "diverse testability") of theoretical objects, processes, events, states, and properties provides evidence that laws about those theoretical kinds are relatively detachable from theories and so confirmable relatively independent of the particular theories in which those laws were expressed.
4. The reality described by our best psychological and social theories is independent of us as observers of, or as thinkers about, that reality.

Measured Realism provides the best explanation for the modest theoretical success of the social and behavioral sciences, particularly the success enjoyed upon the introduction of quantitative methods. This argument is patently abductive, appealing as it does to explanatory considerations, but because we have seen in chapter 3 that there is no special worry about abduction as a form of argument, we can assess the argument for the plausibility of measured realism in the same way that we assess any inductive or nondemonstrative argument—in terms of its plausible handling of the evidence. As an expression of scientific realism, measured realism may appear feeble and hedged. Gone is the familiar commitment to the approximate truth of background theories and the unqualified appeal to the reference of theoretical terms. But in light of the fact that measured realism is designed to be appropriate to the social and behavioral sciences, this modesty is as it should be; the social and behavioral sciences are demonstrably less mature than the physical and biological sciences for which the more daring version of scientific realism was originally and suitably proposed. At the same time, measured realism is stronger than the austere and entity realisms described in chapter 3. According to measured realism, we have evidence for the approximate truth of at least some laws, whereas austere realism is committed only to the existence of dispositions explaining an observed distribution, and entity realism is committed only to the existence of theoretical entities but not to the approximate truth of laws and theories.

Measured Realism is a doctrine designed to explain the reliability of scientific (particularly quantitative) methodology in the behavioral and social sciences. No more and no less. When the subject matter of realist interpretation changes from the mature sciences of physics, chemistry, and (some areas of) biology to the social and behavioral sciences, Measured Realism provides a fitting analysis. Recall that, in the case of mature sciences, Boyd claims that we are led to an interpretation of the history of science as radically epistemically contingent, with the "jumping off" point around Newton's time (Boyd 1981). But no one who regards the history of science as evidential and whose epistemology is naturalistic should expect that our natural endowments and available evidence warrant the same account of realism no matter what the subject matter.

Let us now elaborate on the implications of each thesis. The first thesis does not imply that standard canons of measurement and detection, if applied with mindless devotion and persistence, will support a realistic interpretation of theories. Neither does the first thesis imply that any arbitrarily selected theory in psychology or the social sciences will have some theoretical terms that refer (either partially or fully), nor does it imply that, even for an individual theory advanced as the best in the field, all of its theoretical terms will refer (either partially or fully). The second thesis indicates that no special philosophical reinterpretation of scientific methodology need be effected before the relevant hypotheses are confirmed and no extraordinary scientific requirements need be adopted for confirmation. The methods already in place are fine. Thesis 4 expresses the traditional realist commitment to a mind-independent reality. But the thesis is tricky, because in the psychological and social sciences part of the reality described just is our thoughts (or intentional states generally). This fact appears to entail that thoughts—the reality studied—are therefore independent of themselves. But this would be a mistake. When psychology and the social sciences reveal some aspect of the intentional world, that reality is independent of particular minds or of us as minds. It is in this sense that the reality described by our best social and psychological theories is mind independent.

It is thesis 3 that distinguishes Measured Realism from other brands, so I will devote most of this chapter to a specific defense of that thesis. This defense is best initiated by addressing the following question: What facts about quantitative methods and the social/psychological subject matter made possible theoretical progress in the social and behavioral sciences? I will argue that the most important methodological feature is that of independence: Predictive and explanatory hypotheses are able to be tested without testing every other statement or posit of the theory, and those posits and generalizations can be used in the derivation of phenomena other than those for which they were initially introduced.

For the requirement of independence to be satisfied, both the subject matter and methodology must have a specific character. On the side of subject matter, human behavior and the behavior of institutions must be composed of distinguishable properties, processes, objects, states, and events if independent testability is to be a value. The best model of independence is statistical independence, according to which the probability of one event is not affected by the probability of any other event. Statistical independence is often illustrated by the Bernoulli trial. There, say, the marbles in an urn have a known color distribution—for example, 5:1 black to white. If a marble is blindly drawn from this thoroughly mixed urn, and each time the marble is replaced after being drawn, then each outcome is independent; the outcome of one drawing does not affect the probability of the outcome of the next (or any other) drawing.

Notice the character of these marbles, as proxies for the objects in natural and experimental settings. Their potential causal effects are isolable, if not local. Their differential gravitational influences on the other marbles are negligible. We found similar evidence for relative independence in the measurement case in which the observed value depended counterfactually on a detachable, unobserved value.

On the methodological side, scientific methodology must be sensitive enough to detect and exploit this ontological independence. The fact that the marbles have negligible differential gravitational and mechanical influence on the other marbles makes mixing an appropriate means of achieving randomization. Mixing would not be appropriate if the white marbles were covered with velcro and so tended to stick to other white marbles.

It might be objected to this description of independence that it is difficult to know when two objects are ever sufficiently independent to provide the basis for a good test. Granted, it is sometimes very difficult to determine when independence holds, and chapter 7 will show how theory-guided scientific methodology addresses this challenge. At the moment, one can set out the conditions for independence without laying out the conditions for verifying when those conditions obtain. If these two activities are married, we are left with a kind of verificationism whose problems are well known. To be obliging, however, it is worth noticing that scientific methodology is not at sea when it comes to establishing when such conditions obtain. Often, for example, we can test the reliability of a method on a finite population of known value. If the opponent objects that such cases do not allow us to justify inferential procedures that move from known to unknown parts of a population, the reply is twofold. First, that is a skeptical possibility that none of us can escape and so is not a special problem for the ontological account of independence offered here. Second, the directive of diverse testing is calculated precisely to guard against assumptions whose nonindependence goes undetected. If, for verificationist reasons, one supposes that relevantly diverse testing is unable to achieve this end, then we cannot underwrite the distinction between the measuring procedure and the thing (or quantity) measured. Finally, the consequences of this verificationist objection are sweeping; if it is to be applied consistently, then it also raises doubts about inductions concerning future observable (but as yet unobserved) states.

Inductive inferences typically depend upon premises that are to some degree dependent. One cannot reasonably mean by "independent" that changes in the probability of one premise do not affect the probability of another. For this version of the independence requirement would rule out as question-begging nearly every good inductive argument on offer in science. Consider, for example, early research on what we now recognize as the electron. In the last quarter of the nineteenth century, figures like Crookes, Stoney, and Thomson idealized away from the expected gravitational influences on the small masses. Experimenters of the time knew that these units had mass (even if Stoney had gotten the charge wrong) and so were subject to gravitational influences. But the gravitational influences on the individual units were thought to be negligible. Was this assumption arrived at independently of other assumptions specifying ideal conditions? Not at all. Experimenters reasoned that, if ideal gases allow us to discount as negligible the gravitational influences on individual molecules, we can do so in the case of these even smaller masses as well. So good science flourishes under the deployment of nonindependent assumptions, so long as the assumptions are (relatively) independent in the relevant sense.

The relevant sense of independence, however, is more difficult to determine in the operation of immature sciences—such as current cognitive sciences and late nineteenth-century electrodynamics—than in mature sciences such as contemporary electrodynamics. Since we now understand the theoretical picture in physics in much greater detail, we know which potential differences it is safe to abstract from and thus the relevant sense in which one part of the model (such as the unit charge) can be said to be independent of another (such as gravity).

In chapter 2, I introduced the idea that many of the laws expressing theoretical relations are epistemically bite-sized. The route to an epistemology of such local scale is through the notion of disengaged or adipose theory. For any two measurement procedures applied to the same quantity, there are bits of associated theory in virtue of which the tests or procedures are different. Although any single measurement procedure may engage every piece of associated theory from which it is drawn—and so there is no adipose theory for any single measurement procedure—the fact that two (or three or four) procedures can isolate the same quantity demonstrates that the measurement of that quantity does not depend on any particular theory. If so, then its value can be established independently of any particular theory. This independence from a particular theory supports measured realism, for it shows that we can hold measurement outcomes of a selected science to be cumulative without necessarily being approximately true,[1] and it requires that some of the theoretical knowledge acquired concerns bits of theory larger than the theoretical term (as the argument against Hacking showed in chapter 3).

These notions of approximate truth and partial reference have been tossed about with some abandon, but their role in a defense of realism should be made clear. One class of criticisms that has enjoyed some influence among various antirealists charges that the coherent interpretation of realist claims awaits a semantics for truth and approximate truth and an adequate account of reference to underwrite claims of partial reference. This class of criticisms, however, conveys two misleading impressions. First, it suggests that these notions have highly speculative and specialized functions peculiar to analyses of scientific theories. But these notions underlie ordinary discourse about any knowledge of a mind-independent world. They are required for statements about the size of a table or the distance of a building. Second, it suggests that coherent discourse about a topic is not possible without a prior semantic analysis of its basic hypotheses and terms. But such a demand would rule out ordinary talk about all unobservable phenomena, from electrons to mental states, none of which critics are prepared to consign to nonsense.

Independence and Idealized Philosophical Talk about Theories

At the same time, confirmation does not necessarily spread uniformly from a theory of, say, cellular development to theories of the farthest reaches of the universe. Confirmation relations are thought to follow causal connections, and so confirmation should be expected to be only as holistic as the tightness of causal connections will bear. It is the purpose of the principles of minimal detachment and minimal connection, set out later in this chapter, to characterize the general conditions that obtain when a hypothesis is confirmed. The upshot is that confirmation is holistic but not indiscriminately so; it normally involves more than one theory but not all of the theories to which the target theory might be connected. It is for this reason that theories do not have clear individuation conditions; it is difficult to say when one theory stops and another begins. As a result, it is also hard to make technical points about independence, when such points depend on prior agreement that a test does not presuppose the same crucial part of the theory that is being tested. Many well-intended discussions for and against realism omit considerations of independence and are thus notoriously prone to misleading slogans and oversimplification. Consider the motley of familiar constraints placed on theories implicated in successful abductions, often with little elaboration:

(1) T is approximately true.
(2) Most of the central theoretical terms of T (partially or fully) refer.
(3) Some of the central theoretical terms of T (partially or fully) refer.
(4) Confirmation bearing on one part of a theory bears on all parts of the theory.

---

1. This modest point about the cumulative nature of scientific knowledge is in the spirit of Kitcher (1993), who offers an account of cognitive progress in science designed to do similar service.

It has been said that, without a complete account of the truth of each thesis, any one thesis is without content, false, or otherwise unacceptable.

The fact is, many such suggestions fall silent about the conditions that would make these claims true. For example, in the case of (2) and (3), what makes a theoretical term central? And, if partial reference of some central theoretical terms is a necessary condition for reliability, how minimal can the partial reference be and still satisfy this necessary condition? The theories that scientists actually use are complex and heterogenous objects. Thesis (4) expresses an extreme form of confirmational holism, but what might have led critics to suppose it is true in extreme form?

These are important questions, but too often they are used to raise dust about the case for scientific realism, specifically about the claim that scientific methodology is instrumentally reliable. However, what is important is not that a complete account of approximate truth, partial reference, or confirmation be given but that enough of an account be provided so that we can offer a passable explication of what this instrumental reliability consists in. Scientific success (and the instrumental reliability of scientific methodology) does not depend on providing an account of this success, any more than our knowledge that there are other minds depends on having an account of that knowledge. Similarly, our legitimate treatment of a hypothesis as independent does not hinge on providing an account of independence.

This relative autonomy—analyzed in terms of independence—is the evidential basis of Measured Realism. We can confirm relatively isolable claims of measurement. Theory gets more crucially implicated when we improve measurement and detection procedures by revising them in light of theory, but even then some parts of the theory will bear on the measurement improvement more than others. Measurement claims can be independently confirmed because such claims are typically causal, and causes themselves tend to have experimentally isolable causes and effects. If the effects represent real causal factors, then they will persist independently of our experiments. When the causal claim is not readily tested by experiment, its effects are isolable when our background knowledge allows us to trace them.

In challenging Measured Realism, the critic might adopt an overly simplistic conception of confirmation. Since realists typically hold that scientific realism is an empirical hypothesis and, further, an epistemology that is broadly naturalistic, they heed the actual practices of scientists. And the actual practices of scientists reveal confirmation relations that differ in strength and relevance across the contours of a theory. If one does not attend to such practices, or selects an atypical example, it would be easy to produce a highly idealized, abstract, or otherwise misleading picture of confirmation.

A theory's independence from the evidence has always played an important role in realist accounts of the assessment of hypotheses, as the preceding two chapters showed. Many of the test conditions in confirmation theory surveyed are epistemological: The improbability condition, severity, novel prediction, and bootstrapping all use essentially epistemic notions such as surprise, or unexpectedness, or epistemic probability to describe good test conditions. But we must ask what the world must be like in order for an otherwise unexpected event to be discoverable or for various hypotheses to have different probabilities given the same theory. Minimally, (C) must be true. A theory attributes to (theoretical) objects certain causal powers of a kind and magnitude. To test predictions, we use these differences in causal powers to arrive at particular values that one might expect if the target theory is true or that one might expect if a competing theory is true. These causal powers, whether relational or nonrelational, are typically pretty stable under changes in factors external to them. Because these causal powers can be distinguished and often isolated from the effects of manipulation elsewhere in the experiment (and for a host of other reasons we won't discuss here), we can regard them as relatively causally independent from one another and from the theory that mentions them.

These objects are individuated according to the causal taxonomy of the science under study; these objects are thereby regarded as causally independent. Causal powers differ not just in kind but in their range of influence (or, so to speak, not just in quality but in quantity). To say that two objects are relatively causally independent is not to say that they cannot causally influence one another. Any two molecules are causally independent, in the sense that they can enter into different bonding relations with various other molecules. But they can influence each other as well, in the form of attraction or repulsion.

Similarly, experimental effects can be relatively autonomous from the design. That is, the effect is not a mere artifact of, or completely determined by, the experimental apparatus. This independence is attested to when the same theoretical terms occur in different theories or, put nonsemantically, different theories postulate the same theoretical entities. Diverse testing in the establishment of ontological commitment is a commonplace and is undertaken precisely to exploit this feature of valid posits. Richard Miller (1987) refers to this property as resilience and William Wimsatt (1981), as robustness. The same fact of independence evidenced by survival under diverse tests of contemporaneous theories is evidenced by the ability of successive theories in the history of science to make use of archaic data (see Trout 1994).[2]

2. The theme of diverse tests—implicating different domains—is used to establish the existence of Avogadro's number and with it the existence of molecules. Other such synchronic examples could be added to the list. One research project in genetics concerns the sequencing of bases in one strand of the double helix. To do so, we must separate the strands. Heating is the standard way of achieving this effect. Several different methods can be used to denature DNA. In particular, any method that can break hydrogen bonds without damaging covalent bonds can be used to convert a DNA double helix into two single polynucleotide chains. Because the greater the proportion of GC base pairs in any particular DNA sample, the higher the melting temperature of the molecule, careful measurement of melting temperatures can then be used to determine the base compositions of DNA drawn from different organisms. After all, it takes more thermal energy to break three hydrogen bonds than two, and this difference is measurable by the increase in the absorption of ultraviolet light by DNA as the strands are unwinding. But other methods of measurement can be used, as can methods of separating the strands.

Despite the fact that the realist account of confirmation has carefully attended to actual scientific practice, some have suggested that realists hold an extreme form of confirmational holism, a sort of equipotentiality principle of confirmation difficult to find operating anywhere in science. But by saddling the realist with this principle, the critic implies that the relative independence of evidence from theory has been ignored or missed by realists. For example, Larry Laudan criticizes scientific realism for flouting the very principle to which realists have been most attentive. He first quotes Boyd to the effect that "the sort of evidence which ordinarily counts in favor of the acceptance of a scientific law or theory is, ordinarily, evidence for the (at least approximate) truth of the law or theory as an account of the causal relations obtaining between the entities quantified over in the law or theory in question" (Boyd 1973, p. 1). On the basis of this and other passages, Laudan concludes that, "[f]or realists such as Boyd, either all parts of a theory (both observational and non-observational) are confirmed by successful tests or none are" (1981, p. 229) However, the expression "all parts of a theory are confirmed" is ambiguous. Laudan could be committing the realist to the (strong) view that all parts of a theory are equally confirmed or disconfirmed by the evidence. Or he could be committing the realist to the (weaker) view that, although different parts of a theory are differentially affected by an experimental outcome, all parts of the theory are affected to some degree; no part of the theory is unaffected.

Laudan's misunderstanding of this realist position is instructive. First, as the passage above indicates, Boyd includes laws as well as theories among the objects of confirmation conditions. The lesson that Laudan draws omits reference to Boyd's supposition that laws can be relatively separable objects of confirmation without necessarily conferring an equal degree of confirmation on all parts of the theory. This omission is especially important, because the possibility that confirmation can accrue distinctly to laws undermines the extreme confirmational holism that Laudan attributes to the realism he criticizes. Second, assuming that Laudan is concerned to diagnose deep and general difficulties concerning realism rather than with particular scholars, it is problematic for his view that there is nothing in the realist literature that entails extreme confirmational holism or even hints at it. Quite the contrary. The concept of relevant evidence has animated much realist work on explanation and theory testing (for just two examples, see W. Salmon 1984 and Glymour 1980). And the weak view is compatible with using evidence to support theoretical claims. But to draw so simple and stark a moral from Boyd's brief statement, one must attribute to the realist not just a holism but a holism that is quite extreme. No naturalistic realist such as Boyd would hold this view, because in its extreme form it is incompatible with actual scientific methods of confirmation. But Laudan does not clearly explain why a realist cannot hold a more complicated view of confirmation, according to which experimental tests may differentially affect the level of confirmation of different parts of the theory. He does say that, according to a conception of confirmation that allows just portions of a theory to be tested, "even highly successful theories may well have central terms that are nonreferring and central tenets that, because untested, we have no grounds for believing to be approximately true" and that, "in short, to be less than a holist about theory testing is to put at risk precisely that predilection for deep-structure claims which motivates much of the realist enterprise" (pp. 229–230). As we have seen, the realist is a holist about confirmation but need not be an extreme holist. After all, scientists confirm theories without implicating the "total science" in doing so.

Imperfect Isolation and Imperfect Integration: The Independence of Lawful Generalizations

Close attention to the methods of science display a theory-dependent sensitivity to the relations among the integrated claims of a theory; in virtually any working theory, some claims are utterly disposable, some are differentially revisable by some theory-based metric, and others are centrally associated with the theory's identity. I would suggest that, for a test of a theoretical hypothesis to be independent in the relevant sense and yet for the test to potentially confirm the theoretical hypothesis, the conditions of minimal detachment and minimal connection must hold:

> Minimal detachment condition (where the hypothesis is not the theory itself): It must be possible for a suitably sized body of evidence to undermine the theoretical hypothesis without thereby impugning the entire theory from which the hypothesis is drawn.

> Minimal connection condition: It must be possible for a body of evidence to warrant the theoretical hypothesis without thereby approving the entire theory from which the hypothesis is drawn.

The MD and MC conditions have the notion of adipose theory as a consequence. Neither condition should be unfamiliar, for echoes of these independence conditions of testing[3] are found in Glymour's bootstrap account of confirmation in particular and in the no-miracles strategy generally. But, more important, they express aspects of confirmation that are central to the scientific enterprise.

Together, the MD and MC conditions may appear to say little more than that certain events of theoretical interest are related to a certain degree and unrelated to a degree. Were we attempting to devise a theory-neutral specification of independence, the MD and MC conditions would be woefully inconsequential. One should not be bothered by this initial appearance, however. The MD and MC conditions set out in the most general terms the state of affairs that obtains in routine cases of confirmation. Fortunately, particular theories specify the relations that are causally important.

---

3. These conditions do not state a priori principles; they are contingent, empirical claims that must be true if there is to be such a thing as confirmation. The conditions may approach the sort of banality one associates with conditions asserted to be either conceptual or analytic truths, but there are other sources of banality. In this case, the familiarity of the MD and MC conditions is owed to their centrality in scientific practice, and their status is accordingly a posteriori. For an account of confirmation that, like the MD and MC account, similarly resists a kind of equipotential holism, see Kitcher (1993, ch. 5).

One substantial consequence of the MD and MC conditions—indeed, one of their distinctive merits—is that they explain the instances, quite common in the history of science, in which false theories are able to detect a real object. This is why scientists were not ultimately forced to wholeheartedly endorse the theory whose claims were confirmed. An account of confirmation that denied the MD and MC conditions could not in general count the history of science as a source of evidence. The historical procession of scientific theories often deployed different techniques for the identification of the same object. If one were to deny the MD and MC conditions, one must hold that scientists either have approved all theories when a body of evidence does not distinguish among them, a claim that is demonstrably false, or that they must do so, in which case we have philosophers dictating to scientists once again.

The MD and MC conditions incorporate the ordinary continuity and promiscuity of causal relations—such as those represented in measurement relations—into an account of the conditions required for confirmation. Confirmation can be local or global, depending upon the relevance of evidence to theory. The discovery of a protozoan parasite in cattle with Texas cattle fever was important in the confirmation of the germ theory of disease. This evidence offers less confirmation for the hypothesis of genetic transfer, bears only tangentially on the nitrogen cycle, and applies scarcely at all to the hypothesis of dark matter. So if we recall Laudan's criticism of Boyd, we can see that Boyd's statement of the conditions of confirmation of scientific realism is appropriately hedged. The confirmation conferred by an experimental result can feed either to a law or to an entire theory or both. Given that confirmation can be local, restricted primarily to a law, the realist need not adopt the kind of unprincipled confirmational holism Laudan imputes to the realist, and the condition indicated in Boyd's statement provides sufficient qualification to make one cautious about such an attribution. And, of course, no realist concerned to draw evidence from the history of science would accept commitment to a seeping holism so at odds with the actual practices of scientists.

This description of the independence of a hypothesis not only provides a necessary condition on a test promising confirmatory or disconfirmatory import; it provides a diagnosis of domains whose progress has been slow or whose vulnerability to ideology (in the pejorative sense) has been great. It is a fault of a theory that its claims cannot be separated from background theory sufficiently to have evidence bear on it. I shall argue that this is precisely the problem with narrative methods, and this point will be developed in chapter 8.

The modest version of realism I propose charts a treacherous course, the need for which is perhaps to be expected; unlike the mature sciences of physics, chemistry, and biology, the fledgling psychological and social sciences do not have the history of progress and technical control that deserves easy epistemic praise. Occasional ontological embarrassments are to be expected.

Admittedly, then, the version of realism I defend may be unable to meet the most trenchant epistemological challenges of traditional empiricism. These empiricist challenges propose to threaten realism and associated versions of naturalistic epistemology, for example, by reminding us that theory is underdetermined by evidence or that we can never be certain that a reported effect is real rather than spurious (perhaps the result of a deeply concealed bias or even brute chance). But this signifies no infirmity of realism, for meeting these challenges would carry a price too high to pay—or so I shall argue in chapter 7. The realist can permit that a theory is logically underdetermined by the evidence, and the realist can allow (indeed, insist) that our judgments of the reality of theoretical entities are fallible.

The above discussion of the equipotentiality of confirmation has a simple moral: An appropriate expression of scientific realism about the behavioral sciences must set standards of intersubjective agreement and epistemic reliability, as must a similar expression about the physical sciences: high enough that it would be possible for the facts of scientific practice and history to undermine it but not so high that a single nonreferring term or inaccurate generalization would render scientific realism a mistaken doctrine concerning these disciplines. (The standards should not license astrology but approve, say, late nineteenth-century physics.) After all, even in the history of physics we have instances of nonreferring terms yet—in physics we had to get here from there—a process of successive approximation through inexact measurement. I hope to make the process more familiar in the present chapter.

Let us now briefly consider the conditions we could reasonably expect an account of realism concerning the social and behavioral sciences to satisfy. Any version of realism that is to be supported by evidence from the social and behavioral sciences will likely possess at least two distinctive features. First, it should incorporate a subsidiary account of inexact measurement so that the cumulative character of scientific knowledge can be represented. This is a desirable component for versions supported by the evidence in physics as well but is especially important when questions about progress arise. Second, it should represent the unity of scientific methods and the diversity of tests ordinarily thought to provide independent evidence for causal claims.

Causes in the social and behavioral sciences have always received different philosophical treatment from that of causes in the physical sciences. The reasons for this are many, and most of them are, in my view, based on contingent rather than necessary differences between the two. It is not as though only the behavioral and social sciences propose laws that are stochastic or are prone to exception, for example. One might try to articulate the difference not in terms of the objects of inquiry but in terms of the methods used to study those objects. At the gross level, one might suggest that in physics, chemistry, and biology, measurement by instrumentation figures importantly. In psychology, history, sociology, political science, and economics, measurement by statistical methods plays a more central role.

Failure of imagination prevents us from recognizing an important similarity, insofar as both the natural and social sciences rely on measurement. In the area of statistical measurement, we lack a model that allows us to see the continuity between proper lab instruments and statistical ones. But this comparison will be worked out in detail in the next chapter.

Our next task is to look for evidence that a test hypothesis is independent of the particular theory from which it was originally drawn. Evidence of independence comes in a variety of forms: the metaphysical and semantic form of causal and counterfactual dependence in measurement relations described in chapter 2, the autonomy of experiment described by Buchwald (1992), the historical form of archaic evidence in the confirmation of contemporary theories described in the second section of this chapter, and the epistemic form—what I will call mercenary reliance in science. After surveying these various expressions of independence, we will consider mercenary reliance as an archetypal illustration of how independence is secured by diverse testing and how independence relations in confirmation can focus on small bits of theory.

Diverse Testing

ARCHAIC CONFIRMATION.   One of the most common kinds of confirmation derives from our reliance on past evidence, sometimes archaic evidence. Archaic theories often performed very poorly, by nearly any measure of good-making features of theories. In such cases, we typically find two patterns of ancestral confirmation: (1) Appeals to historically remote experiments that were poorly designed in light of what we know now and whose results can be explained by the current theory, and (2) appeals to historically remote observations that did play an important role in confirming a mediating theory that the current theory depended on, even though the remote observations were not expressly invoked by the current theory or directly responsible for its acceptance.

These patterns of ancestral support are interesting. Remote observations are often counted as confirmatory even if they were made and interpreted under the aegis of a horribly false theory. Reliance on historically remote observation illustrates the kind of methodological independence crucial not only to routine confirmation in science but also to the case for Measured Realism.

Two such cases of archaic confirmation can be found in cometary research and theoretical work on aphasia. In the former case, cometary observations made during the dominant Aristotelian theory—according to which comets are meteorological rather than astronomical phenomena, among many other errant conceptions—are recruited by contemporary theories in order to fix cometary orbits. Because there are so few observations of long-period comets, archaic appeals were essential to the determination of cometary orbits, but such appeals could have been effective only if the archaic and the contemporary theories, no matter how different, isolated the same entities. So too in the area of aphasia research. Ancient Greek theories of speech disorder described various states of speechlessness and speech abnormality that were attributed to excess humidity in the head. Contemporary accounts, by contrast, explain such disfunctions in terms of neurological damage of various sorts. Yet due to the paucity of clinical data early in this century, the record of archaic clinical observations was marshaled as evidence for the current taxonomy of speech disorder. This effective confirmatory role requires that the respective excess humidity and neurological deficit views, though unquestionably different, isolate or detect common mechanisms in the domain of speech disorder.

Notice that we need not suppose that our background theory is approximately true to explain the reliable role of archaic evidence. In fact, a robust theory realism renders this occurrence obscure. After all, a good bit of aphasiac disfunction was understood by the 1930s and 1940s, in the absence of a well-articulated theory of the neurological sources of aphasia. Its association with lateralization was known, and a serviceable taxonomy had been provided by Henry Head in his encyclopedic *Aphasia and Kindred Disorders of Speech* (1926). At the same time, many of the basic neural mechanisms were not understood, certainly not to the extent that those of atomic physics were at that time. Given this balance of theoretical virtues and demerits, it appears that only a measured realism can explain the reliable role of this archaic data and its independence from the elaborate theoretical structure with which it is associated.

AUTONOMY OF EXPERIMENT.   There is a good deal of unevenness in the extent to which a theory gets codified and so considerable variation in the explicitness of the theoretical account that researchers have available to them. Often in the history of science, due to differences in training, researchers who are contemporaries experiment on the same phenomenon even though their techniques reflect vastly different appreciation of theoretical detail. Buchwald considers one such case of the autonomy of experiment:

> One of the great changes in physics began to take firm shape during the 1880s, though its roots go back at least a half century, at first primarily in Germany. Experiments before then were usually done by people who were just as deeply involved in shaping the conceptual apparatus as they were in making and using laboratory devices. This began to change rapidly after the 1880s, and Heinrich Hertz is among the last of a long line of experimenting theorists, or theorizing experimentalists—it hardly makes historical sense to distinguish people in this way. (1992, p. 175)

Although the work of Hertz or Fresnel tied experiment to a clearly articulated body of theory, mucking about was characteristic of much lab research in the nineteenth century. In fact, according to Buchwald, theories were made fruitful by "their resistance to encapsulation in closed, well-ordered schemes" (pp. 175–176). Buchwald selects as a case study the work of Étienne Malus, an early nineteenth century polytechnician. As an alternative to the method of polarization produced by crystals, Malus introduced a mirror method of polarization. Malus

> built his device with a certain understanding, but an understanding that did not generally prescribe what would happen in given circumstances. . . .
> Neither Malus nor Fresnel were guided in the laboratory by anything like a set of codified, or even codifiable, assertions. . . . On the other hand, something did guide each of them in several ways. Something permitted Malus to convince himself through calculation that the light was what it should be. Something permitted Fresnel, in a very different context, to insist on distinctions between kinds of polarization that for many years made little sense to many of his contemporaries. This kind

of thing could rarely be used to provide a blueprint for experiment, but it could powerfully structure the kinds of experiments that seemed important to do; it also provided tools for understanding, and for calculating things about, experiments. It sat for the most part well below explicit discourse, subtly influencing its tone and powerfully guiding the construction of sentences and their material realization in the laboratory. (pp. 176, 178)

The Malus scenario might appear to be an exception in the history of science, but Peter Galison (1987) holds that the autonomy of experiment is a general phenomenon:

> Experimentalists do not march in lockstep with theorists, and quite frequently their experiments span several particular theories, and even groups of theories. Theoretical and experimental breaks frequently do not come together. The periods during which theorists break with tradition do not necessarily correspond to disruptions in the subject matter, methods, procedures and instruments of experimental physics. Especially in modern physics, when the communities of experimentalists and theorists are not the same, it becomes increasingly awkward to assume that the two groups change direction together.
>
> It therefore seems difficult to maintain that when a conceptual break occurs in theory, it follows that one occurs in experimentation as well. (p. 13)

The doctrine of the autonomy of experiment does not undermine the theory dependence of experimentation and measurement that Kuhn and Hanson made a prominent theme in contemporary philosophy of science. Rather, the autonomy of experiment suggests a constraint on the scope of theory dependence. Typically, a particular, favored theory motivates the selection of a particular hypothesis to test, artifacts to control for, and so forth. But this is not to say that only that theory could have selected appropriate test hypotheses or artifacts to control for. To the extent that different theoretical descriptions can pick out the same object (observable or not), or that different methodological practices isolate the same phenomenon, then the measurement or experimental outcomes are independent from any particular theory. In all of these cases, diverse testing reveals part of the theory as adipose, and what is left is often epistemically bite-sized. It is able to be formulated and used by different theories. The epistemic relation of mercenary reliance provides a clear and novel illustration of adipose theory and bite-sized theoretical commitments.

One Model of Independence: Mercenary Reliance

Modern science is the product of an enormous effort of intellectual cooperation, cooperation often made necessary by epistemic restrictions on expertise. A respected expert in one field is a humble novice in another. Yet scientists routinely test a target theory by jointly applying it with a well-confirmed remote theory, thereby expanding the target theory's class of observational consequences; and so the neuroscientist relies on the circuit theorist, the geneticist on the x-ray crystallographer, the psychopharmacologist on the biochemist, and so on. But theory conjunction also demonstrates a type of social dependence that has a striking epistemological feature.[4] Target theorists are typically profoundly innocent of, and without sustained professional interest in, the content of the remote theory. Their reliance on the remote expert is mercenary and at the same time enormously successful.

In defending Measured Realism, my purpose is to transform the fact of mercenary reliance into a powerful objection—different from the standard realist conjunction objection—to contemporary empiricist conceptions of scientific practice. I will first argue that empiricist interpretations of theory conjunction cannot be sustained and, in the case of mature sciences, only a more substantial theory realism can adequately account for the success of theory conjunction. I will close with several observations about how the dependable epistemic role of mercenary reliance in the behavioral sciences can be explained only on a measured realist account of scientific knowledge rather than on either the more modest, minimal realisms or the robust theory realism described in chapter 3.[5]

The Conjunction Objection to Empiricism

The phenomenon of theory conjunction has long been recruited as an objection to empiricist philosophy of science. Indeed, among scientific realists the conjunction objection has served double duty; it has been presented both as a fundamental objection to empiricist accounts of scientific knowledge and as the basis for a realist alternative to them. But none of the realist arguments exploits the epistemological feature of mercenary reliance to their advantage. For example, the conjunction objection was originally posed by Putnam (1973, pp. 210–211) as a logical feature of theory testing: When scientists accept T_1 as true and independently accept T_2 as true, normally they successfully apply them together, demonstrating

---

4. Many forms of epistemic dependence in ordinary and scientific life are too diverse, I suspect, to admit of an account that is general and at the same time illuminating. As laypersons, we rely on doctors' medical knowledge. In unfamiliar surroundings, we often rely on natives for directions. We typically accept the diagnoses of plumbers and mechanics on matters hydraulic and automotive before relying on our own judgment. In science, even similarly trained experts from the same narrow scientific field depend epistemically on one another. They seldom attempt to replicate each others' experiments, even though they would be competent to do so; instead, one simply defers to the research the other has done. Where epistemic dependence is intratheoretic, mutual deference results not from differences in competence but from shared interest in advancing as quickly as possible to the frontiers of research. The best general discussion of epistemic dependence is Hardwig (1985, 1991). Kitcher (1990, 1993) offers the most sophisticated available account of social reliance in science. Also see Lehrer (1977) for an original and illuminating treatment of this issue.

5. The form of this argument is clearly abductive, or, if you like, a miracle argument. Sober argues that "the problem with the miracle argument is not that it is abductive, but that it is a very weak abductive argument" (1990, p. 397). The main problem, according to Sober, is that "the miracle argument fails to specify what the set of competing hypotheses is supposed to be" (p. 397). While some abductive arguments certainly are weak—even some of them about realism—theory conjunction provides the constraints necessary to make the abductive argument for realism stronger. The background theory limits the number or kind of theory that can be the target theory and so specifies the set of competing hypotheses. The means by which this limitation is imposed will be clarified below.

that the practice of theory conjunction is truth preserving and that scientists presuppose the deductive closure of theories under the union operation.[6]

The confidence and success with which scientists routinely infer the truth of the conjunction of two independently well-confirmed theories, it is claimed, is intelligible only on a realist conception of scientific knowledge. According to the empiricist, our knowledge extends only to observable phenomena, and this epistemological restriction does not seem to rationalize successful scientific practice. The fact that, taken independently, T_1 and T_2 are each empirically adequate does not imply that their conjunction (T_1 and T_2) is also empirically adequate. After all, T_1 and T_2 may make contradictory claims about unobservables, and these contradictory claims would then be used, in accordance with the empiricist model of theory testing, to calculate observational values in the deduction of observational predictions.

In its logical form, the conjunction objection meets a ready response from the empiricist. The realist, it is charged, has misunderstood the practice of theory conjunction. Since theories are seldom simply and unhesitatingly conjoined, van Fraassen concludes, "there can be no account of the scientific life of which this simple account draws a faithful picture" (1980, p. 85). Once properly understood, the resulting account of the joint application of theories will honor contemporary empiricist strictures on theory testing and theory choice; joint use implies only the belief that the theories in question are empirically adequate, not, as the realist claims, that they are (approximately) true.

Empiricists and realists alike recognize the methodological importance of relying on remote theories, which are often identified as "auxiliary hypotheses." Boyd (1973) invokes an actual case of the conjunction of bacteriology and an "auxiliary" theory, biochemistry, in defense of a methodological principle whose reliability requires a realist explanation. The methodological principle in question states that a proposed theory must be tested in conditions under which, according to a collateral theory, the tested theory is most likely to fail. Boyd argues that it is only if the collateral field's theoretical claims are accurate, representing probable causal knowledge about underlying mechanisms, that we can adequately explain the reliable operation of this methodological principle.

Since the early versions of the conjunction objection, the realist consequences of the practice of theory conjunction have been made even more explicit. Friedman (1983, pp. 236–263) contends that the results of this practice provide an important further source of confirmation for a literal, realist interpretation of a well-confirmed theory, a source not enjoyed by a formal (Ramsified) representa-

---

6. The picture of theory conjunction drawn by Putnam is clearly intended as an idealization of scientific practice, since he is well aware that no current scientific theory is completely true. Indeed, he indicates that the inference would go through even if the theories taken independently are "highly probable" or "approximately true." So it is somewhat misleading when he states in a later work that the conjunction objection was designed to show that any account of theory acceptance "that lacks the property of deductive closure . . . fails . . . to justify the norms of scientific practice" (1978, p. 102). Nevertheless, the phenomenon of theory conjunction is originally framed as a logical feature of scientific practice.

tion of the observable phenomena. Boyd (1985b, pp. 216–217) argues that theory conjunction has a further striking consequence: An independently well-confirmed theory must be seen as confirming future conjunctions involving that theory.[7]

All of these realist observations about the practice of theory conjunction evade van Fraassen's initial criticism of Putnam's simple account. However, they don't anticipate his empiricist reconstruction of theory conjunction, and they do not highlight the epistemological feature of theory conjunction—mercenary reliance—that represents the primary obstacle to van Fraassen's reconstruction.

The Constructive Empiricist "Rational Reconstruction" of Theory Conjunction

Van Fraassen's constructive empiricist interpretation of theory conjunction first construes the joint application of theories as a process of prior correction, not, as the realist initially claims, one of conjunction. Van Fraassen describes, or perhaps merely advocates, a certain kind of conjunctive behavior:

> in practice scientists must be very careful about conjoining theories, simply because even if (as realists hold) acceptance is belief, it rarely happens that non-tentative, unqualified acceptance is warranted. There was a time when the Bohr-Sommerfeld theory of the atom looked victorious, and at the same time special relativity was generally accepted—you see the point—it would not have made sense to conjoin them: the former would have to be subjected to a relativistic correction. Putting the two theories together would not have meant conjunction, but correction. (1980, p. 84)

Van Fraassen concedes that scientists indeed apply theories jointly and that this practice is reliable, so his normative recommendation that scientists "must be very careful about conjoining theories" is quite irrelevant. The realist has an explanation for the success of the unrevised practice of joint application. The empiricist does not. What we need from the empiricist is either an explanation for the reliability of the joint application of theories or convincing evidence that scientists routinely correct theories before jointly applying them.

The constructive empiricist account of theory conjunction fails first as a description of scientists' behavior. As Demopoulos (1982) points out, the realist

---

7. In his attack on explanationist defenses of realism, Fine ([1986] 1991a) argues that the realist's inference from instrumental success to truth is mediated by the pragmatist's notion of reliability. Therefore, if the explanationist argument for realism is to be non–question-begging and depend only on the instrumental reliability of a science, then the realist's appeal to truth is frivolous, doing no more explanatory work than the instrumentalist's more parsimonious (and therefore preferable) appeal to a pragmatic conception of reliability. Such considerations lead Fine to advance a "proof" of a "metatheorem" that states that "to every good realist explanation there corresponds a better instrumentalist one" (p. 154). Fine ably describes the conditions that an instrumentalist account of theories would need to satisfy for it to be regarded as plausible. However, he offers no independent argument that these conditions are indeed satisfied. And although Fine does discuss the tendency toward theoretical unification, he nowhere squarely addresses the conjunction objection, traditionally thought to be the most damaging criticism of an instrumentalist account of theories.

need not deny this prior process of correction, since the conjunction objection would then apply to the corrected version of the theory in any case. Although this realist response is admirably charitable in conceding to the empiricist that correction sometimes occurs before joint application, it is just as important to recognize that such cases are relatively infrequent. In the typical case, the scientists lack the appropriate expertise in the collateral theory to carry out the prior corrections, and, since our current sciences are still incomplete, often investigators do not yet know prior to conjunction that the corrections are strictly necessary. So the constructive empiricist still must explain why theory conjunction succeeds even though the putatively necessary corrections weren't made. By contrast, the realist is in a position to say that the theories that are in need of correction before consistent conjunction can be successfully conjoined in uncorrected form as long as the theory's projected values for unobservable causal mechanisms are suitable approximations of their actual values. Moreover, van Fraassen draws attention to the process of prior modification to suggest that theory conjunction should be assimilated to the merely pragmatic aim of theoretical unification, in stark contrast to the special epistemic function of theory conjunction required by the realist argument. However, because scientists' reliance on the remote theory is mercenary, their behavior hardly represents a merely pragmatic concern for unification, for "a single theory to cover disparate domains of phenomena" (van Fraassen 1980, p. 86).

Second, according to van Fraassen, the scientist's reliance on the joint application of theories is tentative, an important consideration supposedly misrepresented in the realist's understanding of theory conjunction as the union of two theories believed to be true:

> as long as we are scientific in spirit, we cannot become dogmatic about even those theories which we whole-heartedly believe to be true. Hence a scientist must always, even if tacitly, reason *at least* as follows in such a case: if I believe T and T' to be true, then I also believe that (T and T') is true, and hence that it is empirically adequate. But in this new area of application T and T' are genuinely being used in conjunction; therefore, I will have a chance to see whether (T and T') really is empirically adequate, as I believe. That belief is not supported yet to the extent that my previous evidence supports the claims of empirical adequacy for T and T' separately, even though that support has been as good as I could wish it to be. Thus my beliefs are about to be put to a more stringent test in this joint application than they have ever been before. (1980, p. 85)

Missing from van Fraassen's scenario is the realist appeal to the belief that (T and T') is true. In an effort to cast the scientist's attitude as involving some sort of acceptance weaker than belief, van Fraassen now presents the scientist's doxastic commitment as an antecedent in a protracted pattern of conditional reasoning. The scientist's reasoning must be represented as conditional because her epistemic commitment is thought to be tentative, and her epistemic commitment must be construed as tentative if we are to avoid casting the scientist as dogmatic.

In the case study that follows, we will see just how far van Fraassen's reconstruction departs from actual cases of the joint application of theories and how easy these examples of mercenary reliance are to come by. In particular, these scenarios will illustrate the relation of mercenary reliance between scientists: The target theorist is typically profoundly innocent of, and without sustained professional interest in, the content of the remote theory.

Mercenary Reliance in Theory Conjunction

Evolutionary Biology and Paleontology: Their Dependence on Paleomagnetic Dating

Evolutionary biologists and paleontologists offer explanations for (among other things) the extinction of certain species, the generation of new species, and the flourishing of still others. These explanations typically appeal to climatic conditions and food sources during the species' period of existence. To correlate fossils of a particular species with important changes in climatic conditions and in the availability of food that might have affected the species, evolutionary biologists and paleontologists defer to theoretically remote procedures for dating rock strata.

One dating technique derives from the phenomenon of paleomagnetism. As volcanic flows cool and sedimentary layers are deposited, metallic elements contained in these beds align themselves with the earth's coincident magnetic poles. The earth's poles have spontaneously switched at various periods throughout its history, producing sharp discontinuities in the orientation of metallic components within strata. Because these geomagnetic pole reversals occur in almost entirely random sequences, once the times of the reversals have been fixed by (for example) potassium-argon dating methods, the geologist can use the randomly placed reversals to produce striped maps, providing distinctive "geomagnetic fingerprints" for specific periods in the earth's recent history.

Paleomagnetism has played its most important role in confirming hypotheses about plate tectonics and the rate of seafloor spreading (See Cox and Hart 1986; Piper 1987; Tarling 1971). But paleomagnetic data have also been used successfully to examine the distribution of fossils (Piper 1987, p. 133), the coincidence of polarity changes with the extinction and generation of species (Tarling 1971, p. 127), and the range of oil deposits (Tarling 1971, pp. 148–150). Paleontologists therefore routinely appeal to the results of paleomagnetic dating to confirm a variety of evolutionary hypotheses, the effects of specific catastrophic events, the flora dominant within a particular global range and period, and the rate of the generation, reproduction, and extinction of species. Despite the deep involvement of dating techniques in evolutionary biology and paleontology, it is doubtful that theorists in the field are familiar with even the most rudimentary principles of physics that make paleomagnetic dating possible—details underlying, for example, the hysteresis loop or magnetic dipoles.

Psycholinguistics and the Engineering Implementations of Signal-Processing Theory

Psycholinguists want to know, among other things, what the significant units of speech are, how they are marked, and how they contribute to our comprehension of running discourse. Some attempts to explore these questions require the juxta-position of speech sounds that do not normally occur together. For this purpose, it won't do to splice tape-recorded segments together, since listeners will respond to artifactual discontinuities caused by the splicing. Speech perception theorists circumvent this problem by digitizing the speech, at which time selected segments can be carefully manipulated. This process involves transforming the analog signal (speech or tape recording) into a digital signal by breaking the continuous natural signal into a series of discrete units (called "samples"). Each sample is assigned a specific value. It is now standard to digitize segments at 20,000 samples per second, but the higher the sampling rate, the higher the resolution of the resulting speech. Digitizing speech also allows the scientist to isolate and systematically vary distinctive components of the complex signal, such as formant frequencies and amplitude envelope.

A sophisticated signal-processing theory forms the basis of the digitizing process, a theory whose scope includes not just speech but signals of any kind. Despite their crucial reliance on it, psycholinguists typically know very little about signal processing theory, about the way in which it has been used to produce radar, control satellite attitudes, and analyze harmonic vibrations. They are inno-cent of even those principles that closely guide the appropriate digital reconstruc-tion of speech, such as the transfer function and the sampling theorem.[8]

By indulging his innocence, the psycholinguist is being efficient, not sluggardly. Engineers have designed the reconstruction filters, and computer scientists and signal-processing theorists have developed the speech-editing programs. Therefore the psycholinguist has been free to study, with notable success, the role of such factors as voicing, coarticulation, phoneme boundaries, and stress in speech per-ception.

Faced squarely with detailed analyses of actual cases, van Fraassen's reconstruc-tion of theory conjunction appears strained. Whatever philosophical allure there may be in the sanitized reconstruction of theory conjunction as a process of prior correction and tentative application, evidence of this fastidiousness in real science is difficult to find. Scientists typically haven't the expertise in the relevant fields to make the (allegedly required) preconjunction corrections, nor do they routinely recognize any significant benefits of being tentative in joint applications of theo-ries. In part this is simply because, as novices with respect to the other theory, scientists would not know what they were supposed to be tentative about.

At the same time, no one doubts that theory conjunction is reliable. Therefore if it would be dogmatic for a scientist to unhesitatingly conjoin independently well-confirmed theories, as van Fraassen claims, it would be dogmatic in some sense of "dogma" that is not pejorative. Unlike religious dogmatists who remain committed to their positions no matter how inconsistent or otherwise implausible

---

8. The sampling theorem characterizes an important restriction on the digital reconstruction of natural speech: The analog signal must be sampled at a rate at least twice that of its highest frequency, a rate alternatively called the "Nyquist," "folding," or "aliasing" frequency. See Stearns (1975, pp. 37–40) and Schwartz and Shaw (1975, pp. 33–44) for descriptions of this sampling restriction.

the consequences, scientists are typically willing to revise their positions in light of postconjunction results. Null results issuing from an experimental test involving theory conjunction may motivate the scientist to modify the target theory or (with the guidance of a remote expert) to replace the collateral theory with one potentially more sensitive to the variable being tested. This does not necessarily indicate that it was unwise to have unhesitatingly conjoined the original theories; for, at the time, there may have been no special reason to suppose that the two theories couldn't have been effectively conjoined. In light of the scientist's willingness to revise her original stance, her behavior appears to be far from dogmatic.

Once the specter of dogma has been dismissed, van Fraassen's reconstruction of theory-conjunctive reasoning as conditional appears to be not only unnecessary but inaccurate as well. It does not follow from the scientist's respect for feedback (which sometimes counsels revision) that her original reasoning must have been conditional or her initial epistemic stance tentative. There are certainly cases in which scientists are tentative in conjoining theories that are on the pioneering fringes of research, but this is only because they are tentative in their acceptance of each theory taken independently. Routine and representative cases of theory conjunction, such as those described above, reveal the scientists' commitment to the approximate truth of the resulting conjunction, at least of those parts of the theories that are actually used. Scientists then leave it to the world to correct them when they are wrong, and they revise their beliefs accordingly.[9]

Motivating Epistemic Symmetry

Having abandoned the view that theory conjunction proceeds tentatively and by prior correction, the empiricist may concede the existence of mercenary reliance but argue that its existence is compatible with empiricist strictures. The empiricist might argue as follows. The success of mercenary reliance can be explained in terms of the target scientist's selective familiarity with, or exclusive dependence

---

9. Whatever plausibility van Fraassen's strategy enjoys may derive not from an examination of the psychology of scientific reasoning but from an independent and general dictum that a person's posterior level of epistemic commitment to a certain belief is equivalent to the prior conditional probability of that belief. But, as we discovered above, it would be psychologically anachronistic to claim that the scientist's *actual* reasoning to the prior belief (that two theories can be conjoined) was conditional or otherwise tentative on the mere grounds that this belief is open to revision in light of posterior evidence. Thus, as a psychological account of (scientific) reasoning, van Fraassen's empiricist reconstruction of theory conjunction is subject to the same criticism leveled against Bayesian accounts of scientific reasoning. Glymour states that "particular *inferences* can almost always be brought into accord with the Bayesian scheme by assigning degrees of belief more or less ad hoc, but we learn nothing from this agreement. What we want is an explanation of scientific argument; what the Bayesians give us is a theory of learning, indeed a theory of personal learning. But arguments are more or less impersonal" (1980, p. 74). Giere clearly recognizes the anachronistic character of Bayesian analyses of scientific reasoning: "Scientists, as a matter of empirical fact, are not Bayesian agents. Reconstructions of actual scientific episodes along Bayesian lines can at most show that a Bayesian agent would have reached similar conclusions to those in fact reached by actual scientists. Any such reconstruction provides no explanation of what actually happened" (1988, p. 157).

on, the observational consequences of the remote theory. Of course, when con-joined with the remote theory, the target theory has observational consequences it wouldn't have if taken in isolation. But if these additional observational conse-quences derive entirely from the target theorist's selective dependence on the observational consequences of the remote theory, then we need to presuppose only the empirical adequacy of the conjoined theories, not their approximate truth.

What we will find, however, is that the target scientist also relies on claims about unobservables made by the remote theory, and these claims are crucial to the observational testing of the target theory. Moreover, laboratory settings reveal the target scientist as equally familiar with and dependent upon the observational and theoretical claims of the remote theory and thus (given the distance of the target from the remote theory) as equally innocent of both types of claims. If the "epistemic symmetry" implied by mercenary reliance is vindicated by actual scien-tific practice, a descriptively adequate empiricism could not disregard the theoreti-cal import of the joint application of theories.

The empiricist contention that mercenary reliance involves nothing more than instrumental knowledge of the remote theory is perhaps understandable; the pale-ontologist and psycholinguist rely heavily on the (observable) output of laboratory instruments. But while mercenary reliance is no doubt observationally or instru-mentally reliable, it is just as obviously motivated by theoretical considerations.

The paleontologist uses a magnetometer to determine the orientation of mag-netic components in rock samples. The design of the magnetometer depends in part on principles of magnetism familiar only to the remote theorist, but its use by the target scientist, the empiricist argues, requires only that the target scientist attend to the (observable) report of magnetic orientation yielded by the instru-ment. It might be thought that such technical reliance rests only on these obser-vational consequences of the theory of magnetism. But as a matter of fact, paleon-tologists are concerned to determine the rock sample's age, and they do not treat the (observable) magnetometer readings as a report of the rock's age. After all, paleontologists recognize that there are a variety of ways in which the reported orientation can fail to accurately reflect the age of the rock sample. Igneous intru-sions and lightning strikes can remagnetize or "overprint" the strata, causing the magnetometer to incorrectly report the original (called "primary") remanent mag-netization. Paleontologists are not taken in by such observable values, precisely because they take the instrument to be a detector not of age, but of such unob-servable properties of the sample as magnetic moment. Paleontologists' reliance on claims concerning unobservable magnetic factors is further illustrated by their sensitivity to improvements in measurement and detection procedures: They now insist that samples identified as theoretically problematic receive magnetic scrub-bing, a process that strips away layers of magnetic overprint by exposing the rock sample to an alternating magnetic field or to carefully controlled heating. But the need for magnetic scrubbing could be appreciated only if the paleontologist presupposed that the sample possesses the unobservable magnetic properties re-ported by the magnetometer. So the paleontologist's behavior reflects a sensitivity to both the theoretical claims about magnetic properties and the observational consequences of the conjunction of the theory of (paleo)magnetism and paleontology.

The psycholinguist's position with respect to the instruments of speech analysis is no different from the paleontologist's stance toward paleomagnetic dating instruments. Once conjoined with implementation of signal-processing theory, psycholinguistics has observational consequences concerning the perceptual effects of digitized noise on a range of linguistic abilities. However, when analyzing suitably short segments of speech, psycholinguists don't assume that the signal-processing system detects and transforms perceptually significant features of speech per se but rather unobservable acoustic features of the signal. For example, psycholinguists often strain the perceptual system by adding digitized white noise to the speech stream, to identify those acoustic factors that benefit speech perception under less than ideal circumstances. One such technique adds noise to the digitized speech and then examines the subject's ability to distinguish the noise-only stimuli from the speech-plus-noise stimuli. Perceptual discrimination will be easy if the noise has features starkly different from (e.g., is louder than) those of the speech sound to which it is added. To avoid perceptual effects that are artifacts of detectable discontinuities in the digitized speech, psycholinguists have exploited signal-processing techniques that direct the noise to follow certain important features of the speech, such as amplitude envelope.

Now, although psycholinguists embrace the ability of the analog-to-digital hardware to reconstruct with considerable fidelity the perceptible features of natural speech, they also assume that the individual units or "samples" of the signal are unobservable and that these units are those the digital system processes. This assumption is evident in the methodological choices that psycholinguists make about when to employ particular instruments and techniques. The signal-dependent noise-producing technique developed by Schroeder (1968) should not be used when you want to preserve spectral features of speech, such as periodicity. But, as is evident in the psycholinguistic use of the signal-dependent technique (see, for example, Repp and Frost 1988; Samuel 1987), this methodological prohibition could be reliable (as it indeed is) only if the psycholinguist takes the technique (along with the related hardware) to really be randomly flipping the (+/−) sign of each point, and each point, taken by itself, is unobservable, having no influence on performance. In addition, the technique could yield this specific (amplitude envelope–preserving) improvement over the method it replaced—which instead bases the noise on the digital root mean square of the amplitude of the original segment, not its amplitude envelope—only if there are these 1/20,000-of-a-second points on the speech wave whose amplitude values (or signs) are getting randomly flipped.

These scenarios are important for two reasons. First, they reveal that the remote theory's claims about unobservable causal factors have immediate and direct observational consequences for the target theory, consequences that could not be tested if the two theories had not been conjoined. In conjunction with the suitable target theory, manipulations of digitized speech can produce predictable perceptual effects on performance. The particular magnetic declination of a rock can indicate with some reliability that natural gas deposits will be found near the rock sample's stratum. The presence of a certain level of Ar^{40} can indicate that a particular kind of index fossil will be present in that sample's stratum. Second, the target scientist's tendency to exploit improvements provided by the remote theory can be explained only if we cast the target scientist as recognizing that the relevant instrumentation detects unobservable causal factors.[10] In the case discussed here, the unobservable causal factor is a 1/20,000-of-a-second sample of a sound wave.

Therefore the target theorist's knowledge of the remote domain is not, as our envisioned critic might contend, purely instrumental. Nor is it, in any obvious sense, even primarily instrumental; most of the observational consequences of the remote theory, taken independently, are no doubt lost on the target theorist. And at the same time, the fact that the target theorist is sensitive to some of the remote theory's claims about unobservables hardly constitutes evidence of expertise in the remote domain. This familiarity could be acquired without sustained study. So the target theorist is largely innocent of the remote theory, and at those points of contact between the target and remote theories the target scientist appears to rely in roughly equal proportion on observational and theoretical claims of the remote theory.[11]

Scientific Realism and the Principle of Epistemic Symmetry

The two preceding sections together suggest that mercenary reliance presents quite general difficulties for empiricist conceptions of scientific knowledge. The first of these sections illustrated the symmetry of epistemic innocence; target scientists are so unfamiliar with the content of the remote theory that they are (roughly speaking) equally innocent of the remote theory's observational and theoretical claims. The second of these sections was designed to show that, to the

---

10. In each of these cases of mercenary reliance, the target theory has also been improved by the remote theory's development of more sophisticated instrumentation. Subsequent improvements in the target theory, however, might be regarded as incompatible with the doctrine of mercenary reliance: If the target scientist is truly innocent of the remote theory, how could the former make the type of informed judgment necessary to yield improvement in the target theory? This is an important question, and I think an acceptable answer must address the distinctly social features of epistemic dependence. In particular, the target theorist need not have a detailed understanding of the remote theory but must be sensitive to feedback from conjunction and able to recognize diagnostic features of expertise in the remote domain.

11. The empiricist critic might take a related tack, this time attempting to undermine epistemic symmetry by assimilating the target theorist's reliance on the remote theory to the lab technician's reliance on the remote theory. One might think that the existence of technicians—whose knowledge is primarily observational—is a good counterexample to the principle of epistemic symmetry. But it isn't; the lab technician is not engaged in a theoretical enterprise in the same way that the target theorist is, and the difference in their respective enterprises is a relevant one. In particular, the technician does not design and execute experiments or evaluate the plausibility of one theory in light of its integration with a more secure, affiliated theory. In short, the technician does not normally conjoin theories.

modest extent that the target scientist is acquainted with the remote theory, the epistemic reliability of her methodological judgments depends not just on her familiarity with the observational claims of the remote theory but on her acquaintance with its theoretical claims as well. Together, these two arguments form a single moral, which might be called the principle of epistemic symmetry.

If correct, the principle of epistemic symmetry diagnoses the difficulty empiricists have suffered trying to provide an account of scientific knowledge that both explains the success of scientific practice and accurately characterizes the psychological perspective of the scientist. If theory acceptance involves only the belief that the theory is observationally accurate, and if the principle of epistemic symmetry is correct, then the empiricist cannot explain how the scientist is supposed to exercise a selective and informed reliance on the observational consequences of the remote theory. Indeed, the target scientist is not in an epistemic position to preferentially believe only the observational claims of the remote theory. Roughly speaking, the target scientist either believes all of the relevant information the remote theorist relates or believes none of it; epistemic innocence prevents the target theorist from being discriminating. And, in light of the principle of epistemic symmetry, the target scientist's adoption of methodological improvements reveals a reliance on the remote theory's observational and theoretical claims. The consistent empiricist, then, faces the following dilemma: Admit that, contrary to empiricist epistemic strictures, the target scientist indeed has knowledge of unobservables; or insist that, contrary to the evidence of the cumulative development of scientific knowledge, theory conjunction doesn't yield knowledge even about observables.

The realist, on the other hand, has no difficulty accommodating the principle of epistemic symmetry. In fact, the symmetry of epistemic innocence is exactly what one would expect if, as realists have urged, there is no epistemological motivation for the empiricist's proposed distinction between observables and unobservables. The positive task for the realist is to explain in adequate detail the features of epistemic dependence in theory conjunction that make this form of intellectual cooperation both computationally efficient and enormously reliable. I think that these features can be explained in terms of target scientists' appropriate sensitivity to feedback from conjunction and their capacity to recognize diagnostic features of expertise in remote fields. But that proposal is beyond the scope of the present chapter. Here, I have posed for the empiricist a difficulty that is generated by the familiar, crucial, and pervasive practice of mercenary reliance in science.[12] Since mercenary reliance in scientific practice is so successful, it would be little more than philosophical arrogance to insist on a "rational reconstruction" that treats observational claims as the sole source of the reliability of scientific methodology.

---

12. In any field, of course, there will be a handful of people of unusual background, talent, and stamina who are arguably experts in a target and a remote domain; these scientists do not fully exhibit mercenary reliance. But it is precisely their rarity that makes mercenary reliance so necessary and its success in permitting us to make progress without such special talent that makes it so desirable.

Entity Realism Is Not Enough, and Robust Realism Is Too Much

Once we recognize the antiempiricist consequences of theory conjunction, it is reasonable to ask which version of realism best explains the reliability of theory conjunction. A robust version of realism holds both that the theoretical terms of mature sciences typically refer and that the laws and theories of those mature sciences are typically approximately true (Boyd [1983] 1991a). In an effort to finesse the phenomenon of theory change and the role of idealization alleged to dog robust realism, the more modest entity realism of Hacking (1983) and Cartwright (1983, 1989) only endorses the existence of theoretical entities. Our apparent ability to perennially manipulate unobservable causes is the best evidence of their existence, while the falsehood of (theoretical) laws and theories is ultimately attested to by the obviously idealized conditions that they state and by the historical probability that they will be rejected in the future: "Hence, engineering, not theorizing, is the best proof of scientific realism about entities" (Hacking 1983, p. 274).

The success of theory conjunction, however, depends not just on the existence of postulated entities but also on something like the deductive closure of laws and theories under the union operation. It is, after all, theories, and not entities, that are being conjoined.[13] The fact that the approximate truth of theories is preserved under the taking of unions is therefore still inexplicable on a version of realism—such as entity realism—that eschews the approximate truth of laws and theories. Only a stronger version of realism can vindicate the success of theory conjunction, and the adoption of this stronger version of realism will have dramatic philosophical consequences.

Hacking would insist that his entity realism is not restrictive; manipulability is a sufficient but not necessary condition for realist commitment. It is worth noting, however, that Hacking offers a number of reasons for rejecting more ambitious versions of realism, among them metainductive considerations familiar from Putnam's work (1978). Therefore, to the extent that Hacking's entity realism is more than just the manipulability criterion, it rules out robust realism and restricts us to an ontologically selective version of scientific realism.

Yet, as the phenomenon of mercenary reliance attests, in routine scientific practice there are points of contact between theories whose epistemic accessibility depends not on believing any particular theory to be approximately true but on believing only certain laws to obtain. In consequence, robust realism is not required to explain all successful applications of theory conjunction; for some, only measured realism is needed.

None of this is to suggest that robust scientific realism does not appeal to theories using diverse testing or to the success of this practice. The more elaborate

---

13. It is true that descriptive adequacy demands an account of theory conjunction that permits something like approximate deductive closure, but of course this isn't a special problem for the realist; the empiricist, who agrees that theories are routinely and reliably conjoined, must at least produce an account of the approximate closure of the theories' joint observational consequences.

and detailed the theory, the more effectively one can recruit values to generate specific observational predictions. The theories mentioned in this connection are so specific that the same observed values are unlikely to emerge under different theories. In this respect, diverse testing is far more theory dependent in the natural than in the social and behavioral sciences and is perhaps part of the reason that many behavioral and social-scientific theories are "data driven" rather than "theory driven." But as the scenarios of diverse testing show, from the autonomy of experiment and archaic confirmation to mercenary reliance, not every part of a theory is engaged in testing; some theory is superfluous or, as I have said, adipose. The phenomena illuminated by such settings are local and resilient enough to survive changes of theory; they are phenomena about which there can be stable generalizations or laws. In this way, knowledge of unobservables is possible even in the absence of a true theory; it is possible just to the extent that it is possible to have knowledge of true, modestly counterfactual, general knowledge of objects independent of a particular theory.

Conclusion: Integration, Independence, and Progress by Association

Expressions of independence, then, come in many forms. Perhaps once the results of a discipline are well-enough tested, demonstrations of independence are not as necessary to its realistic interpretation. In the case study of the relation between the engineering implementation of signal-processing theory and psycholinguistics, the physical theory underlying signal-processing implementation is so severely and diversely tested that its success need only be mentioned in its realistic interpretation. In fact, it might be misleading to suggest that the core claims of the theory of magnetism are regarded as credible because tests of its hypotheses meet any single methodological standard of testing. If we apply the same standards to philosophical outcomes as we do to measurement outcomes, then the independence of the causal mechanisms of social and behavioral generalizations is amply attested to by their appearance in settings of mercenary reliance, archaic confirmation, and plausible counterfactual analyses of their causal powers.

In disciplines less mature than physics, methodological evidence of independence is far more central to the establishment of their realistic interpretation. In particular, evidence of survival under diverse tests, recurrent experimental detection in historically remote theories, the epistemic relation of mercenary reliance, and theoretical integration (convergent detection at the borders of disciplines) are crucial to a defense of measured realism. Theoretical integration is not the process of rendering disparate statements consistent, of patching together domains to achieve the desired aesthetic satisfaction. If theoretical integration conduces to the identification of instrumentally reliable theories, it does so because the postulated relations of causal dependence among mechanisms of diverse domains indeed hold. Logical consistency, by itself, cannot sustain integration; too many alternative theories are consistent with the one in fact used. Therefore, the model of integration-as-consistency cannot explain the warranted favor conferred on the specific theory with which the target is jointly applied.

One of the familiar objections to the claimed progress of scientific explanations generally, and psychological and social explanations in particular, begins with the observation that explanations change as new theories of a domain evolve. In consequence, the descriptions of causal factors change with explanatory changes. The modifications in description can be substantial—so substantial, at times, that we are led to suppose that the new theory postulates entirely different underlying causal mechanisms. This putative fact is then recruited to charge that the science in question does not enjoy theoretical progress or perhaps that its progress is not cumulative.

The significance of this phenomenon of explanatory description change is much overplayed, in part because its basis is much misunderstood. For reasons common to the causal theory of reference, we ought first to ask whether the different descriptions serve to isolate similar objects. Description change occurs in physics—as we moved from the Bohr to the wave-particle duality description of the electron—but this would not be cause for claims of stagnation or regression in physics. So it is not clear why similar explanatory shifts in the social and behavioral sciences should be a worry, unless we are willing to hold the behavioral and social sciences to standards the natural sciences aren't held to.

But we have another measure of progress: theoretical integration. Integration is important because it offers evidence that accumulation is more than mere appearance, more than the result of superficial, pragmatic features of explanation that reflect our interest in unification. Moreover, theoretical integration is the explanatory correlate of triangulation in measurement. For, disparate disciplines often have disparate histories. But discoveries frequently lead to unified explanations. The a priori likelihood that unification would occur between two highly specialized disciplines is very low when they have such different histories and when the discoveries that in fact lead to unification have such diverse sources. This effect of unification is especially surprising when respective practitioners never regarded themselves as engaged in a common scientific project.

My inclusion of so broad a survey is a piece of philosophical strategy. Those critical of realist interpretations of a theory might cast any description of a single research area as an isolated program that stands or falls by whatever methodological standards the critic chooses to apply to the case. By so isolating a theory, it may appear that doubts can be raised about the theory without epistemic repercussions. But this supposition runs afoul of one of the few tenets about which realists and empiricists now agree: Confirmation is relatively holistic. One does not reject the results of radiometric dating while leaving intact the physical theory on which it rests. In such a case, we would need to reject, for example, the postulated structure of isotopes and our accounts of decay. What follows is a fairly disparate presentation of theoretical integration in the social and behavioral sciences. The interpretation of these phenomena is complicated, and I won't attempt any such analysis here. Fortunately, detailed commentary on the significance of the integration is not required to present evidence of integration.

Integration of Psychology and Neuroscience

Many well-established effects in psycholinguistics, vision, speech perception, taste, and other areas of psychology depend upon localized brain function. If the argument from diverse testing provides warrant for realist interpretation, then the discovery and exploitation of this neural basis constitutes pointed evidence for the reality of a stable, unobserved structure that subserves these perceptual competencies. The relevant structures are revealed in these domains by very different instrumentation. And their histories, along with the theories on whose basis they were designed, are so different that cross-disciplinary agreement about unobserved structures is less likely to be the result of relevant shared theoretical assumptions than if they had common histories. Visual lacunae, for example, are perceptible blind spots in one's visual field. Typically, visual lacunae are caused by local damage in the visual cortex, damage whose diagnosis requires not introspection but the detection and recording of magnitudes.

Sheer number of examples may underline the centrality of integration. In the case of language, the class of pathologies known as aphasia is associated with specific areas of the brain, such as Broca's and Wernicke's areas. Another kind of localization is hemispheric. Kimura (1967) showed that there is a right-ear advantage in the processing of speech; the left hemisphere of the brain is dominant in speech. There is a biochemical account that details the biochemical changes that underlie color perception: Different cones are maximally sensitive to different frequencies. (McBurney and Collins 1984, p. 66). The processing of semantically anomalous sentences has been studied by using event-related brain potentials garnered from scalp recordings. Specific types of wave patterns are associated with particular types of semantic anomaly. For example, when the reader processes a sentence with a semantically anomalous word at the end, the associated waveform has a peak at about 400 milliseconds after the offset of the final word. If the word is presented in a different typeface, the pattern appears as a trough rather than a spike (Kutas and Hillyard 1984).

Integration of Physiological Psychology and Social Psychology

There is a long tradition of using drugs to treat behavioral disorders of various sorts, from clinical depression and schizophrenia to obsessive-compulsive disorder. Part of this tradition has attempted to trace the interaction of physiological mechanisms and moods. One physiological study (Schachter and Singer 1962) indicates that subjects given adrenaline can be psychologically prepared so that their emotional reaction to their own physiological symptoms is regulated by what they are led to expect. Some subjects were told that they could expect heart palpitations and rapid breathing, others were told nothing. Of those subjects told nothing, when placed in a room with a euphoric person they became amused, and when with a hostile person they become angry. Of those subjects told what to expect from an adrenaline response, there was little emotional reaction to the presence of either the euphoric or hostile person. The explanation given for this difference is that the latter subjects will attribute their arousal to the adrenaline rather than to the social context. (For more on the relation between physiology, arousal, and intensification of emotional states, see Reisenzein 1983; Zillman 1988.)

There is perhaps no better example of global integration of historical, cultural, and physiological evidence than in Nisbett and Cohen (1996). Nisbett and Cohen argue that the culture of the American South is a "culture of honor," in which men are comparatively quicker than those in the North to use violence to protect their reputation for toughness. According to Nisbett and Cohen, this greater tendency among southern males for aggression and violence is to be expected. The North was settled by farmers from England, Germany, and Holland, while the South was settled by herders at the edges of Britain. Because herds can be stolen in a way that crops cannot, herders must be willing to act decisively—typically aggressively—as a display to potential threats to their herd.

In one series of experiments, northern and southern subjects were asked to fill out a demographic questionnaire and to take the questionnaire to a table at the end of a long, narrow hall. As part of the experiment, a person (a confederate of the experimenters) at a filing cabinet blocked the subject's passage and had to push the cabinet drawer in to allow the subject to get by. As the subject tried to squeeze by on the way back (the confederate had just reopened the drawer), the confederate would slam it shut, bump the subject on the shoulder, and call him "asshole." After they returned to the designated room, subjects had saliva samples taken. Cortisol and testosterone hormone levels, both associated with preparation for aggression, were higher after the bump than before the bump for all subjects, though, as predicted, the change was greater for insulted southerners than for subjects in all of the other conditions.

These sorts of results, however, are explicable only if we postulate mechanisms that connect physiological and social factors, and the above research describes an assortment of them. Notice that the cortisol level is taken to be a relatively unproblematic measure of aggressive preparation, and the integration implied by the use of this measure in social psychology can be rationalized only if we interpret the physiological postulates realistically. The latter are regarded as so theoretically well established that no one even tries to replicate the earlier studies purporting to establish those hormone levels as a valid measure of aggressive posture. In other areas of social psychology, the reliance on affiliated hypotheses is direct as well. The existence of evaluation apprehension and race-of-interviewer effects are theses of social psychology, and valid sociological and political research could scarcely be conducted without reliance on them. The affective mechanisms that mediate embarrassment are causally related to the dispositions that underlie honest reports of political and social attitudes. Because attitudes are largely the consequence of social cultivation, this research treats those reports as indicative of the enduring traits wrought by the influences of social class or political affiliation.

Integration of Economics and History

Little imagination is required to see how historical inquiry is integrated with the mechanisms of affiliated disciplines. Many economic, climatic, and agricultural conditions are so potent that they have profound, easily detectable effects in history. During the Reformation, the rise of capitalism was occasioned in part by the tightening of labor. Scarcity of labor was caused by a general reduction in the population of Europe, and this reduction was caused by the plague (Nauert 1977). Such joint applications, as mentioned before, increase the deductive observational consequences of a theory. For example, once we know that the disease in question (the plague) is contagious, and the character of the contagion, we can predict the course that the disease will take, in light of migratory patterns. As a result (other things being equal), we would anticipate a related pattern of scarcity in labor markets if the disease in question is contagious.

This is integration of information, fair enough; but why is any of this theoretical integration? In the first place, many of these historical phenomena are unobserved, even if not unobservable. In the second place, many of the mechanisms invoked to provide a deep explanation for observed patterns are unobservable. The bacterial transmitters of the plague were unobservable, but we now have an account of how their dispositions (along with the environmental conditions that happened to compromise the population by famine in the 1300s) explain the distributional features of the epidemic.

Integration of Social Psychology and Political Science

The use of social psychology in political science research is illustrated clearly in the substantial political science research discussed above. Subjects are interviewed about their feelings of political efficacy. For this research, political scientists deploy theoretical assumptions of social psychology concerning the mechanisms that affect honest report, the social variables that are most likely to intrude in the interview setting. So it is not just that nonreactive methods must be used but that what tells us that a particular method is nonreactive is an articulated theory about the relevant cognitive and affective theory.

But not all research in political science depends upon the report of attitudes. Indeed, some research on voter turnout shuns it (Piven and Cloward 1988). It is true that much of the political science literature that offers various alternative explanations for voter turnout deploys psychological and sociological assumptions. However, these assumptions sometimes identify variables that are not relevant to political structure or subject tasks in political research, even if they are occasionally treated as such in the literature. For example, Piven and Cloward argue that education is not an attitudinal variable, so the relation between education and turnout must be explained by means other than merely the attitudes of voters. Presenting voter turnout data, Piven and Cloward argue that electoral competition forces candidates to court the middle- and upper-class vote and electoral rules make it difficult for lower-class people to vote. Such influences militate against whatever potency attitudinal variables such as motivation might have.

Notice, however, that this theoretical decision disjoining voter turnout and attitude could not be justified were there not a social-psychological account of attitudes that provide the basis for the judgment that they do not interact richly with
voter turnout factors.[14]

Integration of Economics and Sociology

Sociology is rife with functional explanations, accounts of social mechanisms
whose presence or maintenance is said to be explained by the function they serve.
The system of inheritance, for example, is often explained in terms of its effect of
further benefiting the dominant class, by keeping the wealth in the family. The
arrangement for the projection of this largess, along with the laws that allow it,
no doubt require some coordination. But they are not therefore conspiratorial
activities. Institutional analysis attempts to show how dominant social structures
can be preserved by the spontaneous agreement of interests of otherwise independent individuals or industries. In large industries dominated by a small number of
companies, such as the airline and oil industries, there is a remarkable agreement
in the cost of a nonstop flight from Chicago to San Francisco or in the cost of a
gallon of unleaded 87 octane fuel.

Although conspiracy or price fixing is sometimes a plausible explanation for
this remarkable consilience, explicit coordination is not required. In markets that
quickly disseminate information about supply and react rapidly to evidence of
demand, the going price of a good is a faithful representation of what the market
will bear. If we shift to the work force, Michael Reich (1981) argues that labor
markets can suppress wages by exploiting salient social factors such as racism.
Racism in the labor pool reduces cooperation among workers, making it difficult
for unions to bargain effectively. On this view, then, those who own companies
in the sector are the beneficiaries of racism in the market. Racism is not here
promoted by design but arises spontaneously from the congeries of affiliated mechanisms that favor it. The integration of sociology with political science and economics requires common mechanisms at the contacting borders of these disciplines. We have evidence of the causal-dependence characteristic of theoretical
integration when the result of political or economic research making use of the
reigning sociological concept of structure maintenance conduces to the identification of an observationally reliable theory.

The notion of independence developed in this chapter depends on the idea
that not just entities but laws as well are multiply discoverable and confirmable;
they are epistemically bite-sized. Unlike Hacking's extremely modest entity realism and Boyd's robust realism, measured realism is distinctive for its focus on laws.

---

14. Consider as well the theoretical integration represented in research on the social and cultural
traditions that serve to maintain specific political structures. Caste, religion, race, gender, urbanization,
and more influence political activities, and the quantitative methods described above aid in the detection and characterization of their causal influence and their magnitude. Bernstein and Dyer (1992)
contains a systematic presentation of the measurement of variables in political science.

Much more could be said about what laws are, and there is much misunderstanding about what laws must be like. I will not enter that dispute here. For the purposes of measured realism, laws are (approximately) true generalizations that are thought to hold in actual and at least mildly counterfactual circumstances. When social and psychological phenomena support taxonomic generalization, then they have a scale appropriate to make them epistemically accessible and so to form the natural unit of consensus. Similarly, laws are sufficiently independent from particular theories that people can be brought to agreement about the approximate truth of a theoretical law, whether or not the scientists in question share identical background theories.

The social and behavioral sciences advance such generalizations in abundance. What are these generalizations, and how are the objects of social and behavioral theories measured? In the next chapter, I will argue that these objects are detected, and their magnitudes estimated, by a stable physical structure known as a statistical design, which is in the respects relevant to measurement like a proper lab instrument. The improvement and calibration of statistical designs have realist implications. In addition to providing a naturalistic account of psychological measurement, the example of phonemic restoration in the next chapter will also serve as a concrete illustration of the confirmation of a theoretical law. The hypothesis tested—about speech processing—commits us to the existence of speech mechanisms detachable from the particular theory from which it was drawn.

PART II

Epistemological Naturalism and the Measurement of Intention

Statistical Designs
as Instruments

This chapter aims to provide a measured realist conception of statistical designs. They are, on any plausible interpretation, instruments of measurement. These instruments are best understood as detecting theoretical entities, particularly because improvements in design are guided by theoretical considerations. This chapter draws on designs from psychological research on the frequency effect and semantic priming in an attempt to reveal the implausibility of the competing empiricist analysis. As in the case of proper laboratory instrumentation, the calibration and improvement of statistical instruments harbor realist lessons: When improvement in the instrument does occur, it is in virtue of the sensitivity of the instrument to the entities. I then assess how this realist treatment of statistical design fares against empiricist alternatives and argue that they fail for the same reason the operationalist analysis of lab instrumentation failed: The instruments/ (designs) reflect, and scientists treat them as reflecting, sensitivity to real and unobservable causal features of the world. As an instance of a statistical instrument and subsequent refinement, I offer a t-test on speech perception data and show how the design has enjoyed theoretical improvement over time. I then turn to the more sophisticated empiricist work of Bas van Fraassen and contend that, although it may evade the above criticisms, it offers an unsatisfying account of the unification of theories and of the causal direction specified in theoretical models. In consequence, the empiricist rational reconstruction of experimental design can plausibly explain neither the operation of instruments of detection nor scientists' behavior with respect to them.

Epistemically Bite-Sized Theoretical Factors

The naturalism advanced in this book conceives of the methods of psychology as continuous with those of science generally. Whether modeled mathematically or causally, measurement is a central epistemic enterprise in science, and so the achievements of psychological measurement might be deemed an important source of evidence for naturalism in psychology. Measurement in the physical sciences requires instruments, causal arrangements of components that allow the scientist to systematically relate numbers to physical magnitudes. The theory of physical measurement has characterized the role of instruments in securing these achievements in physics, chemistry, and related fields, but at present theories of psychological measurement provide no correlative account of the means by which we relate numbers to psychological magnitudes.[1] Without such an account, it remains unclear how we are to explain the central successes of perceptual and cognitive measurement.

Some philosophers have doubted that there is progress in psychology, though these doubts are seldom accompanied by informed discussion of research in psychology. In the twentieth century, psychology has graced us with striking and secure generalizations that, as in physics, are taken to hold ceteris paribus. The internal mechanisms responsible for the execution of visual rotation tasks appear to follow the actual, mechanical constraints that govern external objects (Shepard and Metzler 1971; Shepard and Cooper 1982; Finke 1989). From studies in social psychology and associated disciplines, we know that people's responses to questions are often guided by their concern over impending evaluation, prompting such phenomena as race-of-interviewer effects and a host of related obtrusion-induced distortions (see, for example, Hatchett and Schuman 1975–1976). In cognitive psychology, we have determined that prototypes (or something very much like them) play a role in cognitive organization that is reflected in specific aspects of performance (Rosch 1975, 1978). This severely truncated list represents both an enormous store of knowledge and a distinct pattern of progress in psychology, despite its having had a shorter history than the natural sciences.

The details that follow are designed to reduce reliance on imagination as well. After all, without vivid description of causal mechanisms and the particulars of research design and analysis, reports of psychological and social research can have the air of fiction. We shall therefore examine the following sort of generalization,

---

1. There is a wealth of literature on psychological testing, a literature that draws liberally from notions of measurement. Much of this work is discussed in chapter 2. But theories of psychological testing and of psychological measurement seldom supply a systematic account of the relation between numbers and psychological magnitudes. One philosophical account can be found in Matthews (1994), who recruits an analogy between propositional-attitude predicates and measure predicates to advance a novel and plausible account of the former that is uncommitted to propositions as the "objects" of the attitudes. Though not directly concerned with instrumentation, Matthews's argument accords nicely with the naturalistic account of the means of psychological measurement developed in the present chapter.

either in the form of predictive or explanatory hypotheses. Consider the following local theoretical explanations of observed effects:

1. The frequency effect: Word entries in our mental lexicon are coded for frequency of occurrence, with the more frequent being more accessible to the mechanisms of search and retrieval.
2. The interaction of vision and semantic memory: Visual priming lowered the activation thresholds of nodes whose meaning is conceptually affiliated with the viewed object.
3. Cognitive dissonance: When counterattitudinal behavior gets well compensated (such as in payment), no change in attitude occurs, but when counterattitudinal behavior goes uncompensated, one's attitudes to the object becomes more agreeable, bringing them into conformity with the behavior.
4. Electoral politics: Reelection pressures tend to produce the largest proportion of shift in (expressed) ideology among American politicians in office.
5. Social stratification: In societies that are intensely socially stratified, there are cultural, religious, and economic mechanisms that maintain and increase the precise character of stratification.
6. Slave economy in U.S. history: Contrary to the traditional view of the causes of the end of the U.S. slave economy, according to which slavery was undermined by its own internal contradictions, slavery continued to be profitable, and from 1840 to 1860 the southern slave economy grew more rapidly than the nation as a whole.

These theoretical interpretations of social and psychological effects sound plausible enough, if a bit mysterious, perhaps in the way that Boyle's atomistic explanations sounded to his contemporaries. Such mystery is the natural consequence of abbreviation. But these statements clearly attempt to address issues of causal primacy. These are the sorts of generalizations that get projected and confirmed in the psychological sciences. It is possible to confirm them because the unobserved dispositions or tendencies expressed are robust and stable enough relative to the instrumentation to be measured. True, the characterizations of these tendencies are incomplete.

I will contend that statistical designs as used in psychology are literally instruments of measurement and that their reliable operation has important realist implications for our philosophical understanding of the objects of psychology. In particular, psychological properties are measured by statistical designs. Statistical methods such as factor analysis are sometimes fancifully described as instruments of discovery or search, but that image of instrumentation has remained an arrested metaphor; the similarities between statistical designs and proper laboratory instruments have not been seriously explored.[2]

---

2. The first reference to the idea of statistical designs as instruments of measurement—at least the first one that I am aware of—can be found in Webb et al. (1966). The reference is metaphorical, but it is there. Since then, it has recurred in Mulaik (1985, 1991) and is taken more seriously in Baird (1987, 1992).

By advancing the claim that statistical designs are instruments whose reliability demands a realist explanation, this chapter invites many opponents. Antirealists may object to the reliance on abduction or to the realist interpretation of psychological measurement. Antinaturalists may resist the assimilation of psychological measurement to measurement generally or resist the idea that our intentional states, primitive or not, can be measured in any illuminating sense.

These objections are worth addressing in detail, but I will attempt no such comprehensive treatment here. Instead, I will broadly outline an unassuming realist account of statistical designs as instruments of measurement. I shall begin by setting out the standard operationalist conception of instrumentation and theoretical measurement and then show how at least a modest version of realism is required to provide an adequate explanation of improvements in measurement, in the absence of any consistent alternative empiricist account of measurement that will explain such refinements. The third section elucidates the concept of a statistical design and establishes that, according to the canonical treatment of scientific measurement and instrumentation, there is no reason to deny statistical designs the status of instruments. The next section illustrates the sense in which a local piece of theory is epistemically bite-sized and how such local theoretical structure can be assimilated by two distinct theories that nevertheless agree about basic issues in the field. The following section provides a detailed analysis of a representative statistical design, in this case used to study the psycholinguistic phenomenon of phonemic restoration, and the penultimate section shows how empiricist alternatives to operationalism prove inadequate as an account of the improvement of instrumentation. The resulting realist analysis of statistical instruments forms the basis of a naturalistic approach to psychological measurement.

Operationalism and Instruments of Measurement

Sophisticated and sensitive instrumentation is responsible for much of the experimental success in the mature sciences, and this fact is part of the experimental realist's point in drawing attention to the antioperationalist insight lost for a generation: Reliable instrument design harbors realist presuppositions. The calibration and improvement of detection and measurement procedures can be adequately explained only if we treat the instrument as responding selectively to a real, unobservable causal factor of which we have knowledge.[3]

A simple and undesigning view holds that detection and measurement, together with calibration and increased precision, consist in a causal relation be-

---

3. As the stock of case studies of experimental measurement grows, so too does the impression that the mature, natural sciences of physics, chemistry, and biology have evidential sovereignty over the behavioral sciences. The cyclotron (Giere 1988), the polarizing electron gun (Hacking 1983), electrophoresis techniques (Jardine 1986), and the cloud chamber (Galison 1987) are all recruited in arguments for the existence of electrons, protons, and polypeptides and for the claim that we have knowledge of their character. Nowhere is it even suggested that this manipulability argument can be extended to the instruments of measurement in the psychological sciences, let alone the social sciences.

tween an instrument and the quantity or thing measured. Along with this simple view of measurement goes a simple and general account of instrumentation. Instruments are whatever we use to measure quantities or properties and whatever we employ to refine and extend the human faculties. Instrument theory compiles and explores the physical and mathematical principles that ground the operation of instruments. As we will see, when used to explain the successful operation of instruments, this account of measurement embodies a realist view: Our knowledge allows us to design an instrument that detects an unobservable quantity and allows us to improve the instrument's ability to measure the real value of that quantity.[4] On this view, the instrument respects no observable/unobservable distinction; some of the things an instrument measures are big enough for us to see, hear, or sense by the other modalities and others are not.

On the operationalist reconstruction of measurement practice, the definition of such theoretical terms as "pH" is given by the set of (observable) laboratory procedures associated with determining pH. The empiricist therefore seeks to reconstitute initially theoretical claims such as "The pH of this solution is 2.3" as a claim entirely about observables, in this case, "If operation O is performed at time t, the result will be R," where O is the observable laboratory procedure and R is the (observable) meter reading. But operationalism could not account for perhaps the most central feature of laboratory practice: Scientists routinely revise measurement procedures, and these revisions are normally introduced to improve the accuracy or extend the application of the instrument. Because these revisions constitute changes in observable operations, according to the empiricist they must reflect a change in what (in this case) "pH" refers to: for each new type of procedure, a different type of quantity. But scientists clearly take themselves to be measuring the same quantity, and the substantial continuity of their measuring procedures appears to vindicate this supposition. So, when applied to an instrument as familiar and well understood as a pH meter, the operationalist account of measurement, squarely within the logical empiricist tradition, supplied a disappointingly misleading account of scientific practice.

From the realist perspective of unreconstructed scientific practice, a pH meter is thought to measure an unobservable property: the concentration of hydrogen ion in a solution. The term "pH" is then thought to refer to this unobservable quantity. This ungarnished account is openly metaphysical. The realist account that replaced operationalism, then, treated the introduction of new procedures in exactly the way that scientists seemed to—as new ways of measuring the same quantities identified by earlier procedures, now improved in response to the instrument's increasing sensitivity to unobservable features of these magnitudes (Byerly and Lazara 1973). The impressive pace and character of the developments in the natural sciences, particularly the fashioning of sophisticated instruments,

---

4. In fact, Gigerenzer (1987) argues that respect for this distinction between true and measured value, already well entrenched in the natural sciences, is one of two chief contributions that statistical methods made to standards of objectivity in psychology. "Probabilistic thinking" achieves this aim by a theory of error, according to which errors for individual measurements cluster around a "true" value.

seemed to warrant the realist claim of theoretical improvement in measurement procedures.

Unfortunately, similar warrant could not be found in the behavioral and social sciences, where progress had been noticeably more modest. It is for this reason, and no doubt due to our comparatively poorly articulated account of psychological and social causation, that operationalist (or at any rate, distinctly empiricist) analyses of social and psychological measurement linger. For example, consider the description of measurement advanced in one of the most widely used and representative textbooks on social research:

> [W]e *can* measure anything that is real. We can measure, for example, whether Pat actually puts the little bird back in its nest, visits the hospital on Christmas, weeps at the movie, or refuses to contribute to saving the whales. All of those things exist, so we can measure them. But is Pat really compassionate? We can't answer that question, we can't measure compassion in that sense, because compassion doesn't exist in the way those things I just described exist. (Babbie 1992, p. 117)

What, then, is it about those "real" things that allows them to be measured? What distinguishes compassion from those behaviors we associate with compassion? Here it is suggested that those "real" things, those things that can be measured, are observable: "*Compassion* as a *term* does exist. We can measure the number of letters it contains and agree that there are ten. We can agree that it has three syllables and that it begins with the letter C. In short, we can measure those aspects of it that are real" (p. 117). Indeed, although the author at first seems to suggest that some aspects of our internal states are real, he then identifies the question of what the term "compassion" means with what is real and judges the reality of the items in terms of observability or verification conditions:

> Some aspects of our conceptions are real also. Whether you have a mental image associated with the term *compassion* is real. When an elementary school teacher asks a class how many know what *compassion* means, those who raise their hands can be counted. The presence of particular entries on the sheets bearing a given label is also real, and that can be measured. We could measure how many people do or do not associate giving money to save the whales with their conception of compassion. About the only thing we cannot measure is what compassion really means, because compassion isn't real. Compassion exists only in the form of the agreements we have about how to use the term in communicating about things that are real. (p. 117)

By itself, it is an innocent idea that observation is an important activity in science. But in this passage from Babbie the idea receives an austere empiricist, if not outright operationalist, treatment.[5] Even in more foundational work on behavioral measurement, the epistemic significance of the observed/unobserved distinction is enforced, particularly

---

5. A passage like the one of Babbie's quoted here can be found in almost any textbook on psychological and social research. These accounts of theoretical definition and measurement have their roots in such early classics as Cronbach and Meehl (1955).

when someone thinks it is important to develop a measure of a psychological property of individuals for which, in fact, there is no real-world measure (criterion).
Mental abilities such as general intelligence, mechanical aptitude, and spatial relations; and personality characteristics such as sociability, dominance, the need for
achievement, and introversion fall in this category. Since such things are hypothe-
sized to exist, but have no direct real-world counterpart (That's why they are *hypoth-
esized* to exist!), the variables in question are called constructs. (Ghiselli, Campbell,
and Zedeck 1981, p. 280)

Philosophers may claim to be less prone than psychologists to the sort of crude
operationalism above, but philosophers have not been quick to provide a more
apt theory of measurement in psychology. There may be nonphilosophical reasons
for this delay. The accounts that died in the physical sciences may have lingered
in the behavioral and social sciences because the latter have no clear conditions
for the improvement of measurement and detection procedures. Fortunately, we
now possess an archetype of an instrument of social and behavioral measurement—the statistical design—that, like the pH meter, detects unobservables and
improves in light of theoretical information.

Statistical Designs as Instruments

Ordinarily, we conceive of instruments as cold, hard and metal. But this conception is unduly restrictive. Although our concept of an instrument is certainly not
perfectly welldefined, the notion of a statistical design finds a comfortable place
within the general theory of instrumentation.

As we saw in chapter 2, an instrument is any device that connects a specific
number to a measurand or property of a physical configuration (for an elaboration
of the theory, see Bottaccini 1975). The physical configuration is the object, subject matter, or body of material—the population, if you like—that possesses the
property on which a series of measurements will be made. If you are measuring
pH, then the physical configuration is the liquid. When the instrument makes a
measurement on a property, it yields a number—the measurent—that reflects an
estimate of the magnitude of that property. There is a difference, of course, between the measurand and the results of a particular measurement—the difference
between the measurand's observed and expected value. The expected value of a
parameter is the value that we would expect to get on an "unlimited" number of
samplings. Suppose we have a population whose mean μ we know and that we
randomly draw a sample from that population. We would expect that this sample
mean from the first drawing would be fairly close to the population mean, especially if the sample size N is large. We would expect the same to be true for
repeated samplings. Under an unlimited number of random samplings of the population, we would expect that the average of the sample means would be exactly
equal to the population mean. The expected value of the population mean is the
average of the (unlimited) sample means. An estimator is unbiased if its expected
value is equal to the parameter that we are estimating. An optimal instrument is

one whose samplings yield estimates that have the statistical property of unbiasedness.[6]

According to this general account, an instrument is composed of elements (e.g., subassemblies, each of which is isolable as a possible source of measurement error), themselves made of even smaller parts or components. The blueprint of an instrument, designating an instrument type, can be characterized abstractly, as an object relating dimensions of the hypothetical configuration or population to measurents. The act of detection, measurement, and calibration must be analyzed in terms of the influence that the physical configuration has on the instrument; these processes occur via actual episodes of causal interaction between tokens or instances of statistical instruments and particular states of the physical configuration. Instances of a design are realizations of abstract plans.

The distinctive feature of a statistical design is that it crosses or combines factors of statistical test and experimental design. A statistical design may combine, for example, an analysis-of-variance test with a repeated-measures design, or a t-test with and independent-samples design, and so on. And like other instruments of experimentation, statistical instruments have an associated reliability estimate for a proprietary population, as well as a source of measurement error; they are subject to the effects of random error, can be modified for special or novel purposes, and can be refined and improved in light of new evidence (particularly from associated domains). As they are normally understood, true statistical designs involve a population of a certain description (the configuration to be measured), a sample or subset of that population, and a treatment to which members of the sample are subjected. This treatment yields a value for each subject based on his or her performance (or the "outcome"), and, as one might have expected, the optimal statistical design is one that employs a sample statistic that is an unbiased estimator of the relevant population parameter.

The fact that statistical designs are subject to, and capable of estimating the value of, sampling error is not peculiar to statistical technique. We will get a different measurement each time we apply a ruler to the same line. But if we measure the line enough times, we will find that the measurements cluster around a mean measurement value. The same goes each additional time we place the same rock sample in a magnetometer, a pH probe in the same liquid, or the same sample in a gas chromatograph. In these respects, statistical designs are like laboratory instruments. In cases where inferential (as opposed to merely descriptive) statistical methods are employed so that causal claims can be supported, the

---

6. Though unbiasedness is the most important property of an instrument in this context, its (statistical) efficiency may also be desirable. The sample mean is a more efficient estimator of the population mean μ than another statistic, if, under repeated samplings, the sample means cluster more closely to the population mean than do the sample medians. The clearest way to express this point is in terms of standard deviations. For example, the sample mean is a more efficient estimator of the population mean than is the sample median because, if we drew many samples from the population, the sample means would have a smaller standard deviation than sample medians. Circumstances under which unbiasedness and efficiency can conflict need not be addressed here.

mean measurement value typically represents the central tendency arising from an enduring causal disposition inhering in the objects being measured.[7]

Objections to this strategy of assimilation run from the technical to the banal. I now want to address three objections to the literal interpretation of the claim that statistical designs are instruments. These objections, I believe, have some intuitive appeal, and they ground many impressionistic conceptions of what is required for reliable and valid measurement. My brief treatment of them is designed to match their relatively impressionistic nature.

First, the distributed character of statistical instruments might be thought to generate a decisive disanalogy with proper laboratory instruments. But once we recognize that instruments often have separable components, their spatial distribution is an incidental fact. Experimental physics gives us some familiar instruments, such as linear accelerators, whose parts are distributed. Statistical instruments too are distributed; the members of the human sample aren't all in one place. The feature that is essential to their status as instruments is that the parts bear determinate causal relations to one another, as well as to the things they measure.

The second objection turns on apparent differences in the respective causal engagements of lab and statistical instruments. When proper lab instruments measure the desired object, they are, at the time of their operation, engaging causally with objects in the measured domain. Not so in certain central applications of statistical design, for some statistical designs are used to analyze historical data, representing causal influences that have long ago perished.

What matters for the antioperationalist argument is that the instrument's reliability be most naturally explicable in terms of its appropriate causal relations to the measured magnitudes or quantities, not that it be currently engaging them. As long as the values assigned to historical kinds are accurate (that is, there is an appropriate relation between the historical circumstances and the values we currently assign), by engaging tokens of those remnant values the statistical design is causally engaged with those historical conditions. The same kind of indirect causal relationship exists between some instruments in physics and the objects measured. The daughter element in a rock sample is a historical remnant of the parent element. When a spectrometer detects a certain amount of daughter element in a rock sample, it allows us, indirectly, to determine the original amount of parent element—but it does so by first causally engaging the historical traces or product currently in that archaic rock. So long as the present product bears an appropriate causal relation to the archaic values, statistical designs used to analyze historical data can be regarded as instruments of measurement.

7. It is important to distinguish statistical methods used for the purposes of mere description—to observe the distribution of characteristics in the sample—from those used for the purposes of causal/statistical inference. For just two sorts of embarrassment that result when causal inferences are drawn on the basis of descriptive statistics, see Keverberg's 1827 letter concerning Quetelet, quoted in Stigler (1986, p. 165), and Claude Bernard's mocking remarks about the analysis of the "*average* European urine" (Bernard 1957, foreword).

Finally, one might raise the related worry that some statistical designs, especially those used in demographic and socioeconomic research, are post hoc or quasi-experimental. If the assimilation strategy defended here governs statistical designs generally, then post hoc or quasi-experimental designs are instruments, and this seems peculiar. After all, in post hoc designs no treatment is introduced, and we do not introduce the relevant controls in an effort to unwind otherwise confounded causal influences; the data analyzed are data gathered without an experimenter's intervention.

True designs differ in important ways from post hoc or quasi-experimental designs. The latter designs do form a special class, but sometimes we recruit parts of the natural, uncontrolled environment as components of a proper instrument, as when we allow errors known to have opposing value and equal magnitude to harmlessly conflict. So long as this objection is not based on the radically skeptical view that theoretical knowledge is impossible, the assimilation strategy is defensible, for then the question is not whether we can ever extract causal information from this sort of correlation data. Path analysis and associated structural equation approaches provide systematic methods for teasing out subtle causal dependencies of this post hoc sort (see Glymour et al. 1987). When the post hoc analysis correctly isolates a causal nexus responsible for correlations, we can assimilate the post hoc design to a proper instrument and measure properties of an unsampled population. These points of assimilation therefore hold for both true experimental and post hoc or quasi-experimental designs.

Certain human artifacts that we perhaps would not call instruments may be used for the purposes of measurement. The point I have made is not one about ordinary language. Many, if not most, of the features that we regard as crucial to the reliability of proper instrumentation are shared by statistical designs. I claim only that the analogy is good enough to enable us to formulate a plausible and modest abductive argument against an operationalist account of psychological measurement of the sort successfully advanced against operationalist accounts of physical measurement.[8]

---

8. The characterization of statistical designs as instruments suggests a certain kind of rigor that some might find misleading. For example, statistical designs, in application, don't typically look at relevant factors that experimenters are averaging across; some instances might assume no difference between distractors in reaction-time experiments. But, it is implied, the sleek instruments of chemistry and physics, such as pH meters, do make such discriminations and guarantees or at least are based on experiments that establish the "negligible effect" hypothesis. There is a straightforward reply to this concern. Often, such negligible-effect hypotheses are not independently established in the phyiscal sciences either, and so this worry has creeping effects, threatening the validity and reliability of core areas of physics and chemistry. It is unlikely that engineers responsible for pH meter design have excluded the hypothesis that there is a difference between Pyrex and other glass beakers (in which a solution is held). It is enough that there is no special theoretical reason to suppose that there is a difference.

Another worry arises at this point: In the psycholinguistics examples used here, isn't there a worry about the validity of generalizations, as with so many university-sponsored social and behavioral research? The class and economic background of student subjects may be systematically different from those of the general language-using population—in this case affecting such linguistic factors as vocabu-

One of the most obvious and important ways instruments get improved is through the introduction and incorporation of controls.[9] This process increases the instrument's sensitivity to the measured variable and thus decreases the likelihood of confounding two causal factors with one. When this disambiguation occurs, the case can be made that this theoretical refinement constitutes an improvement.[10] If we can find such cases of improvement in the behavioral sciences, then we have a prima facie case for realism about the putative objects of measurement.

Manipulation by Law

Cognitive and perceptual psychology provides a variation on the entity realist's argument and a clear rationale for antioperationalist sentiment in the behavioral sciences. In psycholinguistic studies of lexical decision and lexical access—respectively, the processes by which a string of letters is identified as a word and by which the word is retrieved from our lexical memory—some words are made more "accessible" by having been first activated or "primed" prior to the execution of the task. Often, sentence context is used to prime a lexically encoded item. In one prominent study (Swinney 1979), subjects listened to the following passage:

> For years the government building had been plagued with problems. The man was not surprised when he found several spiders, roaches, and other bugs in the corner of his room.

Immediately following the word "bugs," three letters would appear on the screen and the subject would be asked, "Is this a word?" In light of the content of the passage, subjects responded to the semantically related "ant" faster than they did to the word "sew."[11] This effect of semantic facilitation has been replicated many

---

lary. This would be a concern, I believe, were the research generalizing about the vocabulary of people's lexicons. But we are generalizing about psycholinguistic mechanisms, and so it shouldn't be a serious representativeness problem that a substantial body of psycholinguistics experiments is run on college students; their speech mechanisms should be no different from those of the general population, even if the contents of their lexicons are. (I owe consideration of these points to a discussion with Robyn Dawes.)

9. When an artifact is inevitable given the experimental conditions, the best we can do is remain vigilant. This dictum applies to social research using large samples, for a large enough sample can ensure an effect reaching significance. Schuman, Steeh, and Bobo (1988, p. 56) takes great care to reduce the likelihood of such sample size effects. They consider the effects of potentially intrusive measures (p. 66) and introduce a clever method to ensure that a curvilinear trend is not a ceiling effect (p. 220).

10. The epistemological and semantic basis for this realist approach has already been outlined in the literature. The notions of confounding, disambiguation, calibration, and theoretical refinement expressed here have familiar analogs in Boyd (1979, 1981); Devitt (1981, 1991); Field (1973, 1974); Jardine (1986), Kitcher (1978, 1993), and Putnam (1973).

11. The most astonishing result of this particular study is now known as the Swinney effect: In the context in which "bugs" clearly relates to insects, subjects responded to "spy" as quickly as they did to "ant." Further research (cited below) has extended this effect, showing that the presentation of a word *routinely* activates utterly irrelevant meanings.

times over in related research; typically, the lexically encoded item is manipulated by priming it, all in the service of investigating some other (to use Hacking's term) "more hypothetical" process such as lexical access, naming, recognition, classification, and so forth (see, for example, Seidenberg et al. 1982; Friedrich, Henik, and Tzelgov 1991). The otherwise diverse theoretical models invoked to characterize lexical processes agree in considerable detail about the causal powers of these lexical units—how far activation due to priming will spread, the rate at which the activation of a lexical unit will decay, how much of the benefit of priming accrues to the pre-access, and how much to the post-access, stage of processing, and so on. Any review (for instance, Frauenfelder and Tyler 1987, as well as the entire volume in which that paper occurs) will summarize the fundamental consensus concerning the nature of these lexical units, along with the influence that priming has on them.[12] And as far as I'm concerned, if you can prime them, then they are real.

Lexical accessibility is also affected by the frequency with which the word occurs in the particular language (Forster 1976), and the efforts to control for the effects of this influence support the realist interpretation of statistical designs. By introducing a delay between the presentation of the word and the time at which the subject responds, Balota and Chumbley (1984) reasoned that we could isolate and control the influence of frequency on lexical access: Access would have already occurred during the delay. Any further performance differences between high and low-frequency words must derive from post-access mechanisms. To assess the impact of frequency information on each post-access stage of processing, the researcher must devise a design to determine the relative impact of frequency information on the otherwise indistinguishable sources: lexical access and post-access processing.

McRae, Jared, and Seidenberg (1990) also control for post-access influences, allowing us to determine the separate contribution of frequency information. For instance, homophonic high–low frequency word pairs (such as "main"/"mane"), high–low frequency rhymes (such as "cold"/"fold"), and word-pseudoword homophones (such as "scam"/"skam") were used. Although frequency differs, the word pairs are matched for other characteristics known to be relevant to lexical processing, such as word length. It is a better design for having controlled for the effects of word length, because word length interacts systematically with reaction time.

Later in this chapter, I will consider a systematic (constructive) empiricist alternative to this realist interpretation of the experimental setting. But it is worth addressing more generic, less systematic empiricist worries as well. These worries will not necessarily raise doubts about whether improvement in design reflects

---

12. Therefore it would be a mistake to suppose that the postulated entities of contemporary psycholinguistics are not deserving of a realist interpretation just because the literature contains alternative explanations of these psycholinguistic phenomena. Seidenberg and McClelland (1989) provides a nice comparison of serial/register and connectionist approaches to frequency and priming.

empirical progress in psychology, but they will deny that such progress warrants claims of theoretical knowledge. An empiricist might charge, for example, that the above realist understanding of psychological measurement and manipulation runs together two different claims about such experimental contexts: (1) the manipulation of observable factors such as sentence context and word frequency can systematically facilitate the speed with which a string of letters is identified as a word, and (2) this effect occurs via manipulation of some particular internal hypothetical process having to do with lexical access. Only the second claim warrants theoretical commitment to particular unobservable states. One might concede that, although it is extremely plausible that some internal state or other of the subject is affected by the experimental treatment, the above experimental scenario fails to provide good evidence for the reality of the particular internal states postulated by some specific psychological theory; therefore we have support for (1) but not (2).

The primary contention behind this empiricist distinction is that the particular hypothetical internal state is not described by the theory in detail sufficient to warrant a claim of theoretical knowledge. Instead, on this view some internal state or other is assigned some loosely defined function. A battery of realist arguments fights this empiricist distinction; in particular, this empiricist contention radically underestimates the quality of theoretical warrant psychologists possess for the existence of the internal states they postulate.

In addition to the manipulation of lexical encodings, consider the experimental research on visual imagery. If there is any residual worry that we can have at least modest, inexact knowledge of particular unobservable psychological states, we might appeal to the now-accumulated evidence that there is a specific neural basis for particular postulated psychological states. Early research on mental imagery, for example, documented that reaction time on mental image rotation tasks was a rough linear function of the angular disparity between two pictures to be judged for congruity (Shepard and Cooper 1982). And although researchers always showed interest in the possible bearing of neurological evidence on facts of performance (see Farah 1984), at the time no specific neural hypotheses were advanced. But the neurological evidence now suggests that the same unobserved internal mechanisms responsible for perceptual responses to real translatory motion of rigid objects in the environment are activated by image rotation tasks (see Kosslyn and Koenig 1992, especially chapter 4). Appeal to internally represented imagistic phenomena has allowed us to predict effects from tasks involving problem solving, cerebral lateralization, and clinical neural disfunction, to name just a few. Moreover, we have not just predictive success in this domain but explanatory integration as well. The concept of an internal imagistic representation (whose properties depict and preserve actual kinematic relations in the environment) plays an explanatory role, and its explanatory integrity gets tested each time it has been used by scientists in generating new experiments on, and explanations for, diverse phenomena in psychology, neuroscience, and brain anatomy. So it is clear that here, as in psycholinguistics and nearly every other corner of psychology, scientists make essential appeal to unobservables.

How, then, can one manage to raise doubts about the kind of modest theoretical knowledge of internal states that such psycholinguistic and imagistic scenarios suggest? The empiricist distinction between (1) and (2) achieves initial plausibility first by directing attention to the observable parameters that are manipulated and contrasting the perceptual salience of those parameters with the obscurity of features associated with theoretical descriptions of lexical encodings. The realist reply to this reasonable concern over obscurity comes in two steps. First, although the manipulation of sentence context and word frequency is perceptually salient and thus obvious, that fact should not be taken to imply that only observable properties are manipulated in an informed way. After all, no one supposes that only observable properties are manipulated in a linear accelerator, even though observable factors are undeniably being manipulated. The assumption that we have warrant for theoretical claims about proton manipulation but not about the mechanisms of lexical priming turns on the relative difference in the detail with which the respective theoretical descriptions can be articulated in predictions and explanations.

This impression that the evidential warrant for theoretical commitments in psychology is hopelessly vague or abstract is abetted by the recognition that psycholinguistic paradigms often do not offer severe tests of highly specific hypotheses. In some cases, the reasons in psychology are no different from those in physics. The validity of a design may depend on the existence of certain further postulated unobservable entities, but the design may provide no pertinent test of the existence of those entities or the character of those theories. In physics, for example, two different theories may embody different commitments concerning specific unobservables, as late nineteenth-century physicists did about the charge of the electron, even though they agreed that the molecules containing them were roughly spherical and engaged in elastic collisions. To manipulate or otherwise make use of the elastic properties of molecular collisions, all you have to do is assume that the kinetic theory is roughly right; you needn't have the correct and fully articulated theory of the molecule.

Similarly in present-day psycholinguistics. The scenario described above may test different theories (such as serial and connectionist accounts) about the various consequences of lexical access and priming. These alternative theories, however, agree about the nature of some of the fundamental theoretical mechanisms of lexical processing—for example, that lexical encodings store semantic information, that priming makes the information of the relevant node more accessible (by lowering thresholds) to semantically related encodings, that the priming of these nodes yields a determinate decay rate, and so forth. We should not allow the fact that our tests are now more severe, and that our increasingly accurate knowledge is now codified in a reliable theoretical tradition, blind us to the fact that these claims constitute secure theoretical commitments that, years ago, were regarded as substantial, sometimes surprising additions to our theoretical inventory.

A number of points fall out of this impressionistic realist reply. First, if we permit that late nineteenth-century physicists had some approximate theoretical knowledge of the nature of electrons, it is implausible to raise special concerns about the warrant for theoretical postulates in contemporary psychology. Second, an experimental setting may provide ample evidence of the existence of particular unobservable mechanisms without constituting a relevant test of that unobservable, as shown by the common kinetic commitments of competing corpuscular theories. Third, complete theoretical knowledge of these particular internal mechanisms is not required for their manipulation. In short, then, different theories may manipulate unobservables with respect to general properties that both theories agree about and that each theory specifies only incompletely. The empiricist denies this understanding of routine scientific practice at the expense of either assuming the burden of a reconstruction that would eradicate all appearance of theoretical commitment from scientific practice and its history or abandoning a reading of the history of physical science as continuous and empirically progressive.

If we advance for the moment to the specific case of psychology, we might find warrant for a modest realism in the converging evidence of particular internal mechanisms responsible for similar performance on diverse observational tasks (e.g., naming, key pressing, eye fixation, etc.). If we consider the phenomena alone, it is puzzling that tasks that implicate such different motor functions, and are so differently invested in perceptual, attentional, and memory processes, should yield similar observational performance. Such convergence would seem to require an explanation. But what is the best explanation for the correlation in performance on diverse tasks? Eschewing commitment to particular internal, unobservable states, empiricists must take these experiment-induced correlations as an irreducible fact, even if they can say that the manipulation of one observable parameter affects the behavior of another. But the realist has an explanation. At some stage of processing, these diverse tasks implicate common, internal states whose specific character constrains performance.

This realist answer might be less persuasive if explanatory considerations alone supported it. But as it happens, this realist explanation comports with good methodology as well. In designing their experiments, psychologists don't assume that reaction time measures an observed tendency to respond more quickly and felicitously to high-frequency words. Instead, experimenters recognize that a variety of other factors can induce comparably quick and accurate performance—even on low-frequency words. An austere empiricist might contend that observational features can still distinguish performance on high- and low-frequency words, because different observational parameters must be manipulated to prompt fast and accurate responses to low-frequency words. But this rejoinder only invites the question of what is relevantly different between observational contexts that will facilitate reaction time and correct lexical recognition and those that don't. If we don't explain this difference in terms of the operation of different internal mechanisms, then the reasons that some observational parameters, such as sentence context, can prompt low-frequency words to yield performance comparable to that for high-frequency words once again go unexplained. Similarly for the inhibitory influences that priming has on other selected aspects of performance (see, for example, Watkins and Allender 1987). For this reason, psychologists take reaction time to be measuring not observable performance but instead some properties of an internal, unobserved disposition.

The question of whether a particular theoretical commitment is legitimate will always be a question of the quality of evidential warrant.[13] To the extent that these realist arguments are abductive in structure, the patterns of inference they license are certainly fallible; there is always a generic skeptical position from which one could raise questions about warrant. However, approximate knowledge of these unobserved characteristics can survive these concerns because the actual reliability of theoretical commitments is compatible with manufactured, generic skeptical possibilities. Moreover, it is a centerpiece of naturalistic epistemology (which favors a descriptively accurate account of actual scientific practice over a rational reconstruction of it) that philosophers be entitled to the same reliable inference rules, such as appeal to particular unobservable internal mechanisms, as those employed by scientists.

Quite appropriately in this case, then, psychology imitates physics. The idea that statistical designs are instruments of measurement gives manipulability the limited significance it deserves; manipulation of the sort that Hacking describes is just one activity among many that can aid in the determination of a theoretical object's existence. According to the measured realist, detection, measurement, and manipulation are common and continuous epistemic categories.

The assimilation of manipulation to this continuous category will lead us to part ways with the standard experimental, or "entity" realist, position. The consistent realist will be forced to opt for a version stronger than Hacking's "experimental entity realist position"; for, we are able to build and modify manipulative instrumentation just to the extent that we have knowledge concerning the entities manipulated, detected, and measured. This apparent knowledge of the properties of these unobservables presumably consists in knowing true theoretical generalizations of the sort that opened this chapter. These true generalizations have all of the characteristics that are diagnostic of theoretical laws. Therefore, knowledge of entities (at least recognitional capacities impressive enough to guide instrument design) implies knowledge of laws. This is one of several ways in which entity realism proves excessively modest if you are after a descriptively accurate version of realism, and the Measured Realism articulated in chapter 4 indicates the form that realism should take when applied to the social and behavioral sciences. Moreover, I claimed that neither the entity realist nor the empiricist can ade-

---

13. There is an additional argument for realist commitment, distinct from any of those presented in this chapter. Appealing to the individual samples of digitized speech to which we are perceptually insensitive, I argued in chapter 4 that the manipulation of entities whose individual features, taken individually, have no observable effect on the things manipulated nevertheless have a cumulative effect that is observable. The only plausible explanation for this fact is that we really are manipulating unobserved properties of just the sort we proposed. It is not surprising that realism should have a variety of relatively independent arguments in its favor. If it is to be a descriptively accurate account of the reliability of scientific methodology, one would expect this reliability itself to be a robust phenomenon.

quately account for the success of theory conjunction. In the next two sections of the present chapter, this realist argument is recruited for theories that call for the use of statistical instruments. But how shall we test local, epistemically bite-sized pieces of theory?

One class of statistical instruments is defined by a *t* statistic and a related-samples design. The *t* test is a hypothesis testing device, and its purpose is to decide between the null hypothesis—that the treatment had no effect on perfor-mance—and a specific alternative hypothesis. The *t* test determines whether an experimental treatment (the independent variable) affects performance on a cer-tain task (the dependent variable) by examining differences between two groups, one exposed to the particular (level of) treatment, the other not. All other things being equal, the difference can be attributed to a combination of sampling error and the influence of the experimental treatment. In particular, *t* tests measure the size of the difference in the means of two samples. As a crude approximation, if the value of *t* is large, then there is a substantial difference between the sample means and, correlatively, a low probability that this variation occurred by chance. When the difference in sample means is great enough (as indicated on any statis-tics text *t*-distribution table), the null hypothesis is rejected. So when the null hypothesis is rejected, the specific alternative is confirmed.[14]

A Statistical Instrument in Action: Numerical Reflections of Psychological Magnitudes

How does a statistical design measure the properties of a specific object? A con-crete example will help here. One line of psycholinguistic research, specifically in the area of speech perception, concerns the question of how people are able to comprehend speech when the speech signal is so often degraded in natural envi-ronments. People modulate their voices, or change volume without changing dis-tance. Environmental noise such as traffic, construction, and other conversations often interferes with speech at the perceptual level, before the speech signal even has the opportunity to compete for cognitive resources. It is reasonable to suppose that the speech system is capable of compensating for both the natural variability and the poor quality of the incoming speech signal. One such relevant capability is reflected in phonemic restoration, a striking auditory illusion in which people report "hearing" a speech signal as intact even though the acoustic information for a phoneme has been replaced or obliterated by an extraneous sound. This restoration affords speech that is continuous and thus more comprehensible.

---

14. The literature contains arguments, unsuccessful in my view, attempting to show that scientists are wrong for inferring the confirmation of the alternative hypothesis from the rejection of the null. The flavor of my reaction can be conveyed by the following brief consideration: If null hypothesis tests do not support the alternative when the null is rejected, what possible rationale could a physicist provide for regarding his or her alternative as supported when an experimental manipulation produces a substantial difference from an outcome without a manipulation? Without special reason, we should not fault statistical tests in the behavioral sciences for displaying methodological tendencies whose presence would not be criticized in physics.

The discovery of phonemic restoration was by itself a significant accomplish-ment, but questions remain about the mental states or processes that underlie restoration. What features of speech, if any, facilitate or inhibit restoration? Are some speech sounds more restorable than others, and if so, why? We will, of course, want to know how potent a contribution each of these factors might make to the replacement of missing speech sounds as well. Voiced speech sounds, for example, have distinctive acoustic characteristics in virtue of being produced with the vocal chords vibrating. Voiceless speech sounds are produced without the vocal chords vibrating. Among the stop consonants, b, d, and g are voiced, and p, t, and k are voiceless. Stop consonants begin with a plosive burst of energy and spread broadly across the frequency spectrum. However, stop consonants can be classified according to their articulation as well: (b, p) are bilabial; (d, t) are alveolar, and (g, k) are velar. When combined with information about place of articulation, voicing information uniquely specifies each of the stop consonants. The vibration of the vocal chords for voiced stops produces a signal that is peri-odic—acoustically important components repeating themselves in regular pat-terns—and these periodic features are folded into the noisy burst characteristic of stops. By contrast, the voiceless stops are aperiodic. Given the irregular, aperiodic character of noise, one might expect that voiced speech sounds would be less restorable than voiceless speech sounds: Various sorts of background noise would be more like the voiceless speech sound it replaced or obliterated and so less detectable.

We can examine this question by preparing a physical arrangement that, while representative of natural speech situations, will allow us to isolate separate factors causally responsible for phonemic restoration. This physical arrangement satisfies all of the criteria for instrumentation set out earlier. In short, we can construct an experiment that makes use of a statistical design. Below, I provide the data that resulted from just such an investigation of the relation between voicing and phonemic restoration. The human subjects were assigned in such a way that they acted as their own controls, producing a related-samples design. A test of means would be sufficient for establishing a reliable difference in restoration between voiced and voiceless consonants, and so we can use a t statistic for the analysis of the data.

Like any experiment, this one requires careful and elaborate arrangements. In this case, we must prepare appropriate stimulus materials, present those stimuli to subjects with the aid of an experimenter or assistant, score materials, and do other tasks. The list of arrangements continues. The speakers must be native speakers of American English. They cannot have any history of hearing or speech disor-ders. The value of exposing each subject to many stimuli, and thus of increasing statistical power, must be balanced against the threatened distortions produced by subject fatigue. The reliability and validity of the statistical design—the measur-ing instrument—is secured by causal dependencies (elucidated by conditional de-pendencies) between having selected for the property of being a native speaker of American English and subjects' outcomes (owing to mental lexicons with a par-ticular sort of organization and corpus of entries).

If poorly enough understood or ignored altogether, these factors could operate in combination to obscure the evidence of any such capacity to restore missing speech sounds. The stimulus materials might have been improperly prepared, incorrectly presented to subjects, or presented to inappropriate subjects, responses might have been incorrectly recorded, or variables might have been inappropriately scaled. The size of the standard deviation of the difference will affect the sensitivity of the test. And S_D is affected by the magnitude and conflicting directions of differences. Moreover, the size and number of conflicting values are increased by permitting unknown and so uncontrolled sources of variation. I record this litany of components to portray how subtle a tissue is a statistical design.

One might argue that numbers (the performance scores) are operated on by the statistical design, so the relations are not causal in any relevant sense. But this move is no more plausible here than it was for empiricist interpretations of other measurement systems, for one could use the same considerations to show that pH meters are not causal in the pertinent sense, on the grounds that the pH meter operates on numbers too, an influence that explains the readout. But both are arguably causal because the numbers can be plausibly understood as representing and preserving relations among quantities or magnitudes.

The speech-perception experiment outlined above used the standard psychophysical measure of stimulus detectability, d', for phonemic restoration. Two versions of each stimulus word was created: one version in which white noise entirely replaces the critical phoneme and one in which the same noise is added to the original speech segment. The measure of detectability is determined by hits, misses, correct rejections, and false alarms. A hit is a correct report of a replaced item as replaced; a miss is an incorrect report of a replaced item as added. A correct rejection is a correct report of an added item as added, and a false alarm is an incorrect report of an added item as replaced.[15] Because this psychophysical paradigm requires that stimuli be created so that there is a determinate answer to the question of whether a particular stimulus is intact, we have an independent way of determining when the subject is correct in judging that there is speech behind the noise, or that there isn't. As a result we can tell whether the subject is experiencing perceptual restoration of the missing phoneme or whether the subject is simply heavily biased to answer "yes," independently of the character of the stimulus.

Until this methodological improvement, these responses were confounded. Early research on phonemic restoration (see Warren 1970, in which the phenomenon was first established) used a phoneme-monitoring task, in which subjects listened to a sentence containing a phoneme replaced by noise. Subjects were

---

15. See Samuel (1981) for the history and rationale for this improved procedure. On this design, the absence of speech is the signal, and so a hit is defined as the correct report of a replaced item as replaced. Misses, false alarms, and correct rejections are then defined accordingly. The standard treatment of signal-detection theory can be found in Green and Swets (1988; variants of the formula for calculating d' can be found in chapter 12 in that text). For an effective application of signal-detection theory to other issues in the philosophy of mind, see Godfrey-Smith (1991).

asked whether the sentence was intact and to locate on a separate sheet of paper the point in the sentence in which the noise occurred. Subjects reported "hearing" the phoneme that was in fact missing. Unfortunately, because the critical phoneme was always absent, when the subject answered "yes," misses could not be separated from false alarms, and so responses due to perceptual restoration could not be distinguished from those due to response bias.

With the improved design, we can test the hypothesis that voiceless stop consonants are less detectable in noise, and so more restorable, than voiced consonants. Accordingly, d' should be lower for voiceless than for voiced stops. Even eyeballing the scores in table 5.1, one can probably see that the voiceless scores tend to be lower than the voiced scores.[16] But there is natural variability in performance, both within and across individual subjects. So eyeballing is not sufficient for demonstrating significance; if these two sources of variability make a great enough contribution to the effect, then such a distribution could plausibly be the result of chance fluctuation, a fortuitous shuffling of the deck, rather than an effect of the treatment. Table 5.1 contains all of the values required to calculate t. We begin by calculating the standard deviation of the difference, S_D.

$$S_d = \sqrt{\frac{\Sigma D^2}{N} - \overline{D}^2} = \sqrt{\frac{18.82}{24} - (.67)^2} = .58$$

We can then substitute the values of the mean difference ($\overline{D}$), the standard deviation of the differences (S_D), and the sample size (N) in the following formula to determine $t_{(N-1)}$:

$$t_{N-1} = \frac{\overline{D}}{\dfrac{S_d}{\sqrt{N-1}}} = \frac{.67}{\dfrac{.58}{\sqrt{23}}} = \frac{.67}{.12} = 5.58$$

The t value is 5.58, making the effect significant at the $p = .0005$ level. This p level means that the probability that these results would occur (by sampling variation) if there is in fact no relevant difference between groups is less than .0005. So there is a significant difference in the degree of phonemic restoration, depending upon whether the speech sound in question is voiced or voiceless. But which receives the higher degrees of restoration? Recall that d is inversely related to restoration. If we examine the respective group means for V^+ and V^-, we can see that the voiceless speech sounds have a lower d' and so are more easily restorable—they achieve higher degrees of restoration—than their voiced counterparts.

What is being measured in this case is the strength of the unobserved dispositions or activity of mechanisms responsible for phonemic restoration. These may include priming, phonological and lexical encoding, and a host of other theoreti-

---

16. For ease of exposition, here the data will be analyzed using a t-test, though in the published study (Trout and Poser 1990)—which included more conditions than described here—an analysis of variance was used. The results easily reached significance on both tests.

TABLE 5.1 Summary and computation of the test of difference between means for correlated groups. (The values on this table represent the influence of voicing on phonemic restoration.)

S	V+	V−	D	D^2
1	3.36	1.94	1.42	2.02
2	3.00	2.30	0.70	0.49
3	0.47	−0.78	1.25	1.56
4	1.62	0.80	0.82	0.67
5	1.99	0.76	1.23	1.51
6	2.62	1.67	0.95	0.90
7	1.03	0.40	0.63	0.40
8	2.99	2.74	0.25	0.06
9	1.44	1.76	−0.32	0.10
10	1.39	0.87	0.52	0.27
11	1.85	1.60	0.25	0.06
12	2.05	1.85	0.20	0.04
13	1.25	1.50	−0.25	0.06
14	1.38	1.19	0.19	0.04
15	0.92	0.33	0.59	0.35
16	0.78	0.10	0.68	0.46
17	2.54	0.82	1.72	2.96
18	2.56	1.35	1.21	1.46
19	2.55	0.54	2.01	4.04
20	0.65	0.69	−0.04	0.00
21	2.34	1.87	0.47	0.22
22	1.94	1.13	0.81	0.66
23	1.51	1.40	0.11	0.01
24	0.28	−0.40	0.68	0.46
	Σv^+ 42.51	Σv^- 26.43	ΣD 16.08	ΣD^2 18.82

$(\bar{D}) = .67 \ (\Sigma D)^2 = 258.24$

For each subject (S), the d' scores for voiced (V$^+$) and voiceless (V$^-$) consonants are listed. The difference (D) between the two scores is calculated for each subject, and then the difference is squared (D^2).

cal properties described by psycholinguists and considered in the above experiment. Notice that, although we use observed performance—and the scores associated with it—in the measurement of phonemic restoration, the validity and reliability of this psychophysical measure (d') of phonemic restoration depends on having secured at least modest theoretical information about the unobserved dispositions giving rise to these performance scores.

Moreover, in terms of increased sensitivity, the psychophysical paradigm constitutes a clear improvement over the earlier, phoneme monitoring designs. Consider a parallel case in the history of physical chemistry. In 1909, Sorensen used an electromotive force (emf) method for determining hydrogen ion concentration in a liquid. Though dependent on Millikan's incomplete conception of the electron, Sorensen was able to express this factor as a quantity we now recognize as pH. As it happens, at the time there was little reason to suppose that pH readings would vary significantly with the temperature of the solution. But in fact they do.

Temperature affects both the hydrogen ion activity in the solution and the sensitivity of the electrode. Both types of temperature influences constitute sources of error in pH measurement. It is now widely recognized that temperature must be controlled and corrected for in the measurement of pH, and the methods for achieving this are now standard in the field. Drawing our attention to the theoretical work required to determine relationships among temperature, electrical potential, and ion activity, it should be clear that the introduction of this necessary control (for temperature) was guided by theoretical considerations. At the same time, everyone agrees that a pH meter that controls for differences in temperature is better—more reliable and accurate—than one that does not.

Empiricist Alternatives to Operationalism

Of course, one need not choose between operationalism and realism. Other choices exist, in particular empiricist choices, but none looks especially promising. Notice first that no contemporary empiricist would be persuaded by the measured realist's stories of magnitude estimation. The empiricist can concede that, if we measure X, then X exists but deny that we are measuring X. This appears to be van Fraassen's understanding of the measured realist's argument and the vocabulary of discovery. Not yielding to the realist claim that unobservable entities are discovered and measured, van Fraassen assimilates the entity realist's argument to the contention that we obviously get new information about unobservables, and we couldn't get information about something unless it exists:

> When in physics we have a parallel discovery—the electron, the neutron, the magnitude of the charge of the electron—we obtain similarly new information that was not implied by the theory beforehand. This is, in part, information about what the unobservables are like—but surely, unless they exist, there can be no information about them to be had? . . .
>
> And while it may be natural to use the terminology of discovery to report Millikan's results, the accurate way to describe it is that he was writing theory by means of his experimental apparatus. In a case such as this one, experimentation is the continuation of theory by other means. The appropriateness of the means follows from the fact that the aim is empirical adequacy. (1980, p. 77)

We might be disappointed at the vagueness of this account, especially at such a crucial juncture. For the designing of instrumentation that is sensitive to the magnitude of the electron's projected charge would seem to mark a theoretical achievement over earlier instrumentation that simply detected its presence. But despite the apparent dependence of this improvement on theoretical considerations, the empiricist offers as an alternative understanding a rather dim metaphor. What does it mean, exactly, to describe Millikan's discovery of the electron's charge as "writing theory by means of his experimental apparatus"?

On van Fraassen's revisionist account, atomic theory during this period of Millikan's life (roughly 1907–1911) was proceeding slowly, bit by bit. With such piecemeal progress, "many blank spaces had to be left in the theory. Rather than fill such a blank in with a conjectured answer, as hypothesis, and then testing the hypothesis, one carries out an experiment that shows how the blank is to be filled in if the theory is to be empirically adequate" (van Fraassen 1980, p. 75). By filling in this blank with an appropriate value, we are able to "save the phenomena." In a later book, van Fraassen repeats this point and, revisiting that historical period, proposes that in the atomic theory of Millikan's time "a blank is left for the magnitude of the charge." We can proceed with theory construction, he says, by letting

> the experimental apparatus write a number in the blank. What I mean is this: in this case the experiment shows that unless a certain number (or a number not outside a certain interval) is written in the blank, the theory will become empirically inadequate. For the experiment has shown by actual example, that no other number will do; that is the sense in which it has filled in the blank. (1989, p. 232)

Now, this is a striking remark for an empiricist to make—that "no other number would do"—and peculiarly at odds with the empiricist tradition. According to traditional empiricism, numbers outside of the predicted interval could always be written in the blank, so long as appropriate revisions are then made to the background, auxiliary theories. That is, if all that the constructive empiricist requires for such secure reliance on background theories is that they are empirically adequate, then surely a different number could be written in the blank, and the empirically adequate background theories could be revised accordingly or replaced altogether with different but similarly empirically adequate theories. Therefore, if a theory's empirical adequacy depends upon a specific number or interval being "written in the blank," as van Fraassen says, it could only be because tacit confidence in background theories reflected belief rather than mere acceptance. It is only by unwittingly describing a circumstance in which auxiliary theories are regarded as approximately true that the constructive empiricist is able to limit the Duhemian alternatives to just one.

But perhaps van Fraassen wants this case to be understood as one in which the revision of background assumptions is not considered. He might claim that it is only relative to those theories and methods actually accepted (rather than believed, to invoke van Fraassen's distinction) that no other number will do, and thus empirical adequacy is all that is needed to account for the successful use of instrumentation. Two points bear mentioning on this interpretation of van Fraassen. First, scientists do not regard theory revision as beyond their horizon of possible activity. Scientists often revise and refine the theories and methods they actually accept. It is not clear, then, whether this interpretation of van Fraassen's claim offers an acceptable analysis of actual scientific practice. Second, it may indeed be the case that no other number or interval would do given the theories we currently accept, but that may just be because the theories we currently accept are approximately true. So, as a description of this sequence of events in the early history of subatomic physics, van Fraassen's empiricist answer to Hacking's experimental realism fails to rule out a realist explanation: The apparatus writes the correct number in the blank because our available theories, as approximately true, are reliable guides to proper instrument design and measurement.

If empiricism and realism were otherwise equally able to account for facts of scientific practice, a combination of economy and modesty might incline us to opt for an explanation of this episode of measurement in terms of the empiricist notion of empirical adequacy. But when we consider a wider range of scientific activity, it appears that empiricism and realism are not otherwise equally able; there are independent reasons for preferring the realist explanation for the reliability of scientific methods, reasons concerning the integration and unification of theories. Let me close this section with a brief description of this empiricist infirmity and realist strength.

Typically, our experimental options are severely limited by considerations of integration and unification; indeed, the trend toward theoretical integration or unification constitutes, ultimately, both the most potent source of evidence for realism and the most powerful obstacle to all extant empiricist arguments. According to this view, the successful *joint* application of theories reflects approximate theoretical knowledge. This theoretical knowledge was embodied, for example, in Millikan's ability to select exactly those unobservable factors to suppress so that they would not interfere with the effect sought. Background theoretical knowledge is embodied as well in the fact that experimentation allows us to fill in certain "blanks" (as van Fraassen says) left open by theory construction. But van Fraassen's description is vague at just those places that scientific judgments have been intricate and specific. For, unless we characterize Millikan's "blank" as a theoretical entity of which he had specific theoretical knowledge, it will appear mysterious that in filling the electron-charge "blank" Millikan at once filled in a host of others—for the same unit of charge was calculated by diverse means, by Stoney in 1891 using electrodes and by Thomson in 1897 using vacuum discharge tubes. (Later, of course, it could be seen that electrons are implicated in a variety of additional phenomena, such as thermionic emission, the photoelectric effect, electrolysis, and beta radiation, different from those that directly motivated Millikan.)

Many of the psychological phenomena that might have been recruited in defense of measured realism are already achieving integration with developed areas of neuroscience—hardly a disreputable auxiliary field. For instance, one well-established psycholinguistic phenomenon, the Kimura effect, involves a right-ear advantage in language comprehension. This psychological effect explains the direction of performance on dichotic listening tasks, but it is also integrated with established theoretical information in neuroscience concerning the contralateral and ipsilateral neural pathways in the brain. The same applies for receptive fields in vision. Descriptions of such phenomena can be found in any textbook on sensation and perception. Typically, a statistical instrument is used to measure their causal dispositions, and the physiological basis is also identified using neuroscientific instrumentation. The realist explanation for the behavior of contemporary statistical and physiological instruments, like that for late nineteenth-century electrodes and vacuum tubes, is that there exist unobservable phenomena—respectively, lexical units and electrons. The realist explanation for demonstrable improvements in measurement is that we have knowledge of those unobservable factors. Unless the (constructive) empiricist proposes a reconstruction of these activities that is bound to be Byzantine, an empiricist account that is consistent must either fall silent about striking facts of theoretical integration and unification or abandon selective skepticism in favor of an epistemology that is skeptical even about observables.[17]

In the absence of any plausible and natural empiricist explanation for the apparent epistemic role of theoretical considerations, it is not at all clear that van Fraassen has explained this familiar ability in a way that is free from theoretical commitment. At any rate, he has not revealed as doubtful the ungarnished view, often associated with realism, that "by carefully designed experiment we can discover facts about unobservable entities behind the phenomena" (1989, p. 231)

This model of a statistical design as instrument serves three purposes at once. First, although philosophers might evidence astonishment at the claim that a statistical design is an instrument in the sense pertinent to measurement, the details provided here are crafted to transform shock and resistance into understanding and resignation. The stimuli and their exposure to subjects constitute a complex physical arrangement of causally dependent properties formed to estimate the magnitude of some factor of interest in accordance with familiar standards of validity and reliability. Second, it is important to remember that the magnitudes expressed by performance scores are not mathematical fictions. The relations among those numerical values yielded by a psychophysical procedure are grounded in the magnitudes being measured. There is nothing about measurement theory that, by itself, entails an empiricist understanding of the epistemology of measurement. Third, because the above experiment incorporated improved controls, and these improvements must be understood theoretically, then a realist interpretation of measurement is avoided only by an aggressively empiricist epistemology that has not yet been provided. So one might ask the empiricist a simple question: "Is the lexical access design a better design for having controlled for priming effects?" If the empiricist answers "no," then this is akin to having suggested that pH meters are not better for having controlled for temperature. But if the empiricist answers "yes," it is unclear how the affirmative answer can be consistently justified without appeal to the internal state responsible for the effect of decay. By contrast, a measured realist interpretation of measurement will explain why statistical designs succeed in measuring when they do: There are (in the psychological case) unobserved mental dispositions that explain the distribution

17. The preemptory condemnation of empiricist reconstructions as "Byzantine" is intended to indicate that descriptive adequacy may be a reason to prefer one view over another and that empiricist accounts must explain the apparent role of theoretical notions in terms widely regarded as portraying the behavior of scientists as puzzling, even without rationale. Since the aim of descriptive accuracy is independent of the question of the reliability of abduction, the realist's preemptory condemnation is therefore not question-begging against van Fraassen with respect to preference for abduction. In principle, one could prefer realism for its descriptive adequacy, no matter what one's view about abduction. But even if judgments of descriptive accuracy were shown to depend on abduction, it is worth noting that critics of abduction have as yet been unable to show how actual applications of inductive methods are free from reliance on general, background theoretical principles characteristic of abductive arguments.

of numerical values. The dispositions are stable, because they are reproducible by both similar and diverse methods.

Conclusion

Fortified with knowledge of the best science of the time, naturalistic philosophers have advanced distinctive accounts of knowledge, reference, objectivity, intentionality, and the rest. Once naturalized, these notions lead us to a realist conception of psychological measurement akin to realist accounts of physical measurement. I have not addressed questions concerning the particular metaphysical status of the objects of social and psychological measurement, such as how they are individuated. I have not yet raised these questions because, by comparison, the notion of measurement is far less arcane and problematic, and so the realist moral I urge is open to the general public. While I believe that realism about the social sciences and psychology can be defended without claiming that statistical designs are instruments, the case for realism about selected psychological and social sciences is metaphilosophically less complicated if we identify instances of statistical designs with instruments, used to detect and manipulate unobservable causes. And when statistical designs are properly refined in light of theoretical knowledge, they measure the psychological world.

Often the posits of these modestly successful theories persist under a variety of measurement conditions. We rightfully infer the existence of those entities advanced by the theory, along with counterfactual-supporting generalizations about them. The best evidence that these conditions obtain in the social and behavioral sciences is provided by statistical tests, and in the next chapter we consider how statistical measurement, over time, establishes the existence of selected entities and the approximate truth of certain laws.

Statistical Testing and the World's Contribution to Rationality

Measured realism is motivated in part by the fact that many background theories in the social sciences and psychology are themselves unreliable, and so theoretical improvement often requires the experimental strain of statistical predictions. Yet it is sometimes claimed that, for such immature theories, statistical methods are powerless to provide severe tests of hypotheses and so unable to establish the existence of postulated causes. This pessimism, if warranted, would be troubling to the practicing psychologist, because significance testing is the primary method for establishing causal relationships in psychology. Some commentators argue that significance tests and their interpretation are subject to actuarial and psychological biases, making continued adherence to these practices irrational and even partially responsible for the slow progress of the "soft" areas of psychology. I contend that familiar standards of testing and literature review, along with recently developed meta-analytic techniques, are able to correct the proposed actuarial and psychological biases. This chapter presents a natural account of the conditions diagnostic of the reality of a theoretical entity in psychology. In particular, psychologists embrace a principle of robustness, which states that real psychological effects are (1) reproducible by similar methods, (2) detectable by diverse means, and (3) able to survive theoretical integration. The principle of robustness explains why spurious significant findings perish under the strain of persistent tests of their robustness. The resulting vindication of significance testing confers on the world a role in determining the rationality of a method and also affords a measured-realist explanation for the fast progress of the "hard" areas of psychology.

Introduction: Robustness and Significance Testing

If the argument of chapter 5 is sound, then statistical instruments yield measurements, or estimates of the magnitudes, of selected social and psychological kinds. Statistical measurement in the social and behavioral sciences may be based upon statistical tests that are either descriptive or inferential, and in both cases those tests provide quantitative information vital to cumulative progress. But no matter how vital, statistical tests are unable to make all decisions for you. Because not all relevant theoretical information is quantitative, such as the selection and weighting of dimensions, many of the apparently reliable judgments that scientists make are based on informal assessments of the evidence. Can such informal assessments be epistemically reliable? If they can, do normative principles regulate those judgments?

Cognitive research on the frailties of human judgment (for a recent review, see Arkes and Hammond 1986) has quickly made its way into the philosophical literature on rationality (Cherniak 1986; Davidson 1976; Giere 1988; Goldman 1986; Stich 1990), and if you subscribe to the new naturalism in epistemology, you may not like what you see. Laypeople and clinical specialists commit systematic errors when reasoning inductively.[1] These charges are now casting a pall over the more theoretical disciplines as well, particularly psychology and sociology, where research draws heavily on tests of statistical significance. Some quarters allege that significance testing is so problematic that "the usual research literature review is well-nigh uninterpretable" (Meehl 1990b, p. 197), a conclusion that "is precisely the right response of a rational mind" (p. 198) and one that constitutes "a methodological problem of our field that I insist is not minor but of grave import" (Meehl 1990a, p. 108). (For similar charges elsewhere in Meehl's work, see 1967, 1978, and 1985).

Inferential approaches in statistics, such as significance testing (an example of which is the t test of the previous chapter), have been a special target, and not just of Meehl's (Morrison and Henkel 1970, provides a very thorough treatment of the issues; for more recent discussions, see J. Cohen 1994 and Harlow, Mulaik, and Steiger 1997). Because the argument of this book depends upon the claim that such inferential tests display PGE when applied to samples neither terribly small nor terribly unrepresentative of the intended populations, and because this task cannot be completed without the aid of accurate qualitative, taxonomic categories that sufficiently good theories would supply, then our conclusions must be cautious; many areas of the social and behavioral sciences do not enjoy reliable theoretical backgrounds. But with the rationality of this central scientific practice now under attack, the principles and purposes of significance testing deserve closer examination in the philosophical literature than they have so far received. I don't propose to address all of the reasons that have been given for suspicion

---

1. The discussion that follows will focus entirely on errors in inductive reasoning. For experimental evidence from the psychology of human inference indicating the systematic violation of deductive canons as well, see Cherniak (1986) and Wason and Johnson-Laird (1972).

concerning significance tests. Although the methodology of significance testing is often blamed for the slow progress of "soft" (social, personality, counseling, clinical, and educational) psychology, the criticisms of significance testing typically are not presented as depending on the subject matter. Rather, the charge is posed in quite general and neutral terms; significance testing is "a poor way of doing science" (Meehl 1978, p. 806).[2] Following a survey of the charges, I will mobilize three reasons for thinking that the critic's concerns are either peripheral or misleading.

First, to the extent that significance tests could be applied with clearer principle, and interpreted with greater rigor, there are meta-analytic techniques, much discussed in the theoretical literature, designed to refine significance testing in just these ways. Second, the criticisms examined here ignore the methodological and editorial assumption that real psychological phenomena are robust and thus that their effects are (1) reproducible by maximally similar methods, (2) detectable by diverse instruments and measurable by diverse scales, and (3) able to survive attempts at theoretical integration. By contrast, spurious significant findings—effects that reach conventional standards of significance by chance—don't survive in the literature, because they don't survive in the lab or in the field. Finally, the fact that various factors of unknown value influence measurements is not a problem peculiar to significance testing; rather, it is an expression of the more general fact that we fall short of omniscience, a condition that hasn't prevented scientific progress elsewhere.

Continued reliance on significance testing, then, should not be deemed epistemically irresponsible. Far from having established the psychologist's irrationality, the critic of significance testing bears an additional burden; the critic must explain how the "harder" areas of perceptual and cognitive psychology, indebted as they are to significance testing, could have enjoyed such noticeable progress since the 1940s if the methodology of significance testing were as defective as the critics allege.

The Charge that Significance Tests in Psychology Are Unintelligible

In fields such as psychology and sociology, research results are reported primarily in terms of statistical significance tests. Those most commonly used are t tests, F tests, and analyses of variance and of covariance. Let's look at one standard statistical strategy. A population of subjects is identified, and one large group, drawn from that population, is selected and divided into two subgroups or samples. Each sample is given a different experimental treatment, and subject performance under each treatment yields respective sample means. What we want to determine is

---

2. In Meehl's widely cited article, for example, the formal, statistical issues are discussed independently of such substantial issues as the imprecise predictions of "weak" theories. I will examine the statistical problems, and Meehl (1978) covers these in a collection of up to twenty formal and substantial problems in the so-called soft areas of psychology. More recently, Meehl explicitly indicated that his critique of significance testing does not necessarily apply to the "harder" areas of psychology, such as perception and cognition (personal correspondence, September 1996).

whether differences between subgroup means are large enough to be attributed primarily to the influence of experimental conditions rather than chance factors deriving from the assignment of subjects into the subgroups. Variation within the subgroups is used to estimate the amount of variation attributable to chance factors such as sampling error. With the sampling error now estimated, we can determine whether the difference in subgroup means due to experimental factors is great enough to merit treating the two subgroups, originally drawn from a common population, as representative of two different populations.

The hypothesis tested is that the experimental treatment did not have an influence on subjects sufficient to support the conclusion that a significant difference exists between the two samples. When the treatment is understood as an independent variable and the influence or effect as a dependent variable, this hypothesis amounts to the projection that no relationship exists between two or more variables being examined. This is the null hypothesis (H_0). Strictly speaking, a significance test attempts to identify the risk associated with the rejection of the null hypothesis. In light of the particular standard error, the significance test estimates the probability that the difference in subgroup means would be repeated if two subgroups were drawn again from that population. The standard level of risk or significance is normally set at .05; that is, the null hypothesis can safely be rejected if the risk of duplication due to chance falls below .05. The rejection of the null hypothesis is normally interpreted as confirming the test, "alternative" hypothesis.

In relying on these particular significance tests, we risk two sorts of errors. We commit a type I error if we reject the null hypothesis when it is true. In such a case, the effect has reached significance by chance variation in sampling and is not, as we sometimes say, "real." A type II error occurs if we fail to reject the null hypothesis when it is false. Here, again due to chance variation in sampling, no effect materializes even though the two variables are in fact related.

I will be concerned with two factors that complicate the interpretation of significance tests. One factor is largely actuarial, and the other psychological. Both incline the investigator to type 1 errors. The first complicating factor derives from the simple repetition of experiments on the same dependent variable.[3] An effect that reaches the standard .05 level of significance (taken as indicating that there is a 95 percent chance that the effect is indeed real) is reported as significant. Therefore, repeated experiments on the same dependent variable are likely to produce type I errors due to random fluctuation in performance, generating results

---

3. Talk of "replication" or "repetition" here must be qualified. A replication is an instantiation of the same design from a theoretical view. A variety of differences between the original experiment and the replication are unavoidable, even when scientists explicitly attempt to replicate an experiment. Original experiments and their replications are normally carried out at different times, in different settings, often using different technicians. With the qualification now registered that perfect replication is impossible, we can at the same time acknowledge that this limitation seldom presents an insuperable problem. The particular theory tells us which differences make a difference (e.g., is likely to produce a unique artifact, etc.).

that are spuriously identified as significant, even where there is no real relationship between the independent and dependent variables.

The second complicating factor trades on the first.[4] One body of psychological research suggests that psychologists (and other scientists) are subject to an "availability bias," causing them to underestimate the frequency with which "spurious significant" findings get published. Faust (1984) draws on research in cognitive psychology that attempts to demonstrate such systematic errors in both lay and scientific reasoning. The "base-rate problem" is one of the most prominent of these results. People normally underutilize important information about the relative frequency at which a certain event, object, property, or other variable occurs in a population.

In a groundbreaking study, Kahneman and Tversky (1973) constructed personality descriptions of five people putatively sampled from a class of 100 professionals—engineers and lawyers. For each description, subjects were asked to estimate the probability that it belonged to an engineer rather than a lawyer. Subjects were told in one condition that 70 percent of the persons described were lawyers and 30 percent were engineers. In the second condition, the frequencies were reversed. Despite the fact that these personality descriptions were not particularly diagnostic of profession and that under such conditions base-rate information should have had a powerful influence on the probability estimates, subjects ignored base-rate information; instead, they appeared to rely on the stereotype (personality) description, violating actuarial rules in predicting the relevant occupation.

It is not as though subjects were incapable of appropriately exploiting base-rate information. In the absence of any personality information, for instance, subjects used prior probabilities correctly, estimating that an individual randomly selected from the 70 percent lawyer sample had a .7 likelihood of being a lawyer, and so on for the other assignments. However, even when the following, entirely nondiagnostic personality information was presented, subjects once again ignored the base rate: "Dick is a 30-year-old man. He is married with no children. A man of high ability and high motivation, he promises to be quite successful in his field. He is well liked by his colleagues" (Kahneman and Tversky 1973, p. 242). Here, subjects rated the engineer and lawyer likelihoods to be equal—in other words, 50 percent— whether the subjects were provided the 70 percent base rate or the 30 percent base rate. So it appears that, as a class, people respond differently to the absence of information than they do to worthless information; when no specific evidence is provided, prior probabilities are correctly appreciated, and when useless information is provided, prior probabilities are ignored. The moral normally drawn is that people must suffer a woeful lack of appreciation of the importance of base rate information if they can be so easily distracted by such worthless "stereotype" information.

4. As a matter of fact, Meehl's groundbreaking work (1954) on the prediction of performance using actuarial rather than clinical (e.g., configural, stereotype, etc.) guidelines anticipated much of the recent work on the importance of base-rate information.

L. Jonathan Cohen (1986) was the first to raise serious and systematic doubts about this pessimistic interpretation of the experimental results. According to Cohen, the responses of statistically untutored people reveal that they can be led astray in their application of inductive principles; if we recognize a distinction between counterfactualizable and noncounterfactualizable conceptions of probability, and the ordinary dominance of the former over the latter, experimental subjects' violation of normative rules can be rationalized. Cohen concludes that these experiments therefore do not demonstrate human irrationality.

Nothing in the present chapter, however, depends on the truth of Cohen's conclusion. Even if, contrary to Cohen's contentions, laypersons do commit systematic errors of inductive inference, this (putative) psychological bias is subject to correction by the forces described in the sections that follow.

Nor can we secure the integrity of inductive scientific inference by locating the defect entirely within lay reasoning. Faust (1984; also see Chapman and Chapman 1969) argues that the underutilization of base-rate information is not peculiar to lay judgment; insensitivity to prior probabilities produces systemic and fundamental errors in routine scientific judgments as well.[5] As a result, methodological practices such as the literature review are subject to the charge of irrationality if they depend on significance testing and fall in with the evaluative standards for publication that currently prevail.

The way to the base-rate fallacy in psychology is abetted by two institutional biases, one in article submission and another in editorial acceptance. Researchers typically do not submit articles reporting null results, and journals typically reject such articles in the relatively rare instances in which they are submitted. As a result, the journal audience is presented with a population of studies badly skewed toward those reaching significance. And to make matters worse, the audience possesses no base-rate information concerning the frequency with which experimental efforts failed to reach significance; such efforts get filed away and are thus unavailable to the journal audience.[6]

For these reasons, David Faust cautions those who rely on significance tests in psychology and attributes their blind persistence to an "availability bias":

> If base rates are ignored, one might assume that there is a 95 percent chance that the results are indeed significant. If base rates had been considered, it might be shown that the finding of significant results, regardless of external reality, was almost ensured. . . . The far greater availability of concrete instances of significant findings further works against the formation of accurate impressions [of base rates]. . . . That

---

5. Lugg (1987) objects to Faust's move from evidence of error in clinical judgment to error in scientific judgment. Although Lugg is correct to remind us of the presumptive and impressionistic character of Faust's argument, the sorts of practices targeted by Faust, such as literature review, are not peculiar to clinical fields. Nor does the hard science/soft science distinction appear to mark a relevant difference in the standards of literature review (Hedges 1987).

6. On top of it all, pilot studies—which are, after all, experiments in the small—are never counted among the total population of studies, further increasing the total number of experiments executed and thus the likelihood of producing a spurious significant finding.

so little attention has been directed towards gathering base rates for the occurrence of nonsignificant results may also indicate a general failure to appreciate the crucial importance of base rate information. (1984, pp. 93–94)

It has thus grown popular to accuse psychologists with, at best, epistemic irresponsibility, and at worst, epistemic bad faith. Faust seems inclined toward the charge of epistemic irresponsibility, while Paul Meehl is less generous. The most persistent figure behind this accusation, Meehl speculates that students and colleagues haven't responded to his warning "since they might not know what to do next if they took it seriously" (1990b, p. 198). And just in case his diagnosis of denial has not been digested, Meehl adds the following:

As is well known, were some mischievous statistician or philosopher to say "Well, five times in a hundred you would get this much of a difference even if the rats had learned nothing, so why shouldn't it happen to you?", the only answer is "It could happen to me, but I am not going to assume that I am one of the unlucky scientists in 20 to whom such a thing happens. I am aware, however, that over my research career, if I should perform a thousand significance tests on various kinds of data, and nothing that I researched had any validity to it, I would be able to write around 50 publishable papers based upon that false positive rate" (p. 212).

Now, the problems Meehl describes here are real, but they are not as serious (or as willfully committed) as Meehl thinks. Meehl's concerns no doubt derive from his statistical sophistication, along with his frustrated efforts to improve the discipline's testing of "weak" (typically data-driven) theories by largely methodological means. Unfortunately, it is easy to get the impression from the above passage that researchers who rely on significance testing are either dishonest or stupid. Meehl leaves the honest scientist with little recourse but to abandon or radically reform significance testing and to opt for other measures such as curve fitting (or perhaps adopt stricter standards of significance) or remain in the grip of a suspect methodology.[7]

---

7. This impression is aided by the critics' distorting tendency to ignore important aspects of article submission and evaluation, as well as the actual availability of null results. These omissions allow the criticism of significance testing to be presented in the most dramatic and threatening light. But this impression is inaccurate. Articles reporting a single experiment are relatively uncommon. Normally, an article reports two or more experiments, so it is doubtful that fifty experiments that reach significance would yield an equal number of journal articles. Numbers are important here because, first, the psychological plausibility of a hypothesis is sometimes presented as a partial function of the sheer number of articles supporting it and, second, the psychologist's complicity in ignoring the obvious threat of spurious significance, the critic insinuates, should be explained in terms of the psychologist's desire for a lengthy list of publications. Nor are concrete instances of null results unavailable and thus, as Faust implies, involved in "desensitizing" the psychologist to the frequency with which null results occur. Researchers are reminded of null results every time their experiments support the null hypothesis, every time such results are described in personal communication, and every time they are reported among a series of published experiments. Finally, null results sometimes derive from poor design, and referees often reject articles on the basis of poor design. The critics discussed here, however, present the referee's behavior in such cases as a simple reflection of a bias against accepting studies reporting null results rather than as a reliable disposition to reject poorly designed studies.

The problem here, of course, is that we can't tell in advance whether a particular effect reported as significant is authentic or spurious. The value of these actuarial and (alleged) psychological distortions are unknown at any given time, and this is seen by critics as a serious problem rather than just as marking the boundary of our own knowledge at the time. According to Meehl, this uncertainty can be reduced by adopting more stringent testing and review standards. Investigators should predict not just an effect but an effect size, set their statistical power at .9, and report all pilot studies and attempts at replication. Journal editors should generally require a successful replication, tables should report means and standard deviations, and a section of the journal should be devoted to the publication of negative pilot studies. Literature reviewers should, wherever possible, mention the statistical power of the included studies and always avoid the reporting of "box scores," tabulating the number of studies on a particular issue reaching significance and those failing to reach significance, in an effort to estimate a theory's verisimilitude.[8] Finally, theoreticians should attempt to develop alternative methods of deriving predictions from weak theories.

Many of these recommendations would indeed allow us to avoid type I errors, but such standards have a cost that the above critics have omitted from the discussion. Presumably we could always further reduce the risk of type I error by demanding an even greater number of replications and count all pilot studies among the total run, and literature reviewers could always avoid being drawn in by type I errors by assuming a rather large impact for an alleged bias in submission and editorial acceptance. But by doing so we risk committing more type II er-

---

8. This practice of tabulating box scores is mistaken, Meehl states, because it assumes that a significant result does a theory as much good as a null result does it damage. The falsity of this assumption is exposed, Meehl continues, in a moment's reflection on the dynamics of theory testing:

> This is scientifically a preposterous way to reason. It completely neglects the crucial asymmetry between confirmation, which involves an inference in the formally invalid third figure of the implicative syllogism (this is why inductive inferences are ampliative and dangerous and why we can be objectively wrong even though we proceed correctly), and refutation, which is in the valid fourth figure, and which gives the *modus tollens* its privileged position in inductive inference." (1978, p. 822; also see 1990, p. 233).

It's not clear whether Meehl is simply making the point that, when the hypothesis is precise and a test of it is well designed, null results weigh more heavily against the theory than positive results support it or whether he also intends the appeal to the favored status of *modus tollens* in theory testing and the blithe use of "corroboration" and "refutation" as an endorsement of falsificationist philosophy of science. The latter would seem an implausible interpretation, because Meehl is no Popperian. However, since many of those party to the significance-testing dispute are psychologists unfamiliar with the recent developments in the philosophy of science, it might be worth mentioning in such contexts that the last generation in philosophy has witnessed the erosion of the falsificationist program and that there are few real adherents left. The interested scientist might begin with Putnam's (1974) classic "The 'Corroboration' of Theories."

rors—due to designs and reviewing standards that, once reformed, would be insensitive to many real causal factors.

It is worth noting that this actuarial criticism is presented as domain neutral; the statistics of repeated experimentation (on the same variable), not the subject matter, guarantees the production of this study artifact of actuarial bias. Curious, then, that the critics should selectively attack only a few areas of psychology (e.g., social, personality, counseling, clinical, and educational) rather than raise quite general doubts about the integrity of all disciplines—psychological and nonpsychological alike—that employ tests of statistical significance. For instance, this same tendency toward type I error pervades the significance-testing methodology of the quickly advancing fields of perceptual and cognitive psychology, yet the critic doesn't impugn those mature and successful domains. As I will argue later, scientists typically possess knowledge of corrective techniques, are subject to institutional standards of improvement applied at the journal referee stage, or change their views in light of feedback from the world; they don't remain forever innocent of nature's verdict. But for present purposes, the critic is simply mistaken in suggesting that psychologists are unaware of the threat of type I error attendant upon the kind of null-hypothesis testing currently employed. In fact, a separate body of research has arisen to supply the tools to correct the tendency toward type I error due to actuarial bias.

The Development of Corrective Meta-Analytic Techniques

The primary source of statistical vigilance here is meta-analysis, a field that has grown in response to the increasing recognition that literature summaries are initially subject to the actuarial and psychological biases detailed above. Meta-analysis is the study of sets of research results, normally carried out on a number of studies regarding the same research question.

As we saw, psychology journals represent a biased sample of the total number of studies performed on a particular issue. By sheer repetition of studies (on the worst scenario), 5 percent of the studies reported in psychology journals represent type I errors, and 95 percent of the studies showing nonsignificant results (set at, e.g., $p > .05$) are filed away in lab drawers, not regarded as worth reporting or even submitting for publication. This state of affairs, presented by Meehl and Faust as an unrecognized or unacknowledged source of irrational judgment, is so well known among researchers that it even has a name: the file-drawer problem (Rosenthal 1979). To protect against committing a type I error due to simple repetition, we must not underestimate the number of studies carried out on a particular question.

Meta-analysis is particularly well suited to correct such sampling biases predictable from simple actuarial rules. As a remedy for the file drawer problem, meta-analysis offers the tolerance table. The tolerance table tells us how many new, filed, or unretrieved studies with a null mean would be necessary to drag down a population of significant studies (of a certain mean and size) to just below the conventional standard of significance (See Rosenthal and Rosnow 1984, pp. 378–382). For any substantial population of studies reaching significance, the number of null studies it can tolerate is (typically) surprisingly high.[9]

Meta-analysis addresses a variety of other potential artifactual distortions deriving from sampling error, treatment effects, inadequate statistical power, or the strict falsity of the null hypothesis when interpreted literally (known as the "crud factor").[10] Indeed, meta-analysis is one more technique designed to exploit the robustness of psychological phenomena, to which we now turn.

The Robustness of Psychological Phenomena

Given the promise of meta-analysis, we now have reason to think that the biases predictable from actuarial sampling data can be corrected statistically. Although this assurance is encouraging, success does not depend on it. Some properties distinctive of effects are real rather than spurious. In the process of theory construction and literature review, scientists assess the plausibility of theories, and the reality of postulated entities, on the basis of the robustness and integrative survival of reported effects.

Nearly all scientists assume that real psychological phenomena are robust; they emerge and persist under a variety of independent measurements or methods of detection applied to them. It's not surprising, then, to discover scientists employing a certain robustness principle in their literature reviews: Effects that reach significance are more likely to be real if they have been arrived at by diverse, independent methods and reproduced by maximally similar methods. The assumption of robustness is evident in attempts to "triangulate" on research results. If only one procedure is used, the resulting value could always be an artifact of one type or another, and we have no way of checking this possibility. However, if two or more operational procedures are used, the different peripheral causal influences attendant on each could be thought to produce divergent results—were those different techniques not measuring the same persistent object. To confirm the

9. Rosenthal (1979) reports that, of ninety-four experiments on interpersonal self-fulfilling prophecies summarized in Rosenthal (1969), it would take 3,263 unreported studies averaging null results (where the average mean, measured in standard deviation units, equals .00) before we are forced to conclude that the overall outcomes are the result of a sampling bias of the studies summarized in the review. Another review (Rosenthal 1976) of 311 studies of the same area raises the stakes considerably: 49,457 unreported studies are tolerable. As either the population of available studies increases, or the mean (Z) score (in the same direction) increases, the hypothesis that full file drawers could explain such a mean is itself implausible. For the state-of-the-art issues, see Rosenthal (1995).

10. The crud factor is especially influential in the case of large samples. As sample size increases, so does the probability that correlations among the variables under investigation will reach the conventional level of significance (see Lykken 1968; Meehl, 1967, 1990a, 1990b). Although the crud factor does not represent a type I error—these variables are really correlated—it is still a prominent study artifact. Hunter and Schmidt (1990) proposes corrective measures for this artifact and the others mentioned above; also, see Green and Hall (1984).

existence of this object, its presence must be established independently and variously.[11]

In the history of chemistry and physics, attempts to establish the existence and nature of molecules clearly triangulated on diverse research areas and techniques. Dissimilar methods used to measure pressure, temperature, ion exchange, and voltage nevertheless converged to license the full ontological status of molecules.

In cognitive psychology, prototype studies in the 1970s revealed just such a robust phenomenon. When asked to rate how representative an object is (e.g., robin, chicken, etc.) of a certain class (e.g., bird), subjects' performances were the same on both ranking and reaction time tasks (Rosch 1973; Rosch and Mervis 1975; Mervis, Catlin, and Rosch 1976; Mervis and Rosch 1981). The convergent results of these diverse test methods are taken by psychologists to indicate that the prototype effect represents a real (nonartifactual) feature of mental organization.[12] Similar convergence of measurements can be found in personality and clinical psychology, where diverse scales are used to identify the same personality traits and predict the same performance (Norman 1963, pp. 374–391).

Another "test" routinely deployed in the appraisal of an experimental finding is the extent of integration of that effect into a body of information that is already secure. The following methodological principle seems to be at work here: Typically, any single effect is more likely to be real if it coheres with, as opposed to contradicts or undermines, well-established findings. Add to this methodological principle a widely held rule of confirmation: A theory is supported to the extent that the evidence favors it over plausible rivals. This rule of confirmation, when applied to explanatory integration, recommends that findings most appropriately united with the most plausible theory are also the most likely to be real or genuinely significant; integrative survival is diagnostic of authenticity.

Submission and Editorial Biases

Although Faust has charged that psychologists suffer an availability bias, causing them to overlook the frequency of spurious significant findings, this is a substantial hypothesis that still awaits testing. It is not entirely clear that Faust and the multitude of other students of human reasoning are claiming that the availability bias is a clear example of human irrationality. But they do regard it as a sufficiently serious error to warrant normative recommendations for improvement. In the case of editorial and submission biases, Faust claims the root problem is availability:

---

11. The classic description of this procedure is Campbell and Fiske (1959). Wimsatt (1981) is a clear and thorough discussion of the robustness of theoretical objects, events, properties, processes, and states and of the emergence of robust objects under different forms of methodological scrutiny and manipulation. That paper also addresses the threat that, despite the experimentalist's honest efforts, tacitly similar presuppositions of diverse methods conspire to produce converging results, a phenomenon called "bias amplification" or "pseudo-robustness."

12. For an interesting alternative explanation of these results that cites similar mechanisms, see Armstrong, Gleitman, and Gleitman (1983).

The end result is that individuals apply individual judgment guidelines, few or any of which are likely to exploit maximally the valuable information potentially available through knowledge of base rates, and many of which may be in serious error. . . .

They [scientists] could also extend current information about the frequency of unpublished nonsignificant results and its bearing on the likelihood of making false positive errors when interpreting experimental results. One might study scientists' estimates, under commonly encountered conditions, of the base rates for obtaining spurious significant results and determine the extent to which this shapes their conclusions when performing such judgment tasks as evaluating the merits of specific research results. (1984, p. 94)

There are two general problems with this prescription, however, one in estimating the base rates in the first place and another in knowing what to do with the base rates once you have them. To determine the base rate for a certain effect reaching significance, we would first have to estimate the total number of studies, both published and unpublished, that have investigated a particular effect. We could then determine the relative frequency with which the effect reaches significance. But if we are to determine the relative frequency of spurious significant results, obviously we must be able to correctly identify particular significant results as spurious. How might we do this?

Earlier I described a widely held assumption of experimental methodology (the principle of robustness) according to which authentically significant effects should be reproducible by similar methods, measurable by diverse procedures, and, over time, well integrated into a theory's best models. Guided by this principle, we might be able to identify spurious significant results by observing which effects are robust—those results reaching significance that are reproduced and survive integration—and which are not. Therefore, by searching the literature, we can use this diagnostic test for the presence of real phenomena to determine the relative frequency with which spurious significant results are published.

The need to consider base rates, however, was said to derive from the tendency of professional journals to accept papers with results identified as significant. In these journals, over time, real effects survive and prosper and spurious results initially reported as significant give way under the stress of fruitless attempts either to replicate and extend the effect or to use the putative effect as a tool in the testing of other phenomena. Those who criticize the policy of neglecting this base-rate measure, then, are in a peculiar dialectical position. This policy, they claim, is in serious error. Yet they distinguish spurious from authentic significant findings by deploying standards of reliability employed in the very journals whose neglect of base rates is in dispute. If this is correct, there may be very little to be gained by estimating base rates.[13] Over time, the principle of robustness and the

---

13. Accordingly, notice that the present approach is not Bayesian, even though we might believe that in general we must do our best to attend to the normative canons of statistical reasoning emphasized by Bayesians; for example, we need not regard the scientist here as relying on a set of priors.

import of integrative survival work against the perennial commission of type I errors.

The critic of significance testing might object that just because a reported effect disappears or fails integration in future literature does not mean that the reported effect is spurious; these factors are merely diagnostic of actual insignificance, not definitive of it. But, of course, because our science is currently incomplete—we don't yet know how the story turns out—any principles of theory choice will carry with them some epistemic risk, no matter how small. Such principles are ampliative, even if not especially speculative. The critic must therefore tolerate at least some degree of uncertainty in the methods of theory evaluation and choice, or in the standards for distinguishing real from spurious effects, on pain of requiring that researchers be able to correctly predict the future history of science.

The Worldly Regulation of Method

If we are to render intelligible the researcher's behavior, we must attribute to her a belief in the robustness of psychological phenomena; otherwise, attempts at replication, extension, triangulation, and a host of other experimental aims appear either mysterious or unreasonable by her own lights. The psychologist's doxastic commitment to the robustness of psychological phenomena is a special instance of the more general scientific confidence that the robustness of real phenomena will, in the long run and given appropriate background assumptions, guide a reliable (even if imperfect) methodology to the identification of approximately true theories.

Our confidence in the methodology of significance testing and literature review has been vindicated in perceptual and cognitive psychology, disciplines that have enjoyed remarkable progress and consensus in this century and whose successes are nonetheless deeply dependent on reigning standards of significance testing. There are less sweeping criticisms of particular statistical methods (for the best discussions, see Lewontin 1974; Wright, Levine, and Sober 1992), but we have already insisted that particular applications are epistemically irresponsible. Indeed, the theoretical success in cognitive and perceptual psychology would be puzzling if significance testing generally is, as Meehl claims, "a poor way of doing science." Other criticisms of significance testing are typically framed in purely statistical terms and leveled without appeal to the role of substantial theory in guiding statistical method. Here, as elsewhere in science, whether or not a method works depends as much on the character of the world as it does on the intentions and outlook of the investigator. Although normative refinements can yield welcome improvements in methodology, the world, too, is a sobering and corrective influence on theory construction.

Moreover, many of the prior considerations she makes, as well as the corrective mechanisms, are extra-statistical.

As suggestive as robustness is, we have yet to articulate a realist response to the charge of "pseudo-robustness"—that the persistence of entities under diverse tests is merely apparent, the result of nonindependent assumptions or biases in the test setting. Failure to detect pseudo-robustness is sometimes presented as a fatal disappointment of social and psychological theories. The most plausible realist response to this skeptical challenge is a naturalistic one, assimilating the relevant epistemic notions to those of measurement. We now turn to that alternative.

Diverse Tests on an Independent World

This chapter has three broad purposes, and it attempts to satisfy them by integrating issues of scientific methodology and epistemic principles that seldom make contact in the philosophical literature. First, in reply to critics of robustness, I make explicit, and provide a rationale for, a common assumption of typical antiskeptical arguments in contemporary epistemology. The assumption is that some possibilities are just too remote to undermine warrant for an otherwise unobjectionable knowledge claim. Drawing on a family of epistemic notions introduced by Fred Dretske, Alvin Goldman, and John Pollock, I distinguish between relevant and vacuous defeaters of warrant. I offer a strategy for explaining why idle possibilities are vacuous and thus not genuine defeaters. Second, I argue that generic (undisciplined) criticisms of diverse testing in science, criticisms concerning the ubiquitous threat of spuriousness and pseudo-robustness, have the status of mere vacuous defeaters of evidential warrant. The apparent reliability of informed design and of diverse testing survives these attacks and now requires an explanation. The positive part of the chapter therefore turns to the formulation of a naturalistic account of theoretical warrant. I argue that deliberate and unplanned variation in method, both routine features of scientific practice, introduce into the data quasi-random error that tends to wash out bias or systematic error. This account combines a realist understanding of theoretical commitment in the various sciences and a related naturalistic treatment of methodology according to which the world plays a substantial role in the correction of our scientific theories.

Motivating Idle Possibilities

Realists have long held that their ontological commitments, though guided by theory, are in some sense independent of the particular theory in terms of which they are described. This autonomy is expressed in a variety of ways. For example, if my contentions in chapter 2 are sound, then there is a realist account of measurement that explains how these theoretical structures can be detected and measured diversely and so, once again, independently of any particular theory. And if the argument of chapter 3 is sound, then there are theoretical structures accessible to investigations by multiple theories and thus independent of any particular theory. Chapters 4 and 5 explored the methodological and ontological independence expressed, respectively, in the forms of widely held confirmation standards, epistemic relations (making "mercenary reliance" necessary), and unification of disparate domains. Realist knowledge claims are subject to a range of challenges, and the immaturity of the social and behavioral sciences makes them a bit more vulnerable to such contest. In particular, the theory dependence of scientific method is thought to threaten the knowledge claims that scientists makes in light of their evidence. A realist, measured or not, should have an epistemology with the resources to address this skeptical challenge to (some relevant sense of) theory independence of the outcomes of social and behavioral inquiry.

Scientists have never been much moved by the challenges of extreme skepticism. If an evil demon deceives us, his product is a charming illusion, populated by all the appearances of scientific theories that yield instrumental control and theoretical understanding. And if the working scientist were shown that a favored methodological scruple is so exacting that it must have the power to reveal the demon's hypothetical machinations, surely the scruple would be relaxed rather than skepticism embraced. Accordingly, no scientist concerned with appropriate criticism can consistently fault an otherwise reliable methodology for its compatibility with the hypothesis that a demon is deceiving us.

In philosophy, by contrast, the formulation, indulgence, and refinement of such hypotheses yield a cottage industry. Demon skepticism (in its myriad modifications) has its philosophical roots in an epistemology that requires logically conclusive evidence as a condition for knowledge. The assumption is that if you cannot distinguish the experiences and information garnered in an undesigning from those in a demonic world, then it is logically possible that our belief that we live in a demon-free world is mistaken. But if error is logically possible, then our worldly beliefs are not entailed by our evidence, and hence we cannot have knowledge. Because this skeptical demand is thought to cover all knowledge claims, it has the following striking consequence: If any epistemically important principle or method fails to guarantee error-free results, it cannot yield knowledge.

Like this skeptical tendency in some philosophical quarters, a pattern of methodological criticism within science has extreme skepticism as an unintended consequence. This pattern of criticism is often advanced by those scientists and philosophers not officially smitten by extreme skepticism. Even so, as we shall see, their pronouncements move from the possibility that a hypothesis could still be shown false to the claim that the test method in question does not meet any reasonable standard of epistemic warrant. There is no virtue in vanquishing a straw opponent. It may be that the disappointment we will see expressed by philosophers and scientists whenever a method fails to secure certainty is best understood as either routine Humean doubts about induction or an inarticulate worry about the effects of underdetermination. But no matter what the source, these doubts are directed, sometimes with considerable drama, against the general reliability of central scientific principles of theory testing. When made without qualification, the implied skepticism purports to undermine claims to scientific knowledge generally (both observational and theoretical) and, where convenient, selectively (against claims to theoretical knowledge specifically, as in van Fraassen's constructive empiricism). I will look at both sorts of arguments.

The principle I will be concerned with here is that of diverse testing, or "triangulation," whose application led to the "remarkable agreement" that Avogadro found among molecular and atomic phenomena. The epistemic import of diverse testing is explained with clarity and awe by Perrin:

> Our wonder is aroused at the very remarkable agreement found between values derived from the consideration of such widely different phenomena. Seeing that not only is the same magnitude obtained by each method when the conditions under which it is applied are varied as much as possible, but that the numbers thus established also agree among themselves, without discrepancy, for all methods employed, the real existence of the molecule is given a probability bordering on certainty. (1923, pp. 215–216)

The criticism that purports to threaten the principle of diverse testing states that, for any particular experimental or theoretical result, it is always possible that the result is not genuine but rather an artifact of the instrumentation or of nonindependent theoretical assumptions—in short, the result of an undetected bias.

The knowledge claims of working scientists typically express ontological commitments of various sorts, and the justification for those commitments in turn concerns the reliability of the method used to establish the existence of theoretical objects. In the case of a single experiment, we have better reason for holding that a postulated entity is real if familiar canons of experimental design, such as randomization, have been followed. We have even better reason for believing that an effect (or posit) is real if, in a series of experiments, the effect has been arrived at by diverse experimental or theoretical tests. Yet randomization and triangulation, some say, fail to provide the necessary assurance. Some scientists and scientifically informed philosophers express a gloomy methodological worry: It is always possible for a single experiment to yield a spurious effect and, in a series of experiments, for the spurious effect to recur under repeated tests, even when those tests are diverse. These worries are so acute they have even caused some to despair of scientific progress.

Fortunately, there is no reason to despair. The influence of random error tends to work against the formation of a trend in the data over a series of experiments (whether the trend represents a real or a spurious effect), and, as a result, only those effects representing real causal factors remain—the most persistent and causally potent. When applied to cases in working sciences, skeptical doubts about the general reliability of diverse testing have dramatically unacceptable consequences. In fact, I will contend that those critical of the long-term reliability of diverse testing are committed to at least one of two implausible doctrines: (1) that the world conspires to keep information from us (and changes systematically to do so) or (2) that an adequate scientific epistemology must empower the scientist to predict the future history of science. Given the instrumental success of those scientific theories in which diverse testing figures centrally, we should adopt metaphysical and epistemological analyses that rationalize rather than mystify scientific practices. I assume that (1) and (2) fail at this task. Moreover, because the tests in question must be diverse in a sense that is theoretically relevant, a sense that is determined by our best going theories, skeptical challenges to the results of these tests should be understood as incompetently expressed doubts about the quality of associated theory or its parts.[1] Hence I conclude that, because pertinent criticism of the associated theory cannot be offered without extensive familiarity with that theory, contemporary epistemology can either withdraw from its role in the criticism of scientific method or make the special subject matter of science relevant to the development of epistemic principles.

Philosophical Analysis and Scientific Method

Strands of philosophical naturalism have been hard to isolate, particularly when the goals of an "independent" philosophical project coincide with foundational projects of a scientific program. Since a naturalistic perspective doesn't appear at once fully articulated, otherwise naturalistic philosophers sometimes seek to reform scientific practice when it conflicts with philosophical principle; distracted by the morass of methodological details, innocent of the relevant scientific theory, they retreat to orthodox, a priori conditions on epistemic evaluation.[2] Now that it is routine for philosophers to comment on the methods and content of science, retreat to familiar a priori standards is increasingly evident. Moreover, because the normal function of philosophy in these exchanges has been to assess the rational-

---

1. Notice that I have said nothing that would imply that the attempt to demonstrate the independence of several methods is an idle or merely skeptical concern. The demonstration of the independence of diverse tests is an important and interesting scientific practice, designed as it is to establish the immunity of separate tests from similar or systematic biases. Attempts to demonstrate independence in real cases—in specific theoretical contexts—demand what I will call disciplined skepticism, which tempts neither conspiracy nor omniscience. It is only undisciplined skepticism that is subject to this charge.

2. Occasionally, identifiable philosophical influences can be found explicitly in scientific movements. For a brief period in this century, for example, it appeared that the deflationary metaphysics and foundationalist epistemology of logical empiricism motivated the operationalist account of measurement in physics.

ity of methods, pricking the scientist's conscience in matters normative, an impression has been conveyed that an epistemology without "distinctly philosophical," a priori principles must be purely descriptive.

In the first instance, the possibility of spuriousness and pseudo-robustness might be thought to pose an epistemic threat to the knowledge claim that an effect represents a real causal factor. After all, if the effect were actually a manifestation of pseudo-robustness, this fact would undermine the reason we had for believing that the observed effect always represents the underlying cause of interest, thereby defeating the knowledge claim. Spuriousness and pseudo-robustness therefore function as undercutting defeaters, to use John Pollock's phrase (Pollock, 1984, 1986, 1989). So too do most skeptical hypotheses such as deception at the hands of an evil demon or the indistinguishability of dreaming and waking worlds.

Many philosophers express the intuition that mere possibilities cannot defeat actual justification, even if one could not distinguish between the presence of the real object and its skeptic-induced alternative. In "Discrimination and Perceptual Knowledge," Alvin Goldman describes a country drive on which a father (Henry) identifies various roadside objects for his son. Henry points to an object and says, "That's a barn," and in fact he is correct. But now suppose, with Goldman, that there are also some papier-mâché barn facades in the area. If Henry were unable to distinguish from the road between a barn and a barn facade, Goldman suggests, even when Henry is correct we would withdraw the claim that he knows that there is a barn there. Because the prospect that we are experiencing a barn facsimile is, in this environment, a relevant alternative, its specter is an undercutting defeater of the warrant for the claim that the observed object is a barn. Goldman, who first dubbed the concept of a relevant alternative, deploys the notion centrally in his analysis of knowledge: "A person knows that p, I suggest, only if the actual state of affairs in which p is true is distinguishable or discriminable by him from a relevant possible state of affairs in which p is false" (1976, p. 124; also see Goldman 1986, pp. 44–57).

It is doubtful that there is a general account of what makes an alternative relevant. Goldman claims that the actual presence of a barn facsimile makes the possibility of its presence a relevant alternative. As a result, there would be a circumstance in which he could not distinguish between an actual state of affairs in which "That's a barn" is true from a relevant possible state of affairs in which "That's a barn" is false.

Building on the concept of a relevant alternative, we can define a relevant defeater as an actual state of affairs whose presence undermines warrant for a knowledge claim, an alternative one must be in an evidential position to exclude to be credited with knowledge. In this sense, the actual presence of barn facsimiles in the area is a relevant defeater of the knowledge claim that the viewed object is a barn. On the other hand, were there no barn facsimiles around, the possibility that we could be seeing one is not a relevant alternative state of affairs. So, just as merely possible states of affairs are irrelevant alternatives, merely possible states of affairs that would (if true) undermine warrant for a knowledge claim are irrelevant defeaters. I will refer to these as vacuous or idle defeaters, and it will be my contention in what immediately follows that vacuous defeaters are not genuine defeaters.

Goldman's account of relevant alternatives was designed as part of an analysis of knowledge—not as a systematic response to skepticism. The deep and committed skeptic would regard as question-begging Goldman's partitioning of relevant and irrelevant alternatives, as Stewart Cohen (1991) and others have indicated. But notice that there is an important difference between the banal response to skepticism and the causal relevance response considered here. Although in both cases a possibility of defeat raises a worry about warrant, the possibilities have different origins. In the first case, the possible sources of defeat require only a rich imagination and a general familiarity with the epistemic risk associated with inductive judgments. By contrast, in the second case not just imagination and familiarity with inductive risk introduce the specter of justificatory defeat (although they too may be at play) but specific information concerning how this particular body of evidence bears on the knowledge claim. In the context of scientific theory testing, the conditions of justificatory defeat for a specific theoretical claim are given by a rich body of well-established theory telling us which methods are appropriate for certain experimental designs, which potential artifacts are plausible, and so forth, as we will see below. So in Goldman's barn case, we can explain why the presence of barn facsimiles threatens warrant for the claim that some specific observation is of a barn, and we do so without recourse to the claim that the possible presence of barn facsimiles belongs to a virtually limitless class of nonactual possibilities we must exclude.

There is at least one way of demonstrating that the mere possibility of spuriousness or pseudo-robustness is not a relevant epistemic alternative. The first one begins by defining a minimal criterion of relevance, in terms of which we can define a vacuous defeater. A minimal requirement on the epistemic relevance of some condition C to hypothesis h is that being made aware that C obtains should have some influence, positive or negative, on level of warrant for some hypothesis h. Suppose that one infers that hypothesis h is true on the basis of evidence e: For example, if an oscilloscope displays a distinctive 60 Hz pattern, e, and you appeal to e as a basis for your inference that h (that the cluster of neurons you are recording from has a spiking frequency of 60 Hz) is true. You then learn that the oscilloscope is not filtered from ordinary 60 Hz house current. Because the filtering of the oscilloscope controls for a theoretically relevant artifact, its filtering is epistemically relevant. Therefore, the fact that the oscilloscope is not filtered must be excluded in order for there to be sufficient warrant for the hypothesis that these cells have a spiking frequency of 60 Hz. Finally, notice that knowing that the oscilloscope has not been filtered (condition C) will result in a change in the probability assigned to hypothesis h.

By contrast, a vacuous defeater is a condition that does not need to be excluded prior to the establishment of some knowledge claim, a condition that provides no reason to doubt that e offers sufficient warrant for h. One mark of a vacuous defeater is that calling attention to the possibility that it obtains will, by itself, do nothing to the probabilities that you distribute among your various beliefs.[3] For example, the possible existence of an evil demon, once brought to our attention, would not cause us to reassign confidence in our beliefs. Of course, once the possibility is brought to the attention of the demon skeptic making the charge, he would act no differently in light of this information. Since the mere possibility of deception obtains for both the skeptic and the antiskeptic, it ranges over both. In short, vacuous defeaters, like abstract threats of possible spuriousness or pseudo-robustness, don't change any of the probability assignments for levels of rational epistemic commitment, because the threat ranges over all cases. Therefore the same specter of spuriousness and pseudo-robustness hangs over the very research of the scientist making a charge of possible pseudo-robustness.

This latter feature of vacuous defeaters is typically expressed as a kind of ad hominem charge of inconsistency against the skeptic making the charge. As such, this version of the antiskeptical strategy has distinct dialectical limitations. My purpose here is not to refute the thoroughgoing skeptic but to shift the burden to the critic claiming that idle possibilities are genuine defeaters. It also reveals the context sensitivity of knowledge attributions—that our attribution of warrant for knowledge claims is sensitive to the total evidence one possesses.[4] Whether in philosophical analysis or scientific criticism, vacuous defeaters are not genuine defeaters.

Demon Criticism: Error Due to Chance Factors

Broadly speaking, experimental effects reach significance (or patterns in the data occur) for one of three reasons: (1) the design has isolated a real causal factor, (2) ordinary sampling variations introduce chance factors, or (3) the design and instrumentation are biased in the direction of a certain pattern, no matter what the influence of the world. This third sort of error, bias or "treatment error," is systematic: It affects all objects that receive the specific experimental treatment, and the influence may be either positive or negative. The sensitivity of an instrument, size of the sample tested, and specific characteristics of the stimuli selected can all be sources of systematic error. We will discuss the significance of this possibility in the next section. Here we will examine the significance of the second source of error, one that arises from random fluctuations in subject performance. The magnitude of this error varies from subject to subject; random error is, as one might expect from the name, unsystematic. And, unlike bias, random error operates over a series of experiments to reduce the likelihood of the accumulation of either positive or negative instances of a hypothesis.

In any single case, however, we cannot be certain that an effect reaching significance results from chance factors. This anxiety is shared by more than a few

---

3. I am grateful to Stuart Glennan for pointing out an error in an earlier formulation of this point.
4. At the same time, you can hold that knowledge attributions are context sensitive without claiming that their context sensitivity is exhausted by their indexicality. Other, pragmatic features determine the plausibility of the skeptic's epistemic proposals, such as the implicature that the skeptic can do without such machinery. See Dretske's replies to critics in Dretske (1991).

philosophers of science, whether realist, empiricist, or constructivist. And although the skeptical worry is characteristic of empiricist aims, we can also find this undisciplined concern among those of realist inclination who either haven't fully embraced a naturalistic epistemology or are unconvinced of the reliability of certain social-scientific methodologies. Indeed, we can find this concern even among those, such as Paul Meehl, who clearly appreciate the power of diverse testing and who would otherwise count as a disciplined critic.[5] According to Meehl, relying on an experimental result requires that we accept a special kind of ceteris paribus clause, "that there are no *systematic* factors left unmentioned"— confounding factors—that might account for the results: "The ceteris paribus clause amounts to a very strong and highly improbable negative assertion, to wit, *nothing else is at work except factors that are totally random and therefore subject to being dealt with by our statistical methods*" (1990a, p. 111; his emphasis). If this were really the correct understanding of the ceteris paribus clause, it would be surprising that scientists continue their research on the same effect. Why should they, if they really believe their result represents the effect of the intended factor and nothing but the intended factor? But scientists are well aware of their own provisional epistemic position. They are committed to an ongoing program of research. Therefore they attempt to triangulate on the same result, improve the techniques for measuring it, and so on. But, more to the point, if research is to be derogated because it makes this negative assertion, then any experimental result (even any conceivable one) could be criticized on the same grounds. Nowhere in science do we find so ideal an experimental condition. This extreme statement of ceteris paribus clauses ("nothing else is at work except factors that are totally random") has as a consequence a prohibition on routine epistemic risk. Therefore, when used in an attempt to undermine warrant for ontological commitment (as it is here), it is a vacuous defeater.[6]

---

5. In addition to Meehl, I will draw from philosophers such as Howson and Urbach and social scientists such as Gergen and Goffman. Paul Meehl expresses perfectly the attraction of diverse testing:

> *Wherever possible, two or more nonredundant estimates of the same theoretical quantity should be made, because multiple approximations to a theoretical number are always more valuable, providing that methods of setting permissible tolerances exist, than a so-called exact test of significance, or even an exact setting of confidence intervals.* (1978, p. 829; his emphasis)

But because recommendations for methodological improvement can be pitched at various levels of generality, it is not especially surprising that a skilled practitioner or theoretician might lapse into undisciplined, inappropriately abstract skeptical worries or state a position that has skeptical consequences, no matter what the intent. In presenting such lapses, I have not attempted to represent the body of their work as a seamless whole.

6. More pristine empiricist motives can be found in the work of van Fraassen. According to his constructive empiricism, the ceteris paribus clause, the source of such uncertainty on Meehl's view, has a purely pragmatic function. Briefly, laws about unobservables are counterfactual supporting and, to be so, they require ceteris paribus clauses that "fix" particular conditions: "But who keeps what fixed? The speaker, in his mind. There is therefore a contextual variable—determining the content of that tacit *ceteris paribus* clause—which is crucial to the truth-value of the conditional statement" (van Fraassen 1980, p. 116). To the extent that the generalization goes beyond what is observable, the

Although pertinent methodological criticism is always welcome, I will contend that these social scientists and psychologists do themselves and their profession a disservice if they fret over this abstract threat of spurious effects. The disciplined, theoretically informed skeptic will forgo the abstract charge for a more pointed, topic-specific recommendation: "It is not enough to spot flaws in a study; a responsible critic would go on to show how these flaws lead to a counterhypothesis that can explain the observations" (Bross 1970, p. 99).

Undisciplined criticism is also a recognizable tendency among philosophers who are unfamiliar with the specific subject matter and who, in general, disagree with the conclusions of specific research. Given philosophers' facility for producing alternative explanations of the data and their typical innocence of the scientific subject matter, this tendency toward abstractness is understandable. But in the form set out above, the charge is inappropriately abstract, raising the methodological dispute to a rarefied level that is powerless to evaluate the specific content of theoretical claims. This charge also conveys the misleading impression that routine methodological criticism in the social sciences isn't, or at least needn't be, topic specific. Of course, the normal practice of comparing only plausible rival explanations requires disciplined knowledge of the subject matter.

Something like this distinction between disciplined and undisciplined criticism is also at play, at least tacitly, in the familiar recommendation that we take seriously only those artifacts that are theoretically plausible, ignoring methodological criticism motivated by nothing more than remotely possible artifacts. In the social science classic *Unobtrusive Measures*, the authors diagnose undisciplined skepticism and propose a treatment:

> In some logical sense, even in a "true" experimental comparison, an infinite number of potential laws could predict this result. We do not let this logical state of affairs prevent us from interpreting the results. Instead, uncertainty comes only from those unexcluded hypotheses to which we, in the current state of our science, are willing to give the status of established laws: These are the plausible rival hypotheses. (Webb, et al. 1966, p. 10)

In order to decide which hypotheses are theoretically plausible, however, one must be theoretically informed, educated, or disciplined in the particular field. Nevertheless, practitioners continue to repeat this abstract worry: "Given widespread and possibly rapid fluctuations in patterns of human conduct, there is no reasonable hypothesis about human activity for which support (or disconfirmation) cannot be generated" (Gergen 1982, p. 41). Lamenting uncertainty, Gergen despairs of an entire line of social research on dissonance. In-house disputes "ultimately revealed that there was no way in which the psychological basis for behav-

---

ceteris paribus clause is a convention that the speaker (or scientist) adopts, reflecting his or her interests or purposes. This move is characteristic of another empiricist attitude toward the unobservable, according to which the universal character of laws is a superficial feature of our language rather than an epistemic feature of our theories guided by the world. All putative knowledge of true, counterfactual-supporting generalizations, then, is conditioned upon the operation of a pragmatic, context-dependent, *ceteris paribus* clause.

ioral events could be unequivocally demonstrated" (p. 120). Initially, the source
of this epistemological concern is difficult to locate; as often happens, untenable
epistemic commitments are obscured by the concern for methodological improvement. I will argue that this concern represents the residue of various skeptical
theses, from the claim that knowledge requires certainty to the contention that
knowledge requires knowing that you know (for penetrating discussions of various
skeptical theses, see Goldman 1986; Lycan 1988). Of course, I don't mean to
suggest that philosophical critics of this methodological rule would explicitly demand certainty as a condition for knowledge or that they would publicly endorse
the infamous KK thesis (in order to know that p, you must know that you know
that p.) Rather, license for skepticism is implicit in their worries over the possibility of a spurious effect.

In light of the earlier discussion of vacuous defeaters, a rationale can be provided for consideration of only specific, theoretically plausible counterhypotheses
as potential defeaters. The possibility of spuriousness is ubiquitous; for that reason,
recognition of this concern (1) governs the critic's favored theoretical results as
well as the victim's and (2) generates no change in anyone's rational level of
epistemic commitment about pertinent theoretical issues.

Diverse Testing and the Threat of Pseudo-robustness

The diverse testing of a hypothesis is a similar priority in the natural and social
sciences. The existence of molecules was confirmed by the phenomena of thermal
conduction, Brownian motion, and a host of other discovered natural processes,
with each source of evidence having its own specially adapted technique of detection. The virtues of diverse testing are recognized by social scientists as well.
Historians arrived at the existence of a cult of domesticity from diverse testimony
in literary and political sources, and psychologists determined the existence of
stored prototypes by reaction time and ranking methods. In courts of law, converging reports from diverse eyewitnesses, or from physical and eyewitness evidence, constitute powerful grounds for inferring the occurrence of an event or the
guilt of a person. This realist methodological rule concerning the appropriateness
of ontological commitment can be stated generally: We are entitled to infer the
existence of phenomena that survive diverse tests.

Phenomena detected under such varied circumstances can be called "robust"
(Levins 1968; Wimsatt 1981). In chapter 6, I argued that close attention to experimental contexts reveals a principle of robustness that scientists seem to respect
and that only a realist can explain: An experiment provides prima facie reason
for thinking that an effect is real if the effect (1) is detectable by diverse (and
independent) methods, (2) is reproducible by optimally similar designs, and (3)
survives theoretical integration. Of empiricism and realism, only realism vindicates this principle, because the principle is applied equally to observable and
unobservable phenomena. Moreover, the most plausible and natural explanation
for the reliability of this principle—one that does not treat scientists as incompe-
tent in matters of design, as insensitive to feedback, or as otherwise systematically
defective—confers on the world a role in the regulation of scientists' beliefs.

The principle of robustness is one expression of the various realist doctrines concerning evidential conditions and methods that license theoretical commitment.[7] According to some philosophers and scientists, however, we can never be certain that the first condition—detection by diverse (and independent) methods—is ever satisfied in practice.[8] Anticipating these charges, Wimsatt has drawn our attention to a class of effects that he calls "pseudo-robust," effects that appear to satisfy these three conditions (and many more, on Wimsatt's account) but that are nonetheless spurious due to "the failure of the different supposedly independent tests, means of detection, models, or derivations to be truly independent" (1981, p. 156).

As a matter of practice, these standards of robustness are applied evenly to observable and unobservable phenomena. Yet some philosophers deny that diverse tests have the power to yield knowledge of unobservables, citing the ever-present threat of pseudo-robustness. This denial has empiricist motivations of the following sort. Whether or not the net influence of nonindependent assumptions is unobservable, at least at the time of a particular experiment, this impact is as yet unobserved; its operation is uncontrolled and its value is unknown. The resulting lack of certainty concerning the source of the effect compromises any inference to the existence of the studied effect. The critic and sanguine alike recognize the long-term, bias-correcting value of variation in method. But they also concede that, whenever diverse techniques of theory testing share common assumptions, it is possible that experimental (and other) results are artifacts of those conspiring or nonindependent techniques.

Although it is a familiar idea that diverse techniques provide more secure grounds for ontological commitment, genuinely cumulative support requires that the sources of evidence must be reasonably independent of one another: Eyewitnesses should not have had the same preconceptions about what they would see, instrumentation should not be of similar design, and the like. The required sort of independence, however, is not always easy to come by. In fact, the theory dependence of scientific method—one of the most important theses in twentieth-century philosophy of science—is thought by some to compromise efforts to formulate truly independent tests. Different methods for studying the same phenomenon often evolve within the same theoretical tradition. Recognizing the value of diverse testing, scientists deliberately select different techniques. But with a common theoretical source, the handful of diverse methods recognized as theoretically useful can harbor substantial presuppositions that are not truly independent

---

7. See, for example, Boyd ([1983] 1991a), Devitt (1991), Ellis (1990), Giere (1988), Hacking (1983), McMullin (1984), W. Salmon (1984), Smart (1968), and Wimsatt (1981).

8. Establishing independence is no trivial matter. In the minimal, statistical sense of independence, two tests are independent if their results are uncorrelated when one factor is considered: If we have two methods for the assessment of the influence of factor A on factor E, then these two methods are uncorrelated when, besides the influence of A common to both methods, there is no correlation between the two methods when we examine E. There is, in addition, a richer, causal sense of independence among methods. And for familiar reasons of the "third cause" sort, correlational dependence between the results of two tests need not imply causal dependence of one result on the other.

of one another. In short, theory dependence introduces a bias into the selection of methods. The apparent conflict between the fact of theory dependence and the need for sound methodology poses a special problem for realists, who, while insisting on the theory dependence of method, use the survival of an effect under diverse tests as evidence that the object exists.

Partly for reasons of the theory dependence of experimental design, social scientists and concerned philosophers often express a dismal methodological concern about our inability to detect with certainty the presence of nonindependent assumptions. As one representative research psychologist puts the worry: "Experiments invite the researcher to preselect settings that will ensure support for his or her hypothesis. One can never be certain that alternative settings of greater numerosity would not yield findings to the contrary" (Gergen 1982, p. 119). So it is always conceivable, in any particular instance, that the realist rule will mislead us. In an equivocal criticism of social science research design, suggesting either bias or lack of validity generalization, Goffman claims that "the variables that emerge tend to be creatures of research designs that have no substance outside the room in which the apparatus and subjects are located, except perhaps briefly when a replication or a continuity is performed under sympathetic auspices and a full moon" (1971, pp. 20–21).

The threat of pseudo-robustness due to nonindependence can be dramatized by comparing an ideal instance of experimental design with a degenerate one. One might simply rig a theory to produce the predicted result. In such a case, we have a powerful intuition that this theory derives no confirmation from the occurrence of the effect. Of course, any effects issuing from such theories are pseudo-robust, and, precisely because these rigged theories *are* degenerate, actual theories suffer less from nonindependent assumptions. But theoretical assumptions don't have to be purposely so rigged to be dependent; they may have been generated by the same theoretical tradition, a tradition of which some scientists are uncritical.[9] This point can be illustrated rather simply. Because scientists select only those "diverse" tests identified as theoretically plausible rather than as merely possible, not all tests have an equal probability of being selected. In fact, those that have a higher probability of being selected are just those identified by the theory and are thus more likely to share the same theoretical assumptions than those not selected.

---

9. Explanation—the act of "accounting for the data"—doesn't escape these pseudo-robustness concerns. In fact, because explanation occurs after the data are in, it is thought to be even more subject to the threat of nonindependence than prediction. This fear is nicely described by Glymour et al.: "People rightly worry that a theory constructed by someone after seeing the data will be constructed specifically to account for the data. If the theory is deliberately constructed to account for the data, then the data provides no test of the theory and hence no reason to believe the theory. This worry is well founded, but misstated" (1987, p. 58). A good explanation requires more than just consistency or relations of entailment. According to Glymour et al., we have the strong sense that "some theories are unsatisfactory because they are 'cooked' to account for the data. . . . Cooked theories may entail the evidence but they don't entail the evidence in the right way" (p. 59).

This skeptical attitude toward experiment has another aspect, according to which we abandon the hope for assurance of assumption independence for a guarantee that the causal influences not under investigation will cancel each other out in a way that permits the valid measurement of the target variable:

> Whatever the size of the sample, two treatment groups are absolutely certain to differ in some respect, indeed, in infinitely many respects, any of which might, unknown to us, be causally implicated in the trial outcome. So randomization cannot possibly guarantee that the groups will be free from bias by unknown nuisance factors. And since one obviously doesn't know what those unknown factors are, one is in no position to calculate the probability of such a bias developing either. (Howson and Urbach 1989, p. 152)

The considerations expressed here impugn more than just the power claimed for randomization; they could be recruited to show that there is no method, or group of methods, that could "possibly guarantee that the groups will be free from bias by unknown nuisance factors." For any experimental setting, the same doubts could be raised. And when raised against a discipline, no matter how successful, well integrated and otherwise well confirmed, what we have is demon skepticism applied to experimental settings, a vacuous defeater masquerading as a relevant possibility.

Notice that the undisciplined critic is now raising the stakes. What began as a methodological demand to employ diverse methods that are, to the best of our disciplined theoretical knowledge, independent is now transformed into an animated concern that we can never be absolutely certain of the value and direction of possible "nuisance factors." Without certainty of independence, we are awash in contingency.

This is the now-familiar cry of the undisciplined critic, who is trying to make global skeptical hay out of the following epistemological truism: For any given experiment whose hypothesis is confirmed, it is always possible that the positive instance is part of a pattern of pseudo-robust results. But if we recall, it was those scientists with knowledge of the field and with motivated theoretical concerns—disciplined critics—who eventually succeeded in correcting the bias. It appears that this informed skepticism is the appropriate methodological response to the possibility of pseudo-robustness. For the identification of systematic error must specify which causal factors in the subject matter are likely to be confounded, a particular alternative method, and so on. In fact, it is a bit misleading to dub this scrupulousness "skepticism," even if disciplined. For it is not skepticism to which philosophers often retreat when they dislike a conclusion or otherwise want to trip up an opponent. Instead, this vigilance constitutes the sort of methodological care routinely exercised by working scientists. The undisciplined critic's concern, by contrast, would be methodologically inappropriate. Theoretical disputes could not be resolved and progress could not be made if scientists drew back from ontological commitment or suspended judgment about the reliability of an experimental outcome simply because possible artifacts "they know not what" could have produced the effect.

Since pseudo-robustness is actual—with many instances in the history of science and thus no mere fancy of an imaginary opponent—we can now explore the standard methodologies that protect against such theoretical offenses. In so doing, we can guard against the prospect that we are in the grips of a methodology that will, in the long run, license results that are pseudo-robust. Several techniques are routinely employed to guard against pseudo-robustness, techniques that are neither controversial nor especially speculative. But it should be pointed out that these methods, to be applied successfully, must be guided by topic-specific principles. I will argue that, should the undisciplined critic still want to deny that these bias-correcting methods provide adequate protection against pseudo-robustness, she must then either abandon the "no worldly conspiracies" principle, a very weak causal principle, or require the prediction of the future history of science, a very strong epistemic demand. Neither option rationalizes scientific investigation.

Bias-Correcting Techniques

There is a good general reason for valuing diverse tests. Each relevantly different technique engages different causal influences. And since these causal influences are so plentiful and uncontrolled, they are thought to conflict; the variation of measurement techniques constitutes a source of unsystematic or random error in the sample. If the effect keeps turning up, it does so in spite of the abundant, conflicting causal influences that you would otherwise expect to wash out a less robust (or pseudo-robust) effect.[10]

The preference for diverse tests gets satisfied in two ways. Because researchers recognize the importance of the convergent validity purchased by diverse methods, scientists often deliberately formulate different methods for testing the same phenomenon. Call this process deliberate variation. But a certain amount of variation in technique occurs in any case, owing to differences in availability of resources or from lack of explicit coordination of research methodology across labs. Even instances of the same type of design will vary from lab to lab, if for no other reason than setting and resources. Call this process unplanned variation. Deliberate and unplanned variation are routine and familiar ways of achieving convergent validity.

Further corrective considerations can be raised. When the theory's history indicates that it has been especially subject to pseudo-robustness, its current ability to integrate with affiliated theories can indicate just how serious the threat of pseudo-robustness is at present. Therefore, even if diverse methods within the same discipline might conceal the same bias (thus amplifying it when it gets

---

10. If we are to work this argument from the diluting effects of random error, we must respect an important (Gaussian) qualification: The errors must be truly random and thus independent. Now, of course, we can't know when they are, but we know of cases in which they are not; it is this knowledge that allows us to identify potentially interfering artifacts. Fortunately, because independence is a matter of degree, errors need not be perfectly independent for the long-term sequence of quasi-random error to tend toward cancellation or toward summing to zero.

confirmed again by a conspiring technique), it is unlikely that techniques drawn from different sciences, having different methodological histories, would conspire to conceal the same bias and thus produce the same conclusion. This is why the reliable role of auxiliary hypotheses drawn from remote theories provides such good evidence for the existence of the object under study; it is less likely in such cases that the assumptions are common or insidiously dependent. I explore the contribution of theoretical integration to diverse testing in the next section.

An additional reason for supposing the long-term reliability of diverse testing, one already familiar from meta-analysis, is the statistical study of summaries of published research. First, recall that random error varies from object to object in a particular experiment. The total expected value is normally assumed to be zero, because the random (uncontrolled) influences are thought to cancel each other out upon a large enough sample of subjects. Now, suppose we sample a population of experiments that employ diverse methods, perhaps even methods harboring dependent assumptions. If we sample across enough studies, the differences between those studies can be treated as random errors, as we treated the variation from object to object within an experiment. Of course, it is always possible that here, as in the earlier instances of offending designs, the different studies in the sampled population are not sufficiently independent to count the error as random. But by hypothesis, their methods are different in some respects that are regarded as theoretically important, and thus we should not expect the error to be entirely systematic; many of the unknown causal factors contributing to the error term should be of opposing value (if there is any symmetry between observed and unobserved factors, a supposition whose denial would entail enormous argumentative burden). Then suppose that, taken collectively, these studies yield values expected from the presence of the predicted effect. If we acknowledge the fundamental assumption of design—that uncontrolled causal factors cancel each other out over a large enough series of trials—then the presence of an effect in an increasingly large and diversified sample of studies should warrant the claim that the effect is real rather than spurious.[11]

Although similarities exist between my argument and the so-called miracle argument for realism—they are both abductive, for example—they also display important differences in structure and effect. The miracle argument purports to show that, given the instrumental reliability of some theory, it would strain credulity to suggest that the theory and its affiliates are not also approximately true. By

---

11. The bias-diluting or bias-reducing effects of random error is one of the worldly assumptions of experimental design. The independence of each random effect on each subject in a sample (or on each measurement of an instrument) reduces the likelihood of patterned results; that is what makes certain patterns in the data, when they do recur under diverse tests, particularly striking and theoretically interesting. This principle is based on the assumption of the canceling effects of error, an assumption stated (and sometimes even justified) in any standard statistics text. For sheer clarity and simplicity, it is hard to improve upon Guy's statement of the assumption, fashioned over 150 years ago: "[T]he errors necessarily existing in our observations and experiments (the consequence of the imperfection of our senses, or of our instruments) neutralize each other, and leave the actual value of the object or objects observed" (1839, p. 32).

contrast, the argument here does not require the instrumental reliability of the theory in question. Instead, the central contention is that deliberate and unplanned variation in method weigh against the persistence of a particular experimental effect or theoretical commitment—whether or not the theory that supports them is approximately true. Nor do I need to argue that all versions of empiricism have these unacceptable consequences to argue that these empiricist worries do have skeptical consequences.

Worldly Conspiracies and Predicting the Future History of Science

With the qualifications mentioned earlier, robustness normally licenses an inference to the reality of an entity. In drawing this inference, scientists depend on the "no worldly conspiracies" principle. The reliability of this ontological inference is established in much the same manner as the pragmatic justification of induction. In the latter case, the defense proceeds by establishing not that induction is reliable but that it is reliable if any method is. In light of the fact that scientists in no way treat the reliability of induction as conditional, only the claim that the world is uniform in the relevant respects can vindicate the scientist's confidence. Similarly, only the nonconspiratorial character of the world can ratify the scientist's confidence in diverse testing, a point that will be established in the present section.

Because pseudo-robustness is actual, the disciplined critic might legitimately worry even in the face of deliberate and unplanned variation. But reservations about the inductive reliability of diverse testing, like the familiar reservations concerning induction generally, are rooted in empiricist epistemology that has traditionally been understood as infallibilist. The undisciplined critic contends that the inference to existence is in general epistemically unreliable, due to the ubiquitous threat of unobserved and thus unknown "nuisance factors." Such concerns have the form of traditional epistemological challenges, that some knowledge claim that p lacks adequate justification because it is conceivable that p is false (you cannot be certain that p). As I mentioned earlier, I am by no means suggesting that the demand for certainty implied by undisciplined skepticism is the official, considered view of parties to this dispute or is explicitly defended by anyone as a credible view. Rather, I am suggesting that undisciplined skepticism is a (typically unrecognized) consequence of unduly abstract standards for methodological improvement. In their most prominent forms, these epistemological theses are infallibilist because the required justification resides in some set of favored beliefs that are supposedly incorrigible or certain. And these theses appear to be nonnaturalistic, in the end, because they cannot accommodate the insights of causal accounts of perception or extensions of that account to reliable information-gathering processes generally.

The undisciplined critic will no doubt be unmoved by the argument from the corrective power of method variation, and I now want to address two responses in turn. In the skeptical response to the claimed bias-correcting power of deliberate variation, notice how features of a nonnaturalistic epistemology reemerge in more strained form. We can never be certain, the critic says, that deliberate selection of diverse methods has protected against pseudo-robustness. Perhaps researchers thought they were selecting independent (and thus diverse) assumptions when they used two assumptions together. But the assumptions turned out to be misleadingly dependent. Even the most earnest effort toward diversity provides no guarantee of independence.

Next, consider the objection to the claimed bias-correcting power of unplanned variation. We can't be sure, the critic says, that in such cases the variation in methods or sample selection really is unplanned. After all, scientists within the same discipline and generation read the same journals, attend the same conferences, and train with the same texts. Under such highly structured and socially controlled circumstances, it would be surprising if apparently "spontaneous" methodological choices weren't constrained by similarities of training and resources; their choices are spontaneous only in the sense that they are not systematically and expressly coordinated through careful correspondence among labs.

Neither objection to the bias-correcting power of variation is ultimately persuasive, in part because they are simple extensions of the undisciplined criticism described earlier. The fact that unplanned and deliberate variation fails to completely ensure assumption independence is a vacuous defeater. An indictment of this sort would impugn every scientific enterprise, for, philosophers' unreasonable expectations aside, good science persists, even flourishes, under epistemic risk.

Against the second concern that scientific training has already structured choices in such a way that variation in method is never truly unplanned, one might point out that for the virtues of diverse testing to be operative—that is, for the bias-correcting force of random error to have at least some salubrious influence—all that is required is that instrumentation is not actually shared by labs and that special care is not taken to replicate design features. Short of that, uncontrolled differences in method, typically and in the long run, would be expected to wash out the effects of conspiring assumptions. Of course, the undisciplined critic might then claim that unplanned variation contributes too modestly to the error term to have much corrective influence, even if it might have some. This concession to corrective influence, minor though it is, is a step in the right direction. For the quest to determine just how much error is contributed by unplanned variation requires attention to particular methods applied in specific theoretical domains, constituting a move toward a less abstract, more theoretically informed and disciplined critical attitude.

As we saw, variation in method introduces random influences that would tend to wash out the effects of systematic error or bias. The antirealist empiricist holds as significant that variation provides no guarantee of bias reduction. For diverse testing to fail in the long run, however, the world's causal factors would have to change in ways that evade our effort to investigate them: thus the idea that the world would have to conspire to keep information from us.[12] And this paranoid

---

12. I am assuming that there are some systematic philosophical views, such as subjective idealism, that modern scientists and philosophers would not regard as satisfactory explanations for the persistent failure of diverse testing due to nonindependence.

metaphysics is even more presumptuous than it at first sounds, for not just any evasion will do; the evasive change in the world must not increase the likelihood that deliberate and unplanned variation in technique will isolate a real causal factor.

To be certain, before an experimental test, that no artifactual causal factor is uncontrolled, we must already have knowledge of all relevant causal factors, the extent of their influence, the nature of their interactions, and other such matters. If we had such knowledge, however, we would be in a position to accurately predict what discoveries will be made. Therefore, the antirealist critic presupposes an epistemology of science that demands that our theories empower us to predict the future history of science. That is not to suggest that the empiricist is at leisure to make such a presupposition. If the empiricist holds science to standards so high that we must be certain that robustness is not specious, or be certain that theoretical assumptions are independent, then even inductions about observables would fail—an unpleasant consequence for the empiricist and one she would surely reject.

The theory dependence of testing can be a source of nonindependence, and when the theory in question is a bad one, then the test results can reflect systematic error. Fortunately, there is a check on systematic error owing to bad theory: theoretical integration. If we have a handful of reasonably good theories, or at least better than the poor one envisioned above, the process of theoretical integration can act as a reliable constraint on theory acceptance.

Theoretical Integration as Triangulation

It might first appear that I am presenting the empiricist with a certain kind of dilemma: Either rest content with current standards of diverse testing or else demand (unreasonably) that we be able to predict the future history of science. Such a dilemma, the opponent might argue, is too optimistic about our history of theoretical success, particularly concerning the power of internal mechanisms of science to detect specious robustness. I agree. It is worth noticing, however, that the corrective mechanisms needn't be internal. By displaying confidence in the reliability of diverse testing, we needn't have an overly optimistic attitude toward the corrective power of the internal mechanisms of science. For example, external, social criticism of scientific policy and practice exercised just such a corrective influence on theories of intelligence, helping to undermine the racist accounts that dominated much popular and professional psychology in this century (Block and Dworkin 1976). For a time, the psychological community was resistant to the charge that IQ tests produce pseudo-robust effects, treating as independent a student's performance on an "intelligence" test and thus ultimately confounding the diverse but causally related (nonindependent) influences of cultural background, social status, income, and so forth.[13] When the social impact of abortive

---

13. Where good science requires statistical methods, it typically requires far more than that; statistical methods must be correctly applied to a particular subject matter. The fact that statistical methods-

or biased research is great, as IQ research was on the searching educational reforms of the 1960s, external mechanisms such as social organizing, lobbying, riots,
and protests can and sometimes do exert a corrective influence.

Theoretical integration, too, represents a form of triangulation, and so its existence and nature can be parleyed into an argument for the relative independence
of assumptions or (what amounts to the same thing) an argument against the
conspiracy of unknown causal influences. When two or more theories appeal to
the same mechanisms, we often have reason to think that the existence of those
mechanisms have been arrived at by relatively independent means. Our reasons
are two. First, often the integrated disciplines cover phenomena that are otherwise causally remote; for example, the joint application of subatomic physics and
neuroscience made possible the use of magnetic resonance imaging for medical
diagnoses. Second, and in part because of their remoteness, these disciplines have
very different histories. With such differences in their histories and in the causal
powers of their respective objects, these theories are more likely to embody relatively independent assumptions than if their histories had been more closely associated; put negatively, they are less likely to have conspired. Their successful integration therefore provides evidence in favor of the existence of the entities on
which both theories touch.

This same point can be made at the level of theoretical aims. Independence is
strikingly demonstrated when scientists with different aims arrive at the same
value, quantity, or other measurement. Consider the relation between sickle-cell
anemia and differences in resistance to malaria (see Elseth and Baumgardner
1984). Epidemiologists wondered why it is that, in nonmalarial zones, the frequency of the sickle-cell allele in the black population is relatively low. This fact
is tied to the special properties of a particular form of malaria (falciparum) that
fatally claims more victims among homozygotes with normal hemoglobin than
among heterozygotes. In malarial regions, homozygotes are less fit than heterozygotes; the former are less resistant to, and often die from, the malarial parasite.
But where there is little incidence of malaria, heterozygotes have no selective
advantage over homozygotes, and thus selection operates against the sickle-cell

---

can be applied with uneven success across theoretical domains displays that those methods interact
richly with the quality-determining features of theories. Statistical techniques applied to alchemical
theory, no matter how impressive the formal edifice, are unlikely to advance chemistry. Some of the
most dramatically false theories have been introduced, and even sustained, with formal pyrotechnics.

We can find a good example of statistical methods in the service of a poor theory in Richard
Herrnstein and Charles Murray's The Bell Curve, which has by now generated a large critical literature.
Descriptive statistics concerning the distribution of IQ scores, where IQ is considered a measure of
intelligence, does not advance Herrnstein and Murray's argument, which fails to address the wealth of
psychological literature that criticizes IQ as a measure of intelligence and supplies concrete alternatives
to the notion of IQ. To the extent that good science includes routine adherence to standards of peer
review and responsible, detailed reply to alternative positions, The Bell Curve is open to serious criticism as a work in psychological (or, on issues of heritability, biological) science. Of course, in addition
to its methodological problems, its factual errors cannot be mitigated by simply using statistical methods. (For pointed overviews, convincing criticisms, and plausible alternatives, see Sternberg 1995;
Gould 1995; Nisbett 1995; and Block 1995.)

allele. Several disciplines, such as biochemistry, genetics, epidemiology, and population and evolutionary biology, shed light on the nature of sickle-cell disease. Their proprietary explanatory aims, however, are so different that it is unlikely that their integration on the issue of sickle-cell disease is a mere artifact of theoretical conspiracy. Part of our understanding of this distribution is evolutionary, involving the concepts of fitness and selective advantage. But the notions of fitness and selection certainly can't be defined in chemical terms, and doubtfully in genetic terms. The discipline of genetics uses the concept of balanced polymorphism to explain the distribution of the allele in a population, but this notion does not in the first instance engage issues of chemical composition. Chemical accounts characterize the erythrocyte destruction associated with this anemia, but they are not directly concerned with its distribution. With theoretical aims so distinct, one would be hard pressed to account for evolutionary theorists', geneticists', and biochemists' explanatory use of notions like gene and allele in terms of shared training or research aims; the successful invocation of these notions by diverse disciplines (often originating from unanticipated cooperation) speaks to the existence of these entities. Abductive, explanatory considerations such as these play an important role in the realist's argument for the existence of postulated causal factors that have survived diverse tests. On the other hand, by resisting the treatment of these explanatory considerations as evidential, the critic of abduction will be unable to distinguish in an epistemically principled way between reliable scientific methods and the most deplorable epistemic practices. This is a consequence that most critics of abduction don't intend, for the realist and the critic of abduction normally agree that it is the special reliability of scientific methods that merits attention. Objections to abduction often begin locally, as a reservation about the status of a particular inference; but those objections typically do their ultimate damage globally, since abductive arguments are prevalent in nearly every area of intellectual inquiry and certainly in every area of good science.

On one account of theory articulation, integration requires that results in one domain not be inconsistent with those of another. This concern for consistency, especially in light of the merits of epistemic holism, might be thought to compromise the interests of independence, since adjustments in one theory must be logically sensitive to aspects of (and possibly changes in) another theory. Moreover, which adjustments are permissible in affiliated theories is a theory-dependent judgment. Therefore it would seem that theory dependence compromises independence only if tests in one area were carried out with an a priori eye toward theoretical integration; but this kind of formal or logical fastidiousness prior to the joint testing of theories seldom occurs in practice (see Kitcher 1981, 1989). In the first place, the demand for consistency, even if enforced, could not alone explain integration. Specific causal claims get integrated, not entire theories; to use the above example, we document the influence that a causal factor in, say, chemistry has on specific genetic properties. By way of those genetic features, those chemical kinds have a systematic effect on the frequency of the sickle-cell allele in the black population of nonmalarial zones. There are no general requirements that theories never assert causal claims that contradict those of an affiliated discipline; were this a constraint, it would be impossible to discover, as we some-times do, that the results of two domains indeed conflict. As a result, the concep-tion of theoretical integration as representative of robustness survives the failure of perfect integrative fit. If one discipline makes a contribution that turns out to be mistaken, the entire explanatory story is not treated as bankrupt; instead, the problematic fit then becomes a topic of attention and ultimate (often modest) correction. The standards that guide integration, like those that guide appraisals of independence, are topic specific. The piecemeal fashion in which integration proceeds indicates that theoretical integration is an a posteriori matter. And that results can be integrated after the fact—in diverse fields with different theoretical histories—is a reason for thinking that the methods have not conspired.

Morals of Naturalism

If broadly empiricist theorists are to criticize the realist implications of survival under diverse tests, and further to do so in the face of deliberate variation, un-planned variation, and theoretical integration, they must adopt either an episte-mology that is distinctly unnatural or a metaphysical view that is decidedly odd. Recall, the undisciplined critic's doubts were prompted by our failure to guarantee that our current methods are independent. But such a guarantee requires omni-science or at the very least the ability to accurately predict the future course of science. Moreover, if the skeptic abandons the epistemological demand for cer-tainty of independence, but nevertheless rejects the power of diverse testing, it could only be because he or she believes that the world changes in just those ways necessary to keep information from us. The first is an epistemological position so strong it is never satisfied; the second, a metaphysical thesis so peculiar it is never earnestly held.

Appropriate criticism must therefore be informed, or disciplined, by the rele-vant science. Those who think this conclusion insubstantial have perhaps forgot-ten a time not so long ago when philosophers of science presumed to tell scien-tists their business, rationally reconstructing their vocabulary in accordance with the philosopher's foundationalist epistemology and giving typically poor method-ological advice about how theories like that of evolution can be transmuted from pseudo- to genuine science with just a little effort. With an epistemology that defers to the causal knowledge of the informed critic, we can now understand why science has gotten on so well without philosophers dictating appropriate methodology. But more important, we can now make out the contours of a new, more thoroughly naturalistic epistemology. When often arcane causal knowledge provides the basis of reliable epistemic judgments, rather than largely atheoretical and abstract conceptual principles, then we must acknowledge that scientific re-sults regulate the formulation of, perhaps even partly constitute, epistemic tenets.

Philosophers unfamiliar with a posteriori standards of relevance in science will be especially prone to inappropriately abstract criticisms wrought by enforced standards that are theoretically irrelevant. Judgments of relevance are theoretical judgments and so must be sensitive to specific information in a discipline under assessment. When criticizing the methods and results of science, the curriculum of contemporary epistemology—especially high analytic epistemology—did little to underline the benefits of attention to science. It comes as no surprise, then, that when philosophers turn to methodological criticism of scientific results, they are prone to criticisms that are vacuous.

Methodological criticisms drawn from the social and psychological sciences, such as those reviewed above, should be understood as worries about the quality of the scientific theories in question—scientists obviously don't intend to imply deep skepticism about either experimental design or statistical methods. This is not an incidental point; it shows that a common and complex conception of scientific method can survive substantial theoretical disagreement.

Just as bias represents the conspiring contributions of theory, so the influence of random error, because it is beyond our control, represents the independence of the world. The realist can provide a rationale for the methodological directive of diverse testing, because objects have these properties independently of our measuring them. Population-guided estimation with a vengeance. The empiricist must state either that the value we place on diverse testing is unanalyzeable[14] or that it is reliable only at the level of observables.

Realism, then, is one moral of the epistemological approach described here. When a postulated entity survives tests of its robustness, then our realist commitment is warranted. As the passages quoted earlier from Gergen, Goffman, and Howson and Urbach indicate, the actual opponent speaks as an empiricist who is an observational foundationalist of a certain sort, one who would never dream of doubting the existence of barns in the presence of an occasional barn facsimile so long as we tested for its presence diversely (say, by several senses) but all of a sudden worries if the object is too small to observe with the unaided senses. There are, of course, other forms of foundationalism. However, psychological and social scientific methodology was not in the first instance concerned with blocking the infamous regress but with grounding belief in observation. This sort of skeptical worry cuts against knowledge of unobserved observables as much as unobservables.

Without reconstruction or special philosophical reinterpretation, this methodological directive of diverse testing finds its most natural expression in realist terms: Evidence of an unobservable is more reliable when established by diverse methods, and the only explanation for this fact is that the diverse methods are detecting a real, unobservable causal factor. So long as the bias-correcting forces are applied in response to diverse feedback from the world, we can expect the continued adaptation of the inventions of theory to the structure of an independent world, demanding and severe. What emerges from this realist picture of science is not the endorsement of carelessly biased methods but a focused theoretical perspective guided by the world's observable and unobservable aspects. Scientific inquiry, like agency generally, is most free when nature furnishes the bonds.

Not everyone listens to the world's severe injunctions. In fact, our richest heritage in the human sciences places little systematic priority on quantitative meth-

---

14. This is a familiar criticism of empiricist conceptions of measurement. For more on this criticism, see Goldman (1986, p. 150).

ods of the sort enshrined in PGE. The virtues of quantitative approaches have long been established. In addition, the instrumental successes of the behavioral and social sciences seem not to have depended on special features of narrative methods. However, this narrative tradition has proven so resistant to the lessons of quantitative methods, in the face of the latter's successes, that the allure of narrative methods deserves analysis and explanation.

Failed Attempts

The Frailties of
Narrative Methods

> In every history, no matter how contingent, there is
> something general, for someone else can find some-
> thing exemplary in it.
> > Jürgen Habermas, *Knowledge and Human Interests*

> Vomiting, for example, is commonly a sign that the
> person who vomits does not wish to agree.
> > Alfred Adler, *Problems of Neurosis*

This chapter will document the epistemic unreliability of narrative methods as they are used in traditional history, social and political theory, and motivational psychology. After setting out the frailties of narrative methods and the charms that make them so difficult to abandon, we will turn to some of the philosophical background to the narrative methods of figures such as Hegel and Collingwood and to interpretive doctrines such as the "principle of charity." The third section shows how these documented errors, such as the base-rate fallacy, availability bias, and confirmation bias, might be thought to interact with traditional, narrative methods. The next section identifies representative base-rate fallacies and specific biases in the narrative work of such distinguished names as Toynbee, Tocqueville, and Adler. Some of these figures lived before quantitative methods in their fields were available. For such figures, this chapter is not about blame. But deliverance from blame is not deliverance from error. In their work, we will find perfectly good—that is, representative—examples of narrative methods. These methods lead to inferential errors, whether or not the original authors had the resources to avert them. The last section closes the chapter with the contribution that Measured Realism and PGE can make to the diagnosis and correction of these frailties.

Criticizing Narrative Methods: Preliminary Qualifications

The first step in criticizing casual, impressionistic reasoning in the behavioral and social sciences is to provide a clear alternative. Population-Guided Estimation not only describes the distinctive general form that reliable social and behavioral measurement should take, it also depicts the dramatic consequences for traditional, "humanistic" approaches to social and psychological subjects. If psychological and social research should proceed in accordance with the principles of PGE, then we will need to reassess the reliability of traditional humanistic work that relies exclusively on narrative methods and contemporary work that emulates the tradition.

The psychological and social sciences have overcome humble beginnings. Their shaky infancy permitted elaborate theories to be spun from anecdote. Elegant and learned narratives—the classics of early social and behavioral science—led readers through a world of charismatic leaders, diplomats' diaries, peasant uprisings, cartel formation, courtly intrigue, workers' movements, and wars of religion and capital. Whether by literary mood, theoretical orientation, or sheer weight of detail, these texts were designed to instruct, persuade, and transport the reader. Sometimes philosophers drew inspiration from these treatises, distilling ideal versions of social and political organization from the sorry reality of autocracy, inequity, and cruelty.

Modern philosophical conceptions of psychology and the social sciences have been profoundly influenced by this traditional, and quite spectacular, image of the historian of ideas who, with a sure hand, guides the reader through the grand ideas and dramatic contingencies of history. Thucydides chronicles the causes and course of the Peleponnesian War and the collapse of the polis. Tocqueville frames political descriptions of American democracy, documents American and British custom, and illustrates features of the American penal system. Montesquieu speculates about the origin of social laws. All of these texts claim for themselves a certain epistemic authority.

Perhaps because it is so noble and learned, this image has gained undue respect. I will argue that the history of social and behavioral inquiry, and much work on the contemporary scene, is dominated by work of questionable intellectual merit, no matter how learned and well meaning. The question, of course, is, "Are these narrative methods unreliable?"

Although we cannot treat narrative methods as a monolith, characteristic applications proceed by gathering information about an issue of significant interest—a historical period or figure, a political movement, a psychological ability, for example—organizing this information as a kind of explanatory story, and formulating a generalization on its basis. This casual, storytelling model of social inquiry has become familiar from the work of Dilthey, Gadamer, Rorty, Ricoeur, and Charles Taylor and forms the basis of the claim that interpretive or narrative methods of philosophy and literature are better suited to the goals of social science than are the experimental methods of natural science. Narrative methods are characterized by reliance on casual modes of observing, documenting, and generalizing, in the tradition of storytelling. Examples are Verstehen techniques, ordinary attributional procedures, anecdote, and so on. Unfortunately, because narrative methods are also typified by generalization without regard to sample size, effect size, and other standard quantitative considerations familiar from statistics and experimental design, these approaches violate well-understood canons of quantitative reasoning. Moreover, mainstream psychological research on rational inference (see Nisbett and Ross 1980, and Tversky and Kahneman 1974, for the groundbreaking work) indicates that scientists and laypeople alike are prone to serious inferential errors on exactly the sorts of tasks demanded by narrative reasoning.

My reservations about narrative methods are tempered by occasional narrative successes, the significance of which will become clear as this chapter unfolds. Narrative methods can be reliable, and it can be rational to apply them, depending upon the subject matter to which they are applied. Nor should my focus on the frailties of narrative methods be taken as an implicit denial that there are any examples of bad quantitative analysis. In the first place, so far I have provided no more than anecdotal reasons for concern over the reliability of narrative methods; were we to dismiss qualitative social science on the above grounds, we would be guilty of the very impressionistic and anecdotal musing that motivates this call. In the second place, many of the events discussed in narrative texts—the French Revolution, the Crusades, American slavery, and the genocide of Native Americans by European colonialists—are so robust that their important general features can be accurately described without elaborate quantitative apparatus and can be easily checked for representativeness. Finally, inquiry must retain a role for settings of open, nondirected exploration and speculation, in which one may make connections, generate principles, and test out new ideas.

The special vulnerability of narrative methods to bias or unreliability—both epistemically undesirable features—is a complex phenomenon, but we may approach it by considering simple methods that are relevantly like narrative methods but are patently prone to those epistemic vagaries. At the limit of casual observation and generalization is sheer guessing, both about the nature of the objects in the sample and about the nature of the population to which the sampled objects are thought to belong. To the extent that a narrative method is ambitious about the projection of generalizations over unsampled parts of the population on the basis of slim and peripheral evidence, the application of that narrative method is akin to guessing, thus unreliable. And to the extent that a narrative approach is anecdotal in a way that prematurely fixes the theoretical dimensions of inquiry, applications of this method are biased.

This chapter criticizes narrative approaches—the methods most commonly discussed in philosophical treatments of the social and behavioral sciences—by advancing and defending two claims:

(A) There is substantial empirical evidence that the psychological judgments called upon by narrative methods are prone to specific biases that threaten the reliability and validity of generalizations in the behavioral and social sciences.

(B) Independent of the existence and seriousness of these biases, narrative methods are untrustworthy. The narrative approach is indifferent toward careful estimation; it is unconcerned with systematic considerations of sample size, base-rate information, and representativeness.

There are at least two relevant positions critical of narrative methods:

The strong view: Narrative methods cannot be reliable. They are essentially insensitive to quantitative parameters, and so it is always epistemically irresponsible to make use of them.

The weak view: Narrative methods can be demonstrably and systematically unreliable, particularly when applied to any but the most robust phenomena.

I will not defend the strong view. Nothing about narrative methods makes them essentially insensitive to quantitative parameters, and so nothing in this chapter will support the contention that it is always epistemically irresponsible to rely upon them. After all, some works mix narrative and quantitative methods in the same research effort without yielding a product that is the worse for it. In his monumental labor *The Structures of Everyday Life* (which Robert Fogel 1982, p. 22, classifies as a work in traditional history), Braudel manages to provide quantitative information about the economy, agriculture, and demographics of Europe and the Orient in a way that maintains contact with the human lives that are the subject of that history. There, Braudel provides vivid descriptions of such familiar topics as daily foodstuffs, from culinary luxuries to the basic staples. As an item so visible and integrated in human life, food is a robust indicator of the local economy, diet, and culture. It marks cultural differences, both by its presence and by its manner of preparation. Braudel exploits this robustness by combining evidence from cookbooks, agricultural records, and travelers' diaries. (For example, see Braudel's discussion of the centrality of eggs and cheese in European life.) [1] The robustness of these factors makes the convergence of historical evidence relatively easy to secure.

One might still ask, however, why narrative methods exercise such a grip on us, especially when the factors described are ill formulated and of questionable relevance. For example, in another admirable, hybrid text—William Shirer's *The Rise and Fall of the Third Reich*—we find a protracted, primitive quantitative discussion of the economic (inflationary) precursors of World War I that any quantitative historian would approve. Yet the text devotes elaborate narrative descriptions of the behind-the-scenes antics (presumably regarded as theoretically important enough to merit mention) of figures like von Ribbentrop and Göring (see Shirer 1959, p. 1371). Granted, these approaches are varied, and it is doubt-

---

1. Similar virtues can be found in James McClellan's *Colonialism and Science*, a groundbreaking study of eighteenth-century Saint Domingue, modern-day Haiti. (To continue the culinary theme prompted by Braudel, see especially pp. 31–33, though the entire chapter brings some perspective to the question of what life must have been like in Saint Domingue under the Old Regime by close examination of the sheer impact of environmental factors on colonization, from disease and weather to pestilence and the demanding terrain.)

ful that they embody a monolithic motivation. But let me venture three reasons that aim to describe several sources of their attraction:

1. Our educational and cultural tradition is comfortable with the use of anecdote and impression as a basis for generalization about social and psychological phenomena.

2. Narrative methods project familiar psychological attributions to less familiar and less securely understood social structures and situations.

3. These projections are made because of an irresistible urge to decide pressing intellectual concerns on available evidence when appropriate evidence is either unobtainable or inconvenient to gather.

If the argument of this chapter is sound, then the dominant humanistic tradition has grown content with profoundly unreliable methods for psychological and social inquiry. We will see that anecdotal report and chronicler sensitivity are at the bottom of the frailty of narrative methods. What is the alternative, quantitative image of the "human" sciences? Philosophical work on scientific knowledge occasionally pauses to consider the contribution of experiment to knowledge. However, the focus on experimentation has been both narrow and unsystematic. In part, this is due to the special interest of philosophers. Concerned with the favored epistemic role of observation, foundationalists have argued that it is acquaintance with the observable outcomes of experiments that grounds scientific knowledge. The themes of the confirmation literature, for example, are noticeably empiricist. Early empiricist focus on experimentation offered up operationalist accounts of measurement. By contrast, PGE advances an alternative explanation for the significance of quantitative methods, including experimentation. Like instruments, experiments are designed to detect and measure real objects, properties, events, processes, and states. Experiments are often used to detect causal factors that are diffuse, distributed, or latent.

Here is a primitive preview of the narrative features that, in light of PGE, must be regarded as epistemic infirmities:

(1) Selective inclusion of topics based on the chronicler's own impressionistic assessment of the quality of the evidence.

(2) Impressionistic differential weighting in the interpretation of the evidence.

(3) Failure to ensure consideration of alternative plausible explanations of the phenomenon in question.

(4) Failure to examine systematically the variables of moderating influence on the relationship in question.

(5) Failure to address systematically the representativeness of the sample.

(6) Failure to address systematically the possible impact of correctible bias in con-firmation procedures.

Chapter 2 shows that these six transgressions are potential threats to social and behavioral inquiry and offers an antidote in the form of PGE. And if the argu-ment of the third section of chapter 5 is sound, then the transgressions are avoid-able; social and behavioral sciences can reliably estimate even when a proper experimental design cannot be implemented.

In light of the previous qualification concerning hybrid approaches, then, there could be a narrative text innocent of these transgressions. The above sins are not transgressions per se; these are serious intellectual frailties of narrative methods just to the extent that those methods attempt to generalize from a sample of evidence. In short, they are treacherous just to the extent that they engage in inductive generalization.

The best hope we have of systematically avoiding the lot of these intellectual vagaries (what I will call collectively "narrative errors") is to formulate research plans that optimize sensitivity to population parameters and minimize dependence on impressionistic strategies. Adherence to this directive is especially important in the behavioral and social sciences, which, unlike the natural sciences, don't yet have the benefit of a secure theoretical tradition that reliably generates inter-esting research problems, constrains the number of theoretically plausible hypoth-eses, and yields evident instrumental and technical control over their subject matter.

If narrative methods are to be empirically interesting at all (short of providing mere empirical description), the inferences they support must be ampliative. In fact, the most consistent interpretation of the available narrative treatments sug-gests that narrative theorists hold that quantitative behavioral and social science is itself defective. Otherwise, it is difficult to explain why it is so difficult to find narrative texts that include discussion of quantitative methods. We might put the point in this way: If one truly held the weak view, friendly to the quantitative approach, that narrative methods are necessary supplements to the quantitative theorist, then we would expect narrative treatments to bristle with discussion of both interpretive categories and quantitative parameters to which the interpreta-tions are relevant. But that is not what we find in typical narrative works such as Gadamer (1965) or Taylor (1985b). The isolation of narrative from quantitative treatments bespeaks either an implausibly strong methodological isolation thesis or a tacit commitment to the irrelevance of quantitative methods. By contrast, quantitative theorists have always recognized the methodological import of narra-tive insights (the examples are too plentiful to list; see Fogel 1982, where the reader can explore the many references).

The principal model of social and behavioral inquiry was the narrative—often the "great work"—that fit together aspects of a topic into a comprehensive story. Such pretensions to evidential quality are not just the quaint echoes of times past when, lacking quantitative standards in the human sciences and with a classical august sense of the intellectual horizons, the narrator could be excused for ambitious goals and optimism about available tools.[2] Much contemporary social and psychological theory features the same sort of casual declarations and anecdotal reflections represented in the classical literature. The basis of this narrative authority depends on the quality of the evidence, and it is here that the quantitative themes of this book have most to say to traditional, narrative approaches to the social and behavioral sciences. Weighed against qualitative, narrative methods, quantitative methods apply to domains in a way that allows research to be cumulative and makes the data more easily integrated with affiliated domains.[3]

In the sections that follow, it might be charged that I am using the very narrative methods that I am criticizing. Two points must be made here. First, because I argue only for the weak claim, it is not damaging to assert, by itself, that a method used is narrative. In the examples I will provide, I will make an effort to show that a particular case is one in which the fact that a method is narrative is damaging. Second, to the extent that we use intuitive accounts or theories all the time to identify the central theoretical dimensions when beginning inquiry, then we are using a narrative method. But these judgments are revisable in light of new evidence; they are not a priori. Narrative theorists might admit this, but, I will argue, they are often unclear about what counts as evidence, and why it is thought to be relevant. In keeping with the argument of chapter 6 concerning narrative research summaries, some narrative judgments are reliable, particularly those that are regulated by real values of relevant population parameters. Narrative methods are not unreliable per se, but rather whenever they violate the principles of PGE.

The Profile of Narrative Methods

The label "narrative method" is mostly a convenience; it is really a cluster of approaches. It may seem a bit wooden-headed to launch what might appear to be yet another assault on what C. Wright Mills called "grand theory" and to do so in the name of science. But like the "narrative method," "grand theory" itself embodies a variety of methods of inquiry. The tired conflict between traditional and quantitative approaches is often understood as one about the use of imagination over science or the desirability of system building over analysis. But these disputes are executed at a level of abstraction insensitive to the concerns that motivated the dispute.

What is suspect about narrative methods is not that they attempt to be comprehensive, not that they are system building, not even that they are visionary. Rather, they are idiosyncratic in a way that makes them especially susceptible to

2. Bad quantitative work can be guilty of such pretensions as well. Drab data tables and equations may sustain the appearance of precision and rigor, especially when presented without adequate theoretical preparation. But even in such cases, the data are available and treated as relevant.

3. The extreme sensitivity of narrative research to changes in the dimensions of explanation—changing the explanatory subject—partly accounts for the noncumulative character of this qualitative research, a topic alluded to again in the closing section of this chapter.

systematic error and abstract in a way that makes them invulnerable to correction by specific subject matter. The model of the narrative inquirer is that of a person with special skills, able to assess the relative plausibility of competing explanations, even when doing so demands the processing of enormous amounts of information. No matter how reliable and powerful quantitative methods might be, it is sometimes said, "there is no substitute for the brewmaster's nose." (For further discussion of this model of expertise, see Martin 1989.) The attempt to achieve a unified picture of the social world places a heavy burden on a small number of organizing themes, but to present a greater and greater number of specific events, as expressions of those themes, the things these events have in common must be extremely general. Thus the abstractness. Such difficulties arise in motivational and clinical psychology when, for example, all relevant behavior is interpreted as an expression of aspirant sexual superiority or efforts at moral arrogation. At the same time, because these few organizing assumptions are not easy to test independently, their selection is especially prone to bias. Therefore, narrative methods are not to be derogated because they are anecdotal but because they have no means of accommodating considerations of representativeness, sample size, and the other values constitutive of objectivity.

No one would dispute that a comprehensive account of social or psychological phenomena is desirable, nor would anyone doubt the utility of methods affording tests of particular causal claims. But it has never been entirely clear why we must choose between (say) a complete account of the psyche on the one hand and a method of confirmation making it possible to reject an individual claim made by this account on the other. By ignoring relevant quantitative parameters of the population under study, investigators in traditional, narrative social science and psychology routinely marshal evidence too unrepresentative and unsystematic to support the sorts of generalizations about social phenomena typically advanced by scientists. In addition, we must cultivate a respect for these quantitative parameters if we are to increase the likelihood that connections between relatively independent domains of inquiry can be found and exploited. We can expect to find such affiliations, because any real, taxonomic object typically belongs to more than one population and so emerges under a variety of tests.

The suggestion that quantitative methods underestimate the importance of imagination in social and psychological inquiry is a criticism often heard, but it has the sound of desperation.[4] In the first place, if this criticism were correct, it could only be because there is some difference with respect to the imaginative powers required for the practice of the natural sciences on the one hand and those required for social and behavioral inquiry on the other. Quantitative methods typify the methods in the natural sciences, and it is hard to conceive of an intellectual history more rife with the evidence and fruits of imagination than natural science, from brilliant thought experiments to the routinely ingenious solutions to the challenges of theoretical tests. Perhaps the claim is instead that

---

4. For discussion of this claim see Mills (1959). This issue is a centerpiece of L. J. Cohen et al. (1982).

social and psychological inquiry demand a kind of application of imagination—
perhaps that described by Verstehen theorists, of imaginative understanding—
because here the proprietary objects are intentional: People and institutions have
or involve mental states. It is not clear whether the sort of imagination recruited
in addressing questions about human motivation and social organization is different from that used in formulating tests in the natural sciences, and this may be
due to the general unclarity of how to properly individuate (kinds of) applications
of the imagination. But even if we were to concede this difference in imaginative
function, what are we to conclude? Certainly not that quantitative approaches to
the social and psychological sciences are hopeless.

We should understand the dispute instead to be about what kinds of evidence
will be appropriate for the establishment of a certain theoretical claim, view, or
interpretation and about what kind of method is appropriate as a means of gathering this evidence and, on its basis, as a test of the theory. In particular, we should
ask what methods are most able to shape our beliefs so they will reflect theoretically relevant features of the population rather than unrepresentative and theoretically uninteresting ones.

Moreover, the current state of the philosophy of science is considerably different now from what it was in the 1960s. A reassessment of the philosophical
foundations of the social and behavioral sciences is now in order. The positivism
prominent in the quantitative social sciences proved inadequate to characterize
routine features of scientific practice that are epistemically reliable, conducing to
the successes of the social and behavioral sciences. At the same time, many of
the criticisms of positivistic social science and psychology came from within the
emerging quantitative tradition. The theory dependence of scientific methods,
long received as a decisive objection to logical empiricist accounts of measurement in physics, arose spontaneously in quantitative approaches to the social and
behavioral sciences as practitioners attempted to solve routine problems of social
measurement and design validity.

To the extent that these narrative projects attempt, broadly speaking, to identify explanatorily relevant social and psychological causes, as well as to estimate
their magnitude or importance, narration that makes or invites generalization is a
species of measurement. When properly vigilant about the standard considerations
involved in measurement, narrative methods are at their best.

At the moment, measurement is not advanced as the distinctive feature by any
of the dominant approaches in the philosophy of social science. In philosophical
surveys of methods in the behavioral and social sciences (Braybrooke 1987;
Salmon et al. 1992), it is now routine to isolate roughly three approaches: (1)
interpretive, (2) critical, and (3) naturalistic. Interpretive approaches seek to explain psychological and social behavior in terms of rules and conventions of a
particular culture (these include methods employed in participant observation in
anthropology). Critical social science attempts to lay bare the truth-distorting
tendencies implicit in orthodox social sciences as it is practiced in capitalist societies or bourgeois academic institutions. Naturalistic social science attempts to assimilate the ontology of the social sciences to that of the natural sciences. I defend a version of the latter but formulate the doctrine of naturalism much

differently from the logical empiricist variant in extant discussions of naturalism. There, naturalistic stances toward the social sciences are occupied with the nomic status of social phenomena and the reductionist question of whether statements about social and psychological phenomena can be translated into observational claims about the (effects of) physical phenomena. On the account I defend, natu-ralistic social science uncovers causal generalizations about the behavior of indi-viduals and institutions by theoretically established procedures of measurement.

Whether offering an analysis of interpretivism, critical theory, or naturalism, these accounts typically begin with a philosopher's description (or at least, a phil-osophical one) of the standards and limitations of particular methods, and we can find such portrayals in the work of Collingwood, Habermas, or Mill. In what follows, I will treat both interpretive and critical social science as narrative.

There are certain general features that otherwise diverse narrative texts share. By and large, these texts have grand aims.[5] Accordingly, they are given to grand, often hazardous, generalization. Their grand aims do not, however, make narrative methods so feeble. Grandeur, of course, is entirely appropriate when there is grand evidence to back it up. But the required evidence is typically lacking. Thus, Gib-bon claims that "an acrimonious humour falling on a single fibre of one man may prevent or suspend the misery of nations" (1952, p. 492). Such approaches are easy to find, especially in history. Representative examples are Will and Ariel Durant's *The Lessons of History* and the work of Spengler and Toynbee.[6]

Philosophers certainly commented on the significance of historical events and methods, and it is through this commentary that the reigning philosophical ap-

5. If a text has modest, largely descriptive aims, such as a typical biography, then a narrative approach might be appropriate.

6. Not all narrative applications need implicate undefended (or, at any rate, unreliable) generaliza-tions. Lynn White, the historian of medieval technology, offers a carefully defended statement of the impact of the stirrup on the shape of Europe:

Before the introduction of the stirrup, the seat of the rider was precarious. Bit and spur might help him to control his mount; the simple saddle might confirm his seat; nevertheless, he was still much restricted in his methods of fighting. He was primarily a rapidly mobile bowman and hurler of javelins. Swordplay was limited because "without stirrups your slashing horseman, taking a good broadhanded swipe at his foe, had only to miss to find himself on the ground." [footnote deleted] As for the spear, before the invention of the stirrup it was wielded at the end of the arm and the blow was delivered with the strength of shoulder and biceps. The stirrups made possible—although it did not demand—a vastly more effective mode of attack: now the rider could lay his lance at rest, held between the upper arm and the body, and make at his foe, delivering the blow not with his muscles but with the combined weight of himself and his charging stallion.

The stirrup, by giving lateral support in addition to the front and back support offered by pommel and cantle, effectively welded horse and rider into a single fighting unit capable of a violence without precedent. The fighter's hand no longer delivered the blow: it merely guided it. The stirrup thus replaced human energy with animal power, and immensely increased the warrior's ability to damage his enemy. Immediately, without preparatory steps, it made possible mounted shock combat, a revolutionary new way of doing battle.

What was the effect of the introduction of the stirrup in Europe? (1962, pp. 1–2)

proach became familiar with the great works. Prior to the use of quantitative methods in social inquiry, there was little difference between speculative social theorizing of the time and philosophical commentary on the social. Some philosophical interpretations of the social and behavioral sciences bore the peculiar mark of the narrator, even if this required an idealist analysis. In Collingwood, for example, we find the reduction of history to the ideas of the narrator:

> When an historian asks "Why did Brutus stab Caesar?" he means "What did Brutus think, which made him decide to stab Caesar?" The cause of the event, for him, means the thought in the mind of the person by whose agency the event came about: and this is not something other than the event, it is inside the event itself. . . .
>
> All history is the history of thought. . . .
> The history of thought, and therefore all history, is the re-enactment of past thought in the historian's own mind. . . . .
> The historian not only re-enacts past thought, he re-enacts it in the context of his own knowledge and therefore, in re-enacting it, criticizes it, forms his own judgment of its value, corrects whatever errors he can discern in it." (1959, pp. 252–253)

Hegel claims to have found a common and cruel destiny awaiting those rare and magnificent figures through which the winds of history blow. He offers the following as evidence:

> If we go on to cast a look at the fate of these World-Historical persons, whose vocation it was to be the agents of the World-Spirit—we shall find it to have been no happy one. They attained no calm enjoyment; their whole life was labor and trouble; their whole nature was nought else but their masterpassion. When their object is attained they fall off like empty hulls from the kernel. They die early, like Alexander; they are murdered, like Caesar; transported to St. Helena, like Napoleon." (1956, p. 63)

But these dramatic and sweeping generalizations, associated with narrative methods, are typically grounded in undue focus on such factors as personality and other local circumstances that are unrepresentative of the causes of the appropriate phenomena under study. Even the most modest generalization can appear presumptuous if it is supported by irrelevant or insufficient evidence.

Interpretive social science treats understanding as a special goal of the human sciences, to be achieved by explanation. Employing a particular conception of what constitutes understanding, narrators attempted such sweeping claims by anecdote and introspection. These "methods" are so familiar to us, so central to our communication with others and our self-understanding, we are disposed to assign them a special status as procurers of knowledge.

Narrative methods have their roots in our most familiar, folk explanations of behavior. In common accounts of action, we offer a rationalizing explanation, an account of the reasons or motives of that actor. In the social sciences, rationalizing explanations are most prominent in history and anthropology. Dilthey and others argued that, to provide such a rationalizing account, we must achieve some sort of "sympathetic understanding" of the historical actor, allowing us to imagine how we might behave under circumstances similar to those of the actor. This method of attribution, or Verstehen, is at the bottom of a variety of approaches in the behavioral and social sciences, though narrative methods do not depend on Dilthey's peculiar form of intuitionism. We can also find this narrative pattern in the projective techniques of anthropology, in causal attribution in social psychology, and in some aspects of rational choice approaches in microeconomics. But narrative methods are engaged in broader applications, appealing as well to the behavior of nonintentional objects. One might tell stories, for example, about the causes of seismic activity or the process of cell division without appeal to considerations of sample size, magnitude of effect, and other standard quantitative factors.

It is not intentional attribution that makes a method narrative but rather the idea that confirmation and theory choice can rationally be determined solely by appeal to unrecorded, informally retained, and unaided processing of such complex arrays of information. The empathic approach of Dilthey is also reflected in Collingwood, who suggests that the historical method consists in a kind of immediate psychological contact the explorer makes with the explored, when you examine a cultural artifact and say, "I see what the person who made this (wrote this, used this, designed this, etc.) was thinking" (1970, p. 110). Moreover, these treatments conveyed the impression that whether a particular method deserved the title "scientific" depended upon how closely it passed certain tests of meaning interpretation and propositional-attitude attribution that reigned not in the social sciences but in philosophy. To make matters worse, at the time the philosophical tests of rationality were based on crude semantic theses and nonnaturalistic principles of charity.

Although certain otherwise narrative theorists, such as Gadamer and Ricoeur, are critical of empathic approaches, common texts in history, psychology, anthropology, and sociology are thought to proceed by an empathetic or Verstehen process of the sort described above. To the extent that this process constitutes a challenge to translate the experience of another—often from a radically different culture or epoch—into one we can understand, Davidson's principle of charity provides a ready method of rationalizing explanation. This rule was explicitly articulated by Donald Davidson but widely regarded as guiding the practice of interpretation. The historian and clinical psychologist are confronted with much the same interpretive problem as the anthropologist—to describe and render intelligible the behavior of alien actors. Philosophers under the influence of this principle argue that the pressures of understanding favor a method of interpretation that "puts the interpreter in general agreement with the speaker" (Davidson 1980a, p. 169). Charitable interpretation is not a choice we make; rather, "charity is forced upon us; whether we like it or not, if we want to understand others, we must count them right in most matters" (p. 197). Under the strain of disagreement, however, the interpreter trumps the speaker; whoever is doing the interpreting gets to say who is right. If you are the interpreter, of course, this eases the burden of charity. But as long as we are earnest interpreters, our interpretive provincialism requires no apology or bears no shameful mark of epistemic imperfection: Even an omniscient interpreter "attributes beliefs to others, and interprets their speech on the basis of his own beliefs, just as the rest of us do" (p. 201).

This method, however, is not peculiar to history, having gained prominence in anthropology as early studies in the 1920s and 1930s began to grip the imagination of a voyeuristic, often prurient, public. Freud charted the sexual sources of psychological disfunction and normal function, while the public was more than happy to imagine the primitive passions "documented" in Malinowski's *The Sexual Lives of Savages*. Evans-Pritchard's analysis of the Nuer religion is thought to be so indebted to the content attribution elucidated by Davidson's principle of charity that the case of an alien Nuer belief is used by Stephen Stich (1983) to illustrate one of the most stubborn problems for folk psychology. And Goffman's persistent peeking at social behavior, to be discussed later, yields a speculative narrative that draws structural lessons from the dynamics of social settings. These figures described previously uncataloged phenomena but not the sense in which their research was cumulative.

Some have charged that this critical attitude toward the reliability of anecdote and introspection is puzzling at best and at worst incoherent, especially when applied to the improvement of the social and behavioral sciences. After all, in the initial stages of behavioral and social research, it is a summary of our casual experience, anecdotal and impressionistic, that allows us to identify, and aids in the selection of, theoretically interesting phenomena for systematic study. Early work in psychophysics addressed striking auditory abilities with which everyone was familiar. Visual research attempted explanations of robust phenomena such as the Muller-Lyer illusion, the Stroop effect, and the existence of afterimages. Cognitive psychology began many programs of research on the basis of homey observations of problem solving, the acquisition of language, and limitations of memory, along with gripping clinical deficits. Social psychology experiments often start with curiosity about the sources of specific social behaviors. It seems plausible, for example, that we are quicker to blame someone for a destructive act when the actor could have done otherwise. Might we expect, then, that we are less likely to assign blame when the causes of an act are understood as situational rather than dispositional—that is, when the act is the result of circumstances external to the actor or of traits inhering in the individual? In anthropology, do specific rituals solidify social ties, and, if so, is that their function? And so on.

Anecdote and imagination, using the material of intuition, often play a role in the primitive stages of research and in generating research problems. It might be thought, then, that the use of those faculties belongs to the context of discovery, and quantitative methods, where they are appropriate at all, belong to the context of justification. This distinction, at least in stark form, is undermined by the following observation. It is a desideratum of good scientific methodology that theories be tested against their most plausible rivals. To do so, however, plausible rivals often must be created, making the exercise of creative and imaginative capacities a crucial feature of routine scientific method. Far from isolating the epistemology of theory testing from the contingencies of creative imagination and discovery, a satisfactory account of theory justification must include a description of the psychological powers that make sound testing possible.

Commentators in history often term the narrative approach qualitative, because it eschews the scaling of data typified by quantitative approaches. However, methodological developments in history, psychology, anthropology, sociology, political science, and economics have left those disciplines with an array of approaches, some more quantitative than others. These emerging methods bear distinctive marks of their specific subject matter. Of course, no method of inquiry yields pure narration. Even the natural historian, who dutifully describes all he or she sees, makes judgments concerning the classification of data and the details important enough to report. Whether by design or not, all texts embody at least some useful quantitative information. Supplying stereotypes rather than statistics, a text may still give the reader an accurate impression of the causal forces at play in the population of inquiry, in the events, states, and processes within the explanatory purview of the social and behavioral sciences. But this is so only if those stereotypes are representative of the population under study and only if they are causally relevant. Otherwise, generalizations will be unreliable. For example, in a text that is primarily concerned to draw generalizations about the influence of Germany during World War II on the political landscape of Europe, it is a mistake to treat as an important issue—perhaps even as a piece for idle musing—the question of whether Hitler had one testicle or two, a question that has provoked much discussion in purportedly nonbiographical histories of Nazi Germany.[7] In light of the overdetermination of important historical events, or at any rate the complex of swamping causes, if the question is about the causes or broad course of World War II, one would have thought issues such as industrialization and trade would have received primary attention, no matter how pertinent Hitler's testicular status might be to his psychology. About this voyeuristic inclination, C. Wright Mills mentions the taste that much sociological writing has for "a series of rather unrelated and often insignificant facts" (1959, p. 23).

No matter how harsh and dismissive, Mills's verdict is too generous, treating as an annoyance this attention to pointless detail. A more substantial criticism is in order. By focusing on minutiae, a narrative approach can convey the misleading message that the system in question is sensitive to such tiny events or changes when in fact it isn't (even though, implausibly, it can be). This occurs as well in sociology and social history texts in which, though apparently devoted to a description of structural features of a society or movement such as a war or a significant industry, narration turns to the detailed personal dynamics and idiosyncrasies of major players in those settings. This often occurs when there is no good theory guiding us in the identification of facts that are theoretically significant.

One of the most distinctive features of scientific methodology is its ability to partition objects under study into categories of systematic theoretical interest. Indeed, this is part of the purpose of providing a causal taxonomy. Causal properties that are theoretically relevant, such as the charge of an electron or the dispo-

---

7. This preoccupation with personal detail is, of course, standard fare in the biographies of Hitler, such as those of Bullock (1962) and Toland (1977), but one even finds it in work of more general scope, such as Shirer (1959).

sition to worry needlessly, tend to be stable: that is, to play the same causal role under mild changes in initial and boundary conditions. They also tend to be explanatorily deep, affording answers to why-questions concerning the cause of some phenomenon that terminate in a satisfying explanation (judged by the best theoretical standards) rather than resting content with statements of brute correlation. Clearer cases of the role of typicality occur in the physical sciences, where we look at a single object that is representative of a homogeneous class, such as the electron.

Much of this sensitivity, to be discussed in the next section, is due to the fact that narrative approaches present information casually, even if with occasional moral force; the information is not categorized, scaled, or otherwise organized. The casual and unsystematic presentation of information might not constitute a serious difficulty had we, as humans, been cognitively and perceptually unbounded; the human mind cannot reliably and validly process the tremendous amount of information that must be collected, prepared, integrated, and retained, in the typical narrative psychological or social investigation.

At the same time, I will argue that narrative approaches are especially prone to the base-rate fallacy, the availability bias, fallacies of representativeness, and other problems. But these fallacies, as well documented as they are in the cognition literature on inductive judgment, do not express the deepest obstacle to objectivity in the social and behavioral sciences. For these patterns of judgment, or "heuristics," are regrettable not simply because they violate sacred normative rules of reasoning but because a strategy that relies on appraisals of sample characteristics that are intuitive, casual, or otherwise impressionistic does not make it optimally possible for features of the population to regulate our beliefs. Even if we were not subject to specific biases of availability and base rate, our reliance on the narrative approach is irresponsibly neglectful of the nature of the population, normally making use of far less of the relevant available information than we might (and making us extremely sensitive to some information).

The conception of objectivity here is identified with the regulation of judgment by properties of the population. I will rehearse the virtues of this treatment of objectivity throughout, but for now we might notice that this account provides a deeper diagnosis of inductive judgments and, in particular, of the well-documented fallacies associated with making judgments under uncertainty. This literature describes our lay reasoning as a violation of normative rules such as Bayes's theorem. But, of course, it is never irreducibly bad to violate a rule; when it is bad, it is always in virtue of actual or threatened bad consequences. The present description of objectivity has the resources to explain why it is ill advised to ignore base rate, to respond spontaneously to mere availability rather than to representativeness, and so on—to do so is to place yourself in a cognitive relation to the evidence that will not optimally exploit information about properties of the population. Population-Guided Estimation provides not just an antidote to, but a way of understanding the frailties of, narrative methods.

Later in this chapter I will criticize as narrative several representative lines of inquiry in the psychological and social sciences. But for this criticism to be damaging, the inquiry must be narrative in a special way. The basis for this criticism will not be that the text in question occasionally draws an impressionistic general-ization, or that it harbors a peripheral, unprincipled appeal to an aspect of the evidence selected to favor the author's interpretation, unmindful of the character-istics of the population. After all, intellectual activity typically tolerates and occa-sionally encourages moments of daring conjecture or lazy musing. Rather, in the cases I will consider, the narrative distortions are central to the method used and are deployed in a way that will harm the reliability of the projected generaliza-tions.

Biases of Narration and Chronicler Sensitivity

Our evolutionary history has endowed humans with impressive cognitive powers, but it has also imposed severe computational limitations. Moreover, these limita-tions do not result in performance that is statistically representative of the popula-tion of events experienced; the class of events that a person retains represents a biased sample of the events initially processed. To cite just one example set out in chapter 1, we recall the initial and final items on a list with higher frequency than those in the middle. If our methods for drawing inferences from statistical information do not correct and supplement untutored skills with strategies for recording, coding or classifying, and retrieving events, we cannot hope for episte-mically reliable inferences. According to some critics, these facts are objects of shock and shame. As long as those descriptions target attitudes of intellectual arrogance concerning unaided narrative reasoning, the point is well taken. It is unlikely that even explicit but unguided recognition of and attention to these frailties will correct them. Where frailties originate from limitations on computa-tional abilities, on-line vigilance can do only so much. But as computationally limited creatures, we have no more reason to apologize for the commission of statistical fallacies than we do for growing old or getting hungry. After all, there are delicate computer-guided measuring tasks for which the rounding function at the circuitry level constitutes an important source of error or bias. This source of bias is of little consequence when all we are concerned to do is multiply a few values specified to a few decimal places. However, shift the computer task to the multiplication of 10,000 numbers specified to ten decimal places, and rounding bias may present a problem. In short, not all bias is of consequence; it is insidious only if it leads us to erroneous conclusions. But depending upon the nature of our inquiry, the difference between real and measured value may not make a difference.

I will argue that narrative methods are at the bottom of specific frailties of reasoning in the social and behavioral sciences and that these frailties have insidi-ous effects. Two sorts of evidence indicate that narrative methods are unreliable. The first concerns the tendency of narrative methods to reinforce specific psycho-logical biases. The second concerns simple limitations on computational load. Let us consider the evidence for psychological biases in the handling of statistical information. The important theme here is that theory development and the adju-dication of disputes about social and behavioral phenomena involves information so subtle and complex it cannot be done successfully by casual narrative.

Representativeness

BASE RATE.   In the social and behavioral sciences, the central disputes concern claims of causal dependence, and statistical evidence is often used in an attempt to establish the extent and direction of this dependence. Often without specifying the percentage limit that should merit a causal claim, those using narrative methods often report, by appeal to a percentage or rate, the frequency of a certain event. But for the support of a causal claim, we must have information not about the simple frequency with which an event occurs but about relative frequency. (This fact will play a role later in my discussion of Toynbee.) The relative frequency with which an event occurs in a specified population is called the base rate. Suppose I tell you that 15 percent of all surfers at or above the age of 22 have been convicted of a misdemeanor. This is frequency information, but not general base-rate information, for we haven't been told what percentage of the entire population (surfers and nonsurfers alike) at or above the age of 22 have been convicted of a misdemeanor. Does the surfing lifestyle promote petty criminality? To provide a first approximation to an answer, we must determine whether there is anything special about the surfer population compared to the nonsurfer population—something different about it that would yield a difference in misdemeanor crime rate. If 15 percent of the 22–and-above population in general have been convicted of a misdemeanor, there appears to be nothing special about the surfer population in respect of misdemeanor criminality.[8]

Base-rate information is important because having it is a necessary condition for the justification of causal claims.[9] Quantitative studies normally report the known relative frequencies of the events and properties under study so that other researchers are able to make judgments concerning the typicality of just those occurrences cast as theoretically surprising or otherwise special.[10]

It should be clear that one might fall into the base-rate trap in a number of ways. The most common route to this trap fails to even estimate the frequency

---

8. Unless, of course, surfers belong to an additionally special population that is unusually law abiding—in which members would never commit a misdemeanor. In that case, being a surfer may be causally relevant, even though the relative frequency is no greater than base rate. As always, it depends on how the objects are partitioned.

9. Typically we count something as a positive causal factor only when the frequency with which a certain event occurs in one population is greater than the general class property under which that factor falls. The best-known example of this is the admission rates of women into the graduate school at the University of California at Berkeley. As a group, they had a lower probability of being admitted, even though their average standard admissions measures were higher than the average of the entire male-female admissions pool. But this peculiarity disappears once we notice that women applied with higher frequency to departments with more stringent admissions standards. These cases are instances of "Simpson's paradox," in which probabilistic analysis of causal dependence is associated with lower probability. What it shows is that statistical inference is extremely sensitive to the way you partition classes.

10. Kornblith (1993) defends some uses of small-sample stereotype information and nicely reviews the vulnerability that psychologists themselves display toward statistical information.

(expected or not) of a property in the relevant population and nevertheless claims that the possession of a certain property is theoretically important—typically due to its "surprising" frequency. Without such a specification, we cannot tell whether the frequency of the occurrence of that property in the sample is surprising or if it is to be expected. It is always a mistake to infer the existence or significance of a property from relative frequency information when the research provides no base-rate information or any background theory that tells us that a certain frequency is to be expected. More generally, the determination of base rate minimally requires a distinct specification of the population. If the specification of the population vacillates, then the probability increases that the event described will fall under one or another population specification. So the base-rate fallacy sometimes occurs not because we ignore distinctly specified population information codified in base-rate information but rather because indistinct population specification makes it possible to shift base-rate information in an unprincipled, uncontrolled, or untrackable way. As we shall see, the sweeping claims characteristic of the traditional human sciences, found in the work of such figures as Toynbee and Tocqueville, trade on indistinct population specification, allowing explanations with different explananda to masquerade as competing explanations.

AVAILABILITY.   When we reason casually, we draw upon a body of experiences that has not been organized with accurate statistical representation in mind. Instead, memory allows only certain experiences to be retained, most often because they are especially memorable or available. An availability heuristic is employed whenever someone "estimates frequency or probability by the ease with which instances or associations could be brought to mind" (Tversky and Kahneman 1973, p. 208). Ease of access can be a reliable guide to accurate information, even though it needn't be. Clinical psychologists standardly classify a patient's symptoms by comparing this case to similar cases recalled from the psychologist's experience. Using remembered similarities and diagnoses of these past cases, the psychologist assesses the plausibility that the present case is an instance of the same category as those remembered instances, examples available to the psychologist. This availability heuristic may yield accurate information about the probability of a competing hypothesis, but only if (1) the psychologist's experiences are not a biased sample of the population under study and (2) the psychologist's recalled cases are not a biased sample of the population under study.

Unfortunately, just because an event is available does not mean it is representative, and there is much experimental evidence that psychological availability is an unprincipled, sporadic, and consequently poor guide to typicality. Cognitive research on memory shows that we have a way of dealing with on-line demands of memory, but what is available in memory needn't be representative of the information processed. When a variety of information is presented to us, not all of the information has an equal probability of being recalled. As we have seen, the recitation of lists produces a recall curve that is distinctly bow shaped; the first (the primacy effect) and last (the recency effect) events in a sequence are the most easily recalled. The primacy effect is explained in terms of early items receiving more rehearsal or, on average, later items on a list competing with more terms for rehearsal (see, for example, Rundus 1971). Because the recency effect cannot be explained in terms of rehearsal, some other mechanism must be at play. The most prominent explanation holds that, while the earlier words had proceeded to the stage of semantic coding (in terms of meaning), the most recently occurring words are maintained in a speech code in which words receiving the subject's attention are poised for speech production. It is for this reason, it is supposed, that the words occurring at the end of the list, despite poor rehearsal, are usually recalled first.

In narrative inquiry, the articulation of a particular line of argument may depend upon the order in which the chronicler raises particular topics. In attitude surveys, for example, people are more likely to answer in a way that is consistent if the two target questions occur one right after another rather than if separated by many items. Just as there are recency effects in memory, there appear to be recency influences on attitude reports. This effect has been widely studied. In a design executed by Schuman and Pressler (1981), subjects were asked two versions of the same question, each setting out options in a different order. The first form of the question was, "Should divorce in this country be easier to obtain, more difficult to obtain, or stay as it is now?" The second form of the question changed the order of the options, asking, "Should divorce in this country be easier to obtain, stay as it is now, or be more difficult to obtain?" The responses were different in the two cases, despite the fact that the same three (and only those three) options are presented in both question forms. In particular, in both cases the last response yielded the highest percentage.

	easier	harder	same
Form 1	23%	36%	41%
Form 2	26%	46%	29%

The source of the difference in responses between forms 1 and 2 is difficult to see from the above table, but let's reorganize the table in terms of the order of presentation of the options.

	Position 1	Position 2	Position 3
Form 1	23%	36%	41%
Form 2	26%	29%	46%

The moral here, as elsewhere in this section, is that our judgments are regulated by mechanisms that lead to error in these cases, and the only way to correct this tendency is to attend to specific quantitative imperatives of randomization and blocking.

On the basis of the experimental studies reviewed in chapter 6 (also see Gilovich 1991), there is little question that the outcomes of people's reasoning are shaped by an availability bias, whatever its specific explanation.[11] If there is indeed such an availability bias, then a series of psychological phenomena in addition to recency and order effects would make us additionally prone to this bias. Consider, for example, the important occurrence of priming. The speed with which we match a memory representation to some stimulus item—yielding a judgment, say, that a word on a screen and a semantic representation are the same—is in part determined by the representation's level of activation. The level of activation is raised by priming that representation. In a standard priming task, the subject is asked whether two stimuli presented in sequence are the same or different. The first stimulus is called the standard, and the second is called the probe. Subjects are able to identify two letters presented in sequence (such as A–A) as the same more quickly than they are able to respond to A–B as different. That is because the first occurrence of A primes all of the stored features of the representation of A, raising its level of activation and making it more accessible than representations sharing fewer features with the standard (Proctor 1981). If fallacies of availability are abetted by accessibility effects of recency and priming, then the same reasons for concern over the availability bias should be thought to apply as well to processes whose contents are made available by priming and similar effects. Once a schema has been accessed, a connection is easily insinuated between a historical event and an explanation of that event that was preceded by prepared similarities with the event recorded.

When statistical information is relevant to a considered decision, often the decision ultimately made is based on the availability of certain aspects of the statistical population. Salience, either perceptual or cognitive, is one of the most dominant determinants of the availability of an event. An event may be cognitively or perceptually salient because it is representative of the population under study, or its salience could be the result of idiosyncrasy or bias. How might this happen?

If the availability of an event is increased by its salience, an event's salience is sometimes secured by its atypicality or low frequency. Atypical events can be more memorable, presumably because they are thrown into relief against events

---

11. The Tversky-Kahneman inspired literature on heuristics and biases has been reinterpreted in recent work by Gigerenzer (1991), but all parties to this dispute agree that statistical information is important. Gigerenzer argues that the so-called biases described in the Tversky-Kahneman literature are biases only on a narrow, neo-Bayesian conception of the canons of probability theory and statistics. But this narrow neo-Bayesian view

> is not shared by proponents of the frequentist view of probability that dominates today's statistics departments, nor by proponents of many other views; it is not even shared by all Bayesians. By this narrow standard of "correct" probabilistic reasoning, the most distinguished probabilists and statisticians of our century—figures of the stature of Richard von Mises and Jerzy Neyman—would be guilty of "biases" in probabilistic reasoning. (Gigerenzer 1991, p. 87)

Many of the frailties of narrative methods, I will argue, are related to patterns of reasoning that frequentists too would regard as errors.

that are more common and thus less worthy of special attention. Thus, oddly enough, low-frequency events may provide the illusion of higher frequency than is in fact the case. Anecdotal evidence has a way of trading on this low-frequency effect. The maniacal killer and welfare queen are rare figures whose images nevertheless loom large in the public consciousness. Biases of availability—in this case bred by the memorability of atypical, low-frequency events—can make the incidental detail in a narrative text assume undue importance in the mind of the reader.[12]

One of the most powerful influences prompting an availability bias is that of framing, although framing can incline us to a variety of other fallacies. Framing is the process by which a problem is presented to an audience, preparing them to see a certain range of possible options, solutions, evidential bearing, and so on. The audience's intellectual habits and explanatory expectations allow carefully framed narrative descriptions to yield defective inductions. Framing typically gets the reader or listener to ignore important quantitative, sampling information; a number of studies have shown that whether subjects find an option acceptable or not depends upon how the alternatives are presented rather than on quantitative information that, on the typical paradigm of these studies, ensures equally probable alternatives. The following passage is representative of a wide range of instances of framing:

> Respondents in a telephone interview evaluated the fairness of an action described in the following vignette, which was presented in two versions that differed only in the bracketed clauses.

> > A company is making a small profit. It is located in a community experiencing a recession with substantial unemployment [but no inflation/and inflation of 12 percent]. The company decides to [decrease wages and salaries 7 percent/increase salaries only 5 percent] this year.

> Although the loss of real income is very similar in the two versions, the proportion of respondents who judged the action of the company "unfair" or "very unfair" was 62 percent for a nominal reduction but only 22 percent for a nominal increase. (Tversky and Kahneman 1986, pp. 71–72)

---

12. The evident impact of an availability bias vindicates a common indictment, characteristically directed by Marxists toward narrative histories, for giving undue focus to individuals and personalities in historical movements. This criticism has been leveled most often when the event of interest is overdetermined or, at any rate, has multiple causes plausibly regarded, once variously combined, as sufficient to bring about that event. So, to repeat the misleadingly determinist adage, the event "would have happened anyway." It is often contended, for example, that World War I would have happened even if the Archduke Ferdinand were not assassinated (let alone assassinated by Gregor Princip). When such historical events are not recognized as redundantly determined, interpreters may be led to believe that a particular causal factor might be essential to an event. By focusing on details that are in fact irrelevant to the occurrence of the event, no matter how interesting, while ignoring the important ones, the historian makes the details appear causally important.

It is my contention that explanation plays just such a framing role, making some options available and foreclosing others. In such cases, a schema has been accessed; preparing the reader in this way may be an instance of pretest sensitization. And unless explanation is regulated by the relevant properties of the studied population, framing will lead to biases in the assessment of evidence.

CONFIRMATION BIAS.   Laypeople are prone to at least two types of biases directly related to confirmation, and given the experimental tasks employed in this paradigm, there is little reason to suppose scientists would act differently. In the most famous study (Lord, Ross, and Lepper 1979), two groups of subjects were assembled. One group had expressed strong belief in the deterrent effect of capital punishment, and the other had expressed strong belief that capital punishment had no deterrent value. Subjects were divided so that they first read the method and results of an experimental study supporting their respective positions and then the method and results of an experiment that opposed their views. For all subjects, one study compared murder rates for states before and after the introduction of capital punishment (called a "panel" design) and the other compared murder rates contemporaneously (a "concurrent" design) in states with capital punishment versus those without. The experiment was arranged so that, for half of the subjects, the concurrent design study supported their view and the panel design opposed it, and for other half it was exactly the opposite (see Nisbett and Ross 1980, pp. 170–171).

Three results are especially noteworthy. First, subjects found "more convincing" whichever study supported their original view, whether the design was panel or concurrent; they reported recognizing the methodological defects only of the opposing design. Second, subjects' beliefs were strengthened when the study supported their view, whether or not the design was panel or concurrent; at the same time, the initial belief was largely unaffected by studies opposing the subject's original position. Third, not only did the clear expression of an opposing view fail to undermine subjects' confidence in their original views, subjects were *more* committed to their original view *after* having read both analyses.

A second type of bias arises not during the process of confirmation proper but during the posterior operation of integrating study results. This suspect disposition, sometimes called the "hindsight bias," occurs when subjects are asked, after having been told that a certain outcome is "correct," what their decision would have been about the matter had they made a judgment. The answer tends be that the subject would have made the correct decision. In the classic study, Fischoff (1975) employed a "foresight" group and a "hindsight" group of subjects. The foresight group was asked to read psychotherapy case histories and then to assess the likelihood of four possible posttherapy outcomes. The hindsight group was presented the case history and then told that a particular outcome, A, actually occurred. When the hindsight group was asked whether they could have predicted outcome A, they assigned probabilities to outcome A that were 49 percent higher than those assigned by the foresight group. It was only with the benefit of hindsight that outcome A appeared the obvious prediction.

The separate treatment of these fallacies does not suggest that they have independent sources. The hindsight bias, for example, may result from the same mechanism that drives the availability bias; that is, when subjects are asked to judge the probability that they would have predicted outcome A, told of the actual outcome, they access the schema assembled from the prior information about the actual outcome, making it more available than alternatives.

Scientists are not above such biases either, as chapters 6 and 7 observed, and experimenter bias does occasionally threaten the validity of routine research. In perhaps the most famous study of experimenter bias, Rosenthal and Fode (1963) distributed five rats to each of twelve researchers. They were asked to rate, on a twenty-point scale, the degree to which they expected to enjoy working with the rats. Based on their answers to these and other questions, the experimenters were paired, and sets of rats were randomly assigned to them. Six of these sets of rats were identified to the researchers as "maze dull" and the other six as "maze bright." A thirteenth set of rats was assigned to the cohort. In this study, however, the researchers were themselves the unwitting objects of investigation. The authors of the overall study and the cohort alone knew that the rats labeled "dull" and "bright" had been drawn from the same population and randomly assigned to the pairs.

Despite the fact that the rats had been randomly drawn from the same population, those rats labeled "maze bright" scored 50 percent more correct responses in maze tasks than their "maze dull" counterparts. On the basis of information gathered during the maze experiments and from the cohort, the authors of the study concluded that the "maze dull" rats performed worse because they were not treated and trained as well. They cite this effect as a kind of self-fulfilling prophecy. What is interesting, however, is not the direction of the results per se (after all, had anxiety in rats improved their maze scores, the results would have contradicted experimenter expectations) but that the mechanisms regulating experimenter performance are largely beneath the threshold of their conscious inspection.

Confirmation bias interacts with the availability heuristic in research done by Fischoff (1991). Researchers who expected to see a certain phenomenon tended to overestimate the frequency of confirming instances of their hypotheses. The explanation given for this fact turns on the availability heuristic, because matches between theory and data are thought to be more psychologically salient than mismatches. This effect is different from the one described in Rosenthal and Fode (1963), since in this case they hadn't yet observed any such instances. It is therefore a separate effect of availability, consistent with, and perhaps even contributing to, general cognitive tendencies toward confirmation bias.

The experiments demonstrating these biases do not appear especially contrived or unnatural; subjects are asked to make judgments of a sort we make routinely. So it does not look as though subjects need to be specially prepared before they will make such errors. Nevertheless, Dennett seems to hold that they do need to be so prepared:

How rational are we? Recent research in social and cognitive psychology (e.g., Tversky and Kahneman 1974; Nisbett and Ross 1980) suggests we are only minimally rational, appallingly ready to leap to conclusions or be swayed by logically irrelevant features of situations, but this jaundiced view is an illusion engendered by the fact that these psychologists are deliberately trying to produce situations that provoke irrational responses—inducing pathology in a system by putting strain on it—and succeeding, being good psychologists. (1987, p. 52)

If only we could get out of our own way so effortlessly. On the contrary, many of the tasks used in these studies are perfectly representative of those we execute routinely. Indeed, some of the errors are documented from archival data, from voting and other policy records; psychologists did not create the stimulus items, and so there can be no question of psychologists's "provoking" the desired responses (see Gilovich 1991). But there is a closely related concern that does merit some attention.

It might be charged that there is a circularity in attempting to establish the greater reliability of quantitative approaches by appealing to the results of particular empirical, quantitative research. This is a worry only if the greater reliability of quantitative approaches cannot be established independently of particular research techniques. But if the outcomes of, say, reaction-time tasks in psychology are comparable to those of ranking or discrimination tasks—and if there is no theoretical reason to suppose that these diverse methods secrete insidiously non-independent assumptions—then appeal to this agreement in measurement is no more circular in psychology than it is for us to explain the reliability of quantitative methods in physics by appeal to the reliability of other particular quantitative methods in physics. As we saw in chapter 3, many cases of relative dependence of premises in reasoning are misdiagnosed as circularity. And while circular arguments are not acceptable, arguments with relatively nonindependent premises are.

The moral is not that we should all be Bayesian agents, following normative constraints for Bayesian belief revision. Rather, the primary point is that, through vigilance with respect to base rate, representativeness, availability, and sample size, we increase the probability that our inferences will reflect features of the world rather than features of the investigator(s). We know that these population-guiding factors operate on observed samples. Only the empiricist's selective skepticism could license such a restriction on inductive inference, a selective skepticism that received critical attention in chapter 7. Concerns about the above parameters are concerns about objectivity.

Some of these limitations are purely statistical, and so an information-processing system, no matter how sophisticated, would be expected to perform abysmally on such spare data. Other limitations are psychological; they depend on certain psychological assumptions or demonstrated tendencies of individuals to use information suboptimally, even when processing mechanisms are working optimally. Although the argument from psychological dispositions will play a role in my argument for the use of quantitative methods, the argument from statistical limitations will be central.

Given the limited resources able to be spent on a research project, there is a good general reason for doing whatever you can to increase the probability that properties representative of those in the population regulate the properties of theoretical interest embodied in the sample and constrain the methodology used to select the sample. This is just a crass statistical description of circumstances in which the scientist applies a measurement procedure to something that is real. The reason is as follows. By increasing that probability, we thereby increase the likelihood that we will discover and describe other objects of theoretical interest and other properties of the same object. For instance, because World War II actually occurred, it had a number of properties causally responsible for our current beliefs (economic, geographic, etc.—it literally changed the landscape).

The four principles constituting PGE would counsel at least the following five precautions, which are designed to increase the probability that the factors under study are representative of those in the relevant population.

1. Raise considerations about sample size.
2. Raise critical methodological concerns about representativeness.
3. Scale data wherever possible, so that effect magnitude can be assessed.
4. Provide a systematic way of recording research results, so that we have a way of assessing the validity and reliability of research.
5. Test hypotheses diversely.

Chapter 7 provides the rationale for the fifth precaution. Measured Realism requires that one's theory must be *good enough* to identify the approximately relevant natural populations, but Measured Realism does not require that the background theory be approximately true. In any case, there is little reason to be disobliging about the implementation of procedures so reliable in the case of observed samples. We will next examine the frailties of representative examples of narrative reasoning in the traditional social and behavioral research best known to philosophers.

Offending Styles of Narrative Explanation

The contention of this chapter is not that narrators must employ experimental design to inform their audiences. After all, experimental considerations do not exhaust quantitative ones, and quantitative factors can be analyzed in statistical terms. So the estimation of quantitative factors does not require experimental design. The authors of diverse narrative texts of course could not control the world of personal, political, and social activities they described; either the narrator lived after the occurrence of the topical events, was a contemporaneous "participant-observer," or was powerless in the face of institutional social forces. Yet these texts clearly inform. So it would be a peculiar suggestion that informativeness requires experimental control of some sort, and fortunately one I am not making. In short, quantitative methods are distinctive in that they allow us to make the issues of sampling and representativeness a systematic part of social and behavioral inquiry. Those issues play a special justificatory role in the social sciences and psychology.

Instead, I claim that, if these texts are to be epistemically reliable, their authors must make use of available methods that are sensitive to quantitative factors. Prior to the introduction of quantitative methods in the behavioral and social sciences, the diverse explanatory strategies in history, anthropology, motivational psychology, sociology, political science, and other behavioral sciences had a common though perhaps tacit form. The great texts in these fields tested their predictions and defended their favored explanatory hypotheses by appeal to evidence depicted as a sort of story. I have called these nonquantitative methods narrative. But exactly what features are diagnostic of a narrative method is difficult to formulate. Once these features are formulated, we will see that the methodological frailties that compromise narrative methods also threaten the reliability of quantitative methods. My plaint is one of proportion, not of kind; these threatened vagaries are easier to detect and easier to correct in the context of quantitative rather than narrative methods. When added to the intuitive material or hunches regarding psychological and social phenomena, attention to magnitudes pays great dividends, perhaps greater than when applied to the intuitive material or hunches concerning the phenomena of physics.

Even after quantitative methods were firmly in place, philosophers were slow to recognize their potential contributions. In fact, if one were to read the major (or most influential) philosophical treatments of foundational issues in the social sciences published from the mid-1950s to the early 1980s or so, one would get the impression that the only social sciences are history, anthropology, and (on one understanding of social science) folk psychology.[13] We find discussion of war and revolution, ritual practices in traditional cultures, and self-understanding in psychoanalysis. But little attention was given to political science, sociology, economics, or perceptual, cognitive, and social psychology.

The power of quantitative methods resides in their ability to identify enduring or stable causal factors, as well as their magnitude. And identifying such causal factors is essential to providing an adequate explanation of an event. When narrative accounts are tendentious, it is normally because serious questions can be raised about whether the instances (events, objects, states, etc.) described can support the generalizations to which narrative accounts are prone. Admittedly, not all narrative treatments of topics attempt to generalize. For example, Mattingly's (1959) description of the Armada does not attempt to say something about all wars or even all naval battles. There, the goal is a descriptive one, akin to the modest goal of descriptive statistics. Therefore, none of this is to say that narrative approaches are unable to yield knowledge or that there is nothing to be learned from the issues of translation, interpretation, or alien belief. Rather, it is to say that narrative methods are not well adapted to complex tasks or or-

13. I have in mind examples such as Winch's *The Idea of a Social Science* (1958), Habermas's *Knowledge and Human Interests* (1968), and Macdonald and Pettit's *Semantics and Social Science* (1981). Admirable exceptions are Papineau's *For Science in the Social Sciences* (1978), Glymour et al., *Discovering Causal Structures* (1987), and Hausman's *Capital, Prices, and Profits* (1981).

ganizing enormous stores of information about diverse but nonindependent events.[14]

From their focus on particular historical or cultural actors, narrative methods may at first appear to be uniquely associated with individualistic explanations. In one sense, this individualism is inessential to the character of narrative explanations. After all, paradigm nonindividualist explanations in sociology and social theory, designed as generalizations about groups of actors, can be narrative. In another sense, narrative approaches are correctly associated with individualism, for the interpretation theory that underwrites them concerns the utterances and behavior of individuals. Or, put another way, this interpretation theory guides the attribution of intentional states, so only those things having intentional states, or things whose behavior can be grounded in them, are appropriate objects of narrative explanations.

Goffman's work in social theory, or "microsociology," is an influential example of narrative research. Beginning in the 1950s, Erving Goffman studied humans in a "participant observation" setting. He watched routine social interactions and documented the separable structures of motivation and intention ordinarily overlooked in casual exchanges. Common interactions like conversations are not an undifferentiated social monolith, Goffman argued, but a highly structured network of personal interests, defenses, poses, purposes, and conventional protocols of enormous subtlety. What emerged from this research was an elaborate taxonomy and theoretical vocabulary (e.g., unfocused interaction, main involvement, face, dominating and subordinate involvement, situational proprieties and obligations, body idiom, personal front, interaction tonus, etc.) for characterizing the complexities of face-to-face interaction.

Goffman's work influenced a generation of social scientists and philosophers of social science, and there is some consensus that the current state of social psychology and sociology is indebted to the lasting insights of his approach (see, for example, Macdonald and Pettit 1981, p. 105). But it has not been easy to formulate clear expressions of the discoveries so often attributed to him by followers. Did Goffman discover that settings of social interaction are highly structured? One might have thought Shakespeare has just as much claim on that "discovery." Did Goffman discover that people deploy strategies for maintaining their integrity? We learn that, often with shame and embarrassment, from our own case. Or did Goffman merely draw our attention to a structure, as Freud did with the unconscious, whose effects were already recognized?

Whatever his achievements, Goffman recognized and rejected quantitative approaches to the study of face-to-face interaction, employing instead a narrative (what he called "naturalistic") method. Although below Goffman casts his reservations about experimental designs as concentrated on face-to-face interaction, his criticisms are surprisingly general, impugning the nature of social experimentation. In traditional research designs,

---

14. The quantitative theorist's focus on generalizability does not suggest that he/she is concerned with subsuming each described event under some general law, as covering-law fanciers implausibly required of historical events (or that every singular causal statement is tacitly general; see Dray 1957).

The variables that emerge tend to be creatures of research designs that have no substance outside the room in which the apparatus and subjects are located, except perhaps briefly when a replication or a continuity performed under sympathetic auspices and a full moon. Concepts are defined on the run in order to get on with setting things up so that trials can be performed and the effects of controlled variation of some kind or another can be measured. The work begins with the sentence "we hypothesise that. . . ." goes on from there to a full discussion of the biases and limits of the proposed design, reasons why these aren't nullifying, and culminates in an appreciable number of satisfyingly significant correlations tending to confirm some of the hypotheses. As though the uncovering of social life were that simple. Fields of naturalistic study have not been uncovered through these methods. Concepts have not emerged that re-ordered our view of social activity. Understanding of ordinary behavior has not accumulated; distance has. (1971, pp. 20–21)

The antiexperimental sentiments expressed by Goffman are typical of critics of quantitative methods. Aside from his charges of shallowness and corruption, he advances the standard, abstract criticism that experimental variables in the social sciences lack external validity. According to chapter 7, such abstract worries are idle or vacuous defeaters of justification in the absence of a specific counterhypothesis. He provides no evidence for the pejorative claim that variables are (mere) artifacts of design ("creatures of research designs").[15] The documentation of the delicate strands of causal influence in social psychology, according to Goffman, does not require experimental design but rather a sensitive observer with incredible powers of detachment. It is no wonder that the list of credentials for Goffman's ideal social theorist reads like the attributes that alchemists one time claimed were necessary for the practice of their trade—a sort of occult power.

Amidst the animated rhetoric, Goffman proposes several simple virtues of research methodology. Let's take a look at them and consider whether they are genuine virtues.

The power of the narrative approach is in good part the power to exploit similarities through anecdote. One result is that we see an old domain in a new way. But is the reordering of our view, by itself, a good thing? That is, is it conducive to progress in a field? Obviously not. Moreover, it is not always desirable that concepts emerge that reorder our view—in social life or in science. Alchemy and open racism would reorder our view, but not in a way we should want. A systematic account of psychic phenomena would reorient our current conception of psychological life or prompt a new taxonomy of psychological causes. But this would be a bad thing. A reassessment of extant knowledge of some sequence of events is normally borne from confirming events in affiliated domains, events that raise the probability of a certain explanation of the original sequence. And this is why theoretical insights in an associated domain—say economics—prompt us to reassess, for example, a so-called war of religion instead as a war of capital. Let's

---

15. It would be interesting to know what Goffman would have said about the use of experimental design in early modern chemistry. Were those variables "creatures of research design"?

now define, by example, some of the often unrecognized limitations of narrative methods.

Limitations of Narrative Social Science and Psychology

The present concern is over narrative methods that are unchecked by numerical, scalable information, methods unconcerned over the cognitive limits of the narrator. Recall that in chapter 1 I described Toynbee's claim that, from 1588 A.D. to 1918 A.D., there was an "unmistakably cyclical pattern" of war every 100 years or so. As it turns out, Toynbee played fast and loose not only with what was tolerably close to the 100-year interval but also with what counted as a war. What principles grounded Toynbee's selections of war episodes to define the interval? Are particular war episodes discounted so Toynbee could arrive at the 100-year interval (actually, the first interval is 116 years)? Indeed, what would be required to infer that these tabular figures form a significant pattern? During Toynbee's second interval, between 1704 and 1815, England has no fewer than three episodes of war with France (1709 under Marlborough, 1744, and 1803) in proximity to the Continent, and on many more occasions during this period the island was subject to incursions of varying seriousness from the French. The third and final interval here—from 1815 to 1918—is characterized by war with Germany. Unlike the prior two intervals, however, England had very little contact with (what Toynbee identifies as) the aggressor nation throughout this interval, until the turn of the century—or about the last twenty years of the 100-year interval.

So there are telling difficulties with Toynbee's sweeping claims. At the risk of damping the intellectually romantic tendency toward dramatic generalization, we should first observe that, by Toynbee's own dates, the historical intervals he cites are not 100 years in duration but instead vary significantly; they are, respectively, 116, 111, and 103 years. If the claim of recurrence is to be a distinctive feature of these intervals rather than other possible ones, Toynbee must show that there is a low probability that intervals satisfying his criteria would be expected by chance, by random selection of intervals of similar duration within the limits of variability in Toynbee's own 116-, 111-, and 103-year periods. But with no indication of what the base rate is—the relative frequency with which war intervals of such length (including the variation between them) occur throughout history— the claimed significance of this "cycle" is uninterpretable. Second, Toynbee never sets out criteria that exclude a sufficient number of other exchanges to demonstrate the required low probability of such cycles.

Let us proceed on the supposition, as now seems reasonable, that the claimed pattern is not a 100-year cycle and that, whatever the pattern, it was arrived at in a post hoc fashion. In a post hoc search, how surprising is it that we would have found a pattern? Again, this depends upon the specification of the target population. If we are concerned to find any repeating sequence, and we are able to carve up the durational components of the sequences as finely or broadly as we like, then the probability of finding some repeating sequence or other is exactly 1. So we shouldn't be surprised when we find some repeating pattern or other.

Let's begin with a 300-year period. Suppose that we do not restrict the population of events of interest to wars but include famines, epidemics, religious campaigns, catastrophic storms, educational reforms, economic changes, trades agreements, and other significant events. Let us restrict our attention to ten such types of important events. Suppose further that there is an armed conflict of some sort every ten years or so, some sort of famine every ten years or so, and so on and that (contrary to fact but not incoherently) these events are roughly independent. In that case, then, one event of the ten types should occur every year. In any given year in that 300-year period, the probability is approximately 1 that some significant event or other occurs. So by helping ourselves to the same lax, post hoc standards as Toynbee's, one could be virtually certain to identify a sequence that, along one of various dimensions, appears significant.

The actual historical record admits a similarly permissive interpretation. There are, for example, two 24–20–22 sequences between 1068 and 1654, one beginning in 1068, the other in 1562 (Dupuy and Dupuy 1986). If we are looking for some sequence or another, then we can find three consecutive wars (1689–1697, 1702–1713, and 1718–1721) separated by two five–year intervals of peace. We can also find three consecutive wars (1666–1668, 1669–1671, and 1672–1677) separated by two one-year intervals and, in the Ottoman Empire, the same pattern (1547–1568, 1569–1569, 1570–1570) of war and peace. What are the chances? On Toynbee's account, it is impossible to accurately estimate the chances, because he does not clearly state either the time span he is considering or what qualifies as a war. As a result, you cannot count up the number of wars in history and thus determine whether a base-rate fallacy is being committed when the "cycle" is claimed to be significant. In light of this guaranteed confirmation, Toynbee's claimed patterns are compatible with a variety of interpretations of history. One wonders whether the 100-year intervals that Toynbee mentions would hold the same interest for us if our culture had given us a mathematics in base two.

The concern about spurious confirmation I am expressing here has a long history in the philosophy of science. According to a standard qualification concerning confirmation, it must not be the case that the predicted event occur come what may; otherwise, confirmatory support does not accrue to the hypothesis (Glymour 1980). But such patterns probably could be found come what may, especially if one is generous in carving up the appropriate categories. Given that between any two wars there is some interval of time, and that there have been many wars in recorded history, we can view history as a sequence of between-war intervals. Now, for some continuous series of such intervals, a thorough investigation of the hypothesis that this recurrence is significant must address the following questions: (1) what would durational similarity explain, if true, (2) how similar must the duration of interwar intervals be to regard their similarity as theoretically interesting, and (3) what frequency of occurrence would legitimately be regarded as theoretically curious? That is, how often throughout history would such a series be expected to randomly occur? Unless this expectation is specified in advance, Toynbee's interest in a "cyclical pattern" is more numerological than historical. For example, how many wars had England had in its history? How many wars have occurred in recorded history? What are we counting as wars? More generally, Toynbee fails to explain why timing should matter rather than magnitude, the religion of respective sides of battles, the economic success of the aggressor nation, and so forth. Even if these questions were answered, the mechanisms underlying the regularities are not described but instead are termed "curious." Although Toynbee speculates about the relation between this putative cycle and the trend toward a European "Universal State" during that period, the above questions are not addressed. These requests for clarification are not those of an austere positivist demanding that the hypotheses be tested by theory-neutral methods and relegated to nonsense if the hypotheses cannot be tested experimentally.

Even those who deride the vague generalizations based on indistinct population specification find such generalization irresistible. In texts of both scholarly and pedagogical importance, we find authors embracing idle generalizations as they simultaneously distance themselves from them. Ridiculing the "masterminds [who] have sought to constrain the loose regularities of history into majestic paradigms" (1968, p. 88), Will and Ariel Durant nevertheless attempt to explain why "centuries of destitution were followed by the slow renewal and reconcentration of wealth," concluding that "the concentration of wealth is natural and inevitable, and is periodically alleviated by violent or peaceable partial redistribution. In this view all economic history is the slow heartbeat of the social organism, a vast systole and diastole of concentrating wealth and compulsive recirculation" (p. 57). Their considered judgment is virtually uninterpretable, so unspecified are the criteria by which taxonomically interesting instances of the generalization are to be identified—unless their claims are understood as unhelpful platitudes:

> History repeats itself in the large because human nature changes with geological leisureliness, and man is equipped to respond in stereotyped ways to frequently occurring situations and stimuli like hunger, danger, and sex. But in a developed and complex civilization individuals are more differentiated and unique than in a primitive society, and many situations contain novel circumstances requiring modifications of instinctive response; custom recedes, reasoning spreads; the results are less predictable. There is no certainty that the future will repeat the past. Every year is an adventure. (p. 88)

Spengler is guilty of such indistinct population specification as well. In *The Decline of the West*, Spengler details what he calls "higher Cultures" and claims that history reveals to us "eight such Cultures, all of the same build, the same development, and the same duration" (1928, Volume 2, p. 36). Despite these similarities,

> The group of high Cultures is not, as a group, an organic unit. That they have happened in just this number, at just these places and times, is, for the human eye, an incident without deeper intelligibility. The ordering of individual Cultures, on the contrary, has stood out so distinctly that the historical technique of the Chinese, the Magian, and the Western worlds—often, indeed, the mere common consent of the educated in these Cultures—has been able to fashion a set of names upon which it would be impossible to improve. (1928, Volume 2, p. 37)

Evidently, relative-absolute claims had, for Spengler, adequate resilience to frame ambitious cross-historical generalizations of, we might say, iron necessity:

> For Western existence the distinction lies about the year 1800—on one side of that frontier life in fullness and sureness of itself, formed by growth from within, in one great uninterrupted evolution from Gothic childhood to Goethe and Napoleon, and on the other the autumnal, artificial, rootless life of our great cities, under forms fashioned by the intellect. . . . He who does not understand that this outcome is obligatory and insusceptible of modification must forgo all desire to comprehend history. (Spengler, quoted in Durant and Durant, 1968, p. 90)

This is not to say that Spengler's general declarations are literally incompatible with his relativized account of historical necessity, but it is not clear what is purchased by Spengler's qualification—except, perhaps, escape from simpleminded charges of contradiction that state that in claiming that there are no temporally and culturally invariant laws he had created one.

In each case, the population of objects to which the generalization is applied remains indistinct. Contributing to this indistinctness is Toynbee's, the Durants's, and Spengler's silence about the relevant population dimensions along which the explanations are framed. My claim is not that narrative techniques are worthless or that nothing can be learned from them. As a matter of fact, many narrative treatments are ingenious, making their way through testimony, motivations, and chronicles with delicacy and sophistication. In the first instance, then, my claim is that quantitative methods extend our own unaided capacities. Without such aids, our computational and situational constraints render us unable to detect and recognize any but the most powerful and salient effects of theoretical interest. Statistical designs allow us to tease out subtle and otherwise inaccessible causal influences and to correct for some of the biases of availability and representativeness in narrative techniques.

When the historian uses a poorly tested and narrow theory of history—especially an approach less concerned with cultural and geographic facts, well known for flouting interests of converging estimation—converging eyewitness testimony is especially important. Psychohistory, typically committed to one or another psychodynamic account of human behavior and to a view about the historical importance of the psychology of "great figures" or of lesser individuals in a historical setting, is one such area (for an example of the latter, see Winthrop Jordan's *White Man's Burden*). It is possible to find psychohistorical studies of many famous figures, from Martin Luther to Adolf Hitler. Consider Erik Erikson's *Young Man Luther* (1962), in which Erikson relies on an alleged eyewitness report of Martin Luther's "fit in the choir." Erikson begins his analysis of Luther, an analysis that ultimately leads to a diagnosis of neurosis, with a story reported in the secondary literature. According to this story, there was a point in a mass during which there was a reading of the story of Christ's "cure of a man possessed by a dumb spirit" (Erikson 1962, p. 23). At this point, Luther is alleged to have " 'raved' like one possessed, and roared with the voice of a bull: 'Ich bin's nit! Ich bin's nit!' " (p. 23). Erikson allows that Luther may have roared in Latin but says in any case that the meaning conveyed was "I am not! I am not!"

It turns out that, given the suspect character of Erikson's documentation, worries about translation put too fine an edge on the scholarship. Erikson draws the story from a book by Otto Scheel (1929), who in fact raises the oft-told story only to deny that the "fit in the choir" ever happened. Scheel attributes the story to a vicious biography of Luther, written by Johannes Cochlaus in 1549. Never one to give up on a good psychosis story without a fight, Erikson insists that there must be some truth to the story, and makes Scheel himself the subject of analysis: "Scheel does not seem able to let go of the story. Even to him there is enough in it so that in the very act of belittling it he grants it a measure of religious grandeur" (Erikson 1962, p. 25). Of the other detractors of the story Erikson says, "but its fascination even for those who would do away with it seems to be great" (p. 25).

Erikson states that Scheel, as a Protestant professor of theology, is mainly interested in such "fits" as the expression of divine inspiration, mediated by the soul or spirit of a person. It is perhaps understandable that a psychoanalyst instead would interpret such behavior as an expression of neurosis, but what is at stake here is not the priority of psychoanalytic over religious historiography but standards for securing historical accuracy that are not in dispute and that Erikson ignores. A thorough check on the source of the "fit in the choir" story might have revealed that the alleged eyewitness responsible for this report had been responsible for another report that placed a cloven-hoofed tinker in Frau Luther's home just nine months before little Martin was born.[16] One may quibble about the best systematic account of human behavior. But this issue puts too delicate an edge on the dispute if more basic rules of converging eyewitness testimony are routinely flouted; in this case, the event in question may never have happened.

Sociology and Political Science

Alexis de Tocqueville, one of the most vocal admirers of American democracy, fills his most famous text, *Democracy in America*, with a tour of the manners, customs, and laws of the Americans and the British. The sheer number of detailed observations is powerful testament to scholarly devotion. However, the best use has not been made of the details. Although loaded with data, when the text uses this body of information as a basis for generalizations concerning, say, differences between Americans and British, those statements are typically crass and unconstrained, the stuff of porch speculation. Tocqueville reports that Americans rather than the English show more "aptitude" and "taste" for general ideas (1966, p. 402; also see p. 291). Here is a base-rate fallacy due to indistinct population specification, which results from unspecified properties such as "aptitude" and "taste." In

---

16. There is actually a substantial literature on the question of whether Luther was possessed by the devil, in league with the devil, or indeed the devil's changeling. After Cochlaus and Scheel, Herte (1943) provides a way into this literature. On this particular issue, see Herte (1943), pp. 28, 47, 55–56, and 262–263.

consequence, their use could be stretched so that any sort of behavior could be seen as falling within the target population. None of this is to suggest that even the best of methods could compensate for the horrible state of theory at the time. For a pertinent example, one need only examine Tocqueville's alternation between regrettable romanticization and nativist apologetics of "the slave and savage" lives of blacks and Native Americans during his visit.

Failure to assess base rate, to identify theoretically relevant dimensions of explanation, to quantify and scale data, and to estimate relative causal influence had especially unfortunate consequences for Tocqueville's narrative. His treatment yields no serious assessment of the causal relation between American democracy and institutions central to an understanding of its particular function, such as slavery (and the genocide of the Native Americans), however troubling one might have thought an honest investigator would find the apparent harmony of American democracy and slavery. Instead, Tocqueville handles the relation between the institution of slavery and the development of American democracy in the following way:

> I have now finished the main task that I set myself and have, to the best of my ability, described the laws and mores of American democracy. . . .
>
> In the course of this work I have been led to mention the Indians and the Negroes, but I have never had the time to stop and describe the position of these two races within the democratic nation I was bent on depicting. . . .
>
> These topics are like tangents to my subject, being American, but not democratic, and my main business has been to describe democracy. (1966, p. 291)

It appears that Tocqueville's narrative method allows him to abstract from the causal dependence of the leisure of American democracy on the subjection of African Americans and the theft of Native American lands and at the same time to control the story in a way that casts these events as simply unfortunate things that happened to African Americans and Native Americans, not as things done to them by the champions of democracy. Indeed, Tocqueville is generous with his sympathy and often regrets that the slaves and Indians lacked the spiritual or moral resources to overcome their sorry lot. Or their desperate condition is described, but no causal story is provided as to the origin of this condition. Oppression is mentioned, but how it was executed under the aegis of democracy is not.[17]

Again, this passage is not presented in hopes that Tocqueville would be viewed as despicable or stupid. He certainly was neither. Nor is it designed to show that there is nothing of value in his work. Rather, it displays the risks of undisciplined, even if intelligent, reflection upon social exchange. It is worth assessing Tocqueville's work not in light of measurement in physics but in terms of the general canons of measurement outlined in PGE, and doing so can help us to recognize when social and psychological inquiry is flouting standards of careful estimation. Perhaps careful estimation is not the goal of *Democracy in America*. But to the

---

17. The most representative expression of this strategy can be found in Tocqueville (1966, pp. 291–295).

extent that the social phenomena reported in it depend on judgments of kind and magnitude, the process of both report and generalization can be improved by attention to the epistemic category of measurement.

Motivational and Clinical Psychology

Narrative methods dominate in psychoanalysis, the most influential movement of motivational and clinical psychology of this century. The hazards of an approach that ignores the rationale for quantitative information become especially evident when the methods of a discipline are structured to exclude (sometimes even mock) relevant distributional information about the discipline's population. The most influential of the misleading claims of psychoanalysis are those of clinical success. There are two basic problems with such claims. First, if an analyst claims that he or she has been able to cure about 50 percent of their patients, one wants to know whether that 50 percent would have gotten better by chance; that is, we need to know base rates before we can draw conclusions about effectiveness of treatment. Second, an analyst sees an enormous number of patients, too many to track by unaided memory and too varied in terms of disfunction and treatment to trace subtle and often opposing causal influences in the analytic setting to draw conclusions from unaided recollections of patient improvement.

Let's consider a representative example of psychoanalytic practice that set the methodological tone for clinical and motivational psychology in the twentieth century. Alfred Adler's individual psychology, different in its primary postulated mechanisms from Freudian or Jungian psychoanalysis, had in common with those and other approaches the major methodological practices—individual case study, the analytic situation, and the narrative report of treatment and termination. Characteristic of these reports are striking remarks without citation or appeal to any evidence whatever: "I believe that about thirty-five per cent of all persons are left-handed, and most of them unconscious of the fact" (Adler 1929, p. 64). Typically, these projections show scant concern for scaling of appropriate variables (described in chapter 2) and less concern than in the passage above for the identification, nature, and size of the reference class under discussion. In one especially casual use of frequency information designed to support a generalization, Adler says, "the eyebrow on the left side is frequently higher in a left-handed person," but says this without reporting the frequency rate or whether the frequency of higher left eyebrows is greater in the left-handed than in the right-handed population (p. 67). Not only is base-rate information not provided, but there is no redeeming detail about the measures used: "Generally, when I see a very bad handwriting I know it is that of a left-handed person whose courage is below par. On the other hand, if I see excellent handwriting I know it is a left-handed person also, but who has successfully grappled with his difficulties" (p. 64).

In a passage that follows soon thereafter, Adler states that "[i]t is not generally known that left-handed children very often have considerable difficulty in learning to read because they spell reversely from right to left; a mistake which they can correct if it is properly explained to them" (1929, p. 65). Although this passage receives a supporting footnote, Adler's reference is to an article on "these and other facts" appearing in a fledgling journal (*International Journal of Individual Psychology*) whose name honors the approach he founded.

Adler's blithe classification of the sloppy left-hander as "below par" in courage highlights that it is not just base-rate information to which his method is insensitive. Without appeal to evidence that could potentially confirm Adler's analytic triumphs, such as success rate, Adler asks, "How could I cure a stutterer if I believed stuttering to be caused by some subtle and unknown organic deficiencies? I have plenty of evidence that the stutterer does not want to join with others, and he can generally talk quite well when he is alone: he may even be able to read or recite excellently: so I can only interpret his stammer as the expression of his attitude towards others" (1929, p. 63). This explanation of stuttering—the rejection of or contempt for others—would be ultimately unavoidable if it were true and we had a sufficiently developed theory to establish its truth. But given the state of the evidence he presents, Adler's explanation of stuttering as antisocial is unfounded, not to mention cruel and irresponsible.

The focus on Adler, a single analyst, should not be taken to reflect a tacit reliance on a narrative approach, as though the narrative method is so essential to inquiry that in criticizing it I must use it. On a quantitative account, the appeal to single cases is permissible so long as plausible reason is given for thinking that the case is representative. And there is very good reason for supposing that this *approach* in (what we would now recognize as motivational/clinical) psychology is not an abberation of Adler's personality, even if the specific *tenets* of his individual psychology are. If we consult contemporary texts, we find that, given the general methodological features of psychoanalytic theories of the time, the evidence adverted to is insufficient to provide a good test of the (often) rather strong clinical diagnoses or conclusions made.

Notice that the demand for hypotheses that can be tested in a more controlled setting is not a verificationist demand, nor is it proposed as a constraint on scientific respectability, as positivists claimed. This has been the dominant charge against critics of psychoanalysis.[18] When claiming successful treatment, for example, no intervention in the analytic situation would be required and so cannot be used as a reason against doing follow-up studies. Psychoanalysts presumably would agree that, no matter what your scientific scruples, it is in the interest of our common goal of understanding nature that evidence be as publicly available as confidentiality will allow. Because follow-up studies raise no insurmountable concerns about privacy, one is left suspicious of analysts' resistance to studies that might confirm their confident claims of clinical success.[19]

---

18. This charge of "positivism" can be found in many of the psychoanalytic journals, wherever demands for evidence are made. Philosophers of science interested in psychoanalysis are commonly referred to Grünbaum (1984), but a sophisticated treatment of the testability of clinical hypotheses can be found in Edelson (1983).

19. It is worth further notice that my criticism of Adler is methodological and general, independent of any attitude one might have about the content of Adlerian individual psychology or of Freud-

Are these claims justified? Not on the basis of the evidence available to the claimants. It took a meta-analytic study of psychotherapeutic outcomes to establish that some forms of therapy are more effective than no therapy at all. The most famous study on the relative effectiveness of different psychotherapeutic methods was a meta-analytic study by Smith and Glass (1977). Meta-analysis, described in chapter 6, summarizes research not by narrative review but by collecting all the known, relevantly similar studies into one big study. By a kind of statistical averaging of standardized results on a particular research question, meta-analytic reviews are able to arrive at conclusions that are relatively independent of the theoretical perspectives and idiosyncrasies of particular authors of individual studies or their narrative reporters, can handle with facility the large number of studies, and can report not just the direction of the effect but its size as well.

On the basis of 375 studies on psychotherapy outcomes, Smith and Glass concluded that psychotherapy was effective. Although they provide an elaborate analysis of effect size, they offer a more approachable description of the fairly large clinical effect: "The average client receiving therapy was better off than 75% of the untreated controls" (1977, p. 754). We can agree that this is an impressive effect once one sees the numbers, but since there is extensive evidence that even professionals trained in quantitative methods do not perform well when asked to make impressionistic judgments (Tversky and Kahneman 1971), we cannot say that the effect would be recognized by a psychotherapist claiming historical success. But premature and mistaken self-confidence has robust precedent. Extensively trained and licensed therapists also claimed to know that they were more successful than minimally trained professionals in bringing about cure, but Smith and Glass found that this was not the case; those with much training and licensing enjoyed no more success in bringing about cure than minimally trained professionals. There are a number of concerns one might have here, both about meta-analysis in general or about this analysis in particular, but they have been addressed widely in the literature, and the comprehensive reviews tend to confirm the general findings that psychotherapy is more effective than no treatment and that varieties of psychotherapy do not differ in effectiveness. (For representative discussions, see Barber 1994; Crits-Christoph 1992; Smith and Glass 1977; Landman and Dawes 1982; Hunter and Schmidt 1990.)

Aren't we begging the question in claiming, without first having done a meta-analysis, that meta-analysis is preferable to a narrative, anecdotal summary of the psychotherapist's experience? No we are not, for several reasons. Meta-analysis, like other quantitative statistical methods, has proven instrumentally reliable on populations of known value, while anecdotal and impressionistic judgments have

---

ian or Jungian analysis. Moreover, if one has any doubt that Adler's general criteria for neurosis were historically and culturally local—downright bourgeois—his discussion of the three challenges of life is worth reviewing. According to Adler, neurotic disfunction is indicated by the evasion of adjustment to *any* of Adler's three "problems of life": society, occupation, and love. Remaining unmarried, engaging in masturbation or homosexual activity, and inconsistent employment are all mentioned by Adler as evidence of failure at the three problems of life (see Adler 1929, pp. 3–4, 115–116, 148–150).

been shown to be notoriously defective. The argument that meta-analysis is reliable is question begging only if it assumes the very claim that it proposes to establish—that meta-analysis is reliable. But this is not assumed; it is the conclusion of an independent argument that has as its conclusion that quantitative methods are reliable and that meta-analysis is one such method. The reasons for supposing that quantitative, population-guided methods of estimation are reliable concern their successful use outside of the behavioral and social sciences as well; these methods have afforded approximately true predictions at the observable level in areas such as physics and chemistry. Therefore, one charges question-beggingness only at the expense of dismissing the quantitatively based merits of physics and chemistry as well.

Much of the psychoanalytic community has shown enormous resistance to the use of quantitative methods, even though most practitioners take their clinical hypotheses to be empirically testable and show some pride in their own anecdotal successes. The testing of these clinical hypotheses apparently does not require the recording of success rates, the consensual use of control groups and of videotaped sessions, or other confirmatory practices. In fact, many of those familiar with psychoanalysis reject one possible mode of methodological improvement—videotaping sessions to match therapeutic techniques with ultimate success—claiming that videotaping is incompatible with the trust required in the analytic situation; the obtrusive nature of the technique is claimed to compromise the relationship of trust that is supposed to develop between the analyst and patient. An opposing view claims that videotaping sessions promises to improve the effectiveness of treatment by allowing analysts to examine their methods and the patients' responses and to evaluate those treatments in light of the success rates of patients. Should the method threaten to undermine the relationship of trust, perhaps the patient's knowledge that videotaping is designed to help make treatment more effective—intended to help the patient—would reestablish trust. Over time, the video camera, positioned inconspicuously in the room, might become part of the background, little more threatening than the analyst's pad and pencil. Many analysts claim to know that this videotaping process either cannot be made unobtrusive or that its obtrusion cannot be corrected. In any case, the question is not whether the treatment interferes; it is whether the interferences can be controlled or corrected. But they claim to know this without having to test this possibility.

This is a peculiar stand to take for those who claim to no longer be surprised by the astonishing resilience of the mind or by the subtle complexity of the relation of transference. Claimed for psychoanalysis is a power to uncover striking things about the mind: that the subconscious could for decades bear repressed guilt over a tiny transgression or that by recognizing the source of one's obsession one can be released from so powerful a disfunction. Psychoanalytic cures sometimes begin with wrenching epiphanies, but apparently the one surprising discovery that cannot be made is that the video camera (or the fact that one is being videotaped) is a useful tool in psychoanalysis (or, put negatively, does not irreparably subvert the analytic situation).

Given the seriousness with which we treat issues engaging our mental health, and the intellectual integrity we expect from theories claiming the honorific "science," it is not surprising that psychoanalysis has had its scientific respectability more vigorously disputed in the twentieth century than perhaps any other discipline.[20] Another reason the scientific status of psychoanalytic theory has received so much attention in the intellectual community is that psychoanalytic concepts have exercised a powerful influence over a variety of disciplines. Its fundamental commitments to the notions of the subconscious and to the mind as a symbolic representational system embody metaphors whose influence on contemporary academics can be challenged only by the influence of Marxism and evolutionary theory.

Positivist criticisms of psychoanalysis were based on views, now widely regarded as problematic, about reduction as a model of theoretical unification and the foundationalist role of observation in the process of justification. However, the defenders of psychoanalysis were too slow in pointing out these distortions, and there is probably a moral here for both politics and the sociology of philosophy. Rather than simply reject this reductionist picture of science, defenders of psychoanalysis such as Habermas endorsed the picture of prediction and control for natural sciences such as physics and chemistry—whose apparent goal is said to be prediction and control—and postulated a separate domain of inquiry called "the human sciences," like psychology and anthropology, whose goal was said to be "self-understanding." In retrospect, they should have taken the line that there are many different types of causal explanation, all of which satisfy different explanatory interests, and that factors like self-understanding, social class, and witchcraft accusations are all causal and can be implicated in scientific generalizations. This would have blocked the empiricist move (with which we have been living ever since) that conceded the significance of the natural science/human science distinction and then happily observed that the human sciences don't enjoy anything like the explanatory successes or theoretical consensus embodied in the natural sciences, thus raising doubts about the real scientific status of the human sciences.

In any other clinical discipline, a check on enduring cure or clinical success is done by a follow-up study; but not in psychoanalysis. The published case study is the primary medium of professional communication among psychoanalysts and the primary vehicle for reports of successful analysis. These case studies, for the most part, have the same form. The analyst begins by describing the patient and the disfunction that occasioned the initial visit. The analyst then presents the

---

20. An important clarification: When I use the term "psychoanalysis," I intend it to apply to those features of clinical practice common to most theoretical orientations within that tradition. Freudians, Jungians, and Adlerians all assign an important role to the unconscious, to mental functions as symbolic or representational, to analytic relations like transference and countertransference, and to the idea that psychoanalytic cure is achieved through the patient's (and sometimes analyst's) insight about the true causes of his or her behavior. So it won't do to criticize the attack I'm about to make by pointing out that, for Freud, behavior is to be explained by appeal to the desire for sexual satisfaction whereas, for Adler, it is the desire for moral superiority. The aspects of psychoanalytic theory that I'm going to criticize survive differences in motivational outlooks.

information gathered from interaction with the patient, often through long hours of analysis—concerning the patient's personal history, current occupation, attitude toward his/her past relationships, and so forth. Throughout this presentation, the analyst attempts to identify (without the aid of experimental design) specific and recurring themes in the patient's behavior in analysis—which of the analyst's suggestions and interventions are accepted by the patient and which are resisted. By an emerging relation of trust and identification with the analyst (called "transference"), the patient is brought to insights about the actual causes of the disfunction. The analyst describes these changes and their role in dissolving the symptom, then closes the presentation with an account of the patient's apparent resolution of conflict and a schedule for termination of treatment. Call this the "analytic sketch."

Here are some brief but representative descriptions of analytic cure. In the case of one neurotic patient who had a horrible history of rejection by and conflict with those she cared about, "enabling Mary [the patient] to understand the infantile and early childhood roots of her personality difficulties is what led to the patient's ultimate improvement" (Marmor 1988, p. 290). Another patient, who suffered unusual anxiety at the prospect of giving birth (expressed by sadistic wishful fantasies), took the first step toward cure when "she began to be aware of how afraid she had been of the enjoyment and excitement which accompanied those fantasies" (Sandler 1988, p. 323). These descriptions locate as the primary causal mechanism of cure the patient's "awareness" and "understanding" of the source of the disfunction, brought about in the analytic situation. It may be that these are the relevant mechanisms, but, as Dawes (1994) convincingly argues, nothing in the traditional, narrative literature establishes that substantial claim.

What reasons are we given by psychoanalysts for supposing that self-understanding leads to cure or that psychoanalysis is responsible for cure? Follow-up studies are important because they are the only fair and objective test of enduring cure and thus of a treatment's success. First, for a long time psychoanalysts have traded on sophisticated and technical medical terminology. They talk about clinical diagnoses, symptoms, disfunctions, pathologies, and cures. But despite the heavily advertised analogy between medical and psychological notions, it is astoundingly inaccurate as a description of analytic practice. When cancer patients undergo chemotherapy, follow-up studies are an essential part of any evaluation of the effectiveness of treatment. It would be scientifically absurd and morally unconscionable to present chemotherapy as an effective treatment if all the doctor could say in its favor is that it "seemed to make the patients feel better." The way to pin down its effectiveness is to compare the percentage of remissions in the treated group with the percentage of remissions in an untreated group matched for type and severity of cancer. If psychoanalysts really believe that patients are made better by analysis, they should make a good faith effort to show that an untreated sample of patients, matched with the treated group for type and severity of symptoms, would not have improved without analysis. This would prove that, as a matter of professional responsibility, they are not wasting the money, time, and energy of emotionally compromised patients, at least not for that reason. And as a matter of scientific responsibility, there would be, for the first time, evidence that psychoanalysis works. But also, in so doing, we might discover that it doesn't work.

But suppose the experienced psychoanalyst were to claim that the demand for follow-up studies is misapplied in the case of psychoanalysis, that psychoanalytic treatment is complicated in ways that make it distinctly unlike clinical medicine. On this view, medicine treats the patient as an object predictably responsive to chemical treatment, whereas psychoanalysis regards the patient at a dynamic, psychological level, in which fantasies, dreams, and clinical influences like transference affect the patient in subtle and often unanticipated ways. To divine and separate the mechanisms of mental disfunction, the analyst must be a person of unusually sophisticated recognitional skills that only traditional psychoanalytic training will supply. The trained psychoanalyst can spot and respond appropriately to resistances and strategies that may be peculiar to an individual patient. On such a view, follow-up studies are unnecessary because they would only tell analysts what they already know from their practical clinical experience. As a matter of fact, the distinguished authors of one of the scarce experimental studies seem to anticipate this view, placing impressionistic evidence from the couch on a par with experimental evidence:

> When we report that the accuracy of interpretations, which is a solid cornerstone in the psychoanalytic theory of therapeutic change, has been supported by our research, we expect that those of you who believe in the sufficiency of clinical evidence will say, or politely think, "So, what else is new?" For experienced analysts our statement is an obvious restatement of the obvious. But those of you who wish for other kinds of objective evidence will seize this moment as an occasion to cheer. (Luborsky and Crits-Christoph 1988, p. 83)

Rather than derogating the dominant anecdotal approach, the authors appear willing to assign to impressionistic evidence from the clinician's couch a credibility equal to their experimental evidence, citing the latter as merely "other kinds of objective evidence." But I'm afraid that this is a case where professional politeness strains credulity. Quite aside from the question of what they would conclude from these experiments had the studies contradicted conventional analytic wisdom, there is a serious question whether, in the absence of properly designed studies, the analyst could have good reason to believe that analytic interpretations are accurate. (For an interesting experimental approach to the improvement of analytic skills, see Weiss 1988.)

What kind of evidence could the experienced analyst offer to show that particular analytic interpretations of a patient's behavior are accurate? Analysts sometimes claim that a specific interpretation was "useful" or that a clinical intervention was followed by a change in the expression of the patient's neurotic symptom. But, of course, the critic who doubts the accuracy of analytic interpretations doesn't doubt that an interpretation can be useful, perhaps holding with Bertrand Russell that "any theory is better than no theory at all." Nor do critics necessarily doubt that the patient can change as a result of the analyst's interventions. After all, changes can be brought about by intimate conversations with a trusted friend. What they doubt is that the analyst—or anyone else, for that matter—has any good reason to believe that, when patients improve, they do so *as a result* of the accuracy of an interpretation and the reliability of the method leading to it.

If the earlier survey of inferential fallacies is taken to heart, then it is reasonable to suppose that analysts, like the rest of us, are easily misled by information irrelevant to the phenomenon to be explained and insensitive to important factors like sample size. But in the analyst's office, there is no on-the-spot ANOVA and no attempt to check the possibility that four or five of the patient's propensities, all of which vary in strength, are likely to respond favorably to a particular clinical interpretation. You can be as smart, well-trained, and credentialed as you like, but your inferences are still frivolous without such quantitative analyses. And the analyst's reasoning is intuitive and informal in just the ways condemned by the recent research on judgments under uncertainty.

Of course, much more is at stake here than the question of whether psychoanalysis merits scientific status. Psychoanalysis concerns the treatment of ailing patients, and we should be interested in whether psychoanalysis employs reliable methods and effects enduring cures so that, if it does, we can improve its methodology, and, if it doesn't, we can protect the interests of people vulnerable to the psychoanalytic profession's self-conscious styling in the image of the medical profession, its claims to diagnostic authority and objectivity, and its advertised potential for cure.

Follow-up studies (to use Grünbaum's terms, "extraclinical evidence") are necessary not just to evaluate the long-term success of treatment but also to constrain hypotheses about effective clinical techniques, in a way not anticipated by Grünbaum. Suppose, for instance, that we class neurotic patients by type of neurosis. This is a complicated matter, but promising identification strategies are being explored at the University of Pennsylvania Hospital and at the Mount Zion Hospital and Medical Center (see Luborsky et al. 1988). We could then divide this group in two and test specific competing hypotheses about a variety of effects that different analytic techniques could have on the dissolution of the symptom. The independent variable could be the type of treatment (i.e., supportive, confrontational) and the dependent variable the long-term success rate of the respective treatment group. If one group has a statistically significantly higher success rate, we can reason backward, arguing that (all other things being equal) the higher success rate was caused by a superior treatment technique. Now, of course, establishing a causal connection on the basis of a statistical correlation can be a tricky business, but the success of a variety of sciences testifies that it can be done and is done routinely. Among other things, you have to show that the groups had no relevant differences, other than the type of treatment they received, that could have brought about the greater success of one of the treatments.

A number of powerful institutional influences would have to change in the profession of psychoanalysis for such proposals to be taken seriously. But they must change if psychoanalysis is to become a respectable science. If that time comes, we will no longer hear evaluations of an analyst's case study like the following, drawn from a major psychoanalytic journal: "Dr. Karme is to be congratulated for her frank and effective paper as well as on her analytic work. . . . I have the impression of a well-conducted analysis, one which is successful to this point and apparently approaching termination . . . . The sequence of events described is believable and clear, in the sense of 'I know what she means' " (Compton 1988, p. 283). This is a perfectly representative example of clinical judgment and literature review based on needlessly uncontrolled impressions, and often at $120 a throw. My criticism is not that psychoanalysis fails to make patients feel better, that it does not alleviate stress or grief, and certainly not that it does patients irreparable damage.[21] Rather, my contention is that to the extent that psychoanalysis makes claims to cure—and there can be no question that such claims are advanced—it provides little in their defense. And this is epistemically irresponsible, because the route to rudimentary improvement promises to be less complicated than is often supposed.[22]

Prescribing the Antidote: Listening to Measured Realism and PGE

As we have seen, most of the fields in the behavioral and social sciences—psychology, sociology, political science, and history—include narrative or "traditional" approaches in their methodological repertoire; some fields are dominated by them. The criticisms of narrative or "traditional" methods presented here, as disturbing as they might be, cannot be dismissed as the hoary reactions to the dispute between outmoded traditional history and quantitative history. In this chapter, I have offered a specific diagnosis of the frailties of narrative or traditional methods: They are subject to the same experimentally well-established cognitive effects found in the judgment under uncertainty literature, and, more generally, they violate intellectual standards of inquiry that apply beyond those of physical measurement. The account of PGE in chapter 2 illustrates these general standards of inquiry.

If readers have been forebearing enough to sustain this protracted criticism of core narrative methods, perhaps readers have also been patient enough to recognize that my criticisms, while calling for potentially far-reaching revisions to traditional social and behavioral inquiry, are also carefully circumscribed. I have not

---

21. Traditional psychoanalysis is only one of many offending narrative approaches indicted here. Given the combination of space constraints and the especially egregious character of the offense, I can only attempt to leave the reader with a sense of foreboding concerning traditional psychoanalysis. Fortunately, Dawes (1994) provides a wonderfully lucid and serious evaluation of the myths surrounding much contemporary clinical psychology. His criticisms are in the spirit of those advanced here. For a less systematic and more personal critique of contemporary psychotherapy, see Masson (1988).

22. In general, I believe Freud showed greater cognizance of these methodological vicissitudes than some have charged, but his work, particularly his claim to clinical success, is marred by the same fundamental failure to do follow-up studies. I focus on psychoanalysis due to the range of its influence in philosophy, from methodological disputes about the confirmability of clinical hypotheses (Edelson 1983; Grünbaum 1984) to literary exploration about the fullness or "plurivocality" of metaphor resulting from the condensation of symbols (Ricouer 1970; Kristeva 1980).

defended the strong view, that narrative methods cannot be reliable. There is nothing about narrative methods that makes them essentially insensitive to quantitative parameters, and so nothing in this chapter supports the claim that it is always epistemically irresponsible to rely upon them; it is only irresponsible when alternative methods, suggested either by the narrative theorist's own lights or by other reigning or practically available accounts, are blithely dismissed or ignored altogether. All that the evidence indicates, and all I have claimed for it, is the weak view, that narrative methods can be demonstrably and systematically unreliable, particularly when applied to any but the most robust phenomena. According to this weak view, there is substantial empirical evidence that the psychological judgments called upon by narrative methods are prone to specific biases that threaten the reliability and validity of generalizations in the behavioral and social sciences and that, independent of the existence and seriousness of these biases, narrative methods are untrustworthy. The narrative approach tends to be indifferent toward the categories of careful estimation such as sample size, base-rate information, and representativeness. In consequence, the generalizations it advances are not suitably guided by the ways of the world.

While the continued improvement of narrative and quantitative techniques in the social and behavioral sciences will not be easy to achieve, there is no reason to suppose that it is unachieveable. The methodological challenges of social and behavioral sciences are those of science generally, including disagreements about the relative importance of different causes, about how to characterize these causes (endogenous/exogenous, etc.), and about the appropriate *explanandum*, the object of our explanation. We have seen these problems arise in the work of Adler and Toynbee, in psychoanalysis and history generally, and they are nicely described by Wright, Levine, and Sober:

> Assessments of relative importance *among important causes*, even if they can be made rigorously in particular instances, are likely to be so affected by the precise characterization of the explananda and by the range of variation allowed for different causes, that generalizations are likely to be vulnerable to small changes in the specification of the problem. (1992, p. 174)

In light of the research on the cognitive frailties of human judgment surveyed in this chapter, we now have very good reason for supposing that, without following the edicts of PGE, social and behavioral scientists have no hope of arriving at accurate characterizations of important causes. Of course, a good theory could settle all of these disputes at once, but good theories don't fall from the bottoms of cherubs; they typically develop out of the routine work of estimation and explanation. When addressing issues as complex as those in the social and behavioral sciences, nascent research can be limping and misguided. Measured Realism affords an explanation of how progress, however modest, is borne from such sour fruit. Measurement as PGE confers on the world a corrective influence, as does the only plausible explanation for the reliability of the various forms of diverse testing discussed in my treatment of Measured Realism. These considerations cumulatively counsel the adoption of a Measured Realism about the objects of the social and behavioral sciences.

Conclusion

Measured Realism offers an explanation for the success of the social and behavioral sciences upon the introduction of quantitative methods and for the failure of traditional narrative methods, where they have in fact failed. Population-Guided Estimation provides a systematic rationale for scientific realist talk of reliability and approximation. Further, the independence component of Measured Realism allows us to address a historical issue concerning sustained progress in a particular field. Barring utter historical contingency (which may have been responsible for the remarkable advances in physics in the Newtonian era), we can improve upon a poor theory only if particular hypotheses are epistemically bite-sized—sufficiently detachable from a specific theory and evaluable by diverse accounts. Thus neural accounts of aphasia could, by an abundance of intermediary steps, succeed medieval, hydraulic accounts, and computational accounts of vision could follow the extramission theory of the ancient Greeks. In the history of some mature, natural sciences, Measured Realism may provide an accurate account of the progress from poor to serviceable theories, and in some cases measured realist explanation for theory adoption may be preferable to the one of historical contingency in the mature sciences offered by some other scientific realists (Boyd 1981).

A careful critic of scientific realism might notice that even early versions of scientific realism were, in light of what might have been advanced in realism's favor, quite circumspect; these formulations never advanced realism about the behavioral or social sciences, nor about the objects, laws, and theories at the pioneering fringes of physics, chemistry, and biology. Instead, scientific realists restricted their statements to the core claims in the "mature" sciences of physics, chemistry, and biology. In the early 1970s, the full range of the mature sciences was largely philosophically untapped, allowing sweeping generalizations about the overall theoretical success of science—generalizations indicating that something about this overall success is worth explaining. Specific explanations for the success of each domain awaited case studies, and with these studies came both appropriate qualifications and more focused and detailed versions of realism. Sweeping inductions over so enormous a subject matter might have a grand appearance, but vast terrain should not suggest to the critic a correspondingly grand argument.

Philosophers of science seized the opportunity to do case studies, realists and antirealists alike. And no appropriately naturalistic version of realism would formulate its favored metaphysical view independently of historical case evidence. As epistemological naturalism became the stance of choice among philosophers of science, there accumulated in fine-grained analyses of historical episodes an increasingly powerful testament to the instrumental reliability of scientific methodology (for more "local" studies, see, for example, Kitcher 1978, 1984; Boyd 1979; Hacking 1983; Cartwright 1983; McMullin 1984; and Salmon 1984). Realists could now make inductions over a larger and more diverse body of historical evidence. Indeed, this evidence became a standard part of realist arguments. This attention has allowed realists to further refine claims about the character and extent of success, a consideration that motivated Measured Realism. Any global argument for scientific realism, then, will be made in the same way integrative agruments in science are routinely made—by eliciting detailed connections between various domains.[1]

This book is primarily concerned with two issues in the behavioral sciences: realism and naturalism. I contended that the arguments for both realism and naturalism are abductive. If one is neither a realist nor a naturalist in the philosophy of science, then one must embrace a prescriptivism that is radically normative, a kind of epistemology that led positivists to the philosophical shoals.[2] If we are to

---

1. The critical part of this book has focused on the problems with empiricist treatments of science. For an extended discussion and critique of social constructivism, see Trout (1994), in which I argue that social constructivism's defining doctrines are incompatible with a central feature of scientific practice: the reliance on historically remote evidence.

2. In the Afterword to the second edition, Fine (1996) objects to the suggestion that "grand old realism" is a caricature put forward by antirealists. Fine apparently sees in this suggestion evidence of the realist's "instant loss of memory" (p. 181). There is little reason to suppose that Fine would be any less dismissive of the history I have just told here, although I document the extravagant expectations of antirealists in the third section of chapter 4. Indeed, Fine (1996) offers an alternative to the above history of realist literature, portraying it instead as one of realist retreat, with NOA leading the attack. According to Fine's history, scientific realists responded to NOA with a "rather dramatic shift in focus" (p. 181). Reparation of memory and consultation of references reveal that important realist and local ("piecemeal," as Fine calls them) case studies such as those cited above pre-date the appearance of NOA and simply continue the realist tradition that articulates increasingly specific realist proposals. By contrast, the impact of NOA is difficult to trace because the commitments of NOA themselves elude clear description (as has been noted elsewhere; see Kitcher 1993, p. 134, n11). The version of realism advanced here treats history as evidential, and so historical accuracy concerning the development of realist theses themselves is one priority of the realist project.

avoid such philosophical arrogance, we must formulate an epistemology that respects scientific practice and honors recognizable epistemic categories. Measurement is the centerpiece of this realist epistemology.

Still, I tried to include discussion of only those issues essential to the defense of measured realism and naturalism. As a result, many issues otherwise worthy of discussion are not treated. There is no protracted discussion of laws, of approximate truth, or of the social and behavioral dispositions that get measured. There are certainly interesting questions to be asked here, and much contemporary attention has been devoted to them. Fortunately, the initial argument for measured realism can proceed without answering these questions in any decisive way. If realism involves commitment to dispositions, the epistemic basis for this belief must be inference to the best explanation. The versions of empiricist epistemology considered in this book do not have the resources to license such commitment to (unobserved) dispositions, because they cannot endorse inference to the best explanation in the first place. Although I do not think this objection to empiricist epistemology is question-begging—at least to the extent that empiricists and realists alike are concerned to offer a descriptively adequate scientific epistemology—it is not as obliging as it might be. After all, some empiricists might conceivably reply that they are not concerned to draw conclusions about unobservables but only to formulate inferences to future observable states. But when these inferences from observables to observables are reliable, and we agree that this reliability is not brute (and so bears explanation), it is because we have selected the relevant observable states from all those available to form the basis of the inference to future observable states. In such a case, the best explanation for the reliability of the inference from current to future observables is that we had a good enough account (or theory) to identify the relevant respects in which nature is uniform, respects in which our inductions would be supported (see chapter 3).

So even the empiricist needs inference to the best explanation, unless the empiricist resigns to obscurantism about the instrumental reliability of scientific methodology. I therefore defend the use of inference to the best explanation, leaving the nature of dispositions for another occasion. On my account of inference to the best explanation, however, IBE is historically contingent and theory dependent. It is historically contingent in the sense that by "best explanation" I do not mean the best of all possible explanations, the one that would be given by a final or "one true" theory (if there is such a thing) that we clearly do not have in our possession. Instead, I mean the best explanation of those available in the field. These are sometimes horribly false, and in those cases they tend not to provide a secure basis for research in the long run. But an explanation can be good enough to provide a reliable theoretical basis for induction without being true in any unqualified sense of the term. No one supposes that Bohr gave the true explanation for the property of charge, although it correctly isolated some of the properties of charge. As well, according to my account of IBE the criteria of explanatory goodness are theory-dependent considerations and will vary from domain to domain. Comparable explanatory goodness is therefore not to be determined by purportedly domain-neutral measures such as probabilities.

Other questions remain as well. Are laws exceptionless? Do they imply *de re* modality? What metaphysical status should be conferred on properties such as possibility and necessity that seem to be required by the intuitive treatment of laws as counterfactual? What is meant by the approximate truth of a law or theory? In what sense might this be a theory-dependent relation? These questions have received extremely technical treatments independent of their role in arguments for realism, and so I have chosen to engage issues more pertinent to specific questions about measurement progress in the social and behavioral sciences. But there are other reasons to set aside these issues in a book such as this one. For example, many of these topics emerge from a philosophical tradition with pretheoretic conceptions of what an adequate treatment of realism and naturalism must include. Throughout the 1950s, it was quite easy to find arguments that laws had to be exceptionless, bolstered by their formal characterization as universally quantified. But this picture of laws is indebted to a prior picture of theories, typically as a formal, deductively integrated system. Many of these difficulties are not special problems for realism about the behavioral sciences. Any fully articulated account of scientific realism would need to address questions concerning the nature of laws and of approximate truth.

With respect to laws, these issues should be decided by what philosophers want to say about universals or about the logic of subjunctive conditionals. But whatever they decide, it must be informed by scientific concerns about the nature of causal powers in the field. One can, for example, wish that laws have no exceptions, but in fact laws are subject to ceteris paribus clauses (Rosenberg 1988; Hausman 1993). Some philosophers lament this fact, but attempts to eliminate these clauses unnaturally limit the scope of taxonomic generalizations (see Hempel 1988), rendering them infirm.

Lest the doctrine of theory dependence (of scientific method and observation) degenerate into a bland platitude or stark falsity, theory dependence must come in degrees; not all methodological judgments and observations are equally dependent on particular theories. This should not be surprising, since methodological judgments and observations have radically diverse sources. Our background accounts (call them "theories," if you like) have to be good enough guides to the causal powers of their proper objects that our inquiries concerning them can be adequately probed. In the case of psychology, for example, our primitive account of psychological phenomena—which includes an ontological inventory and a characterization of the dynamics of the objects on that list—must correctly isolate the causal roles of psychological phenomena. This primitive account is widely thought to include at least the claims that there are intentional states such as beliefs, desires, hopes, and fears and that they routinely interact (in ways sensitive to stimuli) to produce behavior designed to satisfy the agent's ends.

This condition amounts to the supposition that our familiar folk psychology must be approximately correct, at least in the respects relevant to the use of folk psychology in diverse fields. But how difficult this thesis is to satisfy will depend both upon how substantial a theory folk psychology is thought to be and upon what the ontological retention of its entities depends. Eliminative materialists (see P. M. Churchland 1981 and P. S. Churchland 1986) might worry that such reliance on folk psychology—at least in selected areas of social, personality, abnormal, and cognitive psychology—visits upon those disciplines the same frailties as the folk theory they depend on. This is not the place to formulate and defend a perspicuous version of folk psychology. But a few words are in order about what is not entailed by (initial reliance on) folk psychology. Reliance on folk psychology does not entail that neuroscience is irrelevant to psychological theorizing, that the brain is irrelevant to thought, or that we will never describe mental activity in an exciting and new vocabulary of neuroscience that bristles with nascent discovery and dizzying subtlety. What it does entail is that, however we may someday (re)conceptualize our mental lives, the new taxonomic items and categories will isolate many of the causal roles now occupied by the familiar intentional states. (For an antieliminativist argument for the prima facie scientific respectability of folk psychology, see Trout 1991.)

Alchemists may have made arguments of similar form for the existence of alchemical elements and categories. But alchemy doesn't enjoy folk psychology's core cases of routine success, and so those defending alchemy were less justified (by our lights) in holding such conclusions of success, and those demanding equal treatment had less reason (by our lights) for claiming parity. In the first place, we begin with better natural endowments for detecting causal factors in psychology than those in physics. The endowments regarding folk psychological attributional skills are clearly exportable to many areas of the social sciences.

At the same time, even if we are justified in relying on folk psychology, it does not follow that all applications of folk psychology concepts and principles are reliable. It is possible to apply them to an inappropriate domain, such as physics or geology, or, more likely, to abnormal or sensory psychological phenomena they were not adapted to address. It is also possible to apply folk psychological concepts and principles to an appropriate domain, such as to normal, instrumentally rational behavior, and to do so irresponsibly, as in cases of narrative method surveyed in chapter 8.

Perhaps the most glaring omission is that of social constructivist philosophy of science. Discussions of social constructivism have been very influential in the philosophy of science. Characteristic of social constructivist philosophy of science is suspicion of the very notion of scientific progress, including progress in the natural sciences. As I have claimed elsewhere (Trout 1994), I have doubts about the descriptive accuracy of the consistent versions of constructivism and doubts about the coherence of the alternative versions. The present book, however, is devoted to addressing the question of whether ontological progress in the social and behavioral sciences is possible and actual and, if actual, how it is to be characterized. Given this aim, it would take us too far afield to address the views of those who think that ontological progress is not even possible in the natural sciences.

It is no surprise to the realist that many categories of behavioral science, such as mental illness, are socially constructed in some significant sense (see Hacking 1995). But their historical mutability neither undermines their status as natural kinds nor blocks a realist interpretation of them. Natural kinds are causally (and so taxonomically) important features of a domain. As such, natural kinds are implicated in causal generalizations. Many objects that are in some sense social or cultural artifacts—books, money, institutions—are real in the sense of being natural kinds, causally implicated in taxonomic generalizations. One may have certain pretheoretic preferences concerning what a natural kind must be like, that they must have clear identity conditions, that we must be able to specify the precise sense in which they are physical, and so on, but there is little more reason to honor these pretheoretic expectations than there is to honor other radically normative conditions on scientific respectability, such as verifiability, falsifiability, or semantic reduction, that early logical empiricists attempted to enforce, and there is considerable reason to reject them (for further discussion of these issues, see Hacking 1991; Boyd 1991).

One of the most exciting research programs to which Measured Realism points concerns the psychology of science—in particular, the issues of epistemic dependence and the social character of rationality (explored as well in Giere 1988; Kitcher 1990, 1993; Solomon 1994; Thagard 1993; Goldman 1992; for nice collections, see McMullin 1992 and Schmitt 1994). Chapter 4 illustrates one such relation—that of mercenary reliance. It is now clear that one cannot undermine claims to scientific progress, or to the rationality of scientific method, by showing that individual scientists fail to follow normative guidelines judged rational in individual decision making. It does not follow from this that science is nonrational, for it might be the case that global virtues such as scientific productivity and progress require scientists to act in ways that are, by individual standards, suboptimal. Moreover, once we apply the same quantitative concerns about representativeness and sampling to the emerging tradition of case analysis in the philosophy of science, we can raise questions about what is to be learned from cumulative research in the philosophy of science that treats historical cases as evidential (Faust and Meehl 1992). This philosophical research, like the position in this book, is naturalistic in the sense that it attempts an accurate description of scientific practice rather than rational reconstruction of it, and it takes seriously the epistemic success of unreconstructed scientific practice. The culmination of this naturalistic research does not deliver philosophers from the challenge of interpreting scientific behavior, forcing us to take at face value what scientists say, nor will the naturalistic imperative compel us to abandon traditional philosophical talk of confirmation and explanation in favor of the vocabulary, more common among scientists, of modeling and curve fitting. Any philosophy of science characterizing these activities must be empirical, and it is an empirical question whether scientists are the best chroniclers of their own activities. Measured Realism vindicates our reliance on our best psychological and social theories. With this trust now justified, a naturalistic philosophy of science can reveal the structure of our intentions and the psychological and social forces that shape them.

References

Abramson, P. R. (1982). *Political Attitudes in America*. San Francisco: Freeman.

Achinstein, P. (1991). *Particles and Waves: Historical Essays in the Philosophy of Science*. New York: Oxford University Press.

Achinstein, P. (1992). "Inference to the Best Explanation: Or, Who Won the Mill–Whewell Debate?" *Studies in History and Philosophy of Science*, 23, 349–364.

Adler, A. (1929). *Problems of Neurosis*. London: K. Paul, Trench, Trubner and Co.

Almeder, R. (1991). *Blind Realism*. Lanham, Md.: Rowman and Littlefield.

Alston, W. (1989). *Epistemic Justification*. Ithaca, N.Y.: Cornell University Press.

Anastasi, A. (1988). *Psychological Testing* (6th ed.). New York: Macmillan.

Arkes, H., and K. Hammond, eds. (1986). *Judgment and Decision Making*. New York: Cambridge University Press.

Arkin, M., and G. Maruyama. (1979). "Attribution, Affect, and College Exam Performance." *Journal of Educational Psychology*, 71, 85–93.

Arkin, R., H. Cooper, and T. Kolditz. (1980). "A Statistical Review of the Self-serving Attribution Bias in Interpersonal Influence Situations." *Journal of Personality*, 48, 435–448.

Armstrong, D. (1973). *Belief, Truth, and Knowledge*. Cambridge: Cambridge University Press.

Armstrong, S., L. Gleitman, and H. Gleitman. (1983). "On What Some Concepts Might Not Be." *Cognition*, 13, 263–308.

Augustine. (1993). *Confessions: Books 1–13* (rev. ed.). Indianapolis: Hackett.

Ayer, A. J. (1946). *Language, Truth, and Logic* (2nd ed.). New York: Dover.

Babbie, E. (1992). *The Practice of Social Research*. Belmont, Calif.: Wadsworth.

Baird, D. (1987). "Exploratory Factor Analysis, Instruments, and the Logic of Discovery." *British Journal for the Philosophy of Science*, 38, 319–337.

Baird, D. (1992). *Inductive Logic: Probability and Statistics*. Englewood Cliffs, N.J.: Prentice Hall.

Balota, D., and J. Chumbley. (1984). "Are Lexical Decisions a Good Measure of Lexical Access?: The Role of Word Frequency in the Neglected Decision Stage." *Journal of Experimental Psychology: Human Perception and Performance*, 10, 340–357.

Barber, J. (1994). "Efficacy of Short-term Dynamic Psychotherapy." *Journal of Psychotherapy Practice and Research*, 3(2) 108–121.

Barlow, H. B. (1953). "Summation and Inhibition in the Frog's Retina." *Journal of Physiology* (London), 119, 69–88.

Barnett, V. (1982). *Comparative Statistical Inference* (2nd ed.). New York: John Wiley and Sons.

Beiser, F. (1993). *The Cambridge Companion to Hegel*. New York: Cambridge University Press.

Bernard, C. (1957). *Introduction to the Study of Experimental Medicine*. New York: Dover.

Bernstein, R., and J. Dyer. (1992). *An Introduction to Political Science Methods* (3rd ed.). Englewood Cliffs, N.J.: Prentice Hall.

Bhaskar, R. (1975). *A Realist Theory of Science* (2nd ed.). Atlantic Highlands, N.J.: Humanities Press.

Bhaskar, R. (1982). "Realism in the Natural Sciences." In L. J. Cohen, J. Los, H. Pfeiffer, and K.-P. Podewski, eds., *Logic, Methodology, and Philosophy of Science 6*, pp. 337–354. New York: North-Holland.

Blalock, H. (1985a). *Causal Models in Panel and Experimental Designs* (2nd ed.). New York: Aldine.

Blalock, H. (1985b). *Causal Models in the Social Sciences* (2nd ed.). New York: Aldine.

Block, N. (1995). "How Heritability Misleads about Race." *Cognition*, 56, 99–128.

Block, N., and G. Dworkin. (1976). *The IQ Controversy*. New York: Pantheon.

BonJour, L. (1985). *The Structure of Empirical Knowledge*. Cambridge, Mass.: Harvard University Press.

Bottaccini, M. R. (1975). *Instruments and Measurement*. Columbus, Ohio: Academic Press.

Boyd, R. (1973). "Realism, Underdetermination, and a Causal Theory of Evidence." *Nôus*, 7, 1–12.

Boyd, R. (1979). "Metaphor and Theory Change." In A. Ortony, ed. *Metaphor and Thought*, pp. 356–408. Cambridge: Cambridge University Press.

Boyd, R. (1981). "Scientific Realism and Naturalistic Epistemology." In P. D. Asquith and R. N. Giere, eds., *PSA 1980*, vol. 2, 613–662. East Lansing, Mich.: Philosophy of Science Association.

Boyd, R. (1985a). "Lex Orandi est Lex Credendi." In P. M. Churchland and C. Hooker, eds., *Images of Science: Essays on Realism and Empiricism*, pp. 3–34. Chicago: University of Chicago Press.

Boyd, R. (1985b). "The Logician's Dilemma: Deductive Logic, Inductive Inference, and Logical Empiricism." *Erkenntnis*, 22, 197–252.

Boyd, R. (1990). "Realism, Approximate Truth, and Philosophical Method." In W. Savage, ed., *Scientific Theories*, pp. 355–391. Minneapolis: University of Minnesota Press.

Boyd, R. (1991a). "The Current Status of Scientific Realism." In R. Boyd, P. Gasper, and J. D. Trout, eds., *The Philosophy of Science*, pp. 195–222. Cambridge, Mass.: MIT Press. Originally published in *Erkenntnis*, 19 (1983), 45–90.

Boyd, R. (1991b). "Observations, Explanatory Power, and Simplicity: Toward a Non-Humean Account." In R. Boyd, P. Gasper, and J. D. Trout, eds., *The Philosophy of Science*, pp. 349–377. Cambridge, Mass.: MIT Press. Originally published in P.

Achinstein and O. Hannaway, eds., *Observation, Experiment, and Hypothesis in Modern Physical Science* (Cambridge, Mass.: MIT Press, 1985).

Boyd, R., P. Gasper, and J. D. Trout, eds. (1991). *The Philosophy of Science.* Cambridge, Mass.: The MIT Press.

Bradie, M. (1986). "Assessing Evolutionary Epistemologies." *Biology and Philosophy,* 1, 401–459.

Braudel, F. (1985). *Civilization and Capitalism, Fifteenth to Eighteenth Centuries* vol. 1, *The Structures of Everyday Life: The Limits of the Possible.* New York: Harper and Row, Perennial Library.

Braybrooke, D. (1987). *The Philosophy of Social Science.* Englewood Cliffs, N.J.: Prentice-Hall.

Bridgman, P. W. (1927). *The Logic of Modern Physics.* London: Macmillan.

Bross, I. (1970). "Statistical Criticism." In E. Tufte, ed., *The Quantitative Analysis of Social Problems,* 97–108. Reading, Mass.: Addison-Wesley.

Buchwald, J. (1992). "Design for Experimenting." In Paul Horwich, ed., *World Changes,* pp. 169–206. Cambridge, Mass.: MIT Press.

Bullock, A. (1962). *Hitler: A Study in History.* New York: Harper and Row.

Burian, R., and J. D. Trout. (1995). "Ontological Progress in Science." *Canadian Journal of Philosophy,* 25, 177–201.

Byerly, H., and V. Lazara. (1973). "Realist Foundations of Measurement." *Philosophy of Science,* 40, 10–28.

Campbell, D., and D. W. Fiske. (1959). "Convergent and Discriminant Validation by the Multitrait–Multimethod Matrix." *Psychological Bulletin,* 56, 81–105.

Carnap, R. ([1956]1991). "Empiricism, Semantics, and Ontology." In R. Boyd, P. Gasper, and J. D. Trout, eds., *The Philosophy of Science,* pp. 85–97. Cambridge, Mass.: The MIT Press.

Cartwright, N. (1983). *How the Laws of Physics Lie.* New York: Oxford University Press.

Cartwright, N. (1989). *Nature's Capacities and Their Measurement.* New York: Oxford University Press.

Chapman, L. J., and J. P. Chapman. (1969). "Illusory Correlation as an Obstacle to the Use of Valid Psychodiagnostic Signs." *Journal of Abnormal Psychology,* 74, 271–280.

Cherniak, C. (1986). *Minimal Rationality.* Cambridge, Mass.: MIT Press.

Churchland, P. M. (1981). "Eliminative Materialism and the Proposition Attitudes." In R. Boyd, P. Gasper, and J. D. Trout, eds., *The Philosophy of Science,* pp. 615–630. Cambridge, Mass.: The MIT Press. Originally published in *Journal of Philosophy,* 78, 67–90.

Churchland, P. S. (1986). *Neurophilosophy.* Cambridge, Mass.: MIT Press.

Cochlaus, J. (1549). *Commentaria de actis et scriptis Martini Lutheri.* Apud S. Victorem prope Moguntian: Ex Officina F. Behem Typographi.

Cohen, J. (1988). *Statistical Power Analysis for the Behavioral Sciences* (2nd ed.). Hillsdale, N.J.: Erlbaum.

Cohen, J. (1994). "The Earth Is Round ($p < .05$)." *American Psychologist,* 49, 997–1003.

Cohen, L. J. (1986). *The Dialogue of Reason.* New York: Oxford University Press.

Cohen, L. J., J. Los, H. Pfeiffer, and K.-P. Podewski, eds. (1982). *Logic, Methodology, and Philosophy of Science 6.* New York: North-Holland.

Cohen, S. (1991). "Skepticism, Relevance, and Relativity." In Brian McLaughlin, ed., *Dretske and His Critics,* pp. 17–37. Cambridge, Mass.: Blackwell.

College Board. (1976–1977). *Student Descriptive Questionnaire.* Princeton, N.J.: Educational Testing Service.

Collingwood, R. G. (1959). "History as Re-enactment of Past Experience." In P. Gardiner, ed., *Theories of History,* pp. 251–262. New York: Free Press.

Collingwood, R. G. (1970). *An Autobiography*. New York: Oxford University Press.

Compton, A. (1988). "Discussions of the Case Study." *Psychoanalytic Review*, 75, 283–288.

Cox, A., and R. Hart. (1986). *Plate Tectonics: How It Works*. Palo Alto, Calif.: Blackwell Scientific Publications.

Crits-Christoph, P. (1992). "The Efficacy of Brief Dynamic Psychotherapy: A Meta-Analysis." *American Journal of Psychiatry*, 149(2), 151–158.

Cronbach, L., and P. Meehl. (1955). "Construct Validity in Psychological Tests." *Psychological Bulletin*, 52, 281–302.

Darwin, C. (1859). *The Origin of Species*. New York: Collier.

Davidson, D. (1963). "Actions, Reasons, and Causes." *Journal of Philosophy*, 60, 685–700.

Davidson, D. (1976). "Hempel on Explaining Action," *Erkenntnis* 10, 239–253.

Davidson, D. (1980a). *Inquiries into Truth and Interpretation*. Oxford: Oxford University Press.

Davidson, D. (1980b). "Introduction." In *Essays on Actions and Events*. Oxford: Clarendon Press.

Davis, M., and W. Stephan. (1980). "Attributions for Exam Performance." *Journal of Applied Social Psychology*, 10, 235–248.

Dawes, R. (1994). *House of Cards: Psychology and Psychotherapy Built on Myth*. New York: Free Press.

Demopoulos, W. (1982). "Review of *The Scientific Image*." *Philosophical Review*, 91, 603–607.

Dennett, D. (1987). *The Intentional Stance*. Cambridge, Mass.: MIT Press.

Devitt, M. (1981). *Designation*. New York: Columbia University Press.

Devitt, M. (1991). *Realism and Truth* (2nd ed.). Oxford: Blackwell.

Dray, W. (1957). *Laws and Explanation in History*. London: Oxford University Press.

Dretske, F. (1981). *Knowledge and the Flow of Information*. Cambridge, Mass.: MIT Press.

Dretske, F. (1991). "Replies." In Brian McLaughlin, ed., *Dretske and His Critics*, pp. 180–221. Cambridge, Mass.: Blackwell.

Drew, P., and A. Wootton. (1988). *Erving Goffman*. Boston: Northeastern University Press.

Dupuy, R., and T. Dupuy. (1986). *The Encyclopedia of Military History from 3,500 B.C. to the Present* (2nd, rev. ed.). New York: Harper and Row.

Durant, W., and A. Durant. (1968). *The Lessons of History*. New York: Simon and Schuster.

Eadie, W., D. Drijard, F. James, M. Roos, and B. Sadoulet. (1971). *Statistical Methods in Experimental Physics*. London: North-Holland.

Edelson, M. (1983). *Hypothesis and Evidence in Psychoanalysis*. Chicago: University of Chicago Press.

Ellis, B. (1966). *Basic Concepts of Measurement*. Cambridge: Cambridge University Press.

Ellis, B. (1990). *Truth and Objectivity*. Oxford: Blackwell.

Elseth, G., and K. Baumgardner. (1984). *Genetics*. Reading, Mass.: Addison-Wesley.

Erikson, E. (1962). *Young Man Luther*. New York: Norton.

Erwin, E. (1996). *A Final Accounting*. Cambridge, Mass.: MIT Press.

Farah, M. (1984). "The Neurological Basis of Mental Imagery: A Componential Analysis." *Cognition*, 18, 245–272.

Faust, D. (1984). *The Limits of Scientific Reasoning*. Minneapolis: University of Minnesota Press.

Faust, D., and P. Meehl. (1992). "Using Scientific Methods to Resolve Questions in the History and Philosophy of Science: Some Illustrations." *Behavior Therapy*, 23, 195–211.

Fetzer, J. (1993). *Philosophy of Science*. New York: Paragon.

Field, H. (1973). "Theory Change and the Indeterminacy of Reference." *Journal of Philosophy*, 70, 462–481.

Field, H. (1974). "Quine and the Correspondence Theory." *Philosophical Review*, 83, 200–228.

Fine, A. (1986a). *The Shaky Game*. Chicago: University of Chicago Press.

Fine, A. (1986b). "Unnatural Attitudes: Realist and Instrumentalist Attachments to Science." *Mind*, 95, 149–179.

Fine, A. (1991a). "The Natural Ontological Attitude." In R. Boyd, P. Gasper, and J. D. Trout, eds., *The Philosophy of Science*, pp. 261–277. Cambridge, Mass.: MIT Press. Previously published in Fine, 1986a.

Fine, A. (1991b). "Piecemeal Realism." *Philosophical Studies*, 61, 79–96.

Fine, A. (1996). "Afterword." In *The Shaky Game* (2nd edition), pp. 173–201. Chicago: University of Chicago Press.

Finke, R. (1989). *Principles of Mental Imagery*. Cambridge, Mass.: MIT Press.

Fischoff, B. (1975). "Hindsight ≠ Foresight: The Effect of Outcome Knowledge on Judgement under Uncertainty." *Journal of Experimental Psychology: Human Perception and Performance*, 1, 288–299.

Fischoff, B. (1991). "Value Elicitation: Is There Anything in There?" *American Psychologist*, 46, 835–847.

Fodor, J. (1983). *The Modularity of Mind*. Cambridge, Mass.: MIT Press.

Fodor, J. (1986). "Banish Discontent." In J. Butterfield, ed., *Language, Logic, and Mind*, pp. 1–23. New York: Cambridge University Press.

Fogel, R., and Engerman, S. (1974). *Time on the Cross: Evidence and Methods—A Supplement*. Boston, Mass.: Little, Brown and Co.

Fogel, R. (1975). "The Limits of Quantitative Methods in History." *American Historical Review*, 80, 329–350.

Fogel, R. (1982). " 'Scientific' History and Traditional History." In L. J. Cohen, J. Los, H. Pfeiffer, and K.-P. Podewski, eds., *Logic, Methodology, and Philosophy of Science 6*, pp. 15–61. New York: North-Holland.

Forster, K. and S. Chambers. (1973). "Lexical Access and Naming Time." *Journal of Verbal Learning and Verbal Behavior*, 12, 627–635.

Forster, K. (1976). "Accessing the Mental Lexicon." In R. J. Wales and E. Walker, eds., *New Approaches to Language Mechanisms*, pp. 257–287. Amsterdam: North-Holland.

Frauenfelder, U., and L. Tyler. (1987). "The Process of Spoken Word Recognition." *Cognition*, 25, 1–20.

Frederiksen, J. R., and J. F. Kroll. (1976). "Spelling and Sound: Approaches to the Internal Lexicon." *Journal of Experimental Psychology: Human Perception and Performance*, 2, 361–379.

Friedman, M. (1983). *Foundations of Space-Time Theories*. Princeton: Princeton University Press.

Friedrich, F., A. Henik, and J. Tzelgov. (1991). "Automatic Processes in Lexical Access and Spreading Activation." *Journal of Experimental Psychology: Human Perception and Performance*, 17, 792–806.

Gadamer, H. (1965, English translation 1975). *Truth and Method*. New York, NY: Crossroad.

Galison, P. (1987). *How Experiments End*. Chicago: University of Chicago Press.

Gardiner, P., ed., (1959). *Theories of History*. New York: Free Press.

Gasking, D. (1955). "Causation and Recipes." *Mind*, 64, 479–487.

Gergen, K. (1982). *Toward Transformation in Social Knowledge*. New York: Springer-Verlag.

Ghiselli, E., J. Campbell, and Zedeck, S. (1981). *Measurement Theory for the Behavioral Sciences*. San Francisco: Freeman.

Gibbon, E. (1952). *The Decline and Fall of the Roman Empire* (abridged). New York: Viking.

Giere, R. (1988). *Explaining Science*. Chicago: University of Chicago Press.

Gigerenzer, G. (1987). "Probabilistic Thinking and the Fight Against Subjectivity." In L. Krüger, G. Gigerenzer, and M. Morgan, eds., *The Probabilistic Revolution*, vol. 2, *Ideas in the Sciences*, pp. 11–33. Cambridge, Mass.: MIT Press.

Gigerenzer, G. (1991). "How to Make Cognitive Illusions Disappear: Beyond 'Heuristics and Biases.'" In *European Review of Social Psychology, Volume 2*, pp. 83–115. New York: Wiley.

Gigerenzer, G., and D. J. Murray. (1987). *Cognition as Intuitive Statistics*. Hillsdale, N.J.: Erlbaum.

Gilmour, T., and D. Reid. (1979). "Locus of Control and Causal Attribution for Positive and Negative Outcomes on University Examinations." *Journal of Research in Personality*, 13, 154–160.

Gilovich, T. (1991). *How We Know What Isn't So*. New York: Free Press.

Glymour, C. (1980). *Theory and Evidence*. Princeton: Princeton University Press.

Glymour, C. (1985). "Explanation and Realism." In P. M. Churchland and C. A. Hooker, eds., *Images of Science*, pp. 99–117. Chicago: University of Chicago Press.

Glymour, C., R. Sheines, P. Spirtes, and K. Kelly, (1987). *Discovering Causal Structure*. New York: Academic Press.

Godfrey-Smith, P. (1991). "Signal, Detection, Action." *The Journal of Philosophy*, 88, 709–722.

Goffman, E. (1971). *Relations in Public: Microstudies of the Public Order*. New York: Harper and Row.

Goldman, A. (1967). "A Causal Theory of Knowing." *Journal of Philosophy*, 64, 355–372.

Goldman, A. (1970). *A Theory of Human Action*. Princeton: Princeton University Press.

Goldman, A. (1976). "Discrimination and Perceptual Knowledge." *Journal of Philosophy*, 73, 771–791.

Goldman, A. (1986). *Epistemology and Cognition*. Cambridge, Mass.: Harvard University Press.

Goldman, A. (1992). *Liaisons: Philosophy Meets the Cognitive and Social Sciences*. Cambridge, Mass.: MIT Press.

Gould, S. J. (1995). "Curveball." In Steven Fraser, ed., *The Bell Curve Wars*, pp. 11–22. New York: Basic Books.

Green, B. F., and J. A. Hall. (1984). "Quantitative Methods for Literature Reviews." *Annual Review of Psychology*, 35, 37–53.

Green, D., and J. Swets. (1988). *Signal Detection Theory and Psychophysics*. Los Altos, Calif.: Peninsula Publishing.

Groot, A. D. de. (1965). *Thought and Choice in Chess*. The Hague: Mouton.

Grünbaum, A. (1984). *The Foundations of Psychoanalysis*. Berkeley: University of California Press.

Guilford, J. (1954). *Psychometric Methods* (2nd ed.). New York: McGraw-Hill.

Guy, W. A. (1839). "On the Value of the Numerical Method as Applied to Science, but Especially to Physiology and Medicine." *Proceedings of the Royal Statistical Society*, A 2, 25–47.

Habermas, J. (1968). *Knowledge and Human Interests*. Boston: Beacon Press.

Hacking, I. (1965). *The Logic of Statistical Inference*. Cambridge: Cambridge University Press.

Hacking, I. (1983). *Representing and Intervening*. New York: Cambridge University Press.

Hacking, I. (1990). *The Taming of Chance*. Cambridge: Cambridge University Press.

Hacking, I. (1991). "A Tradition of Natural Kinds." *Philosophical Studies*, 61, 109–126.

Hacking, I. (1995). *Rewriting the Soul*. Princeton: Princeton University Press.

Hanson, N. (1958). *Patterns of Discovery*. Cambridge: Cambridge University Press.

Hardwig, J. (1985). "Epistemic Dependence." *Journal of Philosophy*, 82, 335–349.

Hardwig, J. (1991). "The Role of Trust in Knowledge." *Journal of Philosophy*, 88, 693–708.

Harlow, L., S. Mulaik, and J. Steiger. eds. (1997). *What If There Were No Significance Tests?* Mahwah, N.J.: Lawrence Erlbaum.

Harman, G. (1965). "Inference to the Best Explanation," *Philosophical Review* 74, 88–95.

Haskins, L., and K. Jeffrey. (1990). *Understanding Quantitative History*. Cambridge, Mass.: MIT Press.

Hatchett, S., and H. Schuman, (1975–1976). "White Respondents and Race-of-Interviewer Effects." *Public Opinion Quarterly*, 39, 523–528.

Hausman, D. (1981). *Capital, Prices, and Profits*. New York: Columbia University Press.

Hausman, D. (1983). "Are There Causal Relations among Dependent Variables?" *Philosophy of Science*, 50, 58–81.

Hausman, D. (1986). "Causation and Experimentation." *American Philosophical Quarterly*, 23, 143–154.

Hausman, D. (1993). *The Inexact and Separate Science of Economics*. New York: Cambridge University Press.

Head, H. (1926). *Aphasia and Kindred Disorders of Speech*. New York: Macmillan.

Hedges, L. (1987). "How Hard Is Hard Science, How Soft Is Soft Science?" *American Psychologist*, 42, 443–455.

Hegel, G. (1956). "Philosophical History." In P. Gardiner, ed., *Theories of History*, pp. 60–73. New York: Free Press.

Hempel, C. (1965a). "Empiricist Criteria of Cognitive Significance: Problems and Changes." In *Aspects of Scientific Explanation*, pp. 101–122. New York: Free Press.

Hempel, C. (1965b). "Studies in the Logic of Confirmation." In *Aspects of Scientific Explanation*, pp. 3–46. New York: Free Press.

Hempel, C. (1966). *Philosophy of Natural Science*. Englewood Cliffs, N.J.: Prentice-Hall.

Hempel, C. (1970). "Fundamentals of Concept Formation in Empirical Science." In O. Neurath, R. Carnap, and C. Morris, eds., *Foundations of the Unity of Science* vol. 2, pp. 653–745. Chicago: University of Chicago Press.

Hempel, C. (1988). "Provisos: A Problem Concerning the Inferential Function of Scientific Theories." In A. Grünbaum and W. Salmon, eds., *The Limitations of Deductivism*, pp. 19–36. Berkeley: University of California Press.

Herrnstein, R. J., and C. Murray. (1994). *The Bell Curve*. New York: The Free Press.

Herte, A. (1943). *Das katholische Lutherbild im Bann der Lutherkommentare des Cochlaus*. Munich: Aschendorff.

Horwich, P. (1991). "On the Nature and Norms of Theoretical Commitment." *Philosophy of Science*, 58, 1–14.

Howson, C. (1990). "Fitting Your Theory to the Facts: Probably Not Such a Bad Thing After All." In W. Savage, ed., *Scientific Theories*, pp. 224–244. Minneapolis: University of Minnesota Press.

Howson, C., and P. Urbach. (1989). *Scientific Reasoning: The Bayesian Approach*. La Salle, Ill.: Open Court.

Hubel, D. H., and T. N. Wiesel. (1962). "Receptive Fields, Binocular Interaction, and Functional Architecture in the Cat's Visual Cortex." *Journal of Physiology* (London), 166, 106–154.

Humphreys, P. (1985). "Why Propensities Cannot Be Probabilities." *Philosophical Review* 94, 557–570.

Humphreys, P. (1989). *The Chances of Explanation*. Princeton: Princeton University Press.

Hunter, J. E., and F. L. Schmidt. (1990). *Methods of Meta-Analysis: Correcting Bias in Research Findings*. Newbury Park, Calif.: Sage Publications.

Jardine, N. (1986). *The Fortunes of Inquiry*. Oxford: Clarendon Press.

Kahneman, Daniel, P. Slovic, A. Tversky, eds (1982). *Judgment under Uncertainty: Heuristics and Biases*. Cambridge: Cambridge University Press.

Kahneman, D., and A. Tversky. (1973). "On the Psychology of Prediction." *Psychological Review*, 80, 237–251.

Kimura, D. (1967). "Functional Asymmetry of the Brain in Dichotic Listening." *Cortex*, 3, 163–178.

Kincaid, H. (1996). *Philosophical Foundations of the Social Sciences: Analyzing Controversies in Social Research*. New York: Cambridge University Press.

Kitcher, Ph. (1978). "Theories, Theorists, and Theoretical Change." *Philosophical Review*, 87, 519–547.

Kitcher, Ph. (1981). "Explanatory Unification." *Philosophy of Science*, 48, 507–531.

Kitcher, Ph. (1984). "1953 and All That: A Tale of Two Sciences." *The Philosophical Review*, 93, 335–373.

Kitcher, Ph. (1989). "Explanatory Unification and the Causal Structure of the World." In P. Kitcher and W. Salmon, eds. *Scientific Explanation*, pp. 410–505. Minneapolis: University of Minnesota Press.

Kitcher, Ph. (1990). "The Division of Cognitive Labor." *Journal of Philosophy*, 87, 5–21.

Kitcher, Ph. (1992). "The Naturalists Return." *Philosophical Review*, 101, 53–114.

Kitcher, Ph. (1993). *The Advancement of Science*. Oxford: Oxford University Press.

Klee, R. (1997). *Introduction to the Philosophy of Science: Cutting Nature at the Seams*. New York: Oxford University Press.

Kornblith, H. (1993). *Inductive Inference and Its Natural Ground*. Cambridge, Mass.: MIT Press.

Kosslyn, S., and O. Koenig. (1992). *Wet Mind: The New Cognitive Neuroscience*. New York: Free Press.

Kosso, P. (1988). "Dimensions of Observability." *British Journal for the Philosophy of Science*, 39, 449–467.

Kosso, P. (1989). "Science and Objectivity." *Journal of Philosophy*, 86, 245–257.

Kosso, P. (1992). *Reading the Book of Nature: Introduction to the Philosophy of Science*. New York: Cambridge University Press.

Krantz, D., R. D. Luce, P. Suppes, and A. Tversky. (1971). *Foundations of Measurement*, vol. 1, *Additive and Polynomial Representations*. New York: Academic Press.

Kripke, S. (1971). "Identity and Necessity." In M. Munitz, ed., *Identity and Individuation*, pp. 135–164. New York: New York University Press.

Kristeva, J. (1980). *Desire in Language*. New York: Columbia University Press.

Krüger, L., L. Daston, and M. Heidelberger, eds. (1987). *The Probabilistic Revolution*, vol. 1, *Ideas in History*. Cambridge, Mass.: MIT Press.

Krüger, L., G. Gigerenzer, and M. Morgan, eds. (1987). *The Probabilistic Revolution*, vol. 2, *Ideas in the Sciences*. Cambridge, Mass.: MIT Press.

Kuffler, S. W. (1953). "Discharge Patterns and Functional Organization of Mammalian Retina." *Journal of Neurophysiology*, 16, 37–68.

Kuhn, T. (1962). *The Structure of Scientific Revolutions*. Chicago: University of Chicago Press.

Kutas, M., and S. Hillyard. (1984). "Event-related Potentials in Cognitive Science." In M.S. Gazzaniga, ed., *Handbook of Cognitive Neuroscience*, pp. 387–409. New York: Plenum.

Lakatos, I. (1970). "Falsification and the Methodology of Scientific Research Programmes." In I. Lakatos and A. Musgrave, eds., *Criticism and the Growth of Knowledge*, pp. 91–196. Cambridge: Cambridge University Press.

Lakatos, I., and A. Musgrave, eds. (1970). *Criticism and the Growth of Knowledge*. Cambridge: Cambridge University Press.

Landman, J., and R. Dawes. (1982). "Psychotherapy Outcome: Smith and Glass' Conclusions Stand Up to Scrutiny." *American Psychologist*, 37, 504–516.

Lau, R., and D. Russell. (1980). "Attributions in the Sports Pages." *Journal of Personality and Social Psychology*, 39, 29–38.

Laudan, L. (1991). "Confutation of Convergent Realism." In R. Boyd. P. Gasper, and J. D. Trout, eds., *The Philosophy of Science*, pp. 223–245. Cambridge, Mass.: MIT Press. Originally published in *Philosophy of Science*, 48(1981), 19–48.

Laudan, L. (1990). *Science and Relativism: Some Key Controversies in the Philosophy of Science*. Chicago: University of Chicago Press.

Lehrer, K. (1977). "Social Information." *Monist*, 60, 473–487.

Lettvin, J. Y., R. R. Maturana, W. S. McCulloch, and W. H. Pitts. (1959). "What the Frog's Eye Tells the Frog's Brain." *Proceedings of the Institute for Radio Engineers*, 47, 1940–1951.

Levins, R. (1968). *Evolution in Changing Environments*. Princeton: Princeton University Press.

Lewis, D. (1973). *Counterfactuals*. Cambridge, Mass.: Harvard University Press.

Lewontin, R. (1974). "The Analysis of Variance and the Analysis of Causes." *American Journal of Human Genetics*, 26, 400–411.

Lipton, P. (1991). *Inference to the Best Explanation*. London: Routledge.

Little, D. (1990). *Varieties of Social Explanation: An Introduction to the Philosophy of Social Science*. Boulder, Colo.: Westview.

Lord, C. G., L. Ross, L. and M. R. Lepper. (1979). "Biased Assimilation and Attitude Polarization: The Effects of Prior Theories on Subsequently Considered Evidence." *Journal of Personality and Social Psychology*, 37, 2098–2109.

Luborsky, L., and P. Crits-Christoph. (1988). "Measures of Psychoanalytic Concepts—the Last Decade of Research from the Penn Studies." *International Psychoanalytic Quarterly*, 69, 75–86.

Luborsky, L., P. Crits-Christoph, J. Mintz, and A. Auerbach. (1988). *Who Will Benefit from Psychotherapy?: Predicting Therapeutic Outcomes*. New York: Basic Books.

Lugg, A. (1987). "Review of *The Limits of Scientific Reasoning*." *Philosophy of Science*, 54, 137–138.

Lycan, W. (1988). *Judgement and Justification*. New York: Cambridge University Press.

Lykken, D. T. (1968). "Statistical Significance in Psychological Research." *Psychological Bulletin*, 70, 151–159.

Macdonald, G., and P. Pettit. (1981). *Semantics and Social Science*. London: Routledge.

Magidson, J., and D. Sorbom. (1982). "Adjusting for Confounding Factors in Quasi-experiments: Another Re-analysis of the Westinghouse Head Start Evaluation." *Educational Evaluation and Policy Analysis*, 4, 321–329.

Malinowski, B. (1961). *Argonauts of the Western Pacific*. New York: Dutton.

Malinowski, B. (1987). *The Sexual Life of Savages in North-western Melanesia*. Boston: Beacon Press.

Marmor, J. (1988). "Discussions of the Case Study." *Psychoanalytic Review*, 75, 290–293.

Martin, R. (1989). *The Past Within Us*. Princeton: Princeton University Press.

Masson, J. M. (1988). *Against Therapy*. New York: Macmillan.

Matthews, R. (1994). "The Measure of Mind." *Mind*, 103, 131–146.

Mattingly, G. (1959). *The Armada*. Boston: Houghton Mifflin.

McBurney, D., and V. Collins. (1984). *Introduction to Sensation/Perception*. Englewood Cliffs, N.J.: Prentice Hall.

McClellan, J. E. (1992). *Colonialism and Science: Saint Domingue in the Old Regime*. Baltimore: Johns Hopkins University Press.

McMillan, G. (1984). *pH Control*. Research Triangle Park, N.C.: Instrumentation Society of America.

McMullin, E. (1984). "Two Ideals of Explanation in Natural Science." In P. French, T. Uehling, and H. Wettstein, eds., *Causation and Causal Theories*, pp. 205–220. Midwest Studies in Philosophy, vol. 9. Minneapolis: University of Minnesota Press.

McMullin, E., ed. (1992). *The Social Dimensions of Science*. Notre Dame, Ind.: University of Notre Dame Press.

McRae, K., D. Jared, and M. Seidenberg, (1990). "On the Roles of Frequency and Lexical Access in Word Naming." *Journal of Memory and Language*, 29, 43–65.

Meehl, P. E. (1954). *Clinical versus Statistical Prediction: A Theoretical Analysis and a Review of the Evidence*. Minneapolis: University of Minnesota Press.

Meehl, P. E. (1967). "Theory Testing in Psychology and Physics: A Methodological Paradox." *Philosophy of Science*, 34, 103–115.

Meehl, P. E. (1978). "Theoretical Risks and Tabular Asterisks: Sir Karl, Sir Ronald, and the Slow Progress of Soft Psychology." *Journal of Consulting and Clinical Psychology*, 46, 806–834.

Meehl, P. E. (1985). "What Social Scientists Don't Understand." In D. W. Fiske and R. A. Shweder, eds., *Metatheory in Social Science: Pluralisms and Subjectivities*, pp. 315–338. Chicago: University of Chicago Press.

Meehl, P. E. (1990a). "Appraising and Amending Theories: The Strategy of Lakatosian Defense and Two Principles That Warrant It." *Psychological Inquiry*, 1, 108–141.

Meehl, P. E. (1990b). "Why Summaries of Research on Psychological Theories Are Often Uninterpretable." *Psychological Reports*, 66, 195–244.

Meehl, P. E. (1991). *Selected Philosophical and Methodological Papers*. Ed. C. A. Anderson and K. Gunderson. Minneapolis: University of Minnesota Press.

Mervis, C. B., J. Catlin, and E. Rosch, (1976). "Relationships among Goodness-of-Example, Category Norms, and Word Frequency." *Bulletin of the Psychonomic Society*, 7, 283–294.

Mervis, C. B., and E. Rosch. (1981). "Categorization of Natural Objects." *Annual Review of Psychology*, 32, 89–115.

Milgram, S., L. Mann, and S. Harter. (1965). "The Lost Letter Technique: A Tool of Social Research." *Public Opinion Quarterly*, 29, 437–438.

Miller, G. (1956). "The Magical Number Seven, Plus or Minus Two: Some Limits of Our Capacity for Processing Information." *Psychological Review*, 63, 81–97.

Miller, J. L. (1990). "Speech Perception." In D. Osherson and H. Lasnik, eds., *An Invitation to Cognitive Science*, pp. 69–93. Cambridge, Mass.: MIT Press.

Miller, R. W. (1987). *Fact and Method*. Princeton: Princeton University Press.

Miller, T., and M. Ross. (1975). "Self-serving Biases in the Attribution of Causality: Fact or Fiction?" *Psychological Bulletin*, 82, 213–225.

Mills, C. W. (1959). *The Sociological Imagination*. New York: Oxford University Press.

Mises, R. V. (1957). *Probability, Statistics, and Truth* (2nd ed.). New York: Dover.

Monter, W. (1976). *Witchcraft in Switzerland: The Borderlands during the Reformation*. Ithaca, N.Y.: Cornell University Press.

Morris, A. (1991). *Instrument and Calibration for Quality Assurance*. New York: Prentice-Hall.

Morrison, D. E., and R. E. Henkel, eds. (1970). *The Significance Test Controversy.* Chicago: Aldine.

Moser, P. K. (1991). "Review Article: Justification in the Natural Sciences." *British Journal for the Philosophy of Science*, 43, 557–575.

Moser, P. K. (1993). *Philosophy after Objectivity.* New York: Oxford University Press.

Mulaik, S. (1985). "Exploratory Statistics and Empiricism." *Philosophy of Science*, 52, 410–430.

Mulaik, S. (1991). "Factor Analysis, Information-Transforming Instruments, and Objectivity: A Reply and Discussion." *British Journal for the Philosophy of Science*, 42, 87–100.

Musgrave, A. (1985). "Realism and Constructive Empiricism." In P. Churchland and C. Hooker, eds., *Images of Science*, pp. 197–221. Chicago: University of Chicago Press.

Musgrave, A. (1988). "The Ultimate Argument for Scientific Realism." In R. Nola, ed., *Relativism and Realism in Science*, pp. 229–252. Dordrecht: Kluwer.

Myers, D. (1996), *Social Psychology.* New York: McGraw-Hill.

Nauert, C. (1977). *The Age of Renaissance and Reformation.* Hinsdale, Ill.: Dryden Press.

Newton-Smith, W. (1981). *The Rationality of Science.* London: Routledge.

Nisbett, R. (1995). "Race, IQ, and Scientism." In Steven Fraser, ed., *The Bell Curve Wars*, pp. 36–57. New York: Basic Books.

Nisbett, R., and D. Cohen. (1996). *Culture of Honor: The Psychology of Violence in the South.* Boulder, Colo.: Westview.

Nisbett, R., and L. Ross. (1980). *Human Inference: Strategies and Shortcomings.* Englewood Cliffs, N.J.: Prentice-Hall.

Norman, W. T. (1963). "Personality Measurement, Faking, and Detection: An Assessment Method for Use in Personnel Selection." *Journal of Applied Psychology*, 47, 225–241.

Papineau, D. (1978). *For Science in the Social Sciences.* London: Macmillan.

Papineau, D. (1993). *Naturalism.* London: Blackwell.

Perrin, J. (1923). *Atoms.* Trans. D. L. Hammick. 2nd ed. London: Constable.

Piper, J. (1987). *Paleomagnetism and the Continental Crust.* New York: Wiley.

Piven, F., and R. Cloward. (1988). *Why Americans Don't Vote.* New York: Pantheon.

Pollock, J. (1984). "Reliability and Justified Belief." *Canadian Journal of Philosophy*, 14, 103–114.

Pollock, J. (1986). *Contemporary Theories of Knowledge.* Totowa, N.J.: Rowman and Littlefield.

Pollock, J. (1989). *How to Build a Person: A Prolegomenon.* Cambridge, Mass.: MIT Press.

Popper, K. (1959). *The Logic of Scientific Discovery.* New York: Basic Books.

Popper, K. (1963). *Conjectures and Refutations.* New York: Harper and Row.

Proctor, R. (1981). "A Unified Theory for Matching-Task Phenomena." *Psychological Review*, 88, 291–326.

Putnam, H. (1960). "Minds and Machines." In A. Anderson, ed., *Minds and Machines*, pp. 72–97. Englewood Cliffs, N.J.: Prentice Hall.

Putnam, H. (1970). "Is Semantics Possible?" In H. Kiefer and M. Munitz, eds., *Language, Belief, and Metaphysics*, pp. 50–63. Albany, NY: State University of New York Press.

Putnam, H. (1973). "Explanation and Reference." In G. Pearce and P. Maynard, eds., *Conceptual Change*, pp. 199–221. Dordrecht: Reidel.

Putnam, H. (1974). "The 'Corroboration' of Theories." In P. Schilpp, ed., *The Philosophy of Karl Popper.* pp. 221–240. LaSalle, Ill.: Open Court.

Putnam, H. (1975). "What Is Mathematical Truth?" In *Philosophical Papers*, vol. 1, *Mathematics, Matter, and Methods*, pp. 60–78. New York: Cambridge University Press.

Putnam, H. (1978). *Meaning and the Moral Sciences.* London: Routledge.

Quine, W. V. O. (1963). "Two Dogmas of Empiricism." In *From a Logical Point of View* (2nd ed.), pp. 20–46. Cambridge, Mass.: Harvard University Press.

Quine, W. V. O. (1969). "Epistemology Naturalized." In *Ontological Relativity and Other Essays*, pp. 69–90. New York: Columbia University Press.

Rabinow, P., and W. Sullivan, eds. (1979). *Interpretive Social Science: A Reader*. Berkeley: University of California Press.

Radnitzky, G., and W. W. Bartley (1987). *Evolutionary Epistemology, Rationality, and the Sociology of Science*. La Salle, Ill: Open Court.

Reich, M. (1981). *Racial Inequality*. Princeton: Princeton University Press.

Reisenzein, R. (1983). "The Schachter Theory of Emotion: Two Decades Later." *Psychological Bulletin*, 94, 239–264.

Repp, B., and R. Frost. (1988). "Detectability of Words and Nonwords in Two Kinds of Noise." *Journal of the Acoustical Society of America*, 84, 1929–1932.

Repp, B., and A. Liberman. (1987). "Phonetic Category Boundaries Are Flexible." In S. Harnad, ed., *Categorical Perception*, pp. 89–112. New York: Cambridge University Press.

Ricoeur, P. (1970). *Freud*. New Haven: Yale University Press.

Riley, G., ed. (1974). *Values, Objectivity, and the Social Sciences*. Menlo Park, Calif.: Addison-Wesley.

Rosch, E. (1973). "On the Internal Structure of Perceptual and Semantic Categories." In T. Moore, ed., *Cognitive Development and the Acquisition of Language*, pp. 111–144. New York: Academic Press.

Rosch, E. (1975). "Cognitive Representations of Semantic Categories." *Journal of Experimental Psychology: General*, 104, 192–233.

Rosch, E. (1978). "Principles of Categorization." In E. Rosch and B. B. Lloyd, eds., *Cognition and Categorization*, pp. 27–48. Hillsdale, N.J.: Erlbaum.

Rosch, E., and C. B. Mervis. (1975). "Family Resemblances: Studies in the Internal Structure of Categories." *Cognitive Psychology*, 7, 573–605.

Rosen, S., and P. Howell. (1987). "Auditory, Articulatory, and Learning Explanations of Categorical Perception in Speech." In S. Harnad, ed., *Categorical Perception*, pp. 113–160. New York: Cambridge University Press.

Rosenberg, A. (1988). *Philosophy of Social Science*. Boulder, Colo.: Westview.

Rosenthal, R. (1969). "Interpersonal Expectation." In R. Rosenthal and R. L. Rosnow, eds., *Artifact in Behavioral Research*, pp. 181–277. New York: Academic Press.

Rosenthal, R. (1976). *Experimenter Effects in Behavioral Research*. New York: Irvington.

Rosenthal, R. (1979). "The 'File Drawer Problem' and Tolerance for Null Results." *Psychological Bulletin*, 86, 638–641.

Rosenthal, R. (1995). "Writing Meta-analytic Reviews." *Psychological Bulletin*, 118, 183–192.

Rosenthal, R., and K. Fode. (1963). "The Effect of Experimenter Bias on the Performance of the Albino Rat." *Behavioral Science*, 8, 183–189.

Rosenthal, R., and R. L. Rosnow. (1984). *Essentials of Behavioral Research*. New York: McGraw-Hill.

Rudner, R. (1966). *Philosophy of Social Science*. Englewood Cliffs, N.J.: Prentice-Hall.

Rundus, D. (1971). "Analysis of Rehearsal Processes in Free Recall." *Journal of Experimental Psychology*, 89, 63–77.

Salmon, M., et al. (1992). *Introduction to the Philosophy of Science*. New York: Prentice-Hall.

Salmon, W. (1984). *Scientific Explanation and the Causal Structure of the World*. Princeton: Princeton University Press.

Samuel, A. (1981). "Phonemic Restoration: Insights from a New Methodology." *Journal of Experimental Psychology: General*, 110, 474–494.

Samuel, A. (1987). "Lexical Uniqueness Effects on Phonemic Restoration." *Journal of Memory and Language*, 26, 36–56.

Sandler, A.-M. (1988). "Aspects of the Analysis of a Neurotic Patient." *International Journal of Psychoanalysis*, 69, 317–334.

Sawyer, A. (1986). *Slavery in the Twentieth Century*. New York: Routledge and Kegan Paul.

Schachter, S., and J. Singer. (1962). "Cognitive, Social, and Physiological Determinants of Emotional State." *Psychological Review*, 69, 379–399.

Scheel, O. (1929). *Dokumente zu Luthers Entwicklung (bis 1519)*. Tubingen: J. C. B. Mohr.

Schlick, M. (1991). "Positivism and Realism." In R. Boyd, P. Gasper, and J. D. Trout, eds., *The Philosophy of Science*, pp. 37–55. Cambridge, Mass.: MIT Press. Originally published in *Erkenntnis* (1932/1933).

Schmitt, F., ed. (1994). *Socializing Epistemology: The Social Dimensions of Knowledge*. Lanham, Md.: Rowman and Littlefield.

Schroeder, M. (1968). "Reference Signal for Signal Quality Studies." *Journal of the Acoustical Society of America*, 44, 1735–1736.

Schuman, H., and S. Pressler. (1981). *Questions and Answers in Attitude Surveys: Experiments on Question Form, Wording, and Context*. Orlando, Fla.: Academic Press.

Schuman, H., Steeh, C., and Bobo, L. (1988). *Racial Attitudes in America: Trends and Interpretations*. Cambridge, Mass.: Harvard University Press.

Schwartz, M., and L. Shaw. (1975). *Signal Processing: Discrete Spectral Analysis, Detection, and Estimation*. New York: McGraw-Hill.

Seidenberg, M. S., and J. McClelland. (1989). "A Distributed, Developmental Model of Word Recognition and Naming." *Psychological Review*, 96, 523–568.

Seidenberg, M. S., M. K. Tannenhaus, J. M. Leiman, and M. Bienkowski. (1982). "Automatic Access of Meanings of Ambiguous Words in Context: Some Limitations of Knowledge-Based Processing." *Cognitive Psychology*, 14, 489–537.

Shepard, R. N., and L. Cooper. (1982). *Mental Images and Their Transformations*. Cambridge, Mass.: MIT Press.

Shepard, R. N., and J. Metzler. (1971). "Mental Rotation of Three-Dimensional Objects." *Science*, 171, 701–703.

Shirer, W. (1959). *The Rise and Fall of the Third Reich*. New York: Fawcett Crest.

Smart, J. J. C. (1968). *Between Science and Philosophy: An Introduction to the Philosophy of Science*. New York: Random House.

Smart, J. J. C. (1982). "Difficulties for Realism in the Philosophy of Science." In L. J. Cohen, J. Los, H. Pfeiffer, and K.-P. Podewski, eds., *Logic, Methodology, and Philosophy of Science 6*, pp. 363–375. New York: North-Holland.

Smith, M., and G. V. Glass. (1977). "Meta-analysis of Psychotherapy Outcome Studies." *American Psychologist*, 32, 752–760.

Sober, E. (1990). "Contrastive Empiricism." In W. Savage, ed., *Scientific Theories*, pp. 392–410. Minneapolis: University of Minnesota Press.

Solomon, M. (1994). "Social Empiricism." *Nôus*, 28, 325–343.

Sosa, E. (1991). *Knowledge in Perspective*. Cambridge: Cambridge University Press.

Spengler, O. (1928). *The Decline of the West, Volume 2*. New York: Knopf.

Stearns, S. (1975). *Digital Signal Analysis*. Rochelle Park, N.J.: Hayden Book Company.

Sternberg, R. (1995). "For Whom the Bell Curve Tolls: A Review of *The Bell Curve*." *Psychological Science*, 6(5), 257–261.

Stevens, S. S. (1951). "Mathematics, Measurement, and Psychophysics." In S. S. Stevens, ed., *Handbook of Experimental Psychology*, pp. 1–49. New York: Wiley.

Stich, S. (1983). *From Folk Psychology to Cognitive Science*. Cambridge, Mass.: MIT Press.

Stich, S. (1990). *The Fragmentation of Reason*. Cambridge, Mass.: MIT Press.

Stigler, S. (1986). *The History of Statistics*. Cambridge, Mass.: Harvard University Press.

Suppes, P. (1984). *Probabilistic Metaphysics*. New York: Blackwell.

Swijtink, Z. (1987). "The Objectification of Observation: Measurement and Statistical Methods in the Nineteenth Century." In L. Krüger, L. J. Daston, M. Heidelberger, eds., *The Probabilistic Revolution*, vol. 1, *Ideas in History*, pp. 261–285. Cambridge, Mass.: MIT Press.

Swinney, D. (1979). "Lexical Access during Sentence Comprehension: (Re)Consideration of Context Effects." *Journal of Verbal Learning and Verbal Behavior*, 18, 645–659.

Tarling, D. (1971). *Principles and Applications of Paleomagnetism*. London: Chapman and Hall.

Taylor, C. (1985a). *Philosophy and the Human Sciences*. Cambridge: Cambridge University Press.

Taylor, C. (1985b). "Self-interpreting Animals." In *Philosophy and the Human Sciences*, pp. 45–76. Cambridge: Cambridge University Press.

Tetlock, P. E. (1980). "Explaining Teacher Explanations for Pupil Performance: An Examination of the Self-presentation Interpretation." *Social Psychology Quarterly*, 43, 283–290.

Tetlock, P. E., and A. Levi, (1982). "Attribution Bias: On the Inconclusiveness of the Cognition–Motivation Debate." *Journal of Experimental Social Psychology*, 18, 68–88.

Thagard, P. (1978). "The Best Explanation: Criteria of Theory Choice." *Journal of Philosophy*, 75, 76–92.

Thagard, P. (1992). *Conceptual Revolutions*. Princeton: Princeton University Press.

Thagard, P. (1993). "Societies of Minds: Science as Distributed Computing." *Studies in History and Philosophy of Science*, 24, 49–67.

Thomas, D. (1979). *Naturalism and Social Science*. Cambridge: Cambridge University Press.

Thomson, W. (1891). *Popular Lectures and Addresses*, vol. 1, *The Constitution of Matter* (2nd ed.). London: Macmillan.

Thurstone, L. (1952). *The Criterion Problem in Personality Research*. Psychometric Lab Report No. 78. Chicago: University of Chicago Press.

Tocqueville, A. (1966). *Democracy in America*. New York: Harper and Row.

Toland, J. (1977). *Adolf Hitler*. London: Book Club Associates.

Toynbee, A. (1957). *A Study of History*, 2 vols. (abridged). New York: Oxford University Press.

Treisman, A. M. (1991). "Search, Similarity, and Integration of Features between and within Dimensions." *Journal of Experimental Psychology: Human Perception and Performance*, 17, 652–676.

Treisman, A. M., and G. Gelade. (1980). "A Feature Integration Theory of Attention." *Cognitive Psychology*, 12, 97–136.

Treisman, A. M., and N. Schmidt. (1982). "Illusory Conjunctions in the Perception of Objects." *Cognitive Psychology*, 14, 107–141.

Trigg, R. (1985). *Understanding Social Science*. New York: Blackwell.

Trout, J. D. (1991). "Belief Attribution in Science: Folk Psychology under Theoretical Stress." *Synthese*, 87, 379–400.

Trout, J. D. (1992). "Theory-Conjunction and Mercenary Reliance." *Philosophy of Science*, 59, 231–245.

Trout, J. D. (1994). "A Realistic Look Backward." *Studies in History and Philosophy of Science*, 25, 37–64.

Trout, J. D. (1995). "Diverse Tests on an Independent World." *Studies in History and Philosophy of Science,* 26, 407–429.

Trout, J. D., and W. J. Poser. (1990). "Auditory and Visual Influences on Phonemic Restoration." *Language and Speech,* 33, 121–135.

Truzzi, M. (1971). *Sociology: The Classic Statements.* New York: Random House.

Truzzi, M. (1974). *Verstehen: Subjective Understanding in the Social Sciences.* Menlo Park, Calif.: Addison-Wesley.

Tversky, A., and D. Kahneman. (1973). "Availability: A Heuristic for Judging Frequency and Probability." *Cognitive Psychology,* 5, 207–232.

Tversky, A., and D. Kahneman. (1974). "Judgment under Uncertainty: Heuristics and Biases." *Science,* 185, 1,124–1,131.

Tversky, A., and D. Kahneman. (1971). "The Belief in the Law of Small Numbers." In D. Kahneman, P. Slovic, and A. Tversky, eds., *Judgment under Uncertainty: Heuristics and Biases,* pp. 23–31. Cambridge: Cambridge University Press, 1982.

Tversky, A., and D. Kahneman. (1986). "Rational Choice and the Framing of Decisions." In K. S. Cook and M. Levi, eds., *The Limits of Rationality,* pp. 60–89. Chicago: University of Chicago Press.

van Fraassen, B. (1980). *The Scientific Image.* Oxford: Clarendon Press.

van Fraassen, B. (1985). "Empiricism in the Philosophy of Science." In P. M. Churchland and C. A. Hooker, eds., *Images of Science,* pp. 245–305. Chicago: University of Chicago Press.

van Fraassen, B. (1989). *Laws and Symmetry.* Oxford: Clarendon Press.

Vogel, J. (1990). "Cartesian Skepticism and Inference to the Best Explanation." *Journal of Philosophy,* 90, 658–666.

von Wright, G. H. (1975). "On the Logic and Epistemology of the Causal Relation." In E. Sosa, ed., *Causation and Conditionals,* pp. 95–113. London: Oxford University Press.

Warren, R. (1970). "Perceptual Restoration of Missing Speech Sounds," *Science,* 167, 392–393.

Wartofsky, M. (1968). *Conceptual Foundations of Scientific Thought.* New York: Macmillan.

Wason, P., and P. Johnson-Laird. (1972). *Psychology of Reasoning.* Cambridge, Mass.: Harvard University Press.

Watkins, M., and L. Allender. (1987). "Inhibiting Word Generation with Word Presentations." *Journal of Experimental Psychology: Learning, Memory, and Cognition,* 13, 464–468.

Webb, E., D. Campbell, R. Schwartz, and L. Sechrest. (1966). *Unobtrusive Measures: Nonreactive Research in the Social Sciences.* Boston: Houghton Mifflin.

Weinstein, N. D., and E. Lachendro. (1982). "Ego-centrism and Unrealistic Optimism about the Future." *Personality and Social Psychology Bulletin,* 8, 195–200.

Weiss, J. (1988). "Testing Hypotheses about Unconscious Mental Functioning." *International Journal of Psychoanalysis,* 69, 87–95.

Westcott, C. (1978). *pH Measurements.* New York: Academic Press.

Weston, T. (1992). "Approximate Truth and Scientific Realism." *Philosophy of Science,* 59, 53–74.

White, H. (1973). *Metahistory: The Historical Imagination in Nineteenth-Century Europe.* Baltimore: Johns Hopkins University Press.

White, H. (1987). *The Content of the Form: Narrative Discourse and Historical Representation.* Baltimore: Johns Hopkins University Press.

White, L. (1962). *Medieval Technology and Social Change.* New York: Oxford University Press.

Wiley, M., K. Crittenden, and L. Birg. (1979). "Why a Rejection? Causal Attribution of a Career Achievement Event." *Social Psychology Quarterly*, 42, 214–222.

Wimsatt, W. C. (1981). "Robustness, Reliability, and Overdetermination." In M. B. Brewer and B. E. Collins, eds., *Scientific Inquiry and the Social Sciences*, pp. 124–163. San Francisco: Jossey-Bass.

Winch, P. (1958). *The Idea of a Social Science and Its Relation to Philosophy*. London: Routledge and Kegan Paul.

Woodward, J. (1988). "Understanding Regression." In A. Fine and J. Leplin, eds., *Philosophy of Science Association 1988*, vol. 1. East Lansing, Mich.: Philosophy of Science Association.

Wright, E., A. Levine, and E. Sober. (1992). *Reconstructing Marxism: Essays on Explanation and the Theory of History*. New York: Verso.

Wylie, A. (1986). "Arguments for Scientific Realism: The Ascending Spiral." *American Philosophical Quarterly*, 23, 287–297.

Zillman, D. (1988). "Cognition–Excitation Interdependencies in Aggressive Behavior." *Aggressive Behavior*, 14, 51–64.

Index